FAST and FANCY
Revolver Shooting

by Ed McGivern

Anniversary Edition

NEW WIN PUBLISHING, INC.

Printing Code

19 20 21 22 23 24 25

Library of Congress Catalog Card Number: 84-62402

ISBN 0-8329-0557-7

TO MRS. JENNIE M. McGIVERN

Realizing full well that but for her encouragement, co-operation, and tireless
efforts my work in the field of exhibition revolver shooting, research
and training would never have been developed as it has, nor
would my unaided efforts, ability and patience have been
sufficient to produce and record the results of the numerous experiments which I am now presenting to the
public in book form, I take this opportunity
to express my gratitude and love to

My Dear Wife

to whom this book is dedicated

ED McGIVERN
of Montana

TO MY FRIENDS

I wish at this time to extend my sincere thanks and appreciation to the following persons and firms for their very kind consideration, assistance and co-operation during various contacts and transactions necessary while preparing the material for this book: The American Rifleman; Sports Afield; Outdoor Life; Field & Stream; Bob Nichols, of Field & Stream; F. L. Wyman, of American Rifleman; Phil Sharpe, of All Western and Outdoors; Ed Crossman, of National Sportsman; Chas. Askins, Jr., El Paso, Texas, instructor Border Patrol; R. G. Walker, Bausch & Lomb Optical Company; Major Earl Naramore, Yalesville, Conn.; Col. W. A. Tewes, Peters Cartridge Company; Roy Riggs, Western Cartridge Company; Capt. Charlie Hopkins, Western Cartridge Company; Wallace H. Coxe, ballistics engineer, Dupont Power Company; Leonard C. Davis, Colt's Patent Firearms Co.; M. H. Bingham and Cy Bassett of the Smith & Wesson factory; Roy S. Tinney, Chatham, N. J.; Capt. Paul A. Curtis, formerly of Field & Stream; Monroe H. Goode, of Sports Afield; J. Edgar Hoover and T. Frank Baughmann, of the Federal Bureau of Investigation.

Also Walter Groff, of Philadelphia, Pa., co-operation and assistance in development of exhibition revolver shooting; Frank Fish, Lewistown, Mont., gunsmith, supervision, construction and operation of electrical timing equipment; Emmett McGivern, Great Falls, Mont., exhibition revolver shooting and development; O. H. Graham, business associate, Dick Tinker, Helena, Mont., revolver shooting experiments; Capt. Fred Bullock, Company K, 163d Infantry, also First Sergeant Waldo Vangsness, Company K, 163d Infantry, and Sergeant Leonard Larson, Company K, 163d Infantry, Lewistown, Mont., extensive co-operation in revolver shooting experiment and exhibition development; James Harney, Benchland, Mont., assistant and co-worker in research and experiment; Harry Fitton, secretary Midland Empire Fair Association, Billings, Mont., sponsor of several special exhibition programs and development; Duke Wellington, Harlowtown, Mont., assisting with photography; Chauncey Fowler, Lewistown, Mont., Past Commander American Legion; Lou Boedecker, Helena, Mont., Supervisor Montana Highway Patrol; Capt. Rudy Schmoke, District Supervisor California Highway Patrol, San Francisco, Calif.; Eugene Cunningham, El Paso, Texas, Western writer and recognized authority on guns, belts, holsters, gun carrying rigs and equipment; Harry "Pink" Simms, Butte, Mont., writer and student of Western history; Herb Titter, Great Falls, Mont., Associated Press photographer; Barger Photo Shop, Lewistown, and the Culver Photo Studio, Lute Musson, Mgr., Lewistown, special photography and valuable technical

To My Friends

experiment; J. E. Teague, Oakland, Calif., special motion pictures and program development; Don Jackson, Great Falls, Mont., supervising action snap shots.

Also the valuable co-operation of the following firms: Hercules Powder Co.; Winchester Repeating Arms Co.; Dupont Powder Co.; Remington Arms Co.; Western Cartridge Co.; U. S. Cartridge Co.; Federal Cartridge Co.; Peters Cartridge Co.; Colt's Patent Firearms Co. and Smith & Wesson, Inc.; W. R. Weaver, El Paso, Texas; Lyman Gun Sight Corporation, Middlefield, Conn.; Sam D. Myres Saddlery Co., El Paso, Texas; Kohler Bros., Saginaw, Mich., and X-Ring Products Co., Peoria, Ill., target holders, steel backstops, bullet catchers, gallery and outdoor exhibition equipment.

CONTENTS

Contents

Contents

— 11 —

Contents

INTRODUCTION

This book is intended to make readily available to the revolver shooting public the somewhat unusual, as well as the sometimes quite unexpected and very surprising, results secured through the extensive experiments and research as conducted by the author, over a period of years, in his study of fast and fancy revolver shooting, for the purpose of combining effective accuracy with unusual speed.

The value of such results so secured is due to the fact that the experiments and tests were carried on in connection with electrically controlled timing equipment, specially constructed for the purpose, and various other necessary devices to assist in definitely clearing up certain angles of argument connected with the probabilities and reasonable possibilities of accomplishment; while at the same time making rather thorough tests of many of the long-established customs and beliefs which existed, and were quite generally accepted as absolute facts in relation to revolver shooting.

It is the wish of the author at this point to state very clearly that the results of our efforts towards research and experiment in the various branches of revolver shooting, as set forth in this book, are not in any way intended to be any part of any so-called "debunking" process or movement that could be in any way considered as being directed at any of the early West's shooting history or of any of the earlier or later shooting exploits or performances of others, either individually or collectively. The object of all effort and experiment was to establish facts, by and from the results of actual tests, and to support such facts by the actual evidence of the results so secured, and in so doing to definitely determine certain points of value, and to eliminate certain other points that were detrimental to success.

By outlining and passing on to revolver shooters the methods of procedure that were successfully employed, and attempting to make these methods still more clearly understood by the use of in-action pictures, the author sincerely hopes that such action on his part will prove beneficial to each individual revolver shooter who may study the material herein contained.

It will be readily seen that some of the results secured by the experiments conducted, have disturbed, and in some cases actually reversed, some very well-fixed opinions and beliefs that formerly were regarded by many as well-established truths. The hope is entertained that the facts which have replaced these opinions will prove of much more value

Introduction

to the shooter, and that a great deal of good to every one (and no harm to any one) will be the result of the change.

There will be no attempt made to go into the general history of fire-arms or ammunition, as there are now available several very fine books covering such subjects in considerable detail. "Text-Book of Pistols and Revolvers," by Julian Hatcher, is recommended, also "Pistols and Revolvers and Their Use," by the same author. Ballistics data and charts, with extensive tabulations, can be secured on request from the various firms engaged in the manufacture of arms and ammunition, also from the several makers of reloading equipment, and other sources. The addresses of these firms can be secured from various sportsmen's magazines. Among such books will be found "Hand-loading," by Mattern; "This Handloading Game" and "Complete Guide to Handloading," by Phil Sharpe; "Ideal Handbook," by Lyman Gun Sight Corp., with latest data by Major Earl Naramore; "Belding and Mull's Handbook" the handbook and catalogue of Pacific Gun Sight Company, Reloading tool department, and "Six Gun Cartridges and Loads," by Elmer Keith.

Exhibition shooting and the experiments necessary for its preparation is the source from which the greater part of the material for this book was originally developed, consequently special attention has been given to arranging interesting combinations of gun-handling performances for the exhibition revolver shooter, as well as for those who may wish to develop and improve their skill by trying out the various fancy stunts and combinations listed and illustrated.

The training methods employed by the author to develop speed combined with accuracy were found to be readily adaptable to the training of police officers and members of law enforcement organizations generally. It was very apparent that they could be easily incorporated in a general course of training arranged to meet their special requirements.

After investigating the various problems involved in police work and law enforcement, with due consideration of the probable situations wherein the officer would most likely be called upon, in the line of duty, to use his revolver, such a course of training in revolver shooting was worked out on what was considered as a practical basis, governed by the conditions under which most of such shooting by officers might be, and, in all probability would be, done if and when forced to shoot.

The urgent necessity of performing well and getting positive results under a variety of surprise conditions, that may occur at any moment, with no advance warning, has been carefully considered and emergencies provided for. The submitted targets, located in the police training section of this book, show the actual results secured by various officers under the greatly varied conditions liable to occur in actual battle, after only a short period of practical training under the supervision of the author.

Introduction

The practical value and effectiveness of this type of training is thus firmly established. These successful results, as shown, were secured by the methods of procedure set forth and clearly explained in the later following descriptive matter accompanying the target photos mentioned, and relating thereto, which, as will be noted, constitutes a decided departure from the usual methods, but which has proven extremely effective and positive in securing results.

The same system of education in revolver shooting technique has also proven of great value in training bank officials, messengers and other employees for emergency action under surprise conditions, which, I wish to point out here, is the most important angle of value of such training to a bank employee, when occasion may demand it. It gives me great pleasure to announce that the women bank employees made just about as much progress and became just about as proficient in this work as the men.

The average citizen also comes in for attention. In this class we have the revolver enthusiast who works on targets, and the person who shoots only in quest of the pleasure and satisfaction that comes from accomplishing something just a bit out of the ordinary, and doing it exceptionally well; perhaps mastering it completely. The value of such training to a citizen, when forced by circumstances to protect loved ones, home or property in times of sudden disorder or similar emergency, cannot be overestimated.

It is desirable at this point to mention that shooting revolvers by the double-action method is the important thing that contributes to success in the various branches of revolver shooting outlined in this volume. In the field where more than usual speed is to be combined with the necessary accuracy required to accomplish the various stunts as described in the following pages, the double-action method of operating the gun is absolutely essential.

The author wishes to have it very clearly understood that double-action shooting is not recommended with the idea or intention of entirely taking the place of single-action shooting for all purposes, but when the time factor must be taken into account, and the shooting be completed within a certain limited space of time (or not at all), then, and under such conditions, double-action shooting is absolutely necessary and very positively in a class by itself. Various combinations of effective shooting performances can be, and have been, accomplished by this method, that have never been accomplished by any other method of operating revolvers. In support of this statement speed of performance and accuracy of results have been combined and completed within the very short-time periods found numerously illustrated and convincingly demonstrated and verified on the following pages.

Introduction

It will also be made quite clear by investigation of these results that double-action shooting is not a substitute for single-action shooting, but is, instead, a very necessary advanced or postgraduate course for the revolver shooter who has already, by deliberate effort, become proficient in pointing, holding, sighting and releasing the shots in the proper manner. By this method he can be not only reasonably sure of hitting what he is shooting at, but at the same time maintain somewhat consistent grouping of the shots in the immediate vicinity of the point selected for the bullets to hit, on the object aimed at.

In all manner of quick-gun producing methods where one shot or several shots are to be delivered in the shortest period of time possible after the hand starts for the gun—such as is quite liberally illustrated in the police section—the double-action revolver seems to hold the lead. All of the shooting material of which this book consists,—aerial target shooting, superspeed group shooting demonstrations, and the greatly varied one and two gun stunts against time,—were all developed and gradually mastered by the double-action method of firing and controlling the shots.

All of the widely varied program of shooting stunts and combinations presented in this volume, as a reference and guide for others, were dependent for success on the reliability of the standard regulation double-action revolvers, as illustrated herein.

COMMENTS BY THE AUTHOR IN REFERENCE TO ILLUSTRATIONS

The illustrations relative to the activities described in the various sections will be found arranged in the order of their relationship, in the latter part of each section to which they apply, as indicated by the titles.

In presenting the following in-action pictures illustrating and making clear the methods of procedure employed to secure the results described and illustrated in the following pages, I wish to mention the fact that during December, 1936, while a guest of Mr. Walter Groff of Philadelphia, Penn., who has been my pupil and understudy for a period of four years, and having just completed a strenuous tour of the gun and ammunition factories and a visit with Mr. J. Edgar Hoover and his associate officials at the Federal Bureau of Investigation at Washington, D. C., a very severe attack of arthritis was incurred that brought all of my shooting activities to an end immediately and considerably delayed the progress of the book.

Seven months later, with recovery slow and somewhat doubtful and being still unable to take an active part in the shooting performances necessary to conclude several unfinished sections of the book, I was successful in getting Mr. Groff to come to Lewistown during August and September to assist in finishing up the various shooting performances of which the in-action photographs were urgently needed.

This cooperation made it possible to complete the unfinished sections and I believe these photographs and descriptive data will particularly interest the reader due to the fact that Mr. Groff has developed into an efficient performer and an understudy of whom I openly acknowledge my pride and appreciation, through the same training methods outlined and suggested herein and now available to all.

Reproductions of the various targets made at the longer ranges (from one hundred up to and including five hundred yards) were shot with the S. & W. .357 Magnum Revolver on the Fort Harrison Range, and were made available through the kind cooperation of Mr. Richard Tinker of Helena, Montana. Deputy State Game Warden Waldo Vangsness of Lewistown, Montana, and high individual rifle shot of the Montana National Guard, representing Company K, 163rd Infantry, was responsible, in cooperation with Mr. Groff, for the successful results secured with the S. & W. .357 Magnum Revolver and the Winchester .357 cartridge on the Langrish limbless targets and the Colt silhouette (white) targets placed at the quite surprising range (for revolvers) of six hundred yards. (Section 26)

ED McGIVERN'S BOOK

SECTION 1

PISTOLS, REVOLVERS AND THE LAW.

"Practical" revolver shooting covers a wide field that has many very interesting angles, closely interwoven with what we like to refer to as organized society. Under this heading are considered the government, the financial and the business institutions, and the home, in the building, maintenance, and the protection of which, since the beginning of our pioneer American history to the present moment, the pistol and revolver, and (this is most important) the effective and intelligent use of them, have always played a very important part.

All through history there have been many outstanding characters on both sides of the law, famous for their proficiency with such arms, equally active and determined in the seemingly endless struggle. Many famous law officers were matched against equally famed outlaws, each depending on his skill with the same sort of weapons in this battle for "the survival of the fittest." Law, order, and organized society on one side and the contempt for law and order, by the element that defied society, on the other. A careful study of all such history when stripped of its glamour and romance shows clearly that in the end, when the check-up was finally completed, the law was supreme, and organized society, through its representatives, has always triumphed, for law, in the final analysis, is but the desire of the majority.

The situation that confronts us today is still very much the same as in the earlier days, with the addition of a few modern angles.

Facts and figures will show that the arms of "Law and Order," as one slogan in reference to pistols and revolvers terms them, are very much more numerous and are in the hands of much better trained men on the side of organized society, than against it. It can also be very clearly shown, by reference to the official records of any of the big pistol and revolver matches, that we have many officers of the law, in various capacities, much more expert in the use of such arms than can be found among the most proficient performers on the opposing side. This statement is made, and supported by facts, in contradiction to the great American custom of hero worship which, at times, has been so lavishly displayed towards some of the characters who have opposed the law, while being often thoughtlessly and wrongfully withheld from our most deserving officers, no matter how brilliant or heroic the performances of these officers may have been.

As a result of the reaction against such sentiment influential executives in Washington, as well as in several of our other large cities, have been successful in promoting the organization of police training schools, with both indoor and outdoor shooting ranges for pistol and revolver practice. Under the supervision of capable men well qualified by experience to handle this work, remarkable progress is being made, and new methods are being developed that will successfully cope with all angles of the situation. The very efficient men at the head of these organizations will continue to prove that the law forces of organized society can and will triumph.

The significance of this new development in police training has not been fully realized by the average citizen, or in fact by any great part of the general public. The establishing of criminal research laboratories by and for our leading law enforcement organizations, and the great progress made in crime detection, as well as in the various branches of criminal identification through these agencies, are just a little too big for the mental processes of the uninitiated who chatter about the expense without being capable of realizing the far-reaching benefits that are daily derived from this source.

When we consider the facts, as shown by statistics and supported by the report of the New York police department officials and others, that approximately eighty per cent of the firearms taken from offenders or otherwise gathered in by the police in various parts of the country are of foreign manufacture, and often are of the cheapest sort procurable, it certainly justifies the special training of police and the establishing of such laboratories, together with the purchase of the special equipment required to cope with the situation, and I am glad to state that there is abundant proof that the various officials and the police are making good.

During my own experience covering more than fifteen years of activity in connection with court cases dealing with expert testimony, firearms identification, and kindred subjects, the bulk of murder guns and weapons used in various crimes, and attempted crimes, coming to my attention has been quite generally of the very cheapest sort obtainable, and, as a rule, not in any manner the type of arm used by the members of organized shooting clubs, or the side arms carried by sportsmen, or the better type of home protection weapons usually kept by the reputable citizen.

This feature of the case makes one wonder about our radical agitators who want to enact a law against manufacture, sale, or possession of firearms anywhere within the United States; such law to apply to weapons that can be concealed on the person. Just how could such a law be enforced so as to disarm the crook—he being the target aimed at; and, we are quite sure, he will be the very one **that would not be hit.** As the crook has no re-

Pistols, Revolvers and the Law

gard for the law and does not submit to the rulings or provisions of any angle of the law, just how is he going to be reached through such a law in any better way, or as well, as he is today, and when there is still a chance that the citizen **may** be armed, and so enabled to protect himself; in the other case the law-abiding citizen will be disarmed, making it absolutely safe at all times and places for the crook to attack him, his home, his family, or his property. The officer of the law will also be "hemmed in" and handicapped (much as he is today in many ways) by provisional restrictions, technicalities, and red tape, by the public remedy specialists who would then be in charge.

The crook, through very easy bootlegging operations, can secure a full supply of illegally made or foreign arms and ammunition, a much easier thing to smuggle, or make, than moonshine, thereby opening to him another very profitable field. He will then be the only one to "own and bear arms," while that privilege, originally given to the **citizen** by the Constitution of these United States, will be denied that citizen.

My own efforts and activities in developing, improving, and advancing revolver shooting and methods of instruction have ever been, and always will be, in support of and in behalf of law enforcement, and my opinions and conclusions relative to the subject are based on actual experience. As a result I am most definitely opposed to any method of disarming the law-abiding citizen by any indirect system that we may be misled into thinking has been, or is, aimed only at the crook.

The solution to the problem of the shooting public to preserve their liberty and maintain their right "to have and bear arms," per the Constitution, can be brought about through their united effort, concentrated toward that one objective, taking their cue from and following the example of the opposing forces, but in exactly the opposite direction. If such liberty is taken from us it will be through our lack of activity in defense of our constitutional rights, and through the lukewarm or entire absence of any support to the N. R. A. (National Rifle Association of America) or U. S. R. A. (United States Revolver Association), the two greatest champions of organized, practical, and recreational shooting privileges, development, and protection that has ever existed in this still wonderful country of ours, with all of the opportunities and privileges open and available equally to each and every individual member. The slogan **"We Do Our Part"** never was nor could be applied to any institution created by man where it could possibly fit better than it does when applied to the National Rifle Association of America, Incorporated 1871, and the United States Revolver Association, Incorporated 1900.

In the year 1871 we still had a pioneer spirit that was active and efficient—a class of men that made possible the growth and development of this country into one of the great nations of the earth. We had not as yet developed a group of meddlers and fixers, tampering and experimenting with the Constitution of these United States, to my belief the most wonderful system of government ever devised by man. From this class of men came the organizers of the National Rifle Association, and also the United States Revolver Association, which was founded in March, 1900, at the request of the Rifle Association for the purpose of developing revolver and pistol shooting, to establish and preserve records, to classify arms, and to encourage **friendly** matches between **members** and clubs, and, I may add, to encourage genuine sportsmanship, which is a vital factor in such organizations.

Loyal support and cooperation with the National Rifle Association and the United States Revolver Association, on the part of the rifle and revolver shooting public, in a campaign of education open to and embracing all branches of the general public, is of very great importance. Efforts should be made to secure wide newspaper publicity regarding the activities of the local clubs and members, giving full credit where credit is due, and cooperate individually and collectively with the police and other officers' organizations, local, state, and national. Cultivate and spread the spirit of sportsmanship in all matters relating to the shooting game. Be reasonably modest and graceful as winners, "be good losers" when the break comes that way—it pays dividends. Help the other fellow to solve his problems and to overcome his faults, real or imaginary. The individual shooters make up the clubs and the organizations whose influence extends to the community, the state, and the nation. What you and I, as individuals, grow and develop into, is what later determines what "**we** do," which, in turn (as such combining and organizing continues) comes to be and determines what "**they** do," as our combined actions will be referred to. Each one of us and our activities, or our inactivities, are what makes "The Government." Each one of us has our part and must play it out—we either help to make or break, and to either maintain or destroy, "organized society."

The careful conduct of "we" shooters, along these lines, will do much to solve the firearms problem and much of the ignorant prejudice against firearms that we know exists, and which is almost invariably the result of lack of knowledge of the subject under consideration. It matters little whether the subject is firearms, as in this case, or something else—this truth applies equally well; trying to keep the general public under passive control, through ignorance, is a theory that belonged to the Dark Ages and not to the present. The field of activities that interests us here must not be conducted in any such manner.

SECTION 2

REMOVING THE MYSTERY. MY OWN EXPERIENCE.

In presenting the material contained in this book to the vast army of revolver enthusiasts, police organizations, and the shooting public generally, the effort is made to remove as quickly as possible the veil of purely imaginary mystery that seems to surround the development, within the last few years, of what is generally regarded as phenomenal speed, combined with accuracy, or sure hitting possibilities coupled with the surprisingly high rate of speed that can be attained by the use of the double-action feature of the modern revolver, which has been the subject of intensive study by me for a number of years.

Systematic study of the possibilities of this branch of the revolver shooting game has made it possible to secure some rather surprising results that have been quite generally considered at the least "unusual" as compared to the "extreme rapid fire" or high speed shooting considered to be the limit of possibility only a few years ago. This quite naturally gave rise to the attitude of mystery with which some of the uninitiated, unfamiliar with the method of procedure, tried to cloak such performances. The truth of the matter is that there is no mystery of any kind that could possibly be connected with any of the shooting as herein outlined, all of which will be explained in detail as we proceed.

This book is intended as a reference work and guide, and my purpose is to give clear and definite instructions for the benefit of the reader or student in what is to me the most fascinating branch of revolver shooting.

After years of much varied shooting with all sorts of revolvers, pistols, rifles, and shotguns, and all sorts, sizes, and varieties of targets, including live game, the aerial or flying target shooting with revolvers seems to require, from me at least, more careful study and persistent practice than any other type of shooting, and never lacks interest. As my mind goes back to the days when I decided that I wanted to, and would, in spite of all obstacles and handicaps, stay on the job until I became reasonably proficient in ultraspeed group shooting, and various other attempted "superspeed" stunts, with the then spoken-of "new fangled" double-action revolvers, as well as with the then very generally used—and much worshipped—Colt single-action "Peacemaker" that held the place of honor in the minds of many of the revolver shooting "fans" of that day, I little realized that I would some day be describing my experiences and trying to save others the disappointments that I had to face in my early efforts to master the new and (mostly) untried angles of the game.

Fast and Fancy Revolver Shooting

Part of the price of such proposed success was the large quantities of ammunition consumed in the usually unsuccessful trials, for which I was very generally criticized.   I soon discovered that I was **not** a "natural-born wizard"—I was almost anything but that, so maybe this fact may serve to encourage some of my readers to persevere, in the case that success doesn't smile on their first efforts.   I have vivid memories of certain incidents and failures, and the wails of the immediate members of the family, together with the cheerful advice of some of my shooting associates, against such "absurd ideas."   "Why, the conceited upstart!" as they liked to express it, "no one in the world has ever been able to do such nonsensical things, as those, thus and so—stunts, with revolvers."

Some of the more serious-minded advisers even insisted that certain of the proposed stunts (that were later successfully demonstrated) were quite impossible, for the (to them) very apparent reason that no revolver or any make of ammunition ever produced was, or ever would be, equal to the demands thus put upon it; also, that it was beyond the power of the human hand and eye to master such things.   Most of this wise counsel so generously bestowed has since been proved to be just as unreliable as gratuitous advice generally is.   No doubt the successful results finally secured were due, in part at least, to the fact that although human nature is still much the same now as then, the revolvers and the ammunition have been greatly improved.   At that time there were no instructors to whom one could turn for help, there were no books of reference as a guide, nor any very reliable information available.

I recall that it most certainly looked, at that time, as though the voluntary and always very willing critics were going to have the best of the argument; some similar views and prophesies later appeared in print, in some cases with very well-meaning and, no doubt, honest conviction on the part of the writers.   At other times such advice was coupled with much sarcasm, and a generally "know it all" attitude.   Time, however, with the very funny way that time so often has of doing such things, showed that these wise ones were—well—"just slightly in error."   Memories of this very well-defined spirit of opposition towards my efforts in early life laid the foundation, and no doubt had its influence, towards bringing out the present volume for the benefit of the many interested shooters with whom I have come in contact and who have convinced me that they really desire such information, which I gladly pass along with the very earnest wish that it will assist them to develop their skill to an at least satisfactory degree.

The work of getting together much of the available data so as to be able to pass it along was made into a very pleasant sort of experience by the great interest created by the writings of the better informed and liberal minded gun and ammunition authorities of the present day. The development and wonderful improvement of revolvers, joined with the superior quality of the ammunition being produced for use in these revolvers, made successful results a somewhat regularly repeated performance, which is a very outstanding example of the cooperation mentioned herein, without which we could not possibly have developed the material for this book.

Much of the remarkable progress made recently in this particular field of endeavor and the successful outcome of the experiments conducted to determine vital facts for the benefit of my readers, have been made possible through the invention of the electric timing devices and appliances, and the improvement of various other testing machines and accessories in the several ammunition factories. Among the most notable is the spark photography equipment in the ballistics laboratory of the Peters Cartridge Company at Kings Mill, Ohio. Some of the results secured with this equipment are illustrated and described under the title of "Visible Ballistics." These new scientific instruments have had a powerful influence toward removing haphazard results secured by haphazard methods, and replacing them with positive timing data secured by a very definite system of procedure and carried on to the absolutely definite and positive conclusions outlined and explained in an effort to make them as clear as possible for the interested readers and to remove, so far as possible, the "bogey man" attitude of "it can't be done," as well as the false impression that one must be born with some sort of superhuman qualities in order to be successful.

The instructions and the outline of the methods used to develop the necessary skill to perform these different feats as described are the exact methods used by me in originally working out the problems, minus the wasted efforts due to the general lack of knowledge at the start. By carefully avoiding the angles that were originally responsible for some of the most annoying mistakes and delays, the student of today can work his way safely around the pitfalls that beset the path of the adventurer into the new shooting field at the time of which I write.

Special emphasis is placed on the fact that there is no mystery of any kind connected with successfully mastering any and all of the stunts set forth, or of the entire series being successfully worked out in a satisfactory manner. Another point I wish to bring prominently to the notice of the reader is in relation to the very firm belief, based on my own experience, that **any** "average person" sufficiently interested in this branch of revolver shooting, as treated in the following pages of this book, who is willing to **study, practice,** and **persist** in the effort, can master every subject treated. There are no "magic mixtures" which will take the place of ability developed by practice and study, and, contrary to popular belief, there is no need of any supernatural or out of the ordinary ability, or supermental development required. There is no need of possessing any of the qualifications of a "wizard" in order to achieve success.

Any of the standard revolvers listed herein, just as they leave the hands of the experts at the factory, can and will give highly satisfactory results. Drastic alterations or radical changes are very seldom, if ever, necessary for the use of the average person. Sensible alterations and adjustments can usually be secured on standard revolvers and pistols at the factory, by paying for such special work and for the time and supervision of the experts who are in charge.

The more pronounced alterations and variations in the general outline of grips, trigger adjustments, hammer spurs, etc., that may be desired by the individual, due to some personal peculiarity or decided preference, can usually be secured from a competent gunsmith equipped to take care of special jobs of that nature, several of which are mentioned herein, with examples of such special work done on the certain guns shown.

The great variety of ammunition now obtainable on the open market affords the shooter a choice of some particular cartridge adapted to the most exacting special purpose, leaving very little, if any, room for alibis or criticism. Almost any, or perhaps all, of the standard makes of revolver ammunition, when used in the standard better grade revolvers and pistols, and for the purpose recommended by the makers, will equal and generally, if not always, prove superior, over long continued tests, to the holding ability of the majority of top-notch performers. It will also average, in every way, as regards dependability and accuracy, far better than the general run of fairly "good shots" can hold.

I have fired many thousands of revolver cartridges, of various makes, and under widely varied conditions, with a decidedly small margin of complaint of any kind whatsoever. It will be readily admitted, I believe, that one of the most severe tests that can be given revolver ammunition, aside from those for extreme accuracy, is during the superspeed tests conducted in the attempts to secure the fastest time results possible, when operating revolvers by the double-action mechanism, either by hand or by the gear-operated machine, herein described and illustrated.

Misfires, hangfires, or faulty ignition generally would mean nothing short of disaster during such tests, and might prove practically suicidal should they occur. Such things could not be tolerated under any conditions. The opinion, as expressed regarding standard factory ammunition, is based on experience covering many years of such experiments, without any serious accident.

While on this subject of the danger connected with speed tests, we desire to point out that the practice of mutilating the working parts of revolvers, and of weakening the mainsprings, etc., as an aid toward gaining speed, is to be emphatically condemned as a very possible source of serious trouble. I have always carefully avoided any such drastic changes in any guns that were to be used for speed tests. Standard guns used with standard factory loaded ammunition can be depended on to give standard results, with a sensible margin of safety—a most important fact that should not be overlooked.

SECTION 3

LEARNING THE SHOOTING GAME.

When the average person wishes to learn to play any game or enter any line of sport it is generally the custom to look up some one prominent in that game, or in some manner leading in or promoting the particular line of sport in which he may be interested, and arrange for a course of instruction to be taken care of at certain hours of certain days, and at some certain place, where such equipment as may be necessary is kept in order and properly cared for.

With the person becoming interested in pistol and revolver shooting this course is not always followed. If it was it would be a much easier matter for the student to learn the proper method of handling his gun or guns, to become familiar with their operation, to exercise care and caution in their use, and to acquaint himself thoroughly with the general rules of safety, thus avoiding the general tendency to form bad habits at the start that usually prove quite difficult to correct later on.

In the more settled districts the ambitious student of revolver shooting will be able to find in or near the larger cities and towns one or more clubs affiliated with the United States Revolver Association, or the National Rifle Association, and such clubs will have all the necessary target shooting facilities. The beginner can do no better than to join one of these clubs, where he will generally find a very friendly attitude on the part of the shooting members, and the instructors, as a rule, willing and anxious to assist and coach him along lines that will enable him to decide the many perplexing problems that confront him, regarding equipment and methods of training, and who are in a position, as a result of their experience, to give him the desired information.

If our student does not already possess a suitable gun, it will be wise to talk things over with the club members and be guided by the advice so received. The choice of arms, of course, will depend greatly on the particular purpose for which this pistol or revolver is going to be used, what kind of shooting will be done with it in the main, and what objective the shooter has in mind. If the student merely wants to become fairly proficient in the use of the revolver for defense purposes, when and if the necessity might arise, that will require one sort of training which can be carried on with quite limited equipment. But if he wishes to go in for the finer lines of target shooting it will then be an entirely different matter, and will require selection of different types of guns, several of which will be discussed later.

In the less settled portions of the country it is usually quite easy to find a safe place to practice, where natural backstops may be found or easily erected from some suitable and readily available material. Here in the West (Montana) we are very fortunate in being able to find many suitable places for practice, as well as the so-called "great open spaces," where flying targets or aerial target shooting, as it is generally referred to, can be indulged in with safety. This is, perhaps, one of the reasons the writer took such interest in and followed up aerial target shooting to such a great extent as has been done. Opportunity and convenient surroundings, no doubt, entered into the situation and helped somewhat to assist in promoting this branch of the game.

Our very candid advice to the beginner, along either line, would be to start with a good grade of .22 revolver, either Colt, Smith & Wesson, or Harrington & Richardson, as preferred. Personally, I would recommend target sights, thus calling for either the K-.22 Smith & Wesson, the .22 Colt Officers' Model, or the Harrington & Richardson Sportsman Model, with heavy frames in each case. The frames of the Colt and the Smith & Wesson are the same as those on which the .38 special revolvers are built.

These .22 guns mentioned will do all of the things that the larger guns can do in the way of speed and accuracy, and will give entire satisfaction as to durability and service. The .22 short cartridges can be used in them for practice, and the long rifle for accuracy at the longer ranges, as well as the .22 long rifle with hollow point bullets for small game. The Hi-velocity hollow point bullet long rifle cartridges are most effective, hard hitting and very damaging.

These .22 caliber guns are not in any way playthings or toys. They are very effective guns, and when the student learns to handle one of these well, he can also handle the regular .38 guns about equally well, and easily develop into mastering all of the larger calibers also. These are the guns with which I train my police classes for all of the early speed development exercises. The saving on ammunition, by using these instead of the larger bores at the beginning, will enable the student to have a lot of practice, by actually shooting, until he masters the principles of the game, at a very reasonable outlay.

I am very positive about expressing the opinion that the best known method of learning and mastering any branch of the revolver shooting game is by actually shooting. Intelligent study of the subject together with persistent practice, in an honest effort to make progress coupled with a close analysis of results, and a determination to correct any faults that may develop, instead of resorting to alibis, will bring success. With any of the above guns and a standard brand of ammunition there will be no justified alibis available—only personal error.

We learn and profit and progress mainly by the trial and error method, in our government as well as in our private life and industry. It is not necessary to become discouraged over a few failures during our efforts towards perfect results. Well-directed effort will always win out and can secure surprising results in the way of developing proficiency. As sure hitting, with all shots fired, is the objective in any branch of the shooting game, I will feature that angle throughout the book.

Having had considerable success in teaching with methods that were just a little different from some of the "cut and dried" iron-clad rules, I will offer a few suggestions, and also a few comments, in my effort to help and encourage the student. We will also try to get away from too many "proper this" and "proper that" rules and arguments, and reduce the "don't do this" and "don't do that" to the smallest number with which we can get along.

One of the main factors that tends toward success is the shooting position. Always try to be comfortable in mind and body. A strained, uncomfortable position of body, legs, arms, neck, etc., are to be avoided. A mistaken idea is often advanced that the shooter can be, or may be, steadier standing this way, or that way, in a strained position, rather than in some other much more sensible and comfortable position, just because some individual of an entirely different build and temperament may have had some success while assuming some such "freak" pose, for which, physically, he individually may have been adapted. Adopt a position that is suitable and comfortable for you—never mind the other fellow.

In my estimation there is no **one best position** that is suitable for everybody. The main object to be considered is **steadiness** and **comfort,** freedom from muscular strain, discomfiture or fatigue. Keep in mind that you are striving for extreme steadiness, which, at times, must also be coupled with much speed and necessary freedom of movement, and in order to maintain this you must be free from undue strain of any kind. You should, as stated above, make every effort to be comfortable and at ease in mind as well as body. Positions suitable and effective for the several styles of shooting will be found very clearly defined in the "in-action" pictures used to illustrate the different stunts.

No two persons are alike mentally or physically; no two persons eat, talk, sing, dance, act, work, or play alike. No two persons (except identical twins) even look or measure up alike. Why, then, should we try to make them all stand, pose, breathe, reach, hold, and see alike—let alone think and act alike as regards revolver shooting. It just isn't written that way in the Book of Life. Each one, in fact **all,** of us who come into this old world are simply a new mixture of old material. The mixtures are not of the same age or of the same chemical composition or proportion. What a foolish idea it is to try to control or develop these different combinations of chemical matter, so to speak, by some exactly "cut and dried" formula, or method, and expect it to work exactly and equally well with all of these wonderful and very interesting combinations of living matter called persons.

Learning the Shooting Game

Here enters the danger of "the rule of the dead men," "**tradition,**" custom, habit, inherent prejudice, a hundred and one or more quirks and angles of race characteristics, etc., all of which enters into the game and adds angles and obstacles that should be given serious consideration for the reason that they react, in no small measure, either for or against success.

These things must be studied, given consideration, and encouraged or discouraged, as the case may require. The individual is, and will ever remain, **the individual,** and should be regarded, treated, coached, and handled as such, in order to secure the best results for the particular one under instruction. We must find the way in which these various angles can be handled successfully, so that they can be adjusted and combined eventually into some sort of smooth working whole, without destroying the individuality and the personality of The Shooter.

It is quite necessary that guns of certain models be made very much alike, in order to have successful quantity production and interchangeable parts and replacements; in the case of persons we seem to have the quantity production, all right, but not exactly the interchangeable parts and replacements, nor with the ability to maintain functioning or operating completeness. If we had the interchangeable feature applied to man, the matter would be greatly simplified. We, of course, could then devise a set standard of rules and measurements, with a series of tolerances and clearances that would mechanically guarantee certain uniformly high grade results, just as we now do with the guns. And that is exactly the point—we do not have any such things in relation to humans, and we have no means whatever of getting them, therefore, the best we can ever expect to get out of our human units, by following any **set rule** or **general formula,** would be just some sort of a fair average, and that is the very thing we are trying to get away from.

Instead of just generally fair results being satisfactory for us here, we must strive for clearly specified special results, therefore we must have some sort of specialized formula and improved methods of procedure to apply to the subject at hand. Consistent production of quality results in individuals is dependent entirely and exactly on specialized effort. **"Positive movements, properly controlled, correctly timed and accurately directed,"** form the necessary basis for success in this field of endeavor. This sort of specialized effort is the method by which the writer expects to enable the student to master the various angles of fast revolver shooting, and to practically apply the knowledge of such methods to such training and development.

If a shooting instructor expects to get more than the above-mentioned general, or perhaps a little better than medium, average results out of his pupils, he must be equal to the task of properly developing each shooter's

mental and **physical** equipment. In order to reach production of the right kind of ideas and activity to get these superior results, it must be done from and by the development of the shooter's individual natural qualifications. Care should be taken not to submerge this individuality under too many general rules and regulations.

More or less difficulty is sometimes encountered when instructing pupils along this line, which usually arises from the fictitious "100% rating" that many persons like to flatteringly credit themselves with being able to attain, but which, as cold facts have so very clearly proven, very few have ever been able to develop. The average person who has had no experience with pistol or revolver shooting, who places himself under the guidance of a competent instructor, and willingly and consistently follows the instructor's advice, and observes the rules as outlined (all of which are based on experience), will make more progress and develop more ability, in a shorter period of time, than the quite familiar type of person who has had just enough of haphazard experience to make him think he knows a lot about the game, and enjoys being stubborn and contrary, taking great delight in arguing every point and persisting in the many faults that are usually and quite consistently—as a rule—developed by beginners.

SECTION 4

SHOOTING STANDARD REGULATION STATIONARY TARGETS.
DEVELOPING SPEED AND SURE HITTING ABILITY.
TRAINING FOR PRACTICAL CONDITIONS AND EMER-
GENCY SITUATIONS.

When beginning your training the most effective plan is to try careful and very deliberate slow fire, at fairly large targets and at fairly short ranges, gradually working along and slightly increasing the range, until reaching the standard distances at which certain sized bull's-eyes and targets are regularly used. It is best to stick to the standard targets and the standard distances that are very plainly stated in the regular target shooting rules as authorized by the National Rifle Association and the United States Revolver Association. If these rules are complied with, every shot that has been carefully fired is a benefit to you and assists you along the way toward entering regular competition events, and in addition to that is the fact that you can correctly estimate your progress in comparison to other shooters' scores as made in the regular matches, the accounts of which are very easily obtainable. There are two conditions under which American target competitions are held, indoors with artificial light, and outdoors by daylight, as prescribed by the rules.

When slow fire becomes fairly accurate in results, and sure hits on the standard targets at the standard distances become pretty regular occurrences, and giving reasonable average scores, it is a good idea to try timed and rapid fire in compliance with the governing rules, on a basis of five shots in 20 seconds, five shots in 15 seconds, and five shots in 10 seconds. All strings of shots on these targets and in these time periods can be fired by raising the hammer of the revolver to full cock position with the thumb, then firing the shot by squeezing the trigger, which is called the single-action method of firing the revolver.

Next, after rapid fire on standard targets has been learned well, the shooter can start his training towards hitting various sized objects quickly, placed at various distances; large objects placed fairly close to the shooter at first, then gradually increasing the distance and varying the size of the objects used as targets, later increasing the distances, say 5 yards, 10 yards, 15 yards, etc.; if targets are of medium size this practice will develop distance judgment also. This sort of procedure is quite necessary if the shooter desires to develop proficiency in the use of a revolver for self-defense or other legitimate purpose as a law enforcement officer, guard, or for other official duty.

You do not, of course, have bull's-eyes to help you with the aiming problems when called on to use the revolver for practical defensive purposes, or in performance of official duty in protecting yourself or the lives and property of others. Preferred positions cannot always be selected at the instant one may be called upon to use his revolver; one is forced by these actual surprise conditions to shoot in almost any direction from almost any position, and score sure hits if he expects to get out of the jam alive. Thus we will hereafter name this style of shooting and training, "practical conditions," by which is meant actual surprise conditions under which a person would be expected to do, and would also hope to do, his best work in protection of life and property.

When using the term "practical conditions" there is not the least slight intended or expressed toward any other form or branch of revolver shooting or careful target shooting of any nature, the writer's honest opinion being that any shooting that is done with **care and attention** as a result of the intelligent study of certain important angles, relating to improving and developing the shooter's ability along certain well-defined lines, is a benefit to such shooter always, instead of a hindrance. By trial and error and correction do we learn—not by theory and argument.

The real purpose of target shooting in all branches, from the simplest to the most complicated, is to build up an ability to actually hit things, in certain predetermined places or spots, and do it regularly with reasonable certainty, whenever we shoot at them. This is the underlying rule and the motive all through the game, from A to Z. What we are pleased to here call practical shooting simply means doing the same things as we do on the targets, but without any guides or marks of any kind to assist us. We must do these things much more quickly and with less preparation, and conclude the performance with less lapse of time, and be able to do it repeatedly within the much shortened time periods until the desired results become a certainty of performance. Failure to connect properly with sure hits on an opponent under actual conditions which exist during hold-ups, bank robberies, etc., for which it is generally understood we are preparing and training our pupils, would, no doubt, mean that said pupils would "fade out of the picture" entirely, and perhaps permanently; therefore, training for practical conditions is a very different matter than ordinary target shooting for recreation or in competition for prizes or medals. There are no re-entry rules that apply after you are dead, such as are in force in certain target shooting matches.

Shooting in competition with crooks and other enemies of the law requires entirely different methods of procedure and different technique, but still requires almost equal accuracy with a very active time limit —the more accuracy the better; and the less time required to secure said accuracy makes it still better. Another difference between target shooting and the—as I call it—practical use of a revolver, is, that much of such practical shooting must be done in the dark, or very poor light at best, where sights are generally hard to see, consequently at times almost useless, therefore only thorough familiarity with your revolver will count for anything, **and the fact** must be recognized that there is never any other place where hits are quite so necessary, or really so desirable, as under such conditions.

Therefore, we may be pardoned for creating a distinction and calling this branch of revolver shooting "practical shooting," to identify it and the training named as outlined, "for practical conditions" and for "practical purposes." In this way we can keep it separate from the regular, more careful, high class target shooting. The farthest thing from the intention of the writer would be to make light of any angle, branch, or field of revolver shooting.

Regardless of the many arguments that have been advanced on the subject, it is the writer's opinion that proper training in slow fire stationary target shooting, which develops steady holding, sure hitting, and good grouping, cannot possibly be and is not—as some have claimed—a detriment to later development in rapid fire or to superspeed group shooting either, or to flying and other aerial target shooting, or sure hit quick-draw shooting, or fast sure hitting after the draw. All of these latter stunts are dependent for success on—sure hits. When sure hits are the boiled down essence of the entire field of endeavor, just how can any method that will assist in developing the ability to make **sure hits** be detrimental?

In my early days my ears were continually being filled with such chatter, "don't do this and don't do that—it will surely ruin some one thing or another," or "spoil your this or that natural qualification, or inherent ability," etc. This chatter is ever present and in print in many books and booklets on revolver shooting **today.** My direct answer to most of it is—that it is just empty chatter and nothing else. Any practice, or any system of training or method of procedure that will guarantee **sure hits,** is a most important part of a proper foundation on which to build for future success, in **any branch of any shooting game,** where regular hitting is the all-important point to be considered and achieved. When a person can build up and maintain absolutely sure hitting ability regularly and positively, with absolute certainty of directing and controlling the location of such hits, and confining them to certain definite areas or groups, the main problem of the whole situation is most certainly solved. When once sure hitting ability has really been well and properly developed none of this senseless superstitious "chatter" about "don'ts and dare nots" will have any power to work "black magic" or "wizardry" on your shooting sense and mysteriously spoil your aim, or your hold, or your style.

SECTION 5

THE TRAINING METHODS FOR HITTING SMALL AERIAL
TARGETS. CLOSE GROUP SHOOTING ON AERIAL TARGETS.
CUTTING CARDS IN THE AIR. SIX SHOTS IN CAN WHILE
IN THE AIR. HITTING MARBLES, DISCS AND DIMES. HOW
TO USE THE SIGHTS ON AERIAL TARGETS. DRIVING TACKS
AND NAILS WITH BULLETS.

Years ago when I launched this series of experiments and began accumulating knowledge about aerial target shooting and building the necessary timing machines and other equipment for timing various gun handling performances, arguments were just as plentiful as they still are, advice was just as varied and just as freely distributed. We received our share and profited or lost accordingly.

As a result of some of the superwisdom "dished up" in this way we developed a "curiosity complex" regarding just why we either could, or could not, hit certain sized objects tossed in the air some stated number of times out of so many trials. This is where the value of group shooting stepped in to play its very important part, the great importance of which I, at that time, had not fully realized. In these early experiments we used clay pigeons, which are four and a quarter inches in diameter, also hollow composition balls, three and a half inches in diameter, Chamberlain Cartridge Company's hollow clay balls, two and a quarter inches in diameter, and also their solid clay balls, one and a half inches in diameter, wooden blocks (cubes), two inches in diameter, flat lead discs, two, one and a half, and one and a quarter inches in diameter, and penny size as well. I also had plenty of marbles, one and an eighth inches in diameter, and plenty of others, $\frac{3}{4}$, $\frac{5}{8}$, and $\frac{3}{8}$ inches in diameter. At this point my education regarding aerial target shooting with revolvers was broadened and intensified in relation to **group shooting** and trigger squeezing, and the **why,** looming large and prominent, was made very clear to me, much more so than it had ever been through any sort of stationary target shooting or experiment.

I will endeavor to outline the matter here so as to bring out some of the peculiar angles that made themselves manifest at that time. I started this game by tossing up clay pigeons and shooting at them with revolvers, and with pistols, both single shot and automatic, of all sorts and calibers. The results were very flattering. After a few weeks' training I found it rather easy to hit clay pigeons regularly with almost any kind of a pistol or revolver, but the double-action revolvers seemed to be more suitable for the purpose.

Training for Aerial Targets

Here was the birth of a real idea for me and I promptly started to work on it. The fact of the matter was that I decided I would attempt (whether successful or not) to do most of the stunts that comprised the programs of exhibition shooters in general, and for which they were using various shotguns, rifles, and revolvers. I determined, by persistent study and practice, to develop ability enough, if possible, to do the greater part, if not all of these feats with the more modern double-action revolvers, or if not able to cover such exhibition programs in their entirety with the double-action revolvers, I would persist in my efforts until I approached as closely to them as possible.

At about this time in my progress I made the personal acquaintance of the wonderful exhibition shooting team, Mr. and Mrs. Adolph (Ad) Topperwein of San Antonio, Texas, Mrs. Topperwein being, in my opinion, about the cleverest and most expert, as well as entertaining and unassuming lady shooter that ever appeared before the American public. She is very pleasingly expert with all types of firearms in the many quite unusual fancy shooting stunts that she has completely mastered. Mr. Topperwein also is one of the best known and most proficient performers, skillfully handling large and varied programs of very difficult and interest compelling fancy stunts, comprising the expert use of shotguns, rifles, and revolvers.

Opportunity was still tapping at my door. I was, at this time, fortunate in having an opportunity to watch several programs of very excellent exhibition shooting, as performed by Mr. Charles Flannigan of Great Falls, Montana, who is one of the foremost all-around exhibition and competitive shooters known to the game, and who has been performing before the public for more than twenty-five years. Charlie, as he is familiarly known to his many friends of the shooting fraternity, is proficient and very clever in the use of shotguns, rifles, and revolvers, in a very large assortment of clever stunts in greatly varied exhibition programs.

One of the very interesting feature performances of Mr. Flannigan's exhibitions on the occasions mentioned, which particularly struck my fancy, was the throwing of four, five, or six clay pigeons high in the air— all tossed up at one time by the shooter himself; these he would usually break before they could fall to the ground, using a hand-operated repeating shotgun for the purpose (see page 67). This performance requires perfect timing rhythm, precision movements, correctly controlled and accurately directed, exactly the foundation on which is built superspeed revolver shooting.

From similar interesting exhibitions the idea was developed that five, or perhaps six (at once), aerial targets could be successfully handled with double-action revolvers.

Soon after this I had the extreme pleasure of meeting personally Mr.

Fast and Fancy Revolver Shooting

Rush Razee, now of Denver, representing the Remington Arms Company, and being in attendance when he presented one of his high class shooting exhibitions, comprising a great assortment of fancy and difficult stunts with shotguns, rifles, and revolvers. Mr. Razee is a remarkably expert and very entertaining performer in an extensive and intensely interesting program, showing quite conclusively that he is thoroughly a master of this difficult branch of the shooting game.

At a later date I had the opportunity to observe and study the work of the very well and favorably known exhibition shooter, Captain A. H. Hardy, formerly of Denver, Colorado, and now of Beverly Hills, California. Captain Hardy is an excellent showman and entertainer and his programs consist of an excellent variety of unusual and very interesting combinations. The captain is a very pleasing and proficient performer.

After watching and reviewing these excellent programs and witnessing the amazing skill of these very expert performers, I fully realized that attempting to perform all such stunts while using double-action revolvers only would constitute some large order for me, with the possible or probable goal of success, somewhere perhaps, in the, as I hoped, not too distant future.

This should, I believe, help somewhat to make clear to many interested persons just why I "hung on" so persistently to the double-action revolvers for all purposes, over the period of years required to develop the well-mixed program that was eventually built up with such equipment. While the multiple aerial target idea was suggested by very clever exhibitions with repeating shotguns, I had confidence in the possibilities of the revolvers and went forward with the trials. Enough skill was finally developed to break three clay pigeons thrown in the air at one time; following up this system it was arranged to have the assistants throw the targets in that manner. By using two throwers, either four, five, or six targets could be tossed in the air at once, or in any other order of delivery or timing arrangement desired.

The size of targets was later reduced to the 3½-inch balls, then to 3-inch, the present size of **Duvrock** targets, and there it remained for some time.

As progress was made with the early target shooting under discussion, it was very natural to develop and profit by experience so that later I could quite regularly make **hits** on any kind of targets tossed in the air one at a time, the size being reduced gradually down to and including the one and a half inch clay balls. It also developed that a good average of hits could be scored on doubles (two tossed at a time) on these and the wooden blocks mentioned.

Then it came up to the one and an eighth inch marbles for a try-out, as a test of development and skill, but at this point I seemed to falter and get somewhat erratic. This situation required study. There would be several hits, then several misses (perfectly natural, of course), but why? At this point activities were transferred to the smallest condensed milk cans, measuring two and a half inches in diameter, throwing them up singly and firing two shots, sometimes three, and later four at each can. When four hits were scored it was soon learned from a study of the groups made on the cans that the one and an eighth inch marbles usually had plenty of room to go between the shots so fired, and I then started working on the two-inch lead discs and large iron washers. It was found, much to my surprise, that the grouping on these large discs often showed space enough for the marbles to get through between the bullet holes. This was finally determined after firing several shots on the same disc by tossing it in the air repeatedly and shooting only one shot at it each time it was tossed.

This was the proverbial "turn in the road" where progress was really started towards becoming an aerial target shot with revolvers. How? Well, it can be quite easily explained in a very simple way: I had learned to "squeeze and control the trigger," and also had learned to align the sights about even with the bottom of the marble, or any other target, letting it sort of ride on the top of the sights somewhat as military shooting is done. In this way, if a good central line shot was made, the target while falling had to cross its entire diameter in front of the gun muzzle or line of the bullet's flight to escape being hit, something it was found it could not, or at least did not, do. Here enters in a big way the time factor.

Soon I learned that if the gun was held in the position above-described in relation to the marble, or other small target, and the body was very gradually bent forward, thus gradually moving muzzle of gun downward, that this action would enable the shooter to keep the muzzle of the gun in correct alignment, and also in correct relation to the downward, or falling, movement of the marble for a very short distance during which time the trigger was being squeezed, the hammer falling, the ignition taking place and the bullet speeding out to connect with the target.

This new method of procedure helped very greatly in offsetting much of the time factor and finally developed into an extremely effective system, and hitting soon became reasonably sure and regular and was continued into unbroken runs of reasonable length that were quite surprising to the critics, and, of course, very satisfactory to me. This, I regarded, in a measure at least, as reasonable reward for the time, energy, effort, and ammunition devoted to the development of this branch of revolver shooting.

Now the question—how and why the success in making the several fairly long series of hits by this system? The answer to that is really the answer to the whole puzzling situation which so stubbornly confronted us in the beginning. **I had learned to use the sights quickly and accurately on** moving targets and had learned to squeeze and control the trigger properly while also keeping the movements of the revolver under perfect control, which, "boiled down," means that I had learned to hold the gun steadily with the "wabble" taken out and left out, while doing the trigger squeezing. I had learned to keep the gun in proper relation to the target during its travel over a short part of its downward path. I had learned to move the gun at the proper relative speed, in keeping with the movement of the target, and last, but by no means least, I had learned to fire a perfect line shot, and do it in a regular and approximately uniform space of time. Thus the time factor, the very important item mentioned above, was taken care of properly, and the problem of hitting small objects in the air had been solved.

Three of the very important things that were so profusely branded as "impossible" and "can't be done" had been mastered completely, and had been very properly done, and could be repeated successfully with surprising regularity. The real secret of the whole matter was that I had developed enough skill to shoot close groups in relation to the point of aim, and in direct relation to the center of the small targets, all of which would cause the opening that would be left within the center of the group, so to speak, to be too small for even the marbles to squeeze through, without getting at least some small part of their surface in the way of the bullet, and thus result in a hit which, as described, made the performance a fairly sure hit program. From this successfully mastered combination of correct principles and correctly executed movements, there has been developed the many stunts and variations, and interesting combinations that are outlined here and in the following pages.

If a stationary target shot can shoot groups in direct relation to the center of his target so that an object the size of his "ten ring" cannot get through the central opening of the group he will, of course, score all "ten ring" hits just the same way as the moving target shooter would do on marbles. This is a rule that cannot be side-stepped. When we first dropped down in the marble size to the small ones, the percentage of hits dropped off surprisingly, due to the fact that the opening in the center of the group, in relation to the point of aim, was not quite small enough in relation to this central point to prevent the marbles from getting through untouched. It must be kept in mind, however, that the actual group, as made while shooting at aerial targets, is done under the ever-present handicap of a constantly changing central point of aim, which is not the condition under which stationary target groups are made.

Another item that should also be kept in mind is the fact that the relative visibility of very small aerial targets, when looking over sights, does not prove quite equal to the clearer visibility of the larger ones. The more quickly established relative position of the larger target and the gun also makes considerable difference in the regularity with which hits can be registered over a long series of shots. However, the experienced aerial target shot with revolvers can concentrate particularly on a small target and quite often succeed in hitting it the first trial. It is also quite possible, by keenly concentrated effort, to hit doubles, or two thrown at a time. This has been demonstrated many times, yet runs of ten straight hits in succession on the small targets are not at all common enough to grow monotonous.

In direct variance with what we shooters generally like to believe, or at least often think and would like to have others think with us—**we do not shoot exact center** except on very rare and widely separated occasions. The highest possible winning target scores from the biggest matches will very generally support this statement. These are easily available for study. Instead we usually shoot our shots individually and collectively, one shot or many, just a little off center. This is absolutely true and a very surprisingly general fact. Careful examination and study into this subject will reveal some most interesting angles and this is really the exact principle that establishes and controls the size of our "ten rings" and various other high count centers on our standard regulation targets as used for different matches and under different rulings.

To show the incorrectness of the term used as "shooting center," making tack head groups, etc., if a shooter, shooting at the head of a tenpenny nail or a regular carpet tack, with .38 S. & W. Special revolver bullets, can shoot a group within a circle the size of a nickel, regularly and consistently, he will hit the edge of the nail head or the tack every time. Substitute the head of a .22 caliber cartridge for the nail and the result will be much the same. A three-fourths inch group (inside of the circle) made with the .38 caliber bullets will ruin nail head, tack, or the head of a .22 caliber cartridge regularly.

If a revolver shot, using the .38 Special cartridges, can shoot a group the size of a quarter, that is, keeping the bullets within the outline of the quarter, he can regularly hit three-eighths inch marbles. When the revolver shooter can shoot a circular group where the width of the bullet on each side of the center will make the space between them slightly smaller than the object being shot at, then he will score all hits just so long as he does not permit the group to open up enough to make this opening in the center of group large enough for the object that is used as the target to pass through without touching. Such a shooter could hit any number of such three-eighths inch marble targets without ever even touching the central point of the target on or around which the quarter size group is shot. Note this carefully—**three-eighths inch marbles do not require three-eighths inch groups** in order to score consecutive hits either stationary or in the air. These are the points on which some critics "bump their heads."

Fast and Fancy Revolver Shooting

A stationary target shooter or an aerial target shot could shoot perfect scores for an entire lifetime without ever having to place a shot in the exact center of any target. This is an important point that is well worth remembering.

The person who starts out to acquire sufficient skill to "put his bullets right on top of each other," has a false ideal. It is not at all necessary, and likewise **very hard to do.** The aerial target shooting enthusiast who wishes to become expert in such shooting, while using revolvers for the purpose, who believes the rumors that "So and So" always waits for the tossed-up target to **stop momentarily** at the top of its flight "just as it is turning and where it hesitates slightly just before it starts dropping," is going to waste a lot of energy and form a lot of very useless habits. This is the biggest line of misinformation ever handed out to anyone who ever hopes to hit such targets regularly or to be successful when more than one object at a time is to be thrown for him to hit.

When placing or, more correctly perhaps, trying to place several shots on one target while in the air, this very wise "watchful waiting" attitude—while the target hesitates—is a very practical illustration of the familiar saying, "He who hesitates is lost." Instead of waiting and trying to make still (or stopped) targets out of rapidly moving ones, just follow the outline of the methods described a short time ago in the account of the marble shooting. Bend the body forward for downward movement. Bend the body back for upward movement. Swing or twist body sideways for side movement, and hold arms and hands and revolver in direct relative position to the eye and in line with, and as near as possible at, the correct elevation of target, while making these body movements as described. Study the foot movements described in hip shooting and quick draws. They will be found valuable in aerial target shooting also.

The body movement is "The Big Bad Wolf" in the aerial target shooting game. When studied and developed until it is brought under prompt and positive control, it is the thing that makes it possible to really destroy the aerial targets with regularity, and is not a mysterious matter at all. Experience will then gradually develop proficiency sufficient for hitting groups of targets, two and three or more thrown at once, etc., all in due time, depending of course on persistent practice and systematic study of the principles involved.

A person cannot even throw rocks down a well unless he has skill enough to control the rocks so that they will at least strike within the area of the opening of the well, otherwise he is just throwing them at the well. The same rule applies to aerial target shooting. When pointing skill has been developed to where the gun can be consistently directed so as to group the bullets within the approximate area occupied by the target to be hit, then progress has been started. That is the reason the writer

Training for Aerial Targets

advises large targets, at short distances, sort of "close-ups" like the movie folks play it sometimes.

The "big idea" of not using sights in this work, as advanced by the "posers," or "puzzle putters" as the writer generally considers the "public-minded director geniuses" who can offer free advice on every subject from "birth control" to "reincarnation," without ever having actually experienced either, has just about the same value as trying to get aerial targets to stop and wait for you while you shoot at them. That sights cannot be, and are not used, in this kind of shooting is a radically wrong impression based entirely on theory and lack of actual knowledge of the subject.

That triggers are **not** squeezed and controlled in much the same way as for other shooting, is also quite a wrong idea. THEY ARE! The apparent difference lying in the fact that it is done much more quickly and with a longer sweep when using double-action methods, yet very evenly, very carefully, and quite smoothly, as a result of practice and practical experience which must be developed, of course, by persistent effort and sensible study of the subject and the principles involved.

As a result of the foregoing I feel confident that the details, as given here, have very thoroughly "blown up" the quite generally prevailing idea strong in the minds of many, even among some very expert stationary target shots, that the aerial target expert, when shooting re-volvers at rapidly moving targets in the air, just snaps at them, jerking both gun and trigger, sort of point blank, or "slam bang," trusting to luck or to a kind or unkind providence, as the case may be, to help him to connect regularly. Such opinions are interpreted perhaps, in this case, as **kind providence** if you hit regularly and **unkind** if you miss regu-larly. My experience leads me to believe that providence, or "Lady Luck," as the case may be, is very calmly indifferent as to a hit or a miss, and the success, if any, that can be secured depends on the method of procedure as outlined.

A reassuring comparison for the aerial shooter can be found in the fol-lowing: When shooting three targets at a time in a mixed program, com-bining one stationary target and two aerial targets, the stationary target always requires much more time for getting the shot away and scoring a hit than the aerial targets do. The arrangement calls for the stationary target to be shot at in between the two aerial targets, as follows: The stationary target is placed on the ground or other convenient location about twenty feet from the shooter, then when ready the two targets are tossed in the air—the first aerial target is shot, then the gun is lowered to place a bullet on the stationary target, then the gun is raised again to shoot the second aerial target. The whole performance must be com-pleted before either of the aerial targets can fall to the ground.

Fast and Fancy Revolver Shooting

To make clear what is really meant by sure hits, that are **properly controlled and accurately directed, so that they can be confined to some specified area or group, of some certain size or shape,** I have made the many experiments and tests herein outlined to determine several of the factors entering into the controlling of bullets fired from revolvers, at objects of various sizes and shapes which were tossed in the air for the purpose, and have succeeded in securing the very interesting results set forth that are, I believe, of great value when discussing the aerial target branch of revolver shooting.

The experience gained through the experiments carried on in the early attempts on aerial targets generally, developed the idea of attempting to place all six bullets from a revolver into a can before it could fall to the ground. An interesting problem entering into this game at this time was that the can had to be, or at least should be, tossed up in some uniform manner so as to make it possible to work out some sort of system of procedure to handle the situation. The can should also be tossed or thrown so that it traveled slightly in towards the shooter to avoid drifting too much in some contrary direction from the repeated impact of bullets when "Lady Luck" was favoring the shooter.

In the beginning all of these things were not quite so simple, or so easy to figure out correctly, as was later the case, and as usual we had plenty of critics working overtime, and no doubt they were responsible for the success that came later by keeping us everlastingly at it. Shooting fast double-action groups of six shots within the very limited time period required for the can to fall eighteen or twenty feet to the ground, had not been thoroughly mastered by anybody as yet, so we were frequently informed. Controlling the gun and repointing it accurately after the disturbance caused by recoil of each shot had not as yet been quite completely mastered either. The can would be falling rapidly and at each shot the gun would jump up and obscure vision of the can entirely, sort of making a now-you-see-me and now-you-don't game out of it. To move the hand down and repoint the gun at the lower part of the can each time after the disturbance of recoil, was very difficult and to complete these movements six times, with any very accurate pointing, while the can was still in the air, was a somewhat bewildering job.

The action of gravity being constant, and over which the shooter could have no control, made the time periods very uniform. It being impossible to change this governing influence so as to prolong the time in any way, the only solution possible was to greatly simplify the movements and then completely master them, so that the time period that would be required for successfully completing them would be reduced to much less than the time period required for the can to fall to the ground, which was usually around one and a half seconds, generally less. The big question

Training for Aerial Targets

The high hand hold on revolver grip and the trigger finger position used by the author for all aerial target shooting and fast double-action shooting.

The end of the trigger finger only is used and is held low down, very close to the end of the trigger, thus getting the benefit of all possible leverage.

up for consideration was how to go about working out these very important changes.

It will be remembered that in my writings I have often expressed the opinion that very fast double-action group shooting, aerial target shooting, quick-draw shooting and hip shooting are all dependent for success on body balance and control of body movements, and are all inter-related, sort of "in-laws" from the same family. It was this idea which I put to work to solve the problem of many hits on any single aerial target regardless of what type might be used.

The training methods for preparing to fire six bullets into a tin can were entirely changed at this particular time, and practice for many weeks was confined to shooting six shots at certain sized portions of paper targets just as rapidly as it was possible to operate the revolvers by the double-action method. The recoil of the .38 Special cartridges was controlled and finally almost completely overcome by a system I had been

Fast and Fancy Revolver Shooting

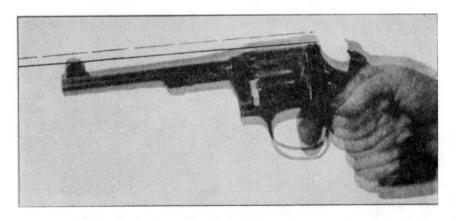

SLIGHT LIFTING MOTION OF ENTIRE GUN

The above cut illustrates the method employed for utilizing the beneficial effect of gravity for fast revolver shooting.

Working away from or in opposition to gravity has been found to be a very positive system for accuracy in fast shooting. It consists of leveling the gun just slightly below the point where you wish the bullet to strike, then, while maintaining the proper sight alignment, raise the entire gun up to the correct elevation (as indicated by the shadows and lines) for the bullet to connect with the desired spot or object which constitutes the target, whatever it may be. It will be found that gravity will greatly assist in arresting the motion of the gun momentarily while the shot is being fired.

When the upward muscular movement ceases, the influence of gravity immediately stops the gun; but, when moving the gun in any direction, except when opposed to gravity, the influence of the weight of the moving gun has a tendency to cause the gun to continue its movement for a fraction of time after the shooter's intentional muscular movement has ceased. As a consequence it goes slightly past the point at which the gun was intended to be aimed. This fact is the cause of and accounts for most of the poor results usually secured by what is generally referred to as "snap shooting." This very important matter can be and has been quite easily overlooked entirely by many shooters. A reasonable amount of study of the regularity with which this "non-stop" action occurs under the conditions just described should make it quite evident that much helpful effect will result from making use of the influence of gravity and having it work in your favor instead of against you at all times.

This upward movement is only slight and must not be overdone. Bottom line shows position from which the upward movement should start, and the top line shows the elevation at which the gun should hesitate or come to rest in line with the spot selected as the target. This movement is better controlled by causing the hand and gun to be raised as a result of moving the upper part of the body backward slightly. The arm and hand can be elevated just slightly without the body movement, if preferred, but will not be found to be quite so successful consistently as when combined with body movement.

The reference so often heard about throwing down on a target with a six shooter, and snapping the shot away at the proper instant, seems to have its successful results made more difficult by this same downward pull of gravity, which can be so helpfully effective when made use of from the opposite direction.

If the gun is used with the "throw down" movement and "snapped" at the spot or an attempt is made to "snap" the shot away correctly while the gun is passing the spot, only a few trials will be required to convince the most skeptical that when the gun is going up and away from gravity it is much more under control than when the "throw down" method is used.

Training for Aerial Targets

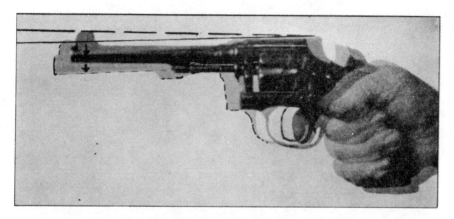

THE FORWARD POKE

The secret of recovery from recoil and repointing of revolver for fast, accurate shooting

The above cut shows the favorite method used by the author for quickly repointing and leveling the run after the recoil. As indicated by the shadow the gun is pushed slightly forward toward the target, which brings the front sight down and in proper relation to the rear sight.

When attempting superspeed group shooting on stationary targets and multiple aerial target shooting also, this slight forward poking motion is very helpful for getting the gun placed in proper relation to the same stationary target or on another aerial target for the next shot. If you can learn to control the gun so that all necessary changing movement from point to point will cease at the instant that deliberate muscular effort in any stated direction is discontinued, then fast and close group shooting on stationary targets becomes a rather positive performance and the hitting of aerial targets is very much simplified.

The two methods of handling a revolver described under the above and previous cut can be successfully combined. They constitute the secret of success back of many fast performances.

The forward poking motion is controlled by the wrist and forearm, then when the sights come level and in line the slight upward movement of the entire gun away from gravity (as illustrated in first cut) can be combined with the short poke and made use of to direct the gun at the exact spot intended to be hit. The combining of the lifting motion of entire gun with the forward poke is accomplished by tilting the upper part of the body backward slightly which lifts the gun, without any movement by the wrist or arm being necessary after the forward poke mentioned. Tilting the body forward will, of course, have the opposite effect of lowering the gun any amount that may be necessary.

experimenting with and finally successfully worked out. It consisted of holding hand, wrist and arm muscles firm so that the muscular rebound from the tension, so exerted, would put the gun right back into the same relative position, regarding the target, as it had been before the recoil disturbed the holding and pointing position of hand and gun. To the arm tension was added the help of the shoulder muscles and the body weight was behind that, aided by a slight leaning forward to buck the lifting effect of the recoil.

Fast and Fancy Revolver Shooting

THE GREAT IMPORTANCE OF FOOT MOVEMENT REQUIRES STUDY

Left—Showing the shooting position of Ted Renfro of Montana, one of the foremost topnotch all-around wing shots of all time, as well as the international champion. A close study of his foot position and movement will prove very valuable in the study of fast and fancy revolver shooting.

Right—Weight is carried on one foot and the other foot used as a stabilizer to control the body swing just as is necessary in all aerial target shooting and other fast action shooting with revolvers.

As the shooting speed was increased, with the recoil coming faster, of course, it was necessary to add more pressure and weight, by body movement, until finally the body, shoulder, arm, wrist and hand action combined became a steady forward and downward pressure, very similar to holding down the handle of a plow. It was later found that this pressure could be regulated to overcome recoil of any caliber of cartridge used.

The result accomplished by this system, as here outlined, was to control the groups to well within the outline of the hand and very often well within the outline of an ordinary playing card, which can be noted on many of the submitted reproductions of ultraspeed targets. As conclusively demonstrated by the time periods recorded on these targets the time factor was whipped to a standstill. The grouping accuracy on the paper targets was sufficient for quart cans, with room to spare, and

Training for Aerial Targets

EMMETT McGIVERN DEMONSTRATES METHODS OF DEVELOPING AERIAL TARGET SHOOTING
Shooting rapidly revolving target. Excellent training for aerial target shooting.

Shooting targets while revolving vertically. Excellent training for aerial target shooting while lying on back and shooting above one's head.

Fast and Fancy Revolver Shooting

EMMETT McGIVERN SHOOTING TARGETS WHILE HANGING HEAD DOWN
Excellent training which is helpful in many ways in connection with fancy shooting performances and demonstrations.

the next thing necessary was to determine just how to get these groups well placed on the falling can. This was accomplished by developing the correct system of movements to control the gun, so as to keep it pointed at the lower part of the can while each succeeding shot was being fired.

After a prolonged period of intensive training for development of the actions and movements necessary for this particular sort of performance, and the firing of around thirty thousand assorted cartridges at various sized cans, under various conditions, which were tossed in the air by various methods and mechanical equipment, the stunt was finally ready for public inspection and approval or disapproval. The reception by the public was very satisfactory and the can shooting was made a permanent part of public demonstrations generally. After the intensive training period was over and the performance was successfully mastered on smaller cans, all later shooting was done with cans similar to the well-perforated one (shown on page 68), which measures five by six inches.

It is well to remember that any stunt performed well after, or during, a period of intensive training is going to be much easier to perform right after the close of such period than it will be if attempted two or three years later, without some rather extensive repetition of such training

Training for Aerial Targets

EMMETT McGIVERN DEMONSTRATING

Left--Shooting aerial targets while lying on back and shooting above one's head.

WALTER GROFF DEMONSTRATING

Right—Aerial targets tossed straight up while shooter is on his back. Later in this training the thrower moves farther away from shooter's head—as may be desired.

being again indulged in, before making an attempt to duplicate the best performance that may have been made at some time during the original development period.

During a recent trip east I was several times handed an empty revolver and requested by some person to operate the gun five times in some particular part of a second that happened to strike the person's fancy, just so they could tell what it sounded like. It should be quite easy to understand that while I like to be obliging I didn't try to do it. It would be just about as sensible to expect a swimming expert, while standing on a paved street, to show you how he did his record high dive at some former time.

The systematic training methods and control development employed to successfully accomplish the results outlined in this section, constitute the foundation from which was built up all of the later combinations of fancy stunts and demonstrations. At the time of which I write there were no instructors in this branch of revolver shooting nor any textbooks

TIMING AERIAL TARGET SHOOTING

Left—Emmett McGivern demonstrates aerial target shooting while hanging head down from the shoulders of the author. Note the revolver is connected with electric timing equipment for this and similar experiments.

Right—This view shows how aerial target shooting is timed by having the revolver connected with electric timing equipment.

either. Everyone struggled along through an atmosphere of doubt, uncertainty, and discouragement, depending for success on the amount of determination he had incorporated within himself.

This can shooting stunt caused more comments from critics, who undoubtedly were not any too well-informed regarding the problem involved, than all of the other stunts on our entire shooting program put together. One of the amusing angles connected with it was that the most insistent of such critics at all times, both early and later, were stationary target shots, and not aerial target shots with revolvers at all, and what was still more entertaining, none of them were so very good at fast, positively controlled, double-action revolver shooting on any kind of targets; yet by using one or two boxes of shells occasionally some of

The author breaking aerial target while sighting with aid of a mirror. Note raising effect of the recoil on the lightly held gun. Courtesy *Outdoor Life*.

them would attempt to demonstrate the improbability of anyone's success with such a stunt.

While I was using many thousands of cartridges, backed by plenty of aerial target practice and experience, to prove that it could be done, some others were attempting to prove the opposite with a few shots now and then fired at a can in the air without having had any training or experience whatever in any form of aerial target shooting. No one can simply walk out and make six hits on a can in the air without plenty of training on aerial target shooting and plenty of persistent practice as well. I have been successful in teaching the system to several persons who have made fairly rapid progress.

I do not have any grievances of any kind against any of the critics. They serve a very useful purpose by keeping all of us everlastingly trying until we accomplish what we have set out to do. Without them all of us would undoubtedly have a tendency to ease up a little on our efforts before we quite reached some of the more difficult goals.

The author shooting aerial targets holding revolver upside down.

It is only fair to mention at this time that some of the most valuable ideas that have come to me concerning unusual, difficult, and, at times, spectacular stunts have come from the critics. Some were honest, while others were "just onery." I gave due consideration to all expressions from all sources, studied, analyzed, diagnosed and experimented, with usually the result that later I could and did perform the very things that many of the critics, sincere or otherwise, often stated as being impossible, nonsensical, or of the "couldn't be done" variety.

If some particular performance is generally regarded as being so difficult as to border on the impossible or even the improbable, then it should be quite interesting to both the experimenter and the spectators alike, hence well worth attempting, and, if successfully accomplished, by

MRS. McGIVERN BREAKING FLYING TARGET WITH LEFT HAND
.38 Smith & Wesson Gun, No. 286600

DOUBLES IN THE AIR
Right—With .45 Automatic pistol.

Left—.45 Automatic on high aerial targets. Note ejected shell to the right of shooter. Target thrown by Charlie Flannigan. Courtesy *Outdoor Life*.

Training for Aerial Targets

FOUR SHOTS THROUGH A CLAY PIGEON

Tossed in the air only once. These pigeons were soaked in water for several days in preparation for these experiments, which were quite successful as shown. Automatic pistols were later discarded for double-action revolvers. Courtesy *Outdoor Life*.

Upper Left—Walter Groff demonstrating on two quart-size cans thrown at the same time from trap placed 25 feet from the shooter.

Upper Right—"Three wooden blocks thrown at same time." Trap is arranged to throw these targets on a curve up and in towards shooter.

Lower Left—"Cutting cards in the air," turned edgewise to the shooter.

Lower Right—Walter Groff working on a high one traveling out and away from shooter.

Training for Aerial Targets

Breaking aerial targets thrown diagonally across and away from shooter.

D. B. Wesson throwing overhead targets for Ed McGivern at Ernie Miller's Ranch, Oct. 10, 1935.

Fast and Fancy Revolver Shooting

CHICKEN SHOOTING

The target is kicked high in the air with the shooter's foot instead of throwing it by hand, leaving the shooter in a rather difficult position for the quick shot that must follow

its very nature would be considered somewhat outstanding from the more ordinary class of performances. This fact accounts, to a great extent, for the great variety of stunts successfully worked out **one at a time** over the period of years during which I was actively interested in such development. The methods of procedure for success with these shooting performances have been very materially simplified since the time I first became interested in such things, and I am passing the information along in the hope of helping others towards such success.

As formerly written by me the system of procedure described in the following may help to remove any impression, such as at one time existed, that some amazing skill or super-gunman ability is necessary for success with this stunt. Putting five or six shots into a medium-sized can before it falls to the ground, after it has been tossed up to a height of eighteen or twenty feet, has now no mystery connected with it. As a matter of fact, it is simply the result of common-sense figuring, mixed with plenty of practice,

Training for Aerial Targets

AERIAL TARGETS BEHIND THE SHOOTER
Raise up, turn and shoot.

No TIME FOR FANCY FOOT WORK
Toss target between legs to rear.

combined with systematic training methods, **conducted under very similar conditions and at regular intervals over a reasonable period of time,** backed with plenty of determination and the expenditure of much ammunition.

The method is as follows: Just as the can starts down, I shoot at the lower part and each succeeding shot is held slightly lower in relation to the can until at the sixth shot the gun is, seemingly, pointed a couple of inches below it, which may be due to letting the front sight climb too much. I recall, when working for practice and not throwing the can very high, the can sometimes came to the ground by the time the fourth or fifth shot was fired—quite often just before the last shot was fired. I distinctly remember that in some such cases the last shot was fired just after the can hit the ground, and **although the can stopped, the gun hand kept moving while yet functioning the gun** and the bullet struck several inches under the can. This is the real reason why many people probably thought that the can could not be hit as many times as I have been able to prove that it could be hit.

Most of the later shots will be fired over the can instead of into it if the gun is pointed at the center instead of at the bottom part, or just at

Left—A perfect three-target throw by Mrs. McGivern.

Right—A perfect four-target throw by Mrs. McGivern. Mac says anybody ought to hit these, with throwing like that to help out. Courtesy *Outdoor Life*.

the lower edge of it. Most shooters, lacking experience, will fire all shots, first to last, with gun pointed at or above the center of the can, and of course score beautiful misses. This description applies when the can is thrown into the air in front of shooter when he is standing at a distance of ten to fifteen feet from the thrower.

A careful study of the detailed diagram of the can, when thrown by a trap placed at various distances from the shooter, up to and including twenty-five feet, will give a very clear idea of exactly the distance the can will be away from the shooter at all times, and at all angles, during such demonstration and experiment. A similar careful study of the size of the groups of five and six bullets on the paper targets submitted, which were fired from double-action revolvers in periods of time below a second, and also noting the distance at which they were shot, will make it quite clear that keeping **such groups** within the outline of the length and width of an ordinary quart can, can be, and is, quite possible.

Training for Aerial Targets

FOUR AERIAL TARGETS TOSSED IN THE AIR AT SAME TIME
The three lower targets were shot from right to left. The high target at left was shot last.

Therefore, there is no mystery connected with this performance any more than there is with any of the other demonstrations listed herein. As is quite evident the can requires more time to return to the ground after being tossed twenty feet in the air than is ever required to fire the five or six shots shown on even the slowest of the rapid fire groups. Combining aerial target shooting with rapid fire double-action group shooting is the system that is required in this problem to get the desired results, plainly evident in the photos (page 155). The can in the picture, as was stated, measures five by six inches, and, as plainly visible, there was still plenty of room to spare around the group of shots thereon.

Fast and Fancy Revolver Shooting

Shooting high incoming aerial target with revolver.   Central Montana Fair, Sept. 4, 1931.

Two aerial targets tossed at same time shot with two-inch barrel revolver.   Central Montana Fair, Sept. 4, 1931.   Courtesy *American Rifleman*.

Training for Aerial Targets

Three targets tossed in the air at same time.   Central Montana Fair, Sept. 4, 1931.

Five targets tossed in the air by two throwers.   Central Montana Fair, Sept. 4, 1931.
Courtesy *American Rifleman*.

Fast and Fancy Revolver Shooting

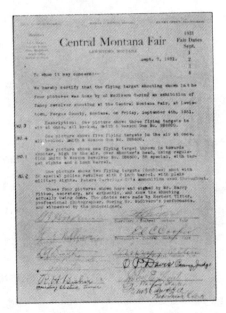

Affidavit of fair officials identifying four pictures of shooting done at Central Montana Fair, Sept. 4, 1931.

We will now give consideration to the methods used for developing another of the more interesting stunts, taking up here the cutting of cards edgewise in the air. This decidedly interesting performance of cutting cards edgewise in the air, or hitting lead discs slightly smaller than a silver dollar (page 71) when thrown edgewise to the shooter, does not in any way border on a miracle even though done with bullets from a .38 Special revolver. The idea for this stunt first percolated through my cranium after an exhibition during which one of the self-appointed critics made light of my having cut some cards held edgewise to me while sighting the revolver through the reflection of a mirror. Of course the cards were stationary, but—well, try the stunt sometime and get acquainted.

Anyway, after listening none too patiently to his line of mild abuse, we made a small wager that I could learn to cut cards thrown into the air. This, the critic stated, sounded like pretty big talk from a little man. (As most folks know, the writer is built rather close to the ground.) So I just naturally **had** to make good. The method of procedure was as follows: Going to a woodworker's shop, we had some full sized four by four timbers of soft pine turned round. These we had sliced on the saw

Training for Aerial Targets

C. L. Flannigan of Great Falls, Mont., shooting six aerial targets within a period of time around 2-4/5 seconds between the first and last shot, using a hand-operated repeating shot-gun for the purpose.   Targets are thrown by himself.

so that they made round slabs four inches in diameter and from a half to three-quarters of an inch in thickness. These were tossed in the air edgewise to the shooter, and in a short time could be hit regularly. As I made progress these slabs were cut thinner and thinner until finally heavy cards were substituted for the wooden discs, and the hits were regular enough so that I was all set to hunt up Friend Critic and "show" him. As practice was continued, care was taken to keep the point of impact of the bullet on the edge of the card as near a certain elevation as possible. Later, the lead discs were substituted at certain intervals, and, as can be seen, the point of impact has been kept quite uniform.

The method of aiming at such objects is to raise the gun from below to get alignment with the card, then as the sights and the bottom of the card come together, the body is bent slightly forward, carrying the gun and sights along with the card for a short distance, **straight down** along with the card's downward travel, keeping gun and card in correct relative

Fast and Fancy Revolver Shooting

SIX SHOTS IN CAN

The author putting six shots into a can that is tossed in the air before it can fall to the ground.   Courtesy *Outdoor Life*.

position to score a hit. The cards (page 71) show fairly well how this worked out by the ones that are shown as cut, and those shown as nipped only. This picture shows the same effect as Peter's Cartridge Company spark photography demonstration shows on a card being cut with a special .38 wad-cutter bullet. The bullet does not, as generally thought, move the card in the air several feet, nor do the separated pieces travel any distance after the bullet travels through the material during the cutting operation. Another thing of a similar nature that has surprised many persons is that an ordinary cigarette paper, turned edgewise to the shooter and held in the fingers or with tips of a nipper clothespin or in some similar manner, can be cut in narrow strips with the blunt-nosed .38 special wad-cutter bullets which, strange as it may seem, do not crumple up the paper and knock it out of the way, as many persons have persisted in arguing that it would. Successful tests and experiments solve many such funny little problems in, at times, very surprising ways.

At this point we have a golden opportunity to study a little closer into the comments and expressed opinions of certain persons who, in all probability, couldn't hit a washtub tossed in the air without the services of a

Training for Aerial Targets

PUTTING FIVE OR SIX SHOTS IN CAN WHILE IN THE AIR

Showing how the five and six shot can shooting stunt was developed. The can in this instance is just 20 feet from the bottom of the pole. Trap is clearly visible at bottom of pole, which is exactly 18 feet high. The impact of the bullets striking the can appears to slightly slow the falling motion, seeming to be as much as a tenth of a second per shot at times. Courtesy *Outdoor Life*.

surveyor to first measure all distances for them, and who probably would also expect the surveyor to hold the tub stationary in the air while they shot at it, but, in a loud voice, assert—or perhaps they just simply pretend to admit—that they know the limitations and also the possibilities of revolvers, including the **impossibility** of aiming or using sights, or squeezing and controlling triggers, during the development and practice of this kind of aerial target shooting.

I wish to state, as a result of my experience, that no man living knows all of the possibilities or exact limitations of revolvers or pistols, either for performance, for effectiveness, for accuracy, or for speed, or for all combined. I am fully aware, of course, when making such statement, that it is directly contrary to the several self-flattering statements made by

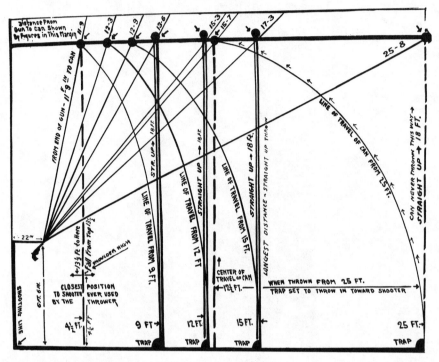

Explanatory—Diagram of can shooting by McGivern when using trap. Showing the distance that can is away from the gun at all distances, all angles, and all trap arrangements. Courtesy *Outdoor Life*.

some others **who have taken full credit of such knowledge to themselves.** The ever-changing methods of construction, material and ingredients used in the manufacture of both the guns and the ammunition, precludes the possibility of any one individual—no matter how conceited he may happen to be about it—ever possessing so much real knowledge of the subject at any one time. The new Smith & Wesson ".357" Magnum revolver and cartridges demonstrated this very clearly, and the surprises for the "wise ones" are still rapidly developing.

One of the most important points stressed in most of these wild outbursts of near scientific "chatter," was the **time factor,** which, we readily agree, is a very important one. I mention these things here at this time for the reason that herein I will be offering a great assortment of evidence very contradictory to such wise statements, regardless of who may have made them. Time and time factors and **correct timing methods and equipment** are indeed a most important part of the material contained

— 70 —

Training for Aerial Targets

CARDS EDGEWISE   LEAD DISCS EDGEWISE

SHOOTING BY THE AUTHOR

Left—These cards tossed in the air edgewise to the shooter were cut by bullets fired from revolvers. Courtesy *Outdoor Life*.

Right—These 1¾-inch lead discs were tossed in the air edgewise to the shooter and were hit with bullets fired from revolvers. Note the uniform elevation register evident by the three different types and weight of bullets and loads which show about the same variation that is generally evident when stationary targets are used. Courtesy *Outdoor Life*.

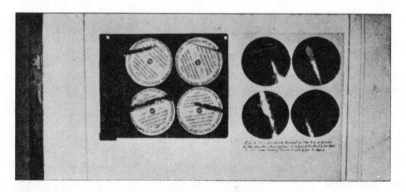

CUTTING CARDS EDGEWISE IN THE AIR

These cards tossed in the air edgewise to the shooter were cut by bullets fired from revolvers and show very clearly the necessity for perfect line shooting and correct holding. September, 1937. Shooting by Walter Groff.

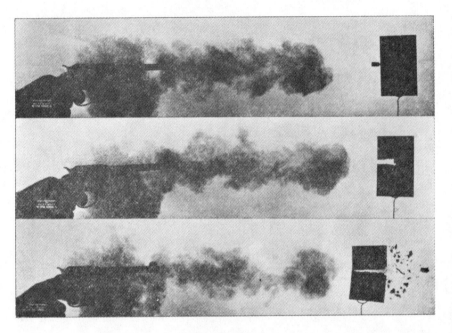

VISIBLE BALLISTICS

Upper—Visible Ballistics by spark photography produced by the Peters Cartridge Co., showing a wad cutter bullet cutting a card edgewise just as it is done in the aerial target shooting on cards herein described.

Center—Shows bullet which has cut halfway through the card turned edgewise to the bullet. Note that while card is only supported by a wire clip the bullet does not move the card during its passage through it.

Lower—Sparkograph of a Peters wad cutter bullet cutting a card edgewise. Note that the upper half of the card is still in approximately its original position. The bullet has a small amount of the cardboard clinging to the point. Although the card was light in weight the bullet, because of its speed, cut the card without moving it to any great extent. The resistance offered by the card was sufficient to tilt the bullet slightly. This is exactly the condition encountered when cutting cards edgewise in the air with similar bullets fired from revolvers.

Note that the card in center cut shows the same wide path, made by the bullet, that is evident in the cards which were cut in the air without any support whatever.

in these pages. I very honestly tried to make the time factor a **much more important part of the research programs** outlined and carried out to successful conclusion, and covering, as it does, a much greater field, with more exact and reliable data and details, **than ever has been attempted in any other book of a similar nature,** or by any other individual experimenter personally responsible for the building and financing of all special equipment. It may be well to point out and make clear that all this was done unaided in any way by anyone who might put me

SHOOTING THROUGH THE MIDDLE

Shooting through the holes of washers which are covered with paper and then tossed in the air, flat side facing shooter.

under any obligations that might make it necessary for me to twist or "flavor" any opinions expressed.

When guns, ammunition or other equipment is herein mentioned favorably or recommended for some special purpose, such opinion is based purely on actual merit as I found it, and from the results secured by actual trials and actual experience with the goods mentioned. Decisions, where stated, are the results of honest effort to find satisfactory answers to certain questions considered important in this line of endeavor, as, and for, a guide to those who may be honestly seeking information and who may not be situated or equipped to secure such information for themselves.

Few, if any, other individuals in the history of the shooting game up to the present time, at least, have ever attempted to cover so wide a field of actual demonstration, or have had any more complete, convenient and practical equipment at hand for determining the actual importance of the **time factor** and its general and also its special effect on revolver shooting. The definite and, at times, quite surprising results which we have been enabled to secure with the aid of such experimental equipment, as stated, are herein set forth as a reference and guide for others in such research.

Fast and Fancy Revolver Shooting

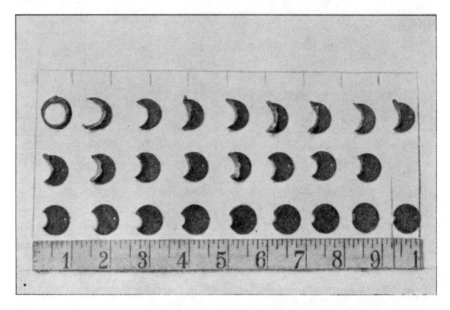

DIME SIZE LEAD DISCS

SHOOTING DIME SIZE DISCS TOSSED IN THE AIR USING .38 CALIBER REVOLVERS FOR THE PURPOSE

The results evident on these twenty-six dime size lead discs constitute a very valuable and practical demonstration of aerial target shooting. There are included in this display the results of two sight adjustments, which are more or less noticeable in the final results. The first six from the right to left on the bottom row show one result. Eight of the next nine from right to left, lower and middle row, show another effect. The fourth one from right in the middle row, which was misplaced, belongs with the two at the left of the middle row, and the rest of the discs ending on the left of top row show a decidedly different effect, finally resulting in a center hit.

These targets were shot by Walter Groff in September, 1937, under the supervision of the author.

The sort of results shown by this display should go far towards removing the quite generally prevailing idea that point blank methods of pointing the gun are made use of instead of correctly adjusted sights.

SECTION 6

TWO-GUN TRAINING. SHOOTING TWO REVOLVERS AT THE SAME TIME ON STATIONARY, SWINGING AND AERIAL TARGETS. SUITABLE SIGHT COMBINATIONS FOR THE PURPOSE.

Developing proficiency in two-gun shooting on stationary and aerial targets is conducted along the following lines: If a person who has mastered shooting one revolver well wishes to become a two-gun, fast-time artist on aerial targets, superspeed groups, etc., all that is necessary is to simply train the other hand in the same way as you did the first one, only do it separately. When both hands are about equally developed, take two guns of the same kind, size, and weight. Shoot one shot from the left hand gun at the selected spot (always starting at short range), then shoot one shot from the right hand gun at the same spot—try for sure hits, remember. Don't sacrifice accuracy for speed.

Shoot the guns alternately (one after the other) in that manner at first, gaining speed by experience and practice, always trying to maintain sure hits. Gradually, by this system, the time between shots can be reduced until both guns can be fired together at the one target and the shots, all hits, will be well-grouped in a surprisingly short time.

The two-gun, two-target work is done in exactly the same way. Alternate—one gun at the first target, then the other gun at the other target. Practice brings confidence and speed until later on the two guns can be shot at once, good groups, good speed. For developing the two-gun draw, start by drawing one gun at a time, working alternately, first one gun, then the other. Work slowly and carefully for sure hits. Work it out until it can be done with each hand about equally well. Experience and plenty of practice will develop speed in the use of both hands, and the two guns, alternately, left, then right; later you can use both together. When equal skill is developed in both right and left hands, the shooter is called ambidextrous. When both guns are fired at the same time, they are shot simultaneously.

If these two-target, two-gun stunts appeal to the student of this fascinating game, he can place the two targets a little farther apart, gradually increasing the distance as his skill develops until they are on opposite sides of the shooter. The distance may be short at first and increased as the shooter's skill progresses.

The big advantage of having both hands trained equally well, or as nearly equal as your physical make-up will permit, lies in the possibility of getting one hand crippled, or perhaps at some time conditions may arise that make it impossible for you to use your preferred hand with which to do the shooting that may be necessary to protect yourself, your home, or your family.

Fast and Fancy Revolver Shooting

Upper Left—Getting the officer's gun. *Upper Right*—Poking it into the officer's ribs. *Lower Left*—Ready for anything that may turn up. *Lower Right*—Two guns can be very well handled when handcuffed in front. This two-gun situation can be adapted to aerial targets or any other arrangment involving two or more targets of any nature.

A trained revolver shot with handcuffs on and hands behind his back can easily and quickly grab a gun from an officer's holster and in less than one second later stick the end of the barrel against the officer's ribs (upper right), and when the officer has been disposed of he is ready for anyone else who may be in his way (lower left).

Two-Gun Shooting

If you are an officer and the protection of the life and property of others is a part of your everyday duty, then the value of being proficient in the use of a revolver with either hand, or with each hand about equally well, and, at the same time, is still more important. As we have stated with reference to several other angles of the shooting game, there is no mystery about becoming a good two-handed, two-gun performer. Just proceed the usual way to train each hand separately but equally and uniformly. Later try alternating the shots. When that can be done consistently, try combining the accurate handling of both guns with both hands at the same time, at the same target in the beginning, as stated, then at two separate targets later on, worked out in various combinations and situations to hold the interest of the performer.

We now step up to moving objects with swinging and aerial targets combined in a program of development. The same training is used and is equally necessary for the moving objects and flying target branch of the game. Start this "change of diet" with swinging targets on a fairly long string, wire or rod, allowing fairly long travel of the chosen object. Start with large objects at comparatively short range so as to get more hits. Long range misses don't mean a thing of value—short range sure hits do, and are good training.

When you can hit the large objects any place that you may designate beforehand, then it is time enough for you to get farther away, or to reduce the size of your target. When it is possible to hit the swinging targets with either hand at any part of their travel at each end or any intermediate point of swing that may be decided on beforehand, then is soon enough to begin on flying targets (aerial target shooting), large ones and at short range to start. When the large target can be hit on any spot called for, with each hand, try two hits, then one hit each on two smaller objects, one with each hand. The same rule applies here—the distance can be increased as regular hits begin to get monotonous, but there should be no immediate hurry. The size of the targets may later be reduced to add to the difficulty and keep things from being "too easy." When it gets to be a case of "Johnny Sure Shot" on single targets, try hitting those easy ones twice or three times with each gun, alternately, of course. Plenty of **practice and determination** will eventually bring success.

A better, and perhaps a more progressive, plan is to throw two targets at once, shoot one gun, then the other, one target with each gun. (Fairly large targets at first, always.) If this becomes reasonably easy, try four, second pair thrown later than the first pair and a little higher, of course, to allow clear vision of the several objects and a little more time for the shots. When regular hitting can be guaranteed on aerial targets thrown two at a time, with one gun, the student may desire to continue his training up to the point where he can break several sets of such targets thrown in pairs or

Fast and Fancy Revolver Shooting

Left—This two-gun situation has many dangerous and decidedly effective angles when the guns are in well-trained hands backed by experience.

Upper Right—With leg irons in addition to handcuffs. A wide range of unusual positions can be made use of and still have decidedly effective results.

Lower Right—Showing position of guns and method of sighting made use of when shooting from position shown at upper right.

Even when handcuffed and leg ironed and flat on his back a two-gun handler is still decidedly dangerous and capable of very effective results. Officers should not take unnecessary chances.

doubles, both targets in the air at approximately the same time. Therefore, we will now expose the deep, dark secret of this seemingly impossible stunt. The "magic mixture" for the success of this trick is in the **subconscious mind** of the shooter, and can be developed in the following way.

If expense is not a matter of importance, secure the services of two persons who are willing to learn to throw properly for you. Have them practice together until each can throw two targets at once with good control so that they will go about the same height every time they are thrown, that height to be governed by the amount of time you require to score two sure hits. At first, have thrower number one toss his two targets—shoot them. Instruct thrower number two to toss his pair of targets into the air just after you finish shooting the first pair, allowing enough time for you to sort of collect yourself. When this can be successfully handled, have thrower number one toss up a third pair of targets shortly after you've shot the second pair. Result—six targets in the air within a reasonably short time. Continue practice with the throwers and shooter working together. When throwers become confident and familiar with the routine the problem becomes very much simplified. Train each hand to shoot alternately, a pair of doubles—two targets thrown at once—for each hand. When you can perform this stunt with a gun in each hand, you will be a qualified two-gun artist. Practice will develop your ability in direct proportion to the amount of study you give the subject.

Thus the **subconscious mind** takes hold—assumes control—over the shooter's movements. The space of time between the throwing of the pairs of targets can be reduced to an almost unnoticed pause. As subconscious control is further developed, as a result of systematic training, one thrower can throw all three sets of targets in any order or arrangement desired by the shooter. Any average interested shooter can learn to hit two targets, or doubles, tossed into the air at once, with revolvers. Persistent study and practice will enable many shooters, who have a little natural ability for such things, to develop it to a point where they can hit four targets tossed in pairs with only a short, almost unnoticeable, space of time between. The pause between the throwing of the two groups of targets can be materially shortened by experience and regular practice.

It is quite important to realize that the secret of successful shooting with revolvers, when groups of two or more targets are tossed in the air at once, does not rest with the shooter alone, but depends to a great extent on the ability of the assistant to control the targets so that they will be placed or grouped one above the other, thereby enabling the shooter to be immediately aware of the location of each of the several targets, and making it possible for him to follow out some plan of procedure for firing the shots in some sort of instantly decided-upon rotation. The time limitation being of paramount importance, the period of deliberation for the selection and

Showing the system of holding and sighting two guns at the same time, one upside down, the other right side up.   In all such two-gun shooting the eye is the point of a triangle; the two lines running to the separated targets complete the triangle.   The sighting is done with the master eye by looking over the sights of one gun and then over the other. Steady holding of one gun is necessary while the other gun is lined up, if the guns are to be fired simultaneously.

On aerial targets both guns are pointed up at about the elevation that the targets are expected to appear and one gun is sighted and fired quickly and then the other is handled in the same way as rapidly as possible; the time interval between shots is usually very short, not generally very noticeable.

choice of targets by the shooter must be reduced to the smallest amount of time possible. When the targets can be tossed in such a way that they are grouped one above the other, the revolver shooter is very materially assisted in instantly locating them and getting the shots away within the short-time period that such targets can remain in the air.

The fact should be fairly well-established by now that target sights are very necessary equipment for aerial target shooting as outlined herein. The formerly existing general belief and seemingly endless arguments about the probability of doing this sort of shooting without using the sights at all, should be permanently set aside. If such shooting can be successfully done without the use of correctly adjusted sights, I, at least, have never been able to master the system.

For my own use, after much study and experiment, I designed and had made for all of my guns what is now known as the McGivern gold bead front sight. This sight has a large, round, projecting gold bead which is set into the face of, and is arranged to fit even with the top and sides of, a one-tenth inch Patridge square top post sight, thereby giving perfect elevation by the use of the top of post sight and combining with it the full advantages of a clearly visible, perfectly constructed for the purpose, brilliant gold bead sight, which has proven, for my use, to be the fastest front sight that I have so far been able to secure. This type of sight is now made by D. W. King Sight Company to fit all revolvers, and is listed as King-McGivern sight. It was first made by Smith & Wesson and is now standard equipment on several of their revolvers, and listed by them as the McGivern Gold Bead.

My second choice in front sights would be the large size King Sparkpoint gold bead. My third choice would be the King-McGivern type with King luminous red bead with chromium light reflector attached. Fourth choice would be the King luminous red post sight with chromium light reflector attached to the sight. The King-Call sight has a round metal insert leveled off flat with the face of the Patridge post sight, and I believe these can be had in several colors and materials for those who may favor this type.

I do not favor any flat faced sight nor any plain black or military style sight for aerial target shooting or for any other sort of fast revolver shooting. The King luminous red post, as mentioned, with chromium light reflector attached, seems, however, to work very well for those who favor post sights in preference to those having beads.

Personally, I use all target model revolvers, both Smith & Wesson and Colt, just as issued by the factories. The only alterations required are the selection of sight combinations. The McGivern gold bead sight is standard Smith & Wesson equipment on some models and will be supplied on any model on special order. I recommend having the sights attached

Fast and Fancy Revolver Shooting

Koehler Brothers compact portable steel bullet backstops as usually arranged for shooting two targets at the same time with a revolver in each hand. These guns are sighted by the master eye as formerly mentioned and positively not by the use of one eye for each gun as some may have believed possible.

The human target element always stimulates interest. Showing the usual arrangement for shooting at two clay pigeons held by assistant. Such targets may be painted white for the purpose. For extra insurance against any danger to assistant the targets may be held with clipper clothespins or on short sticks with clipper clothespins attached. Duvrock targets or clay pigeons do not turn bullets or spatter lead, thus making them a safe target to hold.

at the factory. The King-McGivern front sight can be secured for the Colt guns from D. W. King Sight Company. On the rear sights I use the regular standard, one-tenth inch wide, square notch. A round bottom, wide rear sight slide with extra deep notch can be secured from Smith & Wesson on request, for use with McGivern front sights, if desired. The King white outlined rear sights can be secured for both Colt and Smith & Wesson revolvers, and seem to be helpful to many persons. I have recommended their use on several occasions with satisfactory results. They are furnished in square or round notches as preferred. The white outline is clear cut and very durable.

The King ventilated rib, fitted to both Smith & Wesson and Colt revolvers, which allows any choice and combination of accurately adjustable front and rear sights, will be found suitable for this branch of revolver shooting. The many varieties of aerial target performances listed herein require varied sight adjustments. Many of the situations demand a low point of impact for the bullets. In other words, all bullets must strike slightly lower than the sighting point, or aiming level, for successful results on falling targets, while in several of the other situations illustrated in the "in-action" pictures, where targets are traveling overhead, it is quite readily apparent, from a little close observation and study of the problem which involves the path of travel of the target in relation to the position of the shooter, that, in order to be successful in scoring hits, the point of bullet impact should be, and in fact must be, slightly higher, or just a small but uniform amount above the point of aim, in a manner very similar to the standard bull's-eye shooting on paper targets, wherein the sighting point is just below the edge of the black spot while it is intended that the point of impact, where the bullet will hit, will be the center of the spot and above the aiming point.

By arranging this sort of sight adjustment on certain guns to be used for these special situations, the shooter is enabled to direct the aim at the target without attempting to make complicated allowances while firing the shot, the necessary average allowances having already been made in the sighting arrangement on the guns selected for those certain performances. Close study of these important relative angles help very materially toward success.

In plain terms, if one target is dropping or falling out in front of the shooter and another similar target is passing overhead in a direction toward the shooter, the same pointing won't always hit both targets. The correct sight setting on the guns to be used for similar situations, as when the targets are coming towards the shooter and over his head, would very often overshoot the rapidly dropping target. Clear visibility of targets over sighting level being equally, if not more, important in this game than in paper target shooting, time spent in studying out suitable adjustments

Fast and Fancy Revolver Shooting

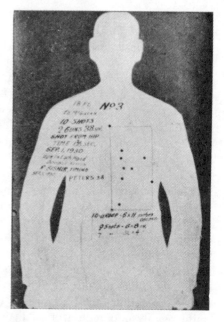

Ten shots at one target at 18 feet, five shots fired from each revolver at the same time double action. The time required was one and two-fifths seconds. Sept. 1, 1930.

A perfect throw on doubles by Mrs. McGivern, both centered.

Wide angle aerial targets using two revolvers. The right hand gun was shot first, which can be easily determined by the positions and attitude of the throwers. Courtesy *Outdoor Life*.

and adaptation of equipment to special purposes is time well spent in very valuable effort.

Such details also constitute an important part of an assistant's training —not to mix up and complicate these angles by improper routine in delivery of targets. The actual difference in the sight adjustments are not very much. In other words, they cannot be adjusted so as to automatically hit the target, but the benefit derived by the shooter from attention to such apparent insignificant details is considerable. These sighting problems are covered in the section on "Sights and Sighting" which follows later.

As a result of these very important conditions and corresponding requirements that exist and are ever present in this game, it becomes clearly evident that the standard regulation, permanently fixed, nonadjustable sight cannot be successfully employed throughout the entire series of experiments and performances. This form of reasoning has been very well supported by my own experience with this type of sights. On the contrary, several guns with clear-cut, easily and accurately adjustable sights are necessary for even reasonable success in this field. In reference to the difficulty of becoming accustomed to using target sights on rapidly moving objects, it may be remembered by many that at the time I started developing advanced training methods for this sort of shooting, I had a very positive idea about it, and was very firm in the belief that a trained mind could direct correspondingly trained hands, eyes, and muscles to handle a revolver so as to positively and quite accurately use such sights on flying targets, and for various tests in superspeed group shooting; all of which seems to be well borne out and quite thoroughly supported by the "actual results" secured, many examples of which are herein set forth.

Describing the sighting process as revealed to me by my own successful experience in this field of endeavor, the image of the sights in relation to the target appears on the field of vision as a silhouette, when properly aimed. When this is not as it should be, as indicated by former experience, the subconscious mind takes charge and makes corrections without any apparent conscious effort. When the perfect silhouette fails to form or becomes disturbed by the gun being incorrectly held, or pointed out of proper alignment of the sights in relation to the object, the subconscious mind can, will, and does make corrections instantly or within a very few hundredths of a second, while the gun and target are moving, and in plenty of time to score hits on such moving target.

Before closing this aerial target discussion a few important things should be given consideration for the benefit of those who may wish to seriously take up this branch of revolver shooting. If expense is not of importance to the experimenter, there are still greater possibilities to be developed than have so far been accomplished. Two very well-trained (until expert)

Two single shot pistols. Right hand gun is sighted by use of a mirror attached to the grip by special bracket.

Two pistols at once at targets on opposite sides of the shooter. One gun is sighted and then head is turned carefully to sight the other gun.

throwers are absolutely necessary for success with multiple aerial target shooting. Each thrower must be able to throw several targets at a time, and so control these targets as to place them one above the other in suitable formation for the shooter to score hits, without the liability of confusing the clear visibility of the targets by broken fragments. The second thrower must keep his group of targets controlled in a similar manner but delivered over to one side of first group, a distance of, perhaps, three feet or more, for the same purpose of preserving clear visibility.

Under these conditions and with such expert assistance, many spectacular and very interesting multiple target stunts are possible of accomplishment. It must, however, be kept in mind that such performances and their problems require long periods of study and preparation, with constant and continuous rehearsing and practice, which will also involve a very considerable expense. There is, of course, a great satisfaction in knowing that such things are within the range of accomplishment, which has been fairly well-demonstrated.

But, if and when forced to depend for occasional assistance on such help as can be secured on short notice and pressed into service without sufficient and proper preparation, the results are very seldom successful and are never satisfactory. All attempts under these latter conditions have been permanently discontinued by us.

"BELLY GUNS"
A successful attempt on aerial targets with two short barrel revolvers

TWO-GUN FORWARD ROAD AGENT'S SPIN

Revolvers are extended towards officer. Guns are dropped sideways so that trigger guard slips over trigger finger. Guns are then flipped so as to spin over with barrel forward and come into position to fire.

Mr. Groff has performed this little stunt and fired the two shots in a fraction less than one second.

View Two of Forward Road Agent's Spin

Two-Gun Shooting

View Three of Forward Road Agent's Spin

View Four of Forward Road Agent's Spin completed. Shots would be fired at this point if necessary.

Walter Groff demonstrating with Officer Joe Young of the Montana State Highway Patrol.

TWO-GUN BACKWARD ROAD AGENT'S SPIN
Turning guns backward with quick reverse movements

Upper—Showing gesture of surrender to officer.

Center—Showing both guns spinning backward to bring grips into shooting position.

Lower—Showing right gun pointing at officer while left hand gun is coming into position to quickly cover any others along the sidelines who might require attention.

Two-Gun Shooting

Two-Gun Border Shift

Upper Left—Toss up left hand gun, pass right gun to left hand.

Upper Right—Catch tossed-up gun with right hand.

Lower Left—"All set to go." Left hand gun is pointed at target, while right hand gun is coming into shooting position.

NOTE: The guns are tossed higher than necessary so as to show the movements clearly in the pictures.

SECTION 7

SUITABLE TARGETS FOR AERIAL SHOOTING. EQUIPMENT
FOR MAKING AND THROWING THEM.

The Peters Cartridge Company's **Duvrock Clay Target Traps** and the **Duvrock** clay targets, for use with them, seem to head the list for convenience of purchase and adaptability to our purpose. These targets are made in a nice size, just three inches in diameter, round, and about $\frac{3}{16}$ inch in thickness, perfectly flat, not dish shape. They come in packages of about fifty, neatly packed in cartons of two hundred and fifty and five hundred, and are the most compact and satisfactory targets ever put out for the shooters who are interested in aerial shooting with revolvers, rifles, and shotguns. They are clean and convenient to handle and ship, or carry in automobiles on a camping or vacation trip, and, what is also somewhat important, they are not expensive.

The Duvrock trap is built to hold about thirty targets at a time in the magazine, and to release one target each time the trigger of trap is pulled. This trigger arrangement can be operated very rapidly when so desired. I mention it at this time for the reason that it is the ideal equipment for aerial target training, particularly where targets are to be thrown rapidly and under uniform conditions. The targets are a satisfactory size for the purpose, and can be released at any desired stated intervals to suit the shooter, and the flight can also be regulated according to his skill and ability to hit them.

The trap can be arranged and tilted at any angle and at any elevation, and will send the targets to any preferred height or distance and at any sort of a slant that may appeal to the shooter. Targets can be thrown straight up, just skimming along the ground, or over the surface of a lake if so desired. Two or three such traps can be arranged to throw targets simultaneously (doubles or triplets) either towards the shooter or away from him, as preferred. The distance they are separated from each other while in the air can also be controlled and arranged to suit the shooter. The spread should be arranged so that the targets can be clearly seen and the broken pieces will not interfere with succeeding shots.

I have tried all sorts of targets tossed in the air by all sorts of methods, and the **Duvrock Targets** and **Traps** seem to be an ideal combination for throwing suitable targets uniformly and rapidly. My recommendation is based entirely on their very satisfactory performance, coupled with compactness and convenience. These Duvrock targets can be thrown by hand also, and handled in a variety of other ways for training and practice, and will be found most satisfactory for such purposes.

Suitable Aerial Targets

The composition balls, so generally referred to as glass balls, and which have been used by most exhibition shooters in circuses, Wild West shows, at fairs, and on the stage, are not glass balls at all, but a composition made of resin, two-thirds, and plaster of Paris, one-third, which is then colored with dry lampblack. The system followed in making these balls consists of melting the resin in a large pot over any sort of fire conveniently at hand. The plaster of Paris is then gradually stirred in with the resin until well mixed, and then dry lampblack is added to the mixture.

This mixture is poured from a dipper into hollow aluminum moulds which have a pouring hole in the top, about the size of a nickel, for convenient free pouring. When the mould has been poured full of the mixture it is immediately turned upside down and the mixture allowed to run out. The surplus spilled on the outside of the mould during the pouring process must be quickly scraped off with a dull knife until the outside of the mould is clean. The mould with the inner coating of material is then dipped into cold water which causes the now hollow ball of material within it to shrink quickly and it is then very easily removed. These ball targets are easily and quickly made and are very satisfactory all-around targets for general exhibition purposes. They can be tossed in the air singly or in groups and can also be hung on strings by the simple process of tying a short nail on the end of the string and, when dropped through the hole in the top of the ball, the nail turns crosswise and anchors the target firmly on the string. This is the way these targets are also attached for the widely circling revolving ball (as shown in photos, page 49).

The moulds for making these balls are in two sizes: the small one (and this size is more generally used) makes the ball target two and a quarter inches in diameter, and the larger size measures three and a half inches in diameter. These targets are easily thrown and controlled, and they do not cause bullets to glance, ricochet, or turn from their course in any way, and as a result are much in favor for public exhibitions where many people are gathered. Wooden blocks, bricks, lumps of coal, glass bottles, and other favorite target material often cause dangerous turning or glancing of the bullets, which can be a very serious happening where many persons are assembled in the vicinity of the shooter. For this reason I can very highly recommend the Peters Duvrock targets and the composition "glass balls" as most desirable targets for general exhibition use and for the safety and protection of the spectators and performer as well.

If smaller flat disc targets are needed I suggest the use of the one and five-eighths inch Duster targets which come in four colors, black, red, orange and light yellow. These targets and the "Van-aumatic" trap which is used with them, is illustrated in the police section, and can be secured from The Fred Goat Company, 314 Dean Street, Brooklyn, New York.

The aluminum moulds used for making the composition ball targets can be purchased in the two and a quarter inch size, for $7.50 each, and in the three and a half inch size for $10.00, from Frank Fish, gunsmith, Lewistown, Montana. These moulds are made to order only and cash must accompany the order. The adjustable trap, as illustrated, for throwing cans in the air, is also built by Mr. Fish and sells for $15.00. Any of the other special equipment used by us and described herein can be built by Mr. Fish on special order.

The Peters Duvrock traps and Duvrock targets can be purchased from The Peters Cartridge Company, division of Remington Arms Company, Bridgeport, Connecticut. They will be pleased to furnish any additional information desired.

SECTION 8

SPEED WITH SINGLE-ACTION COLT REVOLVERS. TWO-HANDED SLIP SHOOTING. FANNING THE HAMMER OF THE SINGLE-ACTION GUNS. THE FASTEST METHODS KNOWN FOR SPRAYING LEAD FROM THE COLT SINGLE-ACTION REVOLVERS.

The single-action Colt revolver has been such an outstanding item in the activities of western frontier history that any book dealing with fast gun handling, quick draws, hip shooting, etc., would not be complete without giving this very deserving and famous six-shooter its rightful credit. When it is taken into consideration that this type of revolver was designed and brought out so many years ago (1873) and has held its own all through the most active part of Western history, and still commands a large sale in all parts of the country, and is also much favored and constantly used by many famed law officers who gamble their lives on the effectiveness of their guns, it is only reasonable to give this type of gun proper credit and favorable mention up to the entire extent to which it may be entitled.

The facts of the matter in relation to the single-action Colt seem to show that these guns will perform almost any necessary regulation shooting service about as well as any other hand gun available. They will stand a great amount of service with a reasonable amount of care. The durability, dependability, quality of material, and workmanship of the present-day output are beyond question. Personally I am still doing some very satisfactory work with several of these guns within the particular field for which they are adapted. I have no criticism to offer regarding the guns; I simply do not always agree with the romantic, nonsensical "chatter" dished up by certain persons who base their opinions on theory and unsupported rumor from "by-gone days," instead of on practical comparative tests of the various revolvers now available.

Many arguments have arisen as a result of the purely visionary belief some persons have had regarding the superiority of these guns over all others. Such claims and beliefs had their origin in early history, wherein these guns played such an important part, and they have ever since been surrounded by and associated with the glamour and romantic hero worship of that period, which, somewhat like a snowball, increases in volume and gathers more and more of the same material which becomes firmly attached to it as it rolls around and travels along.

It is a very well-recognized fact among revolver experts that these guns have in the past been given credit for a great many virtues and possibili-

Fast and Fancy Revolver Shooting

FANNING THE HAMMER
AND
SHOOTING THROUGH THE SMOKE

POSITION PREFERRED BY THE AUTHOR
WHEN FANNING THE HAMMER OF
SINGLE-ACTION COLT

Left—Fanning a single-action Colt, using black powder cartridges. "Shooting through the smoke." Who can see the target out in front of shooter? It's a cinch that the shooter, who happens to be the author, didn't see it after the first shot. Ye Old Timers' speediest method of "spraying lead" from a "six-shooter."

Right—Body and feet position generally assumed by the author when "fanning the hammer" of the single-action Colt revolvers. A much discussed performance—supposedly of much importance in the history of the early day frontiers' fast gun artists. Many claim it was never possible to control the shots, while others claim that very effective shooting could be done this way.

Here is an opportunity to look into the realities of the matter and draw your own conclusions.

ties of accomplishment which they never possessed, and of which they were never capable. It is only fair, however, to call attention to the fact that if there were no other revolvers or pistols available, the army, navy and all law enforcement officers could fulfill all of their hand-gun shooting requirements in a very satisfactory and efficient manner with the single-action revolvers.

The civilian target-shooting enthusiasts could also secure quite satisfactory results by making a few inexpensive adjustments and with the addition of target sights.

After my first boyhood experiences with various contraptions in the form of pistols and revolvers, cap and ball and otherwise, and in the usual assortment of more or less useless calibers of foreign and domestic make, I finally made some serious and fairly successful efforts to master revolver shooting with standard, just as issued, single-action Colt revolvers.

While my progress and development did not in any way startle the world or otherwise indicate that I was anything closely resembling a marvel, I very gradually made headway and by study and persistent practice I was eventually able to perform many of the single-action "show off" stunts that have been handed down through the years as amazing examples of the proficiency necessary to be mastered by "ye old time" gun fighter, in order to insure his living through the numerous gun battles that it was quite generally believed would be thrust upon him from time to time.

Even if the stories as handed out to us about the gun fighters were not exactly correct in all details, the experience gained from such study of, and practice with, the single-action revolvers proved later on to be of very valuable assistance in my research work.

It very naturally followed as a result of this experience that my earlier attempts at aerial target shooting would be carried on with these single-action revolvers, at times assisted somewhat, in mind at least, if not in fact, by alterations in hammer spurs, etc. These guns performed very well up to the point where certain combinations and situations were later introduced that were a little too fast and complicated for any of the methods by which these guns could be rapidly operated and still maintain fairly reliable pointing accuracy.

Attention should be directed at this time to the fact that the standard hammer, just as issued on these guns, is suitable for more fast and fancy stunts than any other modification or remodeling of the hammer that has ever been put on them, and I have tried all of them—up and down—from the Bisley model hammer spur to all of the other modifications, several of which are shown in the various illustrations contained herein.

By grinding the rough checking from the top of the single-action hammer you have an excellent fanning and slipping hammer. Tying or binding the trigger back to the trigger guard with surgeons' tape or with common

FANNING THE HAMMER

Left—This shooting performance is started by moving back the hammer of the single-action Colt with a fanning or sweeping motion of the hand, engaging the hammer spur with the "heel" or bottom part of the palm of the hand as it passes over it, and then —

Right—As the hammer reaches the limit of backward motion the bottom of fanning hand should come in contact with the high part or bump caused by the second joint of the thumb of the hand holding the gun, which causes the fanning hand to turn down slightly, which releases the hammer spur, allowing the hammer to fall and release the shot, and (as shown in next picture) —

tire tape or electricians' tape will keep it out of the way permanently. It is not necessary to take the trigger out or grind the notches from the hammer for this kind of shooting; when use of the trigger is again desired all that is necessary to return the gun to normal condition is to remove the tape from the tied-back trigger.

King's cock-eyed hammer spur, finished smooth on top and slanted left for right-handed shooting and slanted right for left-handed shooting, will help quite a lot in some forms of fast one-hand slip shooting, in connection with quick draws and other forms of fast single-action shooting, either with or without the trigger tied back. This King spur can be adjusted at almost any angle desired on special order, if a correct diagram is furnished.

The single-action Colt can be successfully used on aerial targets tossed in the air, one at a time, with gun in either hand. Continued practice will later develop enough skill to break doubles—two tossed in the air at a time. More persistent practice will enable some shooters to go as high as three tossed at a time, or three targets following each other very closely, or if more interesting to the shooter, perhaps the firing of three shots at one aerial target, such as a can, etc., before it can fall to the ground. Three shots and hits at such targets seem to be about the limit with this kind of a gun while being operated with one hand.

There is a reliable report by Mr. J. E. Berns of Bremerton, Washington, that the late "Packer Jack" Newman of Seattle on one occasion scored four hits on a can in the air while using a slip hammer single-action Colt revolver remodeled to .22 caliber. This was a remarkable performance and not easily duplicated. My own experience, observation and research lead me to set the limit of probable accomplishment at three shots, and the time period required for such shots at aerial targets, by a very expert performer, would be from one to one and a half seconds. A lapse of time of a fraction more than one-half second will usually occur between shots under the conditions mentioned. There are, of course, freak happenings and exceptional occurrences that sometimes appear contrary to worked-out averages, but the above statements will be found to be quite generally correct and outstanding exceptions will be rare.

When firing all shots at the same stationary target by fanning the hammer or slip shooting with two hands, the shots can be delivered much faster than above stated, but such method of shooting the single-action guns is not at all adaptable to aerial target shooting, either singly or in groups, due to the impossibility of accurate pointing.

Much of the false reputation for superiority over all other models that has grown up around single-action guns is based on the fact that the Quick Draw and First Shot with this type of revolver in the hands of expert performers has made frontier history that has no parallel, due in part, perhaps, to the fact that the period in history during which such shooting

FANNING THE HAMMER

Left—The hand continues to turn over and away from hammer spur and must be so moved in order to avoid letting the hammer spur injure the back of the hand as the gun tips up and rears back from the recoil, allowing the hammer spur to pass under the fanning hand instead of gouging into it, which it is almost sure to do when using heavy loads, and —

Right—When the pressure of the muscles exerted against the recoil has caused the gun to again resume the leveled position, the fanning hand is again raised up so as to pass over the hammer with a forward motion (as shown in next picture), and —

Speed with Single-Action Colt

was done has no parallel either. And there is still no satisfactory evidence to show that such guns are superior in any way over several of our more modern guns for this particular purpose. For rapidity of fire and accurate control of shots that follow the first one, the single-action does not hold its own in comparison with some other revolvers, as timed tests reveal. When firing one shot each at several targets where time and accuracy of delivery are to be considered, the single-action guns fail to stay in the lead. All of the faster methods of operating single-action Colt revolvers require two hands where various other revolvers require only one hand.

Fanning the hammer of single-action revolvers is the fastest method ever developed for operating such guns. Fanning a single-action gun is usually done by holding it and pointing it with one hand (either right or left as desired), while operating the gun by slapping or fanning the hammer back rapidly with the lower part (or heel) of the palm of the other hand. This is done by a series of short, choppy, **fanning** motions that strike back the hammer to the full distance of its travel each time, and is continued, if desired, until all the cartridges in the cylinder have been fired. As formerly stated, the trigger is held back, tied back, or removed entirely, as preferred, for this kind of shooting. The same kind of trigger arrangement is used in slip shooting.

It should be kept in mind that fanning the hammer is strictly a two-handed stunt with one gun. No man can fan two guns at the same time, one in each hand, as some not too well-informed Western writers try to describe their heroes as doing, when in a fast-action gun fight.

Fanning the hammer of the single-action Colt revolver, as a means of great speed and effectiveness, has been handed down to us through Western history, romance, and fiction, with variations and general misunderstandings, until the subject has assumed much importance in discussions of guns and gunmen of the early days as well as later days. Many writers have claimed that much speed and accuracy can be, and was, secured, in the early days of the West, by this method of handling revolvers. Other writers go to the opposite extreme and boldly state that fanning by early day gunners, or others, was and is purely a "myth," but we know and have demonstrated that it is the fastest method known for spraying lead from single-action Colt revolvers. (Note targets made by the fanning of the hammer method, pages 102, 104.) These targets, showing well-grouped bullets, are dated and signed by several witnesses.

Two-handed slip shooting is done by holding the gun with one hand and pointing it at the object to be hit, while the hammer is worked rapidly with the thumb of the other hand by pressing or flipping it back to full cock position and letting it "slip" from under the thumb. This "thumb whipping," as it is sometimes termed, may be continued, if desired, until all the cartridges in the cylinder have been fired. This is a quite accurate,

Fast and Fancy Revolver Shooting

FANNING THE HAMMER

Left—When a position about even with the front part of cylinder has been reached the hand is turned over with lower part of palm towards the gun and is then started back towards the hammer spur (as shown at right), and —

Right—The hand continues back with the same circular, or fanning, motion as at first illustrated (first cut, page 98), and another shot can be fired in the same manner.

These motions can be repeated rapidly or slowly in keeping with the desire of the operator, until all loads contained in the gun have been fired. Good control over the movements and also over the placing of the shots is somewhat dependent on persistent practice.

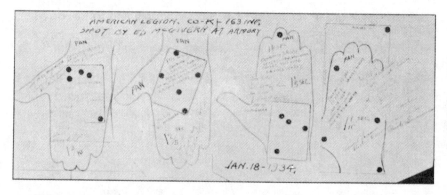

Fanning targets shot by Ed McGivern, Jan. 18, 1934, at American Legion Meet, at Armory, Co. K, 163rd Infantry.

fast method of shooting the single-action revolver, but not so fast as fanning and should not be confused with it.

Reasonably sure hits combined with speed can be obtained by slip shooting. The grinding off of all of the notches cut in the hammer by the factory, as recommended by some writers, will eliminate the necessity of tying back or removing the trigger. It is a matter of personal choice as to which system is used. I do not grind the notches off. I prefer, and use, the tied-back triggers for my own convenience. Either hand may be used to hold and steady the gun both in fanning and slip shooting. I use the left hand for holding the gun and the right hand for doing the fanning and slip shooting.

A great deal of discussion has been carried on regarding the comparative speed of the Colt single-action revolver and the modern double-action gun. The single-action guns require two hands to operate them fast, either by fanning or slipping. Some of the fastest hand-sized groups (shown here in pictures), obtained by fanning the single-action gun, show time periods of one second, one and a tenth seconds, one and a fifth seconds, etc., and it can be readily realized that by the two-handed method of operation required they could not be accurately controlled and properly directed for placing one shot each on several rapidly moving targets. Such performances are out of the question with single-action guns.

Some of the faster witnessed and verified groups shot with double-action guns were done in less than half of the single-action time periods— two-fifths second, nine-twentieths second, one-half second, three-fifths second. These groups (Section 10) have about the same distribution of shots, and occupy about the same amount of space, showing much the same accuracy, but more than doubling the speed of delivery. All of these test targets and speed performances mentioned herewith for comparison of double-action and single-action revolvers have been verified by affidavit of reliable witnesses.

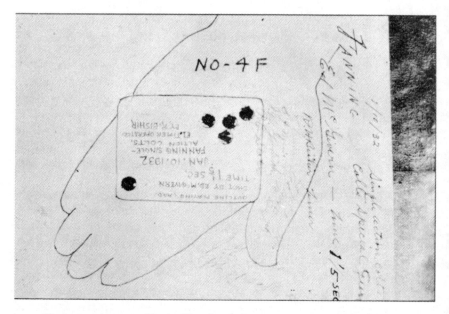

The best group secured in the "fanning the hammer" experiments, Jan. 10, 1932.

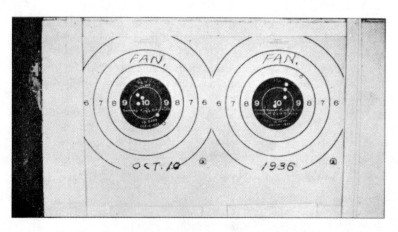

Last two fanning targets made by the author, Oct. 10, 1936.

Speed with Single-Action Colt

TWO-HANDED SLIP SHOOTING

Left—A very accurate method of delivering shots rapidly from a single-action Colt revolver. For two-handed slip shooting. Gun is held in the left hand, trigger finger of left hand is placed in trigger guard and pressed firmly against trigger, or against back of guard if trigger is taken out. The right hand is then placed with first finger ahead of trigger guard, the other three fingers around the lower part of left hand. This enables operator to hold gun firmly and to recover quickly from the disturbing effect of recoil and bring gun back instantly to former pointing position, in which it was held before shot was fired. To fire the shots the ball of the right thumb is placed in the hollow part of the hammer just ahead of the hammer spur and when the hammer reaches the limit of backward motion, caused by moving the thumb sideways, the shooter may hesitate at that point to make sure of his pointing accuracy and, when ready to fire, the thumb continues the backward movement until the ball of thumb slips off of the hammer spur, which usually has all checking removed when used for this purpose.

The movements may be performed slowly for deliberate shooting or may be performed rapidly for speed results. Either way will produce quite surprising results in the way that the shots can be controlled by this method.

Attention is called to the importance of holding the forearms very firmly against the body for steadiness and support. All movement of the gun is to be made and controlled by body movement only and not by any free movement of the arms or hands after once the gun is in position.

As all of this sort of shooting is closely related to, and is actually dependent on, hip shooting proficiency for successful results, the same rules of conduct and methods of control apply equally well to each.

Right—Showing the method of drawing back the hammer, which is now in the position where the ball of the right thumb is slipped off of the spur to fire the shot. Smooth slipping movement is important at this point to avoid jerking the gun. The hand position shown here and recommended has a very steadying effect and helps very materially to avoid jerky movements at the instant of firing the shot.

Fast and Fancy Revolver Shooting

Left—Here is shown the thumb slipped off of hammer spur and it should be deliberately controlled so that when it leaves the spur it goes back over the hump or high place just behind the second thumb joint. If attention is given to this little detail the thumb will be entirely in the clear and safe from injury from or by the hammer spur, when and if a heavily loaded gun rears up backwards, which it usually does as a result of recoil.

Right—The position of hammer spur here shows rather clearly why thumb should be brought back to the hump of thumb joint to avoid being in the way of probable injury when the gun is forced up and back by the recoil. The heavier the load, the more important such details become.

Left—Two-handed slip shooting, using black powder cartridges. A beautiful smoke screen.
Right—A target which was shot through the smoke screen as shown in cut at left.

Speed with Single-Action Colt

A fine job of converting a .45 caliber single-action Colt revolver into a .22 L.R. with recessed cylinder head and relined barrel, Patridge sights. Cylinder is cut off proper length for .22 L.R. cartridges, and barrel is extended through forward frame to proper adjustment. An excellent gun for fanning and slip shooting practice. The work was done by Lee Worthley, Visalia, California, Route 1, Box 439.

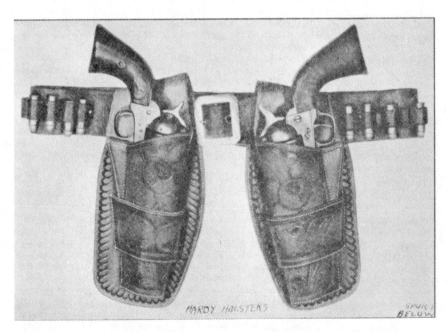

Two remodeled hammer single-action Colts and two very satisfactory Hardy holsters.

Fast and Fancy Revolver Shooting

THE AUTHOR'S METHOD OF COCKING A REVOLVER
FOR FAST SINGLE-ACTION SHOOTING

No. 1. Raising the hammer on double-action gun so as not to disturb the aim or the general alignment of the gun while cocking it by hand, to fire the next shot (single action) in rapid fire work. If handled in this way, the revolver can be kept pointed at the spot during all the string of shots. In the cocking operation the gun is not tipped, or rolled, or moved away from the direct pointing position. The thumb is placed, as on gun No. 1. It is started back with a sliding motion towards the left, as shown on gun No. 2. When hammer comes back to full cock position the thumb continues to slide over and down till it comes in line with trigger finger and lays alongside of frame, as shown on gun No. 3. Note relative position of trigger and of trigger finger during each part of this cocking operation. The thumb can be laid higher up on frame if so desired without altering any of the other motions.

This will give a very good idea of the method used for the fastest cock-the-hammer-and-squeeze-the-trigger system of rapid fire shooting. Note the fingers have not moved or changed position in any way during the cocking operation. This is a fast and accurate method of cocking the gun and shooting it at flying targets thrown one at a time, as fast as one thrower can throw them, or for two at a time. When trigger finger is handled, as shown in the picture, there will be no accidental discharge.

OPERATING THE SLIP HAMMER WITH ONE HAND

No. 2. Shows an O'Meara slip hammer Colt single-action revolver being cocked to shoot by letting the hammer "slip" from under the web, between ball of thumb and finger. Thumb is placed on the low hammer spur, as shown on gun No. 4. Hammer is drawn back, as shown on gun No. 5. When hammer gets into position, as shown on gun No. 6, the thumb slides over across hammer spur until hand is in a position similar to, but not quite as far over to the left, as hand shown on gun No. 3. As thumb slides over to the left on the last move, the spur of the "slip" hammer slips out from under the crotch of the hand, instead of being released by the trigger. The cocking motion is very similar on both of these guns (note position of finger) except that the slip hammer must be held firmly under some part of the thumb (note tension of thumb) until ready to let the shot off. Accidental discharge can happen very easily if this important point is overlooked. As it would be impossible to show the hammer being slipped from under the thumb, the fourth move of slip hammer handling necessarily had to be left out of the picture.

Speed with Single-Action Colt

YE OLD TIMERS' "SIX-GUNS"

No. 6. Single-action Colt, .45 caliber, remodeled by the late J. D. O'Meara, of Lead, South Dakota, has Smith & Wesson rear sight and sleeve front sight, with King-McGivern gold bead and post.

No. 7. A perfect fanning gun, just as issued from the factory, No. 354507, no alterations; top of hammer is smooth, no checking. Electric contact timing equipment can be inserted in the grip, same as the contact equipment in the grip of No. 8. Note studs for connecting battery wires projecting from the bottom of No. 8. These are not necessary in the new arrangement, as the connections pass under the wood grips and are interchangeable for use in several guns if so desired.

Note No. 6 and No. 8 guns have O'Meara slip hammers.

As mentioned in former writings, perfectly adjusted fanning guns, that will stand up under the strain of continued top speed fanning tests, for several hundred shots, are not at all common. This gun, No. 354507, stands continued and prolonged tests and delivers the goods in a very highly satisfactory manner. Plenty of convincing evidence is available and at hand to support this statement. This is practically a perfect gun, built for the purpose, but factory standard in every way, no special features except the smooth hammer spur.

No. 9. A single-action Colt converted into a .22 caliber slip hammer gun, for a fast plaything for practicing slip shooting, etc.

No. 10. A .38 caliber Lightning Model Colt, parrot bill handle, double action, using the .38 Long Colt cartridge. Good 1-1/5 seconds 5-shot group has been made with this gun.

This is the type of gun in .41 caliber claimed to be used by "Billy the Kid."

Fast and Fancy Revolver Shooting

E. W. Ray, former chief of police of Lewistown, Montana, peace officer for more than twenty-five years, and a very good all-around shot, and an enthusiastic supporter of thorough police training in the use of firearms, is here showing the required movements for the single roll.

The double roll is done with two guns, one in each hand, in a similar manner. Sometimes one gun is revolved frontwards and the other backwards, each turning in opposite directions at the same time. The photos show the forward roll, also show how the hammer is raised (Fig. 3) to fire the shot at the latter part of the roll (Fig. 5).

Fig. 1 shows the gun starting down with hand opened flat and with trigger finger extended through trigger guard so that gun can revolve on it.

Fig. 2 shows getting the thumb out of the way so gun can continue the spin.

Fig. 3 shows gun coming over and muzzle going forward. Fingers are being closed around the grip and thumb is just coming over the hammer spur which makes it possible to cock the gun by its own weight and the momentum given it by the spinning motion.

Fig. 4 shows the hammer raised and the gun leveled. The shot is fired as the hammer spur slips from under the web between finger and thumb, as the gun continues its roll forward.

THE .45 REARS BACK SOME

Fig. 5 shows the roll completed and the shot fired and the recoil moving the gun back in the opposite direction. This demonstration was made with a .45 caliber Colt revolver and black powder cartridges, the recoil of which raises the gun up and it also rears back. This fact is often overlooked by some narrators of single and double roll stories. Empty guns do not always rear back, but heavy caliber loaded ones usually do.

SECTION 9

SINGLE-ACTION AND DOUBLE-ACTION REVOLVER SHOOTING IN RELATION TO SPEED AND ACCURACY.

We have now come to the "parting of the ways" in revolver shooting; we have clearly outlined the manner of learning how to hit aerial targets. To hit aerial targets, one at a time, the revolver may be cocked with the thumb and the shot fired by squeezing the trigger in the same way that shooting at stationary targets is generally done. But when we have reached the stage where several targets, perhaps three, or even four, five or six, are to be tossed in the air at approximately the same time, or within a very short period of time, and the program requires that we also try to put three, four, five, or six bullets into or through a single target before it can fall to the ground after being tossed in the air, just how will we do it?

It is not physically possible to do this kind of shooting with a single-action revolver, or by the single-action method of operating a double-action revolver, which means, of course, cocking the hammer of the revolver with the thumb for each and every shot fired. Therefore it can be quite readily observed that, due to the ever-present and frequently mentioned "time element," this system of operating the revolver cannot be made use of in rapid multiple target shooting, due to, and because of, the simple but very clear reason that such single-action shooting cannot be done fast enough by any known method, which would permit the shooter to secure the necessary pointing accuracy required for such purpose. In other words, and to make the matter plain and to the point, such method of operating any sort of revolver or pistol cannot be combined with speed and sure hitting accuracy with sufficient certainty, and regularity, to make it adaptable to the above-described program of performance, for the very obvious reason that the rapidity of gun operating movements that would be required in this situation would add to the difficulty to such an extent that it is not reasonable to believe that it could be mastered, such reasoning being based on the very nature of the specified performance. The firing of the shots alone, without any effort toward directing them, would be beyond the limit of range of human accomplishment. The possibility of accomplishment is entirely dependent on, and governed by, the positively limited time that such targets would be in the air. The falling targets are controlled by natural forces that are constant and at all times active, therefore the time period would be determined by an agency over which the shooter can have no control.

As a result of careful study and what I consider as profitable experience, I am forced to admit that—by me at least—it could not be done by the hand-cocking single-action method of operating any revolver, or by any other method of operating any single-action revolver, so it naturally follows that if done at all it must necessarily be done with double-action revolvers and by the double-action method of operating them. And, right here is where we come "slap bang!" up against a wall of opposition. According to the "sacred" code of the "Rule of the Dead Men," and in accordance with such tradition—"double-action revolver shooting should **never** be indulged in," although double-action revolvers of very fine quality and very dependable actions have been manufactured and sold for years in large quantities in the United States by Smith & Wesson, Colt Patent Firearms Company, and others. A rather odd situation, is it not? Why make such wonderful **double-action** guns as these firms make if they are not intended to be used that way?

I decided this question for myself many years ago, and have been successful in teaching this double-action system of shooting in the face of all opposition, which, I am at this time pleased to say, was brought to bear on me in relation to this subject in rather liberal quantities. Books, catalogues, articles in periodicals and elsewhere denounced it. Surely these writers really believed they were right, and if these, no doubt, very fine and sincere persons were right, I certainly must have been wrong. As I progress with this subject these points can easily be decided, on the merits of the case, and in keeping with the evidence submitted.

Quoting just a little of such opinions in reference to double-action shooting, without any harmful intent on my part toward any particular person, may help to make the situation better understood and furnish food for thought. I quote from a noted writer—"As such shooting (double-action) will ruin any shooter's holding, and still more so his scores, and make hitting or grouping of shots quite impossible." (?) From another of today's books, in reference to quick-draw training—"While it may be possible that there can be a situation wherein double action is necessary."(?) Another reads—"The use of double action in this work (fast drawing, pointing and shooting) is almost sure to throw the aim off." And these are only a few from many that could be quoted.

With this, of course, I did not and do not agree for the very simple reason that it has been demonstrated beyond any reasonable doubt that such arguments against using revolvers "double action" are not supported by facts. The fastest, accurately controlled shooting up to now has been done with double-action revolvers, and all of the fast-shooting results described in this book were secured with double-action revolvers, while using the double-action method and the standard double-action mechanism for operating the guns, all such guns being held in the hands and operated entirely by hand, and entirely free of any other attachments, mechanism, or mechanical device of any sort whatever that could in any way assist in their operation.

Single and Double Action

The important point at issue is—just what caused such positive, though unfounded, opinions to be formed so very generally? Can it be possible that none of these persons ever discovered that astonishingly fast shooting could be done, and excellent accuracy could be secured, by this method of operating these revolvers, or did one writer, basing his opinions on theory, express such views, and other writers repeat them and then keep on repeating what some other one had said, and pass it on in that way from one to another? It now seems highly probable that this was the case, which makes us wonder if at least a great part of our shooting information is not handed out to us in that manner. The results of many of our actual tests carried out to determine the lack of reliability of some such handed-down information seem to point that way quite conclusively.

In the past it was quite a general custom for men to settle disputes by quoting words spoken by some individual or statements from some books; perhaps in some cases this custom is still in favor. I am, of course, interested in this angle of the situation to the extent of wanting to have the material contained in this writing, which relates to this particular subject, to be reliable enough in every way, so that if someone should decide to quote from it, the quotation will at least be fairly correct and reasonably reliable even though we must allow for the usual variations that generally —though possibly unintentionally—creep into quotations.

If this book serves no other purpose than to clear up this situation and kindred matters relating to this system of shooting, and thereby establish only part of the real possibilities of the double-action revolvers, I will surely feel fairly well-paid for the effort put forth to gather together the data and other valuable material so necessary to produce it.

On this basis I will proceed with the description of methods used and the results that can be expected along this line of endeavor.

SECTION 10

SHOOTING REVOLVERS DOUBLE ACTION. COMBINING ACCURACY WITH SPEED.

Judged from my point of view, we are now face to face with the most important part of this book which, I am led to believe, constitutes the first treatise on this form of revolver shooting that has ever been attempted on a detailed, yet extensive, scale, with actual demonstrations of the highly satisfactory practical results possible to secure.

In the following pages we will jointly analyze, study, and outline the various angles of shooting **double-action revolvers** by the **double-action method**, with the definite purpose of combining speed with accuracy while so doing. Surely a big subject to cover, yet one which I hope to do successfully, with absolute fairness and courtesy to all, but, if it is to be of any value when finished, it must be done frankly, fully, and without evasion; it is hoped that it will be received with the same spirit in which it is offered. If, in following this path as outlined, I should, unintentionally to be sure, step on someone's toes—perhaps some of those who are fanatically loyal to the single-action revolvers—it must be kept in mind that such toes must have been knowingly placed in this path by their owner, and, as a natural result, would be stepped on at some time or other during such a discussion. But I earnestly hope that nothing of a serious nature arises from such happening; I will try to tread softly where occasion requires it.

The reason for firing revolvers by the double-action method is based entirely on the urge and the need for speed. Persistent practice and prolonged tests have shown conclusively that greater accuracy can be combined with speed by this method than by any other method by which revolvers have ever been operated. In fact, surprising accuracy, combined with amazing speed, has been developed within the last few years by this method. Convincing results of such tests are herein described and illustrated.

When first attempting to fire revolvers by the double-action method, there are a number of things that must be taken into consideration that will, in the following pages, be set forth in what I believe to be their order of importance.

Unless the student has had considerable shooting experience, I recommend starting and continuing to practice with empty guns for some time. This is generally referred to as **dry shooting,** and will be explained more fully, with reasons for its use for certain purposes, as we go along. Of course, this dry shooting is optional with the shooter and is only expressed

Shooting Double Action

RAPID FIRE DOUBLE-ACTION TIMING EQUIPMENT CONTACT MECHANISM FITTED UP, READY FOR USE

Nos. 30 and 32 show the Smith & Wesson Adapters in place. Nos. 30 and 31 are the McGivern Model .38-44. No. 31 is equipped for timing speed tests. This trigger guard contact mechanism is interchangeable on Nos. 30 and 31. The contact equipment on Nos. 32 and 33 is interchangeable on these two .45 caliber guns. Note construction of contact equipment for Nos. 30, 31, 32, 33, being of later design, is much more sturdy than on 34 and 35, making it accident-proof and very durable; not affected in any way by the heaviest loads used.

No. 34. Smith & Wesson K-.22, equipped with superspeed contact mechanism, also interchangeable on .38 M. & P. model, ready for connecting with electric timer.

No. 35. Colt Officer's Model .38 Special, equipped with the earlier model of boxed-in contact mechanism, capable of very fine adjustment. The later style is available for all models at the present time. These are also interchangeable on the Officer's Model .22 caliber Colt revolver. Separate special control equipment is required for Colt revolvers. These appliances are not interchangeable from Colt to Smith & Wesson, or the reverse. Each make requires special fitting, all of which we have on hand.

as our opinion—not a law nor a positive rule. I am simply trying to offer sensible instructions to those interested persons who may wish to follow them, in order to develop accurate double-action shooting, along the same lines and by the same methods as those used by me in my own development.

If the advice herein given is followed for a reasonable length of time I firmly believe it will bring at the least fair success to the reader student, just as it has brought success to many members of my shooting classes, and there is plenty of convincing proof of this fact available. If the student can figure out better methods after he has mastered the ones set forth here, it will be more than satisfactory to me, and I will be glad to congratulate him on his future success from such source. Arguments from that angle having been removed, we will proceed with the unfinished business.

A very important matter that should be mentioned and clearly stated here in relation to double-action shooting is that it is not in any way intended to entirely take the place of single-action shooting of double-action guns. It is not intended to replace or abolish single-action shooting in any branch of revolver shooting, or in any place or situation where the **time factor** is favorable for the single-action method of operation. Where the time period or time allowance is sufficient for reasonably careful single-action manipulation of the revolver, I most emphatically recommend it.

When the time factor for getting the shots away does not enter into the situation, I do not claim that any person can shoot better or more accurately by the double-action system of manipulating and operating any revolver than he can by the single-action method of doing it. I very firmly believe that most persons, when taking deliberate aim, holding carefully, and squeezing the trigger properly, can shoot more accurately and consistently by the single-action method than they can by the double-action method. But when the time factor enters into the situation and speed of fire must be combined with close grouping of bullets, and those bullets must be released quickly or not at all, then the single-action has no standing whatsoever in comparison with the double-action method. Plenty of reliable proof of this statement is also readily available. In other words—shooting can be done by the double-action method, where speed and accuracy **must** be combined, that cannot be even closely approached by the single-action method.

I wish to make the relative terms (relative to this subject) very clear, so I request the reader to give these statements very close attention; make every effort to be sure that they are thoroughly understood. When this is done, another important angle of argument will have been removed.

It is very generally admitted at the present time and well substan-

Shooting Double Action

Inside view of the old O. K. Corral.

The old O. K. Corral, Tombstone, Arizona. The Earp-Clanton
feud fight started just inside of this gate, Sept. 28, 1881.
Tom and Frank McLowery, and Billy Clanton were killed.

THE O. K. CORRAL, TOMBSTONE, ARIZONA

Photo from famous collection of N. H. Rose, San Antonio, Texas. The Earp-Clanton feud fight at Tombstone, Arizona, Sept. 28, 1881, is one of the most famous gun fights in early Western history. Six man-shaped targets were used in our demonstration to give some basis for comparing and timing the performance with present-day revolvers and their possibilities in such situations.

tiated that I have made some remarkable progress with double-action revolver shooting, and have also been successful with some decidedly different combinations of shots and with many difficult stunts. Many of these were branded as impossible of accomplishment beforehand, due to various reasons ascribed **to imperfections probable, or existing, in double-action revolvers,** and in the ammunition that must be used in them. Included in this doubtful prophecy, of course, was also the physical shortcomings of the shooter regardless of who he might be. It, therefore, gave me great pleasure to announce that in the final demonstrations to secure the stated results, which I had for so long a time been expecting to accomplish, the advice so offered seemed not to be so well-founded, and the many inherent faults of the double-action guns and the cartridges to be used in them seemed somehow to fail to make their appearance at the critical time set for such things to happen.

I now feel justified and quite confident about passing this information and the training and instruction methods along. Instead of getting "chesty" over a little rather hard-earned success and trying to "swell up" to the proper size and proportions to fill the opening for an instructor in this branch of revolver shooting, I preferred to wait until I sort of **gradually developed, and grew big enough,** by actual experience and reasonable success, based on results that would qualify me 'to pass the word along. On this basis I have chosen the pages of this book for transmitting to shooters in general, and interested students of the revolver shooting game in particular, the accumulated knowledge gained from such experience, in the hope that it may save others the unpleasant experiences and disappointments that I was forced to undergo at times in this particular field. It might also save some of the wasted energy, and much of the cash, that can be spent in misdirected effort.

When starting to learn double-action shooting as formerly mentioned in trigger control, it is well to learn the movements first by gradually starting from the single-action method, or short movement of squeezing the trigger, then switching to the double-action system, or longer movement of squeezing the trigger, to operate the gun without wabbling it around the neighborhood in irregular circles every time the hammer rises and falls. (Note the photo of the double-action hold adopted by me and the general position of my hand on pages 46 and 47, with the relative position of thumb and fingers, described in detail in lower paragraph, page 280; these things are all quite important in the beginning.) Slight changes can be made to suit the hands of the different individuals as long as the general principles are understood, and in a general way maintained, until the student can understand the principle of the working movements necessary, and the disturbing movements that must be avoided. After this point is reached the individual may be able to make such changes as

Shooting Double Action

WALTER GROFF USING DOUBLE-ACTION REVOLVERS ON SET-UP OF LANGRISH
POLICE TARGETS

Six-man set-up to illustrate O. K. Corral battle at Tombstone, Arizona, Sept. 28, 1881 Three to six seconds were allowed for delivering the six shots from a double-action revolver at these six-man targets placed 35 feet from shooter. Six trials resulted in only three misses, 33 hits out of 36 shots fired. Note targets. There are no bullets off of the panels, which are 24 inches wide.

In the reports of this battle it is claimed that when the shooting started that the men were about five or six feet apart and about 30 shots were fired, the battle lasting several minutes and three men were killed. The persons involved were all outstanding Western characters and famous peace officers, generally credited with being expert and experienced gun handlers and fighters of that day. The results of our experiment are herewith offered for the benefit and interest of those who may enjoy making comparisons and studying probabilities.

will benefit him individually, also making the muscular movements comfortable and convenient and in keeping with the physical structure of his hands, without disturbing to any great extent the pointing steadiness of the gun.

No matter how discouraging the wabbling around of the gun seems to be at first, do not listen to any of "Uncle So-and-So's" fancy arguments in relation to how "dang foolish" it looks. Remember that the police officers and others, who shot the dime-size groups herein shown (page 343), using the revolvers double action while doing so, did not know anything about it at all just a year before. They simply started following instructions and stayed with it. They were just as skeptical as anybody could be about the double-action idea when first advanced.

My pet scheme for this sort of double-action "dry shooting" training is to place a spot on a looking-glass and then have the student keep the muzzle of the revolver (unloaded, of course) pointed at it while he follows instructions to slowly and carefully **squeeze** the trigger back the full distance of its travel, which is necessary to operate the gun double action and cause the hammer to rise and fall. When the trigger is released forward, which is also necessary in each case, one should try to let it forward slowly, holding the tension of the spring with the trigger finger, so that it releases at about the same rate of speed as that at which it is squeezed backward when raising the hammer. It is well to keep up this training until these motions can be repeated fifty times or so without much wabbling around of the muzzle of the gun from the spot on the mirror. This can be clearly noted by the person who is standing in front of the glass while practicing, and which is the real reason for using the glass as a background for what we will call the training target. If a mirror is not readily available the student may try using a spot on the wall or other convenient location. Any convenient short distance is satisfactory for this practice; long distances are not at all necessary. We leave that for "the puzzle putters."

When reasonable steadiness has been developed (the student can be his own judge), the actual shooting can be properly started somewhat along the following lines: Stand, say six to ten feet away from a fair sized target, or any object that a person may wish to use for a target, line the gun up in the usual way in which the shooter has been accustomed to lining it up for single-action shooting. Take careful aim, squeeze the trigger back slowly, the full distance of travel. This is quite necessary and important at first, in order to maintain a steady hold until you get the shot away. Note the result of the shot without making any changes whatever. Now with the hammer down—not raised by hand—again point the revolver at the spot you desire the bullet to hit, take careful

Shooting Double Action

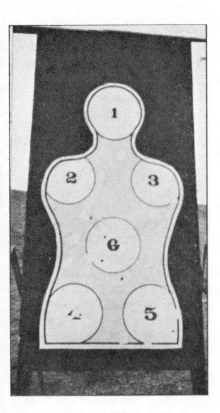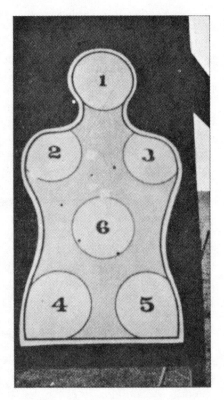

TARGETS USED IN THE O. K. CORRAL SET-UP

Left—Six hits, no misses. One bullet in the figure six; one in upper part of center circle.

Right—Five hits, one miss.

aim as before, and while striving to maintain the aim by steady holding, start again to squeeze the trigger back the full distance of travel, slowly and carefully; do not hurry at all, no jerk, no hurried pulling—just steady, **careful squeezing** till the shot gets away.

Now—don't let the trigger jump forward; instead, let it move slowly forward, hold the tension. Why? Because it is on the forward movement that all superspeed double-action group shooting is balked by not learning properly the smooth, **but full,** forward movement of the trigger finger in the beginning. The balks never occur on the backward movement. Try to keep this important point constantly in mind. The balks always occur on the forward movement. Why, then, should one neglect the careful handling of the forward movement, which is such an important factor toward success? This rule applies equally well, and is equally as important, on the aerial target shooting. While learning to get the trigger back smoothly and evenly, you should also try to learn to let it forward smoothly at about the same rate of speed as that at which you are able to bring it back without wabbling. In this way you train your finger to take care of the spring tension evenly and correctly.

By paying close attention to these seemingly small, but in reality quite important, details, a uniform control can be established which is in keeping with the time periods, that should be about equal, for the forward and backward movements alike. This is a highly important factor when the person wishes to develop into the superspeed five-shot group shooting, in periods of time below a second. The evenness of time period movements, developed by this early practice as outlined, is the secret behind the half second and slightly faster groups herein shown. Do not underestimate or fail to remember, and observe, this forward tension control. No matter how foolish someone—even the shooter—may think it seems to be, I can assure everyone that it is most important for even sure hitting speed. Later, through training, it becomes a natural, smooth, subconsciously controlled action, and from that point on the sure hitting ability and the fairly positive control of the faster fired groups commence to make their appearance.

A good plan to follow is to start with a fairly large paper target of some sort, with a central aiming point marked out at or near the center. The gun should be aimed carefully by sighting as usual, then the well controlled backward squeeze of the trigger should be started. This should be done gradually and as evenly as possible until the hammer is released and the shot fired. It should also be remembered that this early training in the slow, smooth, forward movement of the trigger is going to be quite helpful in the later training for speed. The trigger should be allowed to go forward at the same rate of speed as that at which it was drawn back, whether quickly or slowly. About five groups of five shots each should be fired

Shooting Double Action

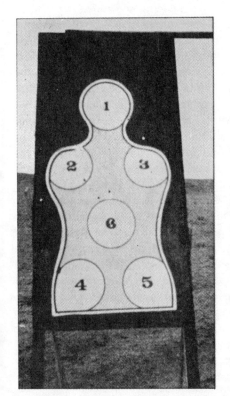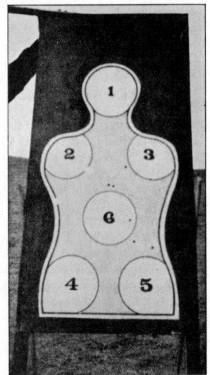

TARGETS USED IN THE O. K. CORRAL SET-UP

Left—Four hits, two misses. Note one bullet hole in the figure six of center ring, one on left of shoulder and one just above right shoulder.

Right—Six hits, no misses.

this way for practice, making a determined effort to group the entire string of twenty-five shots as closely as possible. When fair control over the trigger movement has been acquired by this method, it will be quite all right to increase the speed of the squeezing movements gradually, and in that way develop the muscles of the fingers particularly, and of the whole hand generally, for fast group shooting, which later will be used for aerial target shooting, quick-draw shooting and the continued rapid firing and sure hitting after the draw. These movements are also the necessary foundation for the close group shooting when the gun is held at or near the hip position, and, as shown and explained, is the fundamental basis of all the **quick-draw, sure hitting ability** that can be developed.

As stated heretofore, there is no real obligation attached to this training, to force the student to do these things exactly as directed, unless he should happen to have a sincere desire to be successful, and to hit things when and where he really wants to hit them, and do it quickly and repeatedly. In that case, of course, it is well for him to do as he is told to do, for the very good reason that if he does not make some effort to so do, he is really fooling no one but his own dear self.

It is here that I clearly established the very justifiable reason for double-action shooting, and for the operation of the revolvers by the double-action method instead of the single-action, particularly when several shots must be delivered very quickly and with fairly good accuracy. When using the double-action mechanism, and, by what is called the double-action method, it is quite possible to accurately place five shots on any chosen spot—on a crook's anatomy for instance—in approximately the same amount of time that the average single-action gun, or a double-action gun fired by the single-action method, can generally be made to fire two shots only. If desired the five shots can be distributed and placed accurately on five different spots—or crooks—in the same comparative relation to time as the single-action performance mentioned.

This is the real reason for double-action training and the very thing that no single-action guns can do, nor can they be operated by any means whatever that will give anywhere near the equal speed, with accuracy, that the double-action guns can and will give. The relative speed tests of both types of guns at short distances, where the relative size of the groups of hits are to be about the same, show that the double-action guns are twice as fast by actual electrically timed tests as the single-action guns were, both types of guns being operated in the hands of experts, and by the recognized methods used to secure the highest speed possible with each.

The fairness of this test is also supported by the fact that there are no witnessed records of any greater speed having ever been made anywhere with single-action guns than are shown in photos of targets used

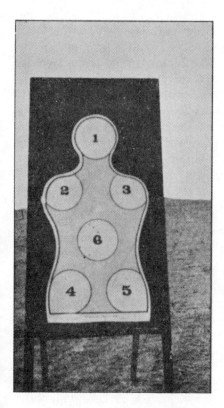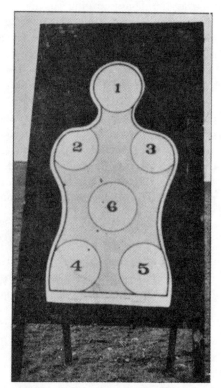

TARGETS USED IN THE O. K. CORRAL SET-UP

Left—Six hits, no misses.　All in center ring.

Right—Six hits, no misses. Note two very close together just above the center ring. **Three** misses in 36 shots.

in these comparative tests. Where the single-action guns fired five shots in one second and in one and a tenth seconds by the fanning method, the double-action guns can be drawn from the holster, at a signal, and the drawing time, as well as the firing time for the five shots, can be included in the one second, and the one and a tenth seconds total that showed on the timing machine at the end of the tests (page 268); therefore the drawing time for the double-action gun was made up for and was included in the same amount of elapsed time as the single-action guns required for the firing only. This result is due to the increased speed with which the double-action revolvers can be fired when operated by the double-action method.

In short, and by well-proven results of very thorough tests, covering a period of years, the double-action guns, tested against electrically operated timing machines, seem to be capable of speed combined with accuracy and bullet grouping that cannot be equaled by any single-action or other type of revolver when used for superspeed close group shooting, and still more particularly evident is this fact when such guns are used on groups of rapidly moving aerial targets. At this particular angle of the game the work of the double-action revolvers stands out in "bold relief" and is supreme by a liberal margin.

SUPERSPEED

Here is the story about the shooting of five shots from a double-action revolver in two-fifths of a second, and at the same time controlling the bullets so that they would form a group on the target that could be covered by the shooter's hand, and later on by an ordinary playing card.

After many years of trying all sorts of fast and fancy shooting stunts with revolvers, the discovery that I could shoot five shots in two-fifths of a second occurred on the afternoon of September 13, 1932, at the Armory headquarters of Company K, 163rd Infantry, at Lewistown, Montana, while making preparations and practicing for an exhibition to be given in the evening for the members of the company and a large number of guests. This group, which was checked by the electric timer on that occasion, is reproduced herewith (page 149).

During the evening the fastest five-shot group (pages 142 and 143) required one-half second, although on August 20, 1932, at Lead, South Dakota, some very small groups had been shot in nine-twentieths of a second, which were verified by the signatures of the witnesses on the targets, which also appear herewith (page 152).

On December 8, 1932, more trials with the electric timing equipment were conducted, and during twenty attempts the two-fifths of a second groups occurred four times, the first one on that occasion being the result of the 11th trial, then again on the 12th trial, again on the 18th trial, and

Shooting Double Action

WALTER GROFF USING DOUBLE-ACTION REVOLVERS ON OLYMPIC TARGETS

Six Olympic targets placed at a distance of 84 feet from shooter. Time allowances arranged for were 3 seconds for the fastest string, and 6 seconds for slower strings which consisted of firing 6 shots from a .38 Spl. M. & P. Model S. & W. revolver, also the Smith & Wesson .357 Magnum revolver, both with six-inch barrels. 180 shots were fired and 33 of them failed to connect with the man figure, but 16 of these came very close and registered on the panels, leaving 17 shots only missing the panels, which are 24 inches wide.

Walter Groff of Philadelphia, the author's understudy for four years, did the shooting under the author's supervision.

The 6 shots, one at each target by the double-action method of operating the revolvers, were repeated 30 times. The bullet marks can be counted on the targets, also on the double exposure target. There were 23 hits on the Olympic target and 18 hits out of 25 shots on the Langrish target, overlapping the upper part of Olympic target. This Langrish target was also shot by Mr. Groff from sitting position, at 200 yards, with .38-44 S. & W. revolver, having plain open sights and using Peters high velocity cartridges (.38-44). (See page 132.)

(Shot latter part of August, 1937.)

The double exposure mentioned was discovered too late to correct the error.

No attempts for superspeed (below 3 seconds) performances with small caliber guns or automatic .22 pistols were conducted on this occasion.

Fast and Fancy Revolver Shooting

again on the 19th trial. The time for the first five trials was four-fifths of a second each for five-shot groups. After that in the order listed, the time was as follows: three-fifths, one-half, eleven-twentieths, three-fifths, four-fifths, three-fifths, **two-fifths,** split between nine-twentieths and full **two-fifths,** four-fifths, three-fifths, **two-fifths,** split between nine-twentieths and full **two-fifths,** split eleven-twentieths and full one-half. Photos of the original list of figures accompany these details (page 150).

In January, 1933, more trials gave more nine-twentieths and two-fifths second results, and at this time an article by me, appearing in the February, 1933, issue of "Outdoor Life" on page 53, carried a statement practically promising a two-fifths second five-shot group would be delivered within a year. On January 18, 1934, before a large gathering at the American Legion headquarters, which was also headquarters for Company K of the 163rd Infantry, during a two-hour fancy shooting exhibition with revolvers, I announced that I would attempt to shoot five shots in two-fifths of a second, as timed by the electric equipment, and if not successful in six or eight trials would postpone further tests until later.

After trying out the timer several times for the benefit of the committee and guests without the use of loaded cartridges, when everything was adjusted and all set to go, at the signal, I tickled the trigger of the double-action revolver No. 640792 and the electric timer showed nine-twentieths of a second for the five-shot performance. After some discussion this first trial was decided to be satisfactory and the target (also reproduced on page 156) was inspected and signed by some sixty witnesses, after which the rest of the shooting program was carried out to conclusion.

Feeling that I still had that two-fifths second group lurking somewhere around in my nervous system, on January 23rd the timing equipment was again fitted up and adjusted in the indoor shooting range, and the committee and spectators assembled for more attempts at superspeed demonstrations. After getting everything lined up and properly inspected and the committee all set, I announced that I was ready, and the firing of five-shot strings was started, and the first results were just a little above three-fifths of a second. They gradually worked down a little at a time until finally I turned out a group just a very slight fraction less than two-fifths of a second, and, as my "lucky star" would have it, three shots of this group were just off the edge of the target. While it was a good enough group it counted for nothing but noise.

The second trial after that gave the two-fifths second target herewith offered, the original of which was presented to Mr. Jim Browne of Big Fork, Montana. The members of the committee whose names appear thereon are very reliable persons. Their affadivit, along with the photos of Mr. Hogan and Mr. Browne inspecting the target, appear on pages 158 and 159. There has been a number of two-fifths second five-shot groups shot at

Shooting Double Action

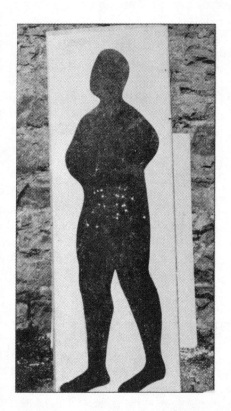

OLYMPIC TARGET SET-UP

Left—W. Groff's Olympic target No. 1 showing 29 hits.
Right—W. Groff's Olympic target No. 2 showing 21 hits.

various times, but there was more noise made about this particular one than about all of the others combined.

There was a great "hurrah" about a statement that appeared in "Adventure Magazine" in 1933, which was written by a friend of mine, in reference to similar performances, which read: "He can fire five shots double-action in two-fifths of a second and group them under a dime, this at twenty feet." When this appeared the "fireworks" became general and caused much comment. This was cleared up in November, 1934, issue of "Adventure," wherein the editor wrote: "This (the chatter) was caused by an ambiguity of statement later cleared up in 'Camp Fire' (a department of 'Adventure Magazine'). McGivern can fire five shots double-action in two-fifths of a second. McGivern can group five shots under a dime at twenty feet. He can't, he hastens to assure us, do both of these at once." This was the catch in the statement—there were two separate and distinct performances, each of which had been done, but could not possibly be done together.

At that time I thanked Mr. W. C. Tuttle, author of "Western Fiction," and Mr. Donnegan Wiggins, firearms authority for the "Adventure Magazine," for their courteous attitude during the discussion, one angle of the opposing argument being that a revolver just couldn't group five shots under a dime at 20 feet, regardless of time, etc. Three groups here submitted, shot on September 22, 1933, in settlement of this argument, seems to offset such theory. Many other groups herein submitted give evidence of the error of such statement.

Shooting five shots fast from two guns, three from one gun and two from the other, can be done in surprisingly short-time periods, and quite often groups that can be covered with the hand, and occasionally some that can be covered with an ordinary playing card, will be the result. Five shots each from two guns can be shot in short-time periods also, and good groups made with each gun. Several such two-gun grouping results are herein reproduced. One pair of such groups (page 145) is each well inside of the outline of ordinary playing cards. The playing card groups are the goal that is usually being tried for, and quite often, but not always secured.

Shooting Double Action

OLYMPIC TARGET SET-UP

Left—W. Groff's Olympic target No. 3 showing 24 hits.
Right—W. Groff's Olympic target No. 4 showing 26 hits.

 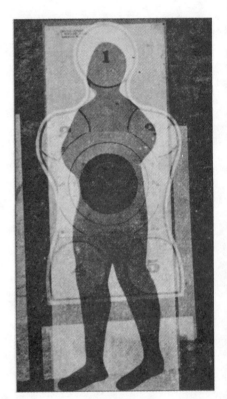

OLYMPIC TARGET SET-UP

Left—W. Groff's Olympic target No. 5 showing 24 hits.

Right—W. Groff's Olympic target No. 6 showing 23 hits.

Also showing Mr. Groff's Langrish target shot at 200 yards scoring 18 hits out of 25 shots. Open sights.

Double exposure by mistake.

Shooting Double Action

The Olympic targets and the assistants after checking the results

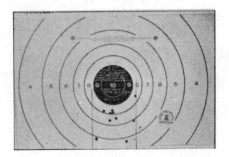

DOUBLE-ACTION SHOOTING

Shooting by Special Agent T. Frank Baughmann, standing with back to target having 5½-inch bull's-eye. Turn and shoot 1 shot each time, double action, at distances from 18 to 25 feet. The time for turning, drawing and firing one shot each time ranged around 1-1/5 to 1-3/5 seconds, under supervision of Ed McGivern, Dec. 8, 1936, at Washington, D. C.

This target is here presented by the writer to illustrate the value of teaching good line shooting as a foundation on which to build proficiency in practical defense shooting for all law enforcement officers.

The bullets were purposely placed below the bull's-eye in this test for a practical demonstration of line shooting control.

Mr. Baughmann's other targets shown herewith, through courtesy of J. Edgar Hoover, fully supports the opinion of the writer in reference to this important matter. Learn to shoot good line shots, double action, then learn to condense the up-and-down distribution of your bullets and effective grouping will be the result, as will be readily seen on the various targets here submitted.

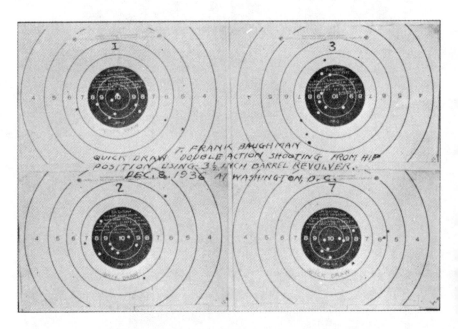

QUICK-DRAW SHOOTING WITH DOUBLE-ACTION REVOLVER

Showing the results of quick-draw shooting by T. Frank Baughmann, using S. & W. .357 Magnum revolver with three and a half inch barrel. Shooting from hip position at eight-inch bull's-eye, twenty-one feet from the shooter, under the instruction and supervision of Ed McGivern, at F. B. I., Washington, D. C., December 8, 1936. Reproduced through the courtesy of J. Edgar Hoover, Director of Federal Bureau of Investigation.

Shooting Double Action

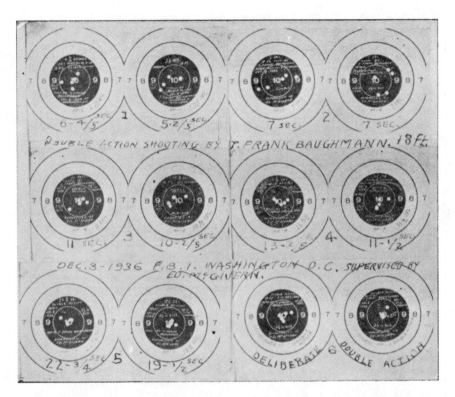

This reproduction of twelve targets, shot by T. Frank Baughmann, of the F. B. I. at Washington, D. C., under the instruction and supervision of the author, on December 8, 1936, furnishes a very valuable demonstration of the importance of the time factor in this very excellent example of double-action revolver shooting. As very clearly evident here the five-shot groups, which show the smaller periods of time required for their delivery, also require a little more space on which to place them. As the time for delivering the various succeeding five-shot groups is gradually extended into longer periods, the grouping becomes closer and more condensed until on the last target, at the lower right, which was shot with deliberate aim but still by the double-action method, there are four bullets almost in the one hole in the center of the target and one just slightly to the right and higher.

This is an exceptional group when it is considered that it, as well as all of the other very good groups, was fired strictly offhand and by the full double-action method of operating the revolver. As stated, the shooting was supervised, and all of these targets were timed, checked, signed and dated by the author, and permission for the reproduction was later requested and received through the courtesy of J. Edgar Hoover, Director of the Federal Bureau of Investigation.

The late F. W. Millington, a double-action revolver shooter, who was a most outstanding performer. A former pupil and associate of the author. This very effective shooting position adopted by Mr. Millington produced the excellent double-action targets herewith presented.

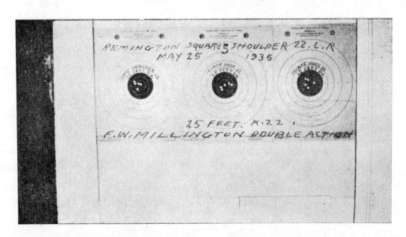

Double-action shooting with S. & W. K-.22 revolver, using Remington square shoulder .22 long rifle cartridges. Range, 25 feet.

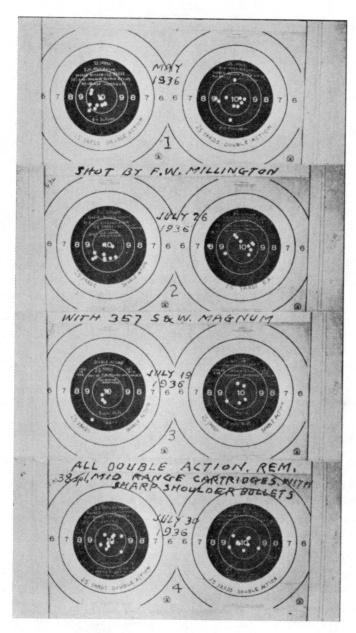

F. W. Millington's excellent double-action targets.   Shot from 25 yards.

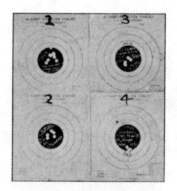

DOUBLE-ACTION SHOOTING

Showing targets 1 and 2, shot by Mr. Bingham of the Smith & Wesson testing department, with a 3½-inch barrel, .357 Magnum revolver on his first trial of double-action shooting, under the author's supervision during a visit to the factory in November, 1936. The close grouping evident here, with which the author was highly pleased, speaks well for both Mr. Bingham and the double-action system of operating the revolver.

Targets 3 and 4, shot by Cy Bassett, Smith & Wesson representative, during his first trials of deliberate double-action revolver shooting, also under the author's supervision, using a 3½-inch barrel, .357 Magnum revolver. Target 4, which is a very valuable demonstration, somewhat definitely explodes the theory that a revolver cannot be accurately sighted and positively controlled while operating the double-action mechanism. By what system could it have been much improved? The upper target, No. 3, shows the group after adjusting the sights, which was the only detail that required any changing.

Shooting Double Action

Double-action shooting from 25 yards by Lewistown police officer, Ben Anderson, June 24, 1937.   5-inch bull's-eye.

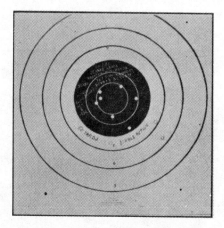

Deliberate double-action shooting by Gerard Lewis from 50 yards, Madison (N. Y.) Range, Smith & Wesson .357 Magnum revolver; witness, Roy S. Tinney, Nov. 3, 1936.

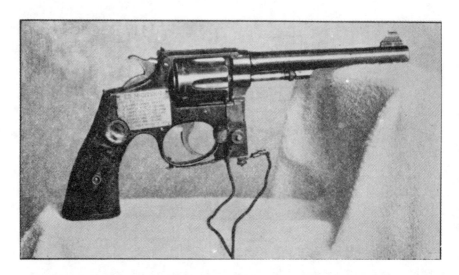

SMITH & WESSON REVOLVER, No. 286600

.38 Special Smith & Wesson with electric contact mechanism, all connected up to operate timing machine. When hammer is released for first shot, the timing mechanism starts the watches. The fifth shot causes the electric mechanism to stop the watches, thereby determining the exact time that has elasped while the 5 shots were being fired. The several watches are interchangeable in several timers—the timers are adjustable to any number of shots from 1 to 10.

Smith & Wesson Revolver, No. 286600, with engraved gold plate now owned by D. B. Wesson.

Shooting Double Action

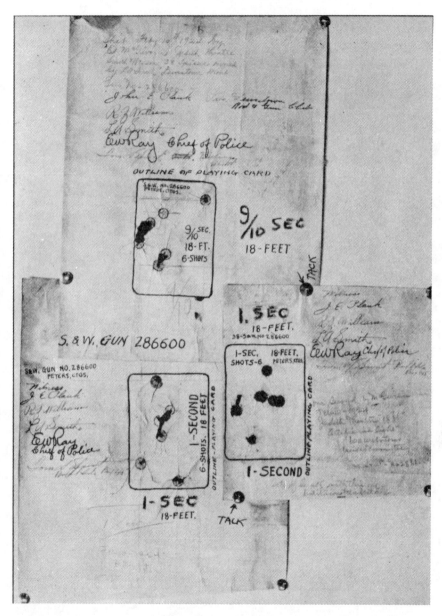

DOUBLE-ACTION SHOOTING

Showing three of the 6-shot groups listed on the gold plate on side of Smith & Wesson Revolver, No. 286600, which were shot in 1924 in Judith Theatre at Lewistown, Montana, before members of the committee and several hundred witnesses.

Fast and Fancy Revolver Shooting

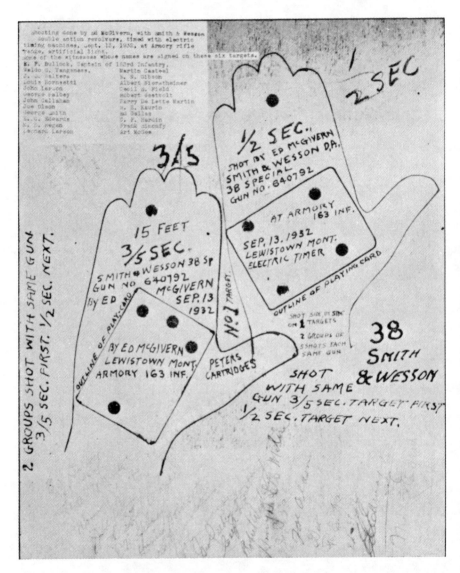

DOUBLE-ACTION SHOOTING

Co. K, 163rd Infantry, Target No. 1, Sept. 13, 1932

Two groups shot on the same target side by side. The 3/5 second group was made first, the ½ second group was made next.

Shooting Double Action

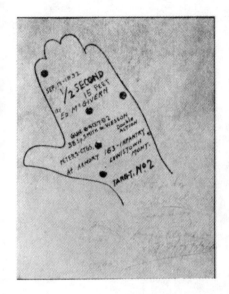

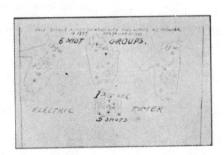

DOUBLE-ACTION SHOOTING
Co. K, 163rd Infantry, Target No. 2,
Sept. 13, 1932.

DOUBLE-ACTION SHOOTING
Co. K. 163rd Infantry, Target No. 3,
Sept. 13, 1932.

.45 DOUBLE-ACTION SHOOTING

There has always been a great hurrah about the old timers shooting .45 caliber revolvers while the modern experts shoot .38 caliber guns for painful accuracy, etc. It would be interesting to see some hard-boiled bad man trying to digest this group of .45's after they hit somewhere around his belt buckle with the compliments of the author. (*Right cut*)

DOUBLE-ACTION SHOOTING

Three groups of six shots each fired from .45 caliber double-action revolver; time required being 1-2/5 seconds, 1-2/5 seconds, and 1-1/5 seconds. The lower small group of five shots required 1-3/5 seconds. Smith & Wesson Revolver, No. 23703. March, 1929.

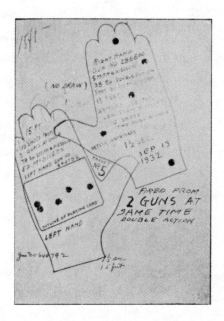

DOUBLE-ACTION SHOOTING
Co. K, 163rd Infantry, Target No. 5, Sept. 13, 1932
Using two guns.   Time for 10 shots, 1-1/5 seconds.

Shooting Double Action

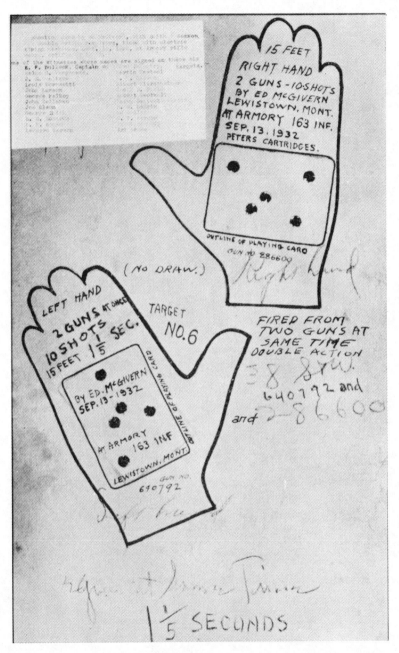

DOUBLE-ACTION SHOOTING
Co. K, 163rd Infantry, Target No. 6, Sept. 13, 1932
Using two guns.   Time for 10 shots, 1-1/5 seconds.

Fast and Fancy Revolver Shooting

Lewistown, Mont. Sept. 14, 1932.

We, the undersigned officers of Company K, 163rd Infantry, were in charge of the program of shooting put on by Ed McGivern at our new armory headquarters, No. 525 Main street, on the evening of Sept. 13, 1932. We operated the electric timer attached, and connected up with, his revolvers, with which he did the shooting shown on the six targets, witnessed and signed by us, and others, on that occasion. The results so outlined, signed and witnessed, are genuine, and the time is correct. The shooting was done with standard Smith & Wesson double action target revolvers, No. 286600 of 38 caliber, and No. 640792 of 38 caliber, both having 6 inch barrels. The 45 caliber Smith & Wesson standard double action target revolver, used was No. 23703. Standard factory ammunition of Peters Ctg. Co. and Remington Arms Co., was used.

Three targets, No. 4-5-6, show 10 shots from the above two guns (five shots from each,) both guns fired at same time, by the double action method. (One gun with each hand) the time for three trials was 1-1/5 seconds each. The 5 shots from the 45 cal. revolver, grouped under outline of hand, was 4/5 of a second, on target No. 3. The distance for all targets shot was 15 feet.

Two groups of five shots each, shot side by side on same target, with gun No. 640792, show time as 3/5 second, for first group, and 1/2 second for second group—each group being under outline of hand, on target No. 1. Target No. 2 shows 5 shots, under outline of hand, in 1/2 second. All targets are signed and numbered for identification. Details are printed in India ink on each target, gun numbers also.

Affidavit relating to the shooting program at Co. K, 163rd Infantry, Armory, Sept. 13, 1932

Shooting Double Action

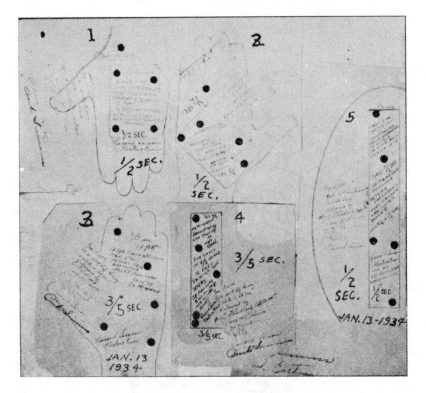

DOUBLE-ACTION SHOOTING
Co. K, 163rd Infantry, Jan. 18, 1934
Target marked Jan. 13 by mistake

Target No. 1 shows five shots fired in a half second without any effort made for definite line control. Target No. 2 shows similar grouping and time. Target No. 3 shows attempt toward better line shooting and slightly slower time. Target No. 4, which measures 1½ x 5½ inches, shows much better line control and more condensing of the spread sideways in a similar three-fifths second period. Target No. 5, which measures 1½ x 9¼ inches, shows concentration on line shooting, also condensing the spread sideways, combined with an effort towards faster time. While successful in maintaining just as much control sideways as on the three-fifths second group, the up-and-down distribution is approximately half again greater. This is due in part, at least, to the concentration being put into effect on these later groups, which is quite clearly noticeable in targets Nos. 6, 7 and 8, which were shot on the same occasion. The names of the witnesses signed hereon are clearly visible.

Fast and Fancy Revolver Shooting

DOUBLE-ACTION SHOOTING
Co. K, 163rd Infantry, Jan. 18, 1934

Target No. 8 made at American Legion and Co. K, 163rd Infantry, headquarters on January 18, 1934, shows nine shots grouped in 1⅞ x 11¼ inches. The first shot from right-hand gun is inside of the 4½-inch spread from the extreme left line. The drawing time in these performances, including the first shot from each gun, usually registers around the half second mark and on that basis the firing of the ten shots in this case would require approximately one and three-tenths seconds. Attention is called to the group made with the left hand which is smaller than the outline of an ordinary playing card. It will be noticed all through the two-gun groups that the left hand quite generally makes the smaller groups.

The two groups, Nos. 6 and 7, show five shots each, within the outline of a playing card, both groups fired from a Smith & Wesson hammerless pocket revolver with a two-inch barrel. No. 6 was done in one and three-tenths seconds and No. 7 required one and two-fifths seconds, or about the same amount of time for each that was required to fire the ten shots from the two guns.

Shooting Double Action

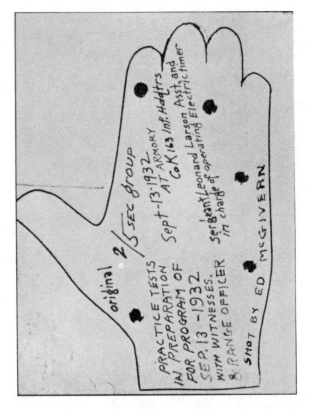

DOUBLE-ACTION SHOOTING

The first two-fifths second group mentioned, shot by Ed McGivern, Sept. 13, 1932

DOUBLE-ACTION SHOOTING

List of the results of 20 attempts for two-fifths second groups shot on Dec. 8, 1932, by Ed McGivern.

Shooting Double Action

Ten Shots in One and Two-Fifths Seconds Using
Two Double-Action Revolvers

Ralph Bishir, the author's chief assistant in the Central Montana Fair programs and the Fox Movietone News activities, is here holding one of the Fox Movietone targets. He was also active in promoting and timing the many repeated attempts for the two-fifths second five-shot groups in the numerous occasions herewith mentioned, and some of which are listed. He was also active in the police training development and many other experiments, the results of which are herewith reported.

Mr. Bishir has had a lot of experience with these experiments against time, and proved to be a very expert electrical timing equipment operator.

Fast and Fancy Revolver Shooting

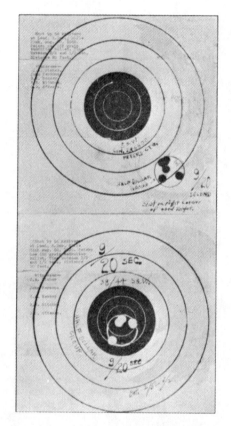

DOUBLE-ACTION SHOOTING

Two groups of five shots each fired from Smith & Wesson .38-44 Outdoorsman in nine-twentieths of a second each. The five shots on each target can be covered by a silver half dollar.

This shooting was done at the range of the Lead Rifle Club Range at Lead, So. Dakota, Aug. 20, 1932. Witnesses' names appear on upper left of each target.

Shooting Double Action

At Ernie Miller's Dude Ranch, Oct. 10, 1935. Douglas B. Wesson and the author examining and discussing the various brands of factory-loaded ammunition being used for the special performances of fast and fancy revolver. shooting which were conducted for the entertainment of Mr. Wesson, Ernie Miller, Mrs. Miller, and their many friends and guests.

The author explaining to Douglas B. Wesson the particular method employed for manipulating the double-action revolver for aerial target and other fast shooting stunts. Combining superspeed with accuracy, so as to hit the objects used for targets with reasonable regularity.

At Ernie Miller's Dude Ranch, Oct. 10, 1935. Ed McGivern presenting Douglas B. Wesson with the gun which was used in January, 1934, to fire the five-shot groups in nine-twentieths of a second and also in two-fifths of a second, as the engraved plate on the side of it clearly states.

Shooting Double Action

This gun, which was used for shooting the 2/5 second and 9/20 second groups herein illustrated, was presented to Douglas B. Wesson on Oct. 10, 1935, at Ernie Miller's Dude Ranch on the West Gallatin near the west entrance to Yellowstone Park at the close of Mr. Wesson's big game hunt.

Engraved silver plate on Smith & Wesson Revolver, No. 640792, relating to the two performances.

Fast and Fancy Revolver Shooting

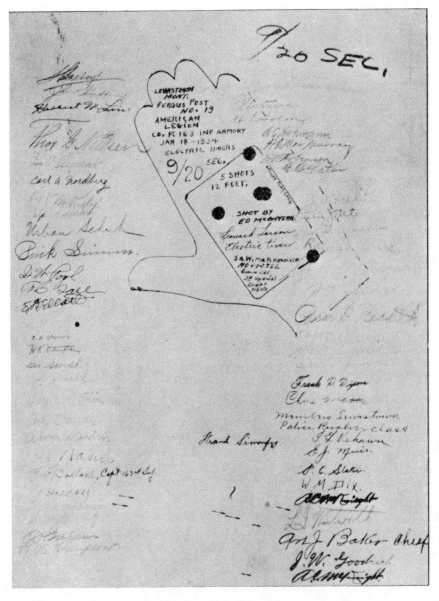

DOUBLE-ACTION SHOOTING

Five shots fired from a Smith & Wesson double-action revolver in nine-twentieths of a second at American Legion headquarters, Jan. 18, 1934.

Shooting Double Action

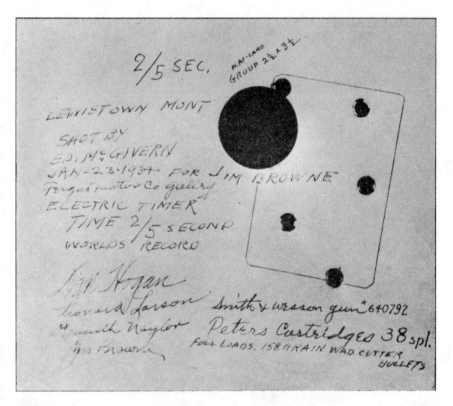

DOUBLE-ACTION SHOOTING

The two-fifths second group made on Jan. 23, 1934, with gun No. 640792, which has engraved silver plate on the side.

Five shots fired from a double-action Smith & Wesson revolver in two-fifths of a second, details and particulars on affidavit accompanying this target (page 159).

This shooting is two one-hundredths of a second faster per shot than the original three-fifths second group of six shots made in 1919, which is also herewith reproduced (page 163).

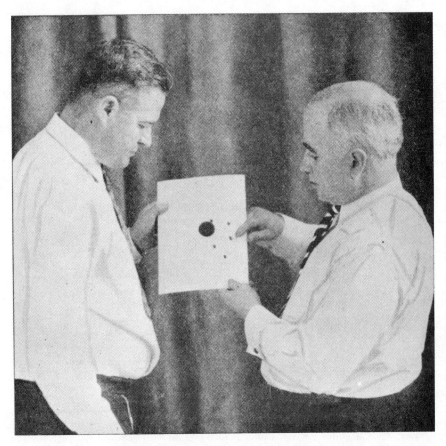

Messrs. Dan Hogan and Jim Browne, two members of the committee, examining the two-fifths second target shot by Ed McGivern on Jan. 23, 1934.

Shooting Double Action

TO WHOM IT MAY CONCERN:

We the undersigned were present during the tests and performances mentioned herein and observed very carefully all operations of electric timing machines and equipment, supervising each operation personally and carefully checking up the correctness of all results.

On the evening of January 23rd, 1934 at the indoor revolver shooting range at Lewistown, Montana, we witnessed the performance of Mr. Ed McGivern, when he fired five shots from a Smith and Wesson Revolver No. 640792 from a distance of 15 feet making a group of the five shots entirely covered with an ordinary playing card. The time required for this performance was exactly two-fifths of a second. Mr. McGivern declared his intention before hand to try for this record and selected this committee to witness the correctness of all timing operations connected with the performance.

This target was shot at the request of and for the personal possession of Jim Browne of Big Fork, Montana, who now has it in his possession.

Date   January 23, 1934   at Lewistown, Montana.

_____   _____

_____   _____

SUBSCRIBED AND SWORN to before me this 25th day of March A. D. 1935.

_____
Notary Public for the State of
MONTANA; Residing at Lewistown,
Montana; My commission expires
January 19, 1937.

Affidavit relating to the two-fifths second five-shot group fired by Ed McGivern from the Smith & Wesson Revolver, No. 640792, on Jan. 23, 1934.

Ed McGivern placing five shots on a target in three-fifths of a second at Kiwanis Boy Scouts District Camp, June 12, 1935.

Shooting Double Action

Affidavit relating to three-fifths second, five-shot group, shot at Kiwanis Boy Scouts District Camp, June 12, 1935.

Fast and Fancy Revolver Shooting

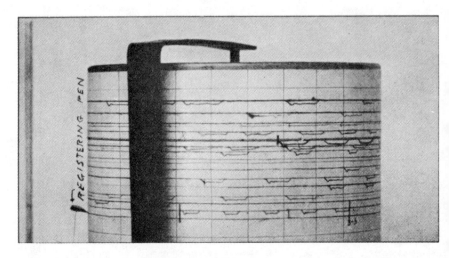

VISIBLE RECORDING OF ELECTRICALLY TIMED RAPID FIRE DOUBLE-ACTION REVOLVER
SHOOTING

This view shows the visible record and spacing of the finger movements involved in firing five shots in three-fifths of a second. In this particular instance these appear on the line next to the bottom. The first short line slanting downward from the continuous line occurred when the trigger was pressed back for firing the shot. At that time the electric contact was closed by the trigger action and the magnets snapped down the marking pen. The little V-shaped spur at the bottom was cause by the rebound of pen carrier when it reached the full downward stroke.

The horizontal mark extending from this little spur and continuing parallel with the upper line, indicates the time that was required for firing the shot, reversing the finger movement and moving the finger forward far enough to release the contact points, which again opens the circuit. When the contact was released the marking pen immediately snapped upward to its original position on the continuous line. This occurs every time a shot is fired by the double-action method while the electrical contact mechanism of the revolver is connected with the revolving drum.

The clear space between these downward bracket marks, and which follows each one, indicates the time required for completing the forward, and again backward, movement which makes it possible for the trigger mechanism to re-engage the necessary operating parts of the revolver which raises the hammer, revolves a new cartridge into place and fires it when the trigger has again reached its full backward travel, all of which occurs during the period of time indicated by the clear spaces showing between the markings which indicate the shots. The total shooting time for the five shots is also checked and registered by the several electrically controlled stop watches entirely independent of the drum, but at exactly the same time that the marks are being registered on the drum by the electrically operated marking pen, visible at the left, which in this case has been moved down in preparation for checking up on another string of shots. These pens simply make a continuous line around the drum until disturbed by the electric contact mechanism on the trigger guards of the revolver. The group checked by the drum in this instance has no connection with the group shot at the Boy Scouts Meet, only in the similarity of time.

Shooting Double Action

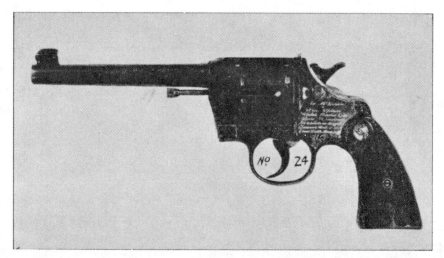

THE DOUBLE-ACTION REVOLVER USED FOR THE EARLIER SPEED TESTS AGAINST VARIOUS TIMING MACHINES AND ELECTRICAL EQUIPMENT

This Colt revolver, which was later presented to Wm. Splan by Ed McGivern, was used to shoot the accompanying targets at Denver, Colo., in 1919. They appeared in *Outdoor Life* in 1920. One of these targets (No. 1), dated Nov. 30, 1919, shows six shots fired in three-fifths of a second.

This three-fifths second performance was repeated at Great Falls, Montana, on July 1, 1920, with this same revolver.

These details are engraved on the gold plate attached to the left side of the gun which is now the property of C. E. Berkner of Great Falls, Montana, assistant supervisor of the Montana State Highway Patrol.

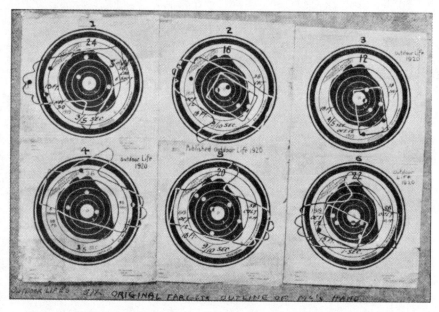

Targets at Denver in 1919. No. 1 shows six shots fired in 3/5 of a second; No. 2, six shots in 9/10 of a second; No. 3, six shots in 4/5 of a second; No. 4, five shots in 3/5 of a second; No. 5, six shots in 9/10 of a second; No. 6, six shots in 1 second. Courtesy *Outdoor Life.*

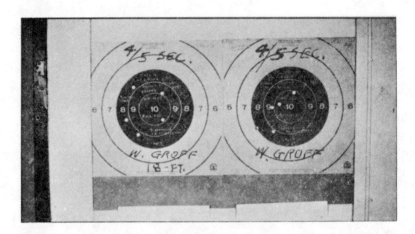

WALTER GROFF'S ELECTRICALLY TIMED SPEED TESTS, SUPERVISED BY THE AUTHOR

Two groups of five shots each fired by Walter Groff from a double-action revolver in four-fifths of a second for each group.

Shooting Double Action

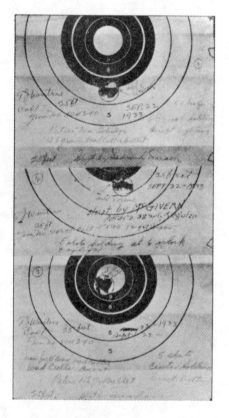

Deliberate single-action·shooting in effort to secure close grouping. Two were shot by Leonard Larson and one by the author.

This shows the three groups of five shots each, shot from 25 feet. Each of these groups can be entirely covered by a dime. These targets were used for the purpose of clearing up the impossible performance theory mentioned in connection with *Adventure Magazine,* and herewith reproduced in fairness to all concerned.

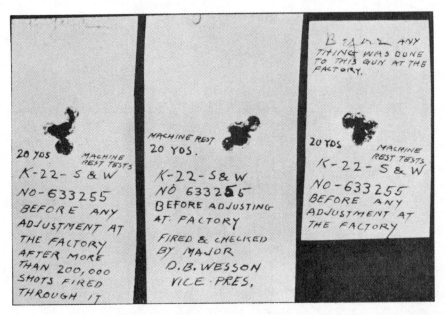

Does your gun lose accuracy on account of a few hundred shots having been fired through or is it just an alibi resulting from the imagination? Here are the results of a few tests to determine such points.

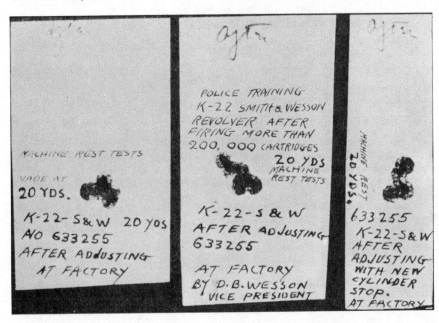

Machine rest grouping from a very much used S. & W. K-.22 revolver.

Shooting Double Action

The gun is entirely hidden in this experiment by the box being held above it in imitation of the early day gamblers who occasionally did their surprise shooting under a table. Alf P. Lane, famous New York pistol and revolver shot and all-around world's pistol champion, at that time, requested this demonstration by the author.

The result of emptying eight double-action guns, firing six shots from each, or 48 shots in all, in this manner, at the 8½ x 11 inch target, is quite clearly evident. There are 16 shots on each of the two upper quarters and 8 shots each on the two lower quarters of target.

This shooting was done at Denver, Colo., Feb. 16, 1920, in the presence of witnesses. Courtesy *Outdoor Life*.

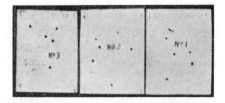

Cut showing targets Nos. 1, 2 and 3, size 8½ x 11 inches, shot by double-action method, while gun was entirely hidden from the view of the shooter, as shown in above cut, distance 20 feet. Feb. 16, 1920. Courtesy *Outdoor Life*.

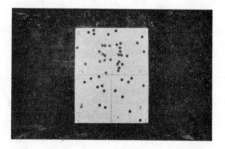

48 shots with guns entirely hidden from view. Distance 20 feet, target 8½ x 11 inches Feb. 16, 1920, Denver, Colo. Courtesy *Outdoor Life*.

Fast and Fancy Revolver Shooting

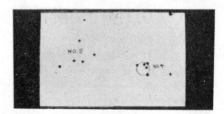

Targets Nos. 4 and 5 shot by the double-action method while gun is held behind the back (as shown and explained below), Feb. 16, 1920.   Courtesy *Outdoor Life*.

Targets under date of Feb. 16, 1920, shot at 20 feet show results of the system of shooting behind the back.   Notice the full length bearing of forearm against and across the back, as formerly mentioned in reference to behind-the-back draw, etc.   The cut of shooter and target make the position of gun and arm quite clear.   Note that gun barrel extends clear of and beyond the left side.   The absence of wide spread feet and general body and leg sprawl or "gun man's crouch," etc., is also noticeable.   These targets are all standard letter-head size, 8½ x 11 inches.   Shooting was done at Denver, Colo., on Feb. 16, 1920, in presence of witnesses.   Courtesy *Outdoor Life*.

Shooting Double Action

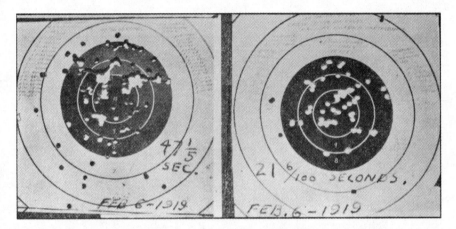

100 SHOTS DOUBLE ACTION   50 SHOTS DOUBLE ACTION

Courtesy *Outdoor Life*

Right—50 shots fired in 21 seconds, February 6, 1919, with double-action revolvers.

The time required for shooting the six shots each time varied between one and nine-twentieth seconds to one and six-tenths seconds. The time for changing guns ranged from one second to one and five-twentieths of a second.

Left—100 shots fired from double-action revolvers in 47 seconds, February 6, 1919.

The average time required for firing each string of six shots ranged from one and a half seconds up to one and six-tenths seconds. The time for changing guns varied between one and five-twentieths of a second to one and a half seconds.

The most important thing upon which success depended was the muscular relaxation secured during changing periods. The first attempts were not successful because this was not understood.

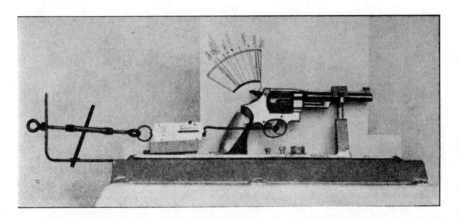

MACHINE FOR WEIGHING THE OPERATION OF DOUBLE-ACTION REVOLVER MECHANISM

In these double-action weighing experiments there is firmly attached to the hammer of the revolver an indicator needle which is used to show the several important points of travel and relative action of the several parts of a double-action revolver during the operation of firing a shot from it by the double-action method.

On this diagram (page 162) will be found indicated and plainly marked the point at which the double-action shooter should, and the successful ones do, momentarily hesitate the hammer-lifting action, while steadying the aim and readjusting the pointing accuracy, after which a slight additional pressure gets the shot away. This is explained in some detail under heading of Trigger Control, Section 11.

Shooting Double Action

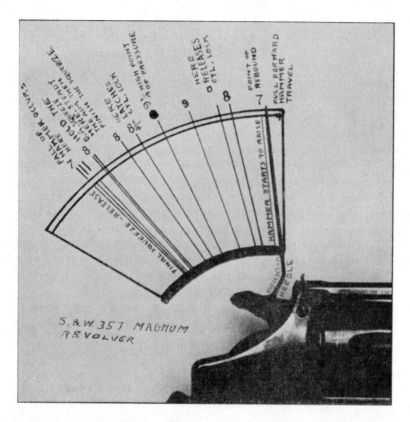

S. & W. 357 MAGNUM REVOLVER

This machine arranged for weighing and determining the number of pounds and fractions thereof required for operating the double-action mechanism of various guns, revealed that the S. & W. .357 Magnum revolver, although one of the heaviest weight standard revolvers manufactured, has one of the smoothest and lightest operating double-action mechanisms available, usually operating at slightly less than ten pounds. A series of trials of various revolvers of all makes shows that many double-action revolvers require as high as twelve and a half pounds trigger pressure to complete the operation of firing a shot by the double-action method. Various guns start lifting hammer at seven and a half to eight pounds and the pressure increases as the working parts of the gun are involved in the operation. Many of the standard high grade revolvers perform well just below eleven pounds while some few models require as high as twelve and a half pounds to operate them.

The author's Shooting Master Colt revolver starts lifting at eight pounds and hammer releases quite uniformly slightly below eleven pounds.

It is usually the case with double-action revolvers, that the more they are operated by the double-action method and the more care and attention they receive, the smoother the actions become and the better they operate.

Attention is called to No. 8 at upper left, the point marked **hold**. The successful, deliberate, double-action revolver shooters hesitate on the trigger pressure temporarily at this point, in order to check up on correctness of aim, etc., just before releasing the shot.

SECTION 11

TRIGGER CONTROL. "HOLD 'EM AND SQUEEZE 'EM."
POSSIBILITIES AND LIMITATIONS. THE TIME FACTOR.

Too much emphasis cannot be put on that ever-popular slogan of the target range, "Hold 'em and squeeze 'em." It is always very much in evidence at all the important matches, on all of the regular ranges, everywhere. The experienced target shot knows that his success, both in practice and in competition, depends more on his ability to squeeze the trigger evenly, steadily, and, what is still more important, to control these trigger squeezing manipulations correctly, than on any other combination of factors connected with revolver shooting, or any other shooting for that matter. Shooting form may be excellent, steady holding ability, taken separately, may be amazing to self and friends and so on, but if a shooter is unable to control the **trigger** properly during the entire time required for getting the shot away, all other accompanying effort has been only **"wasted effort"** and fully as important, **wasted energy** as well. These three essentials of revolver and pistol shooting, Holding, Squeezing, and Trigger Control, are so closely related and so very important that we will discuss them together under the condensed term of Trigger Control when referring to any and all shooting herein described, whether for single-action, double-action, slow fire, timed fire, rapid fire, superspeed, on stationary targets, or for moving targets and the various forms of aerial targets as well.

A little intensive study of the subject will quite readily make the fact apparent that this trigger control idea is the concentrated essence of success in every branch of revolver shooting, and special effort will be made to show how and why it is absolutely necessary, and is directly connected with and responsible for, all successful efforts in each and every kind of shooting—from every angle—as mentioned under the different headings. The most important point of all that can be connected with shooting—of any kind, is **trigger squeeze** combined with **trigger control**, not **pull.** "Pull" is a very wonderful source of results and sometimes of revenue in politics, but it does not help to get results in shooting. On the contrary, it defeats the very purpose for which it is used. **Squeezing the trigger** and developing absolutely positive control over all of the trigger squeezing manipulations involved, is the only successful system of using such mechanism for the purpose of accuracy with pistols and revolvers, whether at the highest rate of speed of which the guns (or shooters) are capable, or for the slowest, most deliberate, super-accurate purposes for which guns may be used or that can be required of them.

When any person can develop and consistently maintain perfect

Trigger Control

"**trigger control,**" perfect scores will usually be the result, for the reason that under such conditions there necessarily must be a regular and consistently uniform result. Perfect trigger control means squeezing the trigger very carefully and properly at all times, while the holding is exactly right and when correct alignment of the sights assures the shooter that the gun is in a perfect position in relation to the object, to score a hit on the certain portion of such object, selected as the most desirable point for the bullet to hit, such, for instance, as the ten ring of the bull's-eye on a paper target, etc. But, when the holding varies or is a little uncertain, or the sight alignment is not just exactly right, or a muscular tremor disturbs the steady pointing and holding necessary for a sure hit, while the trigger is being squeezed, the person who has mastered trigger control will hold the squeeze and not carry it any farther until all things have been satisfactorily arranged again for a perfect registering shot. In short, trigger control means squeezing off the shot when all things are correctly related and in the proper position exactly. It also means with much importance— **not** finishing the squeeze unless everything is relatively correct. In other words, holding the pressure on the trigger at any point at which it may be, while any disturbing influence is interfering with the shooter getting perfect results, and continuing to hold such trigger squeeze at that particular point at which it was when the disturbance occurred, and not continuing it or applying the balance of pressure required for a "**let off**" until everything readjusts itself again to a perfect hold and perfect sight alignment, and when this occurs then carefully finishing the squeeze and getting the shot away while the favorable condition still exists.

Too much emphasis cannot be put on the highly important point that perfect trigger control means **not** squeezing the trigger or finishing the squeeze to get the shot away, at any time, when all conditions are not correct for a perfectly registering hit.

In plain terms—if, for instance, you have a three-pound trigger pull and you have squeezed gradually until two and a half pounds of the required pressure has been applied, leaving only one-half pound more to be applied in order to get the shot away, when, at this two and a half pound point something may occur to disturb either the sight alignment or the normal steady holding, **do not** release the two and a half pounds of squeeze that you already have gained. **Hold** the trigger at or as near that point as it is possible for you to do it, until everything steadies down again, then go on with the steady squeeze and finish the other half pound or so of pressure yet remaining necessary to get the shot off. During such pause for readjustment do not release trigger pressure and allow trigger to go forward again, thereby losing the advantage you have already gained up to that point. Neglect or oversight of this important matter at this particular time will make it necessary for you to start all over again and for the second time overcome the full three-pounds "pull" or squeezing pressure that was originally required to release the hammer, instead of just the remaining half pound necessary, if you had held what you had at the time that you were compelled to hesitate.

Perfect trigger control is, due to average physical conditions, an almost impossible thing to master, but we should try to get as close to it as possible and make an earnest effort to master such conditions to the greatest extent that we are mentally and physically able to, for the specific reason that the "trigger control" is the absolute master-key to **all control** you may ever hope to have over the results of your revolver shooting (or of any other kind of shooting) in any and all branches of the game in which you may engage. It is really the most important thing connected with revolver shooting, and the greatest factor connected with any and all angles of the game.

Trigger control must first be learned by slow, careful shooting, while using the single-action method of operating the gun and of squeezing the trigger. When this point has been reached and reasonable certainty of control has been acquired by this method, the double-action method of operating the revolver should be taken up and studied, so as to develop a similar control over the much longer and heavier trigger movements required, and, of course, in consequence thereof also controlling the movements of the hammer.

In double-action shooting—the hammer should be raised by the **pressure** of the trigger, until the hammer **reaches almost, but not quite,** the full distance of backward travel that is required (see diagram, page 171), and held there at that point until all things are steadied and in proper relation for a hit. Then, but not until then, the balance of the trigger pressure required can be applied to raise the hammer the rest of the way needed for it to slip off of the spur of the "self-cocking" mechanism and be released to fire the shot. This is of course the very important point of hammer balance or temporary hesitation just before the hammer is released, that must be mastered for successful double-action shooting. When this system of operation is completely mastered it will be found that the almost **perfect trigger control** that has been developed by the single-action method can be developed by the double-action method also, with very positive results. The fact of the matter should be apparent by now that under this system the latter part of trigger movement or final let-off to fire the shot, in double-action shooting, is practically the same as the short trigger movement for single-action shooting.

When this double-action trigger control is developed to the point, as described, where the shot can be, and, of course, must be, released at the instant of proper relative position of gun to target, all the seeming mystery of hitting small objects, either stationary or when tossed in the air, with

Trigger Control

bullets fired by the double-action method, from double-action revolvers, quickly vanishes. Trigger control is the "mystery" underlying all of these seemingly marvelous performances, and nothing else can ever take its place for successful results in double-action revolver shooting. And until it is successfully mastered, no certain specified successful results can be secured, nor can reasonably fair high average performances be expected with any degree of regularity, in this branch of the shooting game.

Trigger control, as applying to very short barreled revolvers and pistols, both single-action and double-action, assumes a position of very great importance, just a little more so, perhaps, than when referring to those with longer barrels—in the neighborhood of six inches, etc. Great stress has been placed on the lack of distance between sights, or the very short sighting plane, as it is usually spoken of, when discussing these very short guns and the lack of successful results secured with them by many persons, which has been quite generally ascribed to that particular cause.

The very successful results of the experiments with these extra short revolvers by the two well-known authorities, Colonel Julian S. Hatcher and Mr. F. C. Ness, of the "American Rifleman" staff, with various two and three inch barreled revolvers, as written up in detail in the "American Rifleman" magazine some time ago, wherein they outlined and described rather clearly the various trials and the, as generally considered, unusually good results that they were able to secure by careful study and intelligent effort with these short guns, seem to agree pretty well with the very satisfactory results that have been secured in some of our experiments.

These new-fangled contraptions or "belly guns," as some of the skeptical ones have sometimes rather scornfully referred to these short guns, have been subjected to a great deal of such thoughtless criticism which is entirely unwarranted. The expression "belly gun," as we construe the usual meaning of the term, is in a general way intended to indicate that the user of one of these guns would find it almost necessary to hold the end of the barrel right against the belly of the man he might be forced to shoot, if he really expected to be in any way sure of scoring a hit. However, the actual results do not agree with this view, as a careful survey will reveal.

The practical possibilities of these guns are really very surprising, and, as stated, they furnish a very fine example of the absolute necessity of the development of positive trigger control. The surprisingly good work done by Colonel Hatcher and Mr. Ness, as mentioned, as well as the rather satisfactory work done on various aerial targets and quick-draw groups, and superspeed group shooting, while using assorted models of these abbreviated guns, seems to strengthen the argument very much indeed in favor of the very careful study of trigger control rather than placing too much accent on alignment difficulties, the lack of sighting plane, etc., etc.

Fast and Fancy Revolver Shooting

The possible speed results, as mentioned, and the handiness and adaptability and the greatly varied places and ways in which these guns can be carried and quickly produced, for effective use by federal and other law enforcement officers when in a tight spot, can and certainly should pay very satisfying dividends for the time and effort required to master double-action trigger control sufficiently to at least give these guns a fair opportunity to demonstrate their worth-while qualities, which they very certainly will do, if handled properly.

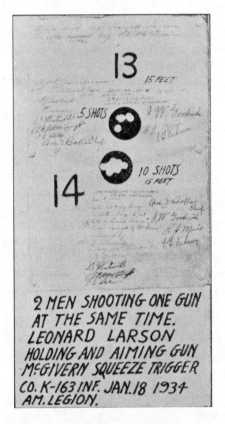

Demonstrating the importance of careful trigger control: one man holding gun correctly lined up on bull's-eye; the author carefully squeezing the trigger without disturbing the shooter's holding. 15 shots were fired in this test.

SECTION 12

PSYCHOLOGY. PRACTICALLY APPLIED TO FAST AND FANCY REVOLVER SHOOTING AND THE VARIOUS ANGLES EMBODIED THEREIN. STUDY AND TRAINING COMPARED TO JUST NATURAL ABILITY. GENIUS. EFFECT OF DANGER AND OF CROWDS PSYCHOLOGICALLY. PSYCHOLOGY AS A FACTOR IN DEVELOPING SKILL, SPEED, ACCURACY, AND PRECISION MOVEMENTS.

This section will deal with the subject of speed development and the various angles and systems of combining speed with accuracy.

This constant urge for speed, through which the human race has ever sought for faster and better ways of doing things, has, no doubt, been responsible for man's gradual, but none the less steady, progress and improvement. This compelling urge has been very closely interwoven with the history of the human race all through the ages; from his very beginning man has ever been changing and developing and seeking new and better methods of accomplishment.

As a result of this, we have reached the present stage of "high speed activity" that enters into all branches of our everyday life, and practically controls our very existence. The same primal urge for speed and improvement was no doubt working in my case and is probably the same driving force that keeps all of us going until our work is finished and the results can be passed along for the benefit of others.

Being a genuine Westerner and a resident of a section of the country that is so rich with the romance of the pioneer spirit of the early days of the West, and the gun handling ability of the famous sheriffs and other hardy characters of the frontier, I naturally became interested in revolvers and the possibilities for speed in their manipulation, and the effective results that could be combined with such proficiency.

I started my training with the avowed intention of mastering **all**—or at least as much as it would be reasonably possible for one average person to master—of the old timers' one and two gun tricks, "killers kinks" (without the killing if possible), quick draws, novelty stunts, and general entertainment features. I very soon realized that to be in any great measure successful in combining and mastering these various outstanding features of six-shooter science, which Eugene Cunningham of El Paso, Texas, so aptly terms "Triggernometry" in his excellent book, which gives a most interesting history of the famous six-gun artists of frontier days, under that title, I would be compelled to make a study of the subject of Psychology and apply it practically to my self-imposed program of accomplishment.

Research along this line soon brought to me the firm conviction that in my chosen field of revolver shooting the perfect development of control of all movements relating to such shooting, by the subconscious mind, is absolutely necessary for success, holding true from the impulse to act, and continuing through with the release of nervous energy which not only starts, but also makes it possible to continue, with the necessary precision movements while in action. Development of subconscious control is, in my estimation, the most important point to be considered when laying the foundation for a working basis.

The more I studied into the Psychology angle, the more convinced I became that, of necessity, it must be only in this way that we humans can develop the so-called marvelous skill, unusual ability, superspeed, dexterity, lightning movements, etc., required in this and various other fields of endeavor, which, by the uninitiated, are generally believed to indicate that the excellent performer in any line must be gifted with unusual powers or talents of some sort, or, as believed in the "Old Days," that he is possessed of some sort of a spirit (or devil) or spiritual influence, good or bad, as the case may be. In fact, everything is either blamed, or praised, for unusual development of expertness except psychological processes. Repeating and studying these processes and experiences is the method of procedure by which we must develop what is termed exceptional ability, if our ambition directs our activities in that direction.

As we proceed with this subject it should be constantly kept in mind that man is an organism for reacting on impressions, his mind is there to help determine his reactions, and the purpose of his education is to make them (the reactions) numerous, immediate, and perfect.

It is to be remembered that muscles are never active except as stimulated to action by the nervous system and it must also be kept in mind that a great part of the essence of success is contained in perseverance. Resolute action in preference to alibis; legitimate excuses, of course, may be used sparingly.

Such persons as may be liberally endowed by nature with the necessary physical qualifications, which specially fit them for such things, will, of course, master the more difficult stunts, and the more spectacular features of the game, with a little less effort, and perhaps in a little less time, than those who may be less favored by nature in their physical make-up. But, because a person does not happen to be born with all of these so-called "natural gifts" there is no reason whatever for discouragement, for the very special reason that proficiency can be developed and maintained by persistent training and practice, in usually a much greater degree than that which is generally in evidence as a result of "just a natural gift."

Psychology

With very few exceptions—if any—expert revolver shots, plain and fancy, are developed by consistent training and study, instead of just being born that way and growing into it. The meaning of this is, that through a system of study, application and training, intelligently persisted in, certain desired results can be quite regularly secured; by properly directed effort during a certain period of time and over a certain prescribed course, such things **can** be accomplished.

Such individuals are "made" into expert revolver shots by, and as a result of, training and experience, and contrary to a rather popular belief, without such "training and experience" they never could or would "grow" into it through some lucky break of being "born that way." The law of averages and the peculiarities of human nature seldom, if ever, combine to produce such "natural wizards." Therefore, the most sensible course of conduct for the student would be to follow the example of the many outstanding revolver "shooting stars" of today, who usually will be very glad to tell you that their experience is pretty well in agreement with my statements. No matter how much natural shooting ability a person may be born with, training and experience will be necessary to properly develop such talent to a sufficient degree where it can be directed in the proper way to qualify one as a real expert in accordance with the standards by which such things are measured.

There are a great many things that enter into being a consistent performer that the "natural-born wonder" without training and experience to develop him does not usually possess, and one of the more important of these is the power to maintain physical and mental balance while under pressure. He is very liable to find himself at the critical moment of hard fought, close competition, entirely deserted by what is usually referred to in the more polite world of sport as "intestinal stamina," and more roughly speaking is known as "fighting guts." This condition arises quite generally in such persons and is an almost direct result of this lack of training and experience mentioned, which in itself is necessary to enable the person to stand up under pressure of the nervous strain placed on him in a tight match, or the disturbing psychological effect of a crowd, which works in very much the same way and is actually as alarming to the uninitiated as when exposed to great personal danger.

When extreme pressure of such a nature is brought to bear on the individual who has not had sufficient training and experience, he is apt to find that he has been thrown entirely out of balance with himself and his usually quite normal actions are completely out of time. His usually precise movements are jerky and irregular, his mental impulses faulty, and the nervous impulses controlling the muscles jerky and stuttering, instead of being guided by the usual smooth flow of energy that under ordinary conditions produces a continued series of positive movements, properly controlled, correctly timed, and accurately directed.

It is this point of resistance that was so important and was built up and developed to the highest degree by the noted characters and famous law officers of the early West, whose remarkable performances in the face of death have been handed down to us with many interesting variations. If someone had mentioned to most of these men at that time anything about the effects of psychological disturbance or physical, mental, and psychological balance, or subconscious control, kinæsthesis, muscle sense, etc., it's a reasonably safe bet that, if they didn't shoot the speaker at once, some of them would doubtless have replied in more or less disgusted tones, "Why, I was never sick a day in my life." "I don't remember of ever having such a disease." Yet these very men had all of these things developed in plenty and to the highest degree. The survivors of the many famous gun battles of that period were the ones who had their impulses and movements always under perfect control; no disturbing influence was great enough to throw them out of normal balance, no danger, no matter how great or close, interfered with their "positive movements, properly controlled, correctly timed, and **accurately directed.**"

With such men it was not a case of lack of nerves, as some try to make it appear; it was a matter of having everything in the way of impulse and emotions absolutely under control at the **psychological moment,** as the ones who are versed in such things generally refer to it.

It was from close observation, study and analysis of somewhat corresponding situations and results, that I conceived the idea of developing subconscious control and making practical application of the principles involved in my own efforts toward developing ultraspeed with fairly dependable accuracy under varied conditions, in some of the, as originally regarded, slightly unusual, or—as by some considered—crazy combinations and angles, of double-action shooting.

How much or how little success this system was able to produce, as applied in a practical way, may be judged at the conclusion of this book by the readers who have been patient and persistent enough to follow that far, through what some may be inclined to regard as "radical ravings" and wild riding of somebody's "pet hobby." But I, like many others, may be forgiven, for the reason that I have been quite "sincere in my faith" in the dependability of what we regard as **the medium of control,** and the very positive realization that it is a very healthy fact that **can be** and **has been** quite well-demonstrated.

Doctors and surgeons and professors, generally interested and well-informed in such things, can, and often do, explain clearly about man's reaction to what is termed "the external stimulus to act." These things are carried out in detail in the definitions of "psychological time" and "reaction time" under the branch of psychophysics; in short, it is the time elapsing between the application of a stimulus and the reaction to it, occasionally called psychophysical time. A brief technical explanation is here given for the benefit of those technically inclined who sometimes like to argue. Using an expression credited to the old West—I will here "turn my wolf loose," in relation to subconscious control, kinæsthesis, muscle sense, etc.

Psychophysical time consists of three periods: First, a period of initial excitation of the sense organ and transmission of the stimulation to the ganglionic center; second, a period of activity in the center; and, third, the period of the transmission of the motor impulse and of the physical reaction. The first and third of these constitute the "psychological time." The simple "reaction time" is, as nearly as possible, made identical with the "psychological time," the period of central activity being reduced to a minimum.

"Complex reaction times" are determinations of various sorts of central time. The usual types are: recognition, perception or discrimination time; choice time; and association time. The reader is urgently requested to take particular note of the several later points mentioned here, which are very vital facts, and factors, that assume much importance in the later explanation of aerial target shooting in groups or where five or six shots are to be grouped on one target, either moving or stationary. Their importance cannot be overestimated by those seriously interested in securing successful results.

We will now go back and take up the matter of **"positive movements, properly controlled, correctly timed,** and **accurately directed."** As the young boy looking over his mechanical toys on Christmas might be expected to remark: "Let us see how this 'jigger' works." First, the "psychological moment" is defined as "the occasion when any action or event is most certain to have full effect on men's minds, the most important moment, as by reason of exceptional interest, excitability, or expectancy." Psychology is defined as "the science of mind, systematic knowledge and investigation of functions of mind," "of or pertaining to the mind; mental; —contrasted with physical," "the science of behavior," etc.

Voluntary action, under normal conditions; an idea works itself out **in action** in the same way and to the degree to which it is the exclusive object of individual attention. But usually more than one idea is present in consciousness at the same moment, each striving, so to speak, to bring out its appropriate action. **Action is thus delayed** by the presence of competing ideas, causing what we call **deliberation, reflection** and **choice.**

We reflect, we deliberate, we choose.

Thus it can readily be seen that deliberate effort, directed entirely by the conscious mind alone, would be subject to this sort of stuttering and more or less interfered-with action, not quite smooth and efficient enough to successfully take care of the situations that confront us here.

We must seek our solutions for the problems outlined, through some more adaptable medium such as I have described and referred to as "subconscious control," the workings and reactions of which I shall try to outline in some sort of a practically applied manner. Therefore, I shall here offer a few explanatory remarks relating to the method I followed in the development of aerial target shooting with revolvers at various sized targets, in groups from three to six, as formerly described, and of firing five or six shots at one target (such as a can) while in the air, before it could fall to the ground after being tossed up by hand or by the use of a trap, to a height around 18 or 20 feet. The time for falling, when the can or other similar target is hit regularly, varies slightly, due to the effect the bullets usually have of slowing it up to a small extent; the most important factor for imposing a time penalty arises, therefore, from missing the target; the more often it is hit, the more time it usually stays in the air.

A great many theories have been advanced as to just how this and similar fast shooting is done, so as to combine the necessary accuracy to score all hits, with the speed required for completing the string of shots in the very limited time allowed, and which cannot be extended to any great extent by any such things as "lucky breaks." The writer's explanation has been for years that it is the result of subconscious control over the combined movements required from start to finish, this control having been developed and built up gradually through much repetition and by the study and close application of the principles involved, necessary for subconscious control.

Let us analyze a few of these factors that might have an important bearing on the matter together with some of the definitions relating thereto for the particular benefit of those interested persons who may wish to develop themselves along similar lines. (I may as well make it plain at this particular time that this is actually the principal purpose in mind when arranging the material for this book.) We will follow step by step a short way along the self-explaining (dictionary) definitions relating to this subject. We will then put the evidence together and compare methods and "motives" with results as established by actual demonstrations, abundance of such evidence being available and at hand. Thus:

"Conscious ideas" are connected by subconscious mental excitations; pertaining to liminal consciousness or to subconsciousness.

Liminal—Pertaining to the limen, or threshold of consciousness.

Subconscious—Of the nature of mental operation,—a designation applied to certain phenomena seemingly of the same nature as the phenomena of consciousness, as subconscious reasoning. Subconscious memory seems to involve the presence of subconscious ideas, sub, or lower degrees of consciousness belonging to the liminal, or threshold margin of consciousness, or to that portion of the conscious field which falls without—outside the range of direct attention, not requiring conscious attention acts performed subconsciously; without the necessity of conscious attention.

Sub—Original prefix, from under, up to. A prefix signifying, in general, under, below, beneath.

Subserve—To serve in a subordinate capacity, to be subservient or instrumental to.

Sub, in Latin origin, expresses an inferior degree, an imperfect or partial state, somewhat or slightly less than usual, or normal, almost, nearly.

The brain is essential to all voluntary activity. Therefore, the brain is the bodily organ most directly associated with consciousness, and conscious action. In other words the source of directed activity.

We have occasionally heard these completed shooting performances referred to in a "jump at conclusion," "very simple" explanatory manner by some persons as the result of brain impulse. We shall now look in on that angle.

"Brain impulse"—The sensory (nervous impulse from a sense organ) is sent to the brain, the brain transforms it into perhaps several related impulses, which are in turn sent to different muscles and sets of muscles, along, with, and through different nerves, and combinations of nerves. Nervous energy starts with the eye (or other sense organ) sensing the danger—or other reason for action, which is called the "external stimulus." This reaches the brain, the brain processes turn this instantly into a command for a combination of movements necessary to fulfill the entire muscular action program, starting and continuing until completing the entire series of impulses, movements, actions, etc., that may be required—as the brain figures it out instantly from what is sent by the sense organ (eye) in that one instant impulse, through what are regarded as the **mental processes.** It is from this process that we have derived the term that we use here as **"mental impulse."**

In short, the impulse is started by the sense of vision, by some external stimulus, goes to the brain where by **mental processes** it is rearranged into its various requirements and **then** sent on in the subdivided and varied forms of impulse and commands, through the very efficient distribution system of nerves, etc., to the various muscles, resulting in the combined action involving a period of coördination of movements toward one objective—the desired result, or the definite conclusion of a situation existing at the time, which is or was instantly recognized, positively identified, and correctly analyzed by the brain through the intellectual mental processes, developed through the process of memory, and from experience, covering like or similar situations that have existed at some time, or perhaps several, times, in the past. This now comes under the head of kinæsthesis, kinæsthetic memory, muscle sense, etc., **kinæsthetic** — which in short means . . . any mental representation of movement sufficient to induce its voluntary performance.

The acquisition of voluntary control over the muscles is due to such kinæsthetic images, etc., the sum of the images representing certain movements to the mind.

This completed combination from the sense impulse to the finished action, or end of the situation, we attribute to mental processes, while the impulses that are finally sent out, as a result of the working over of the first sensory (eye) impulse by the brain, through these mental processes which have their seat or base of operations in the brain and taking place at that point, should—as we see it—be termed "mental impulse," by reason of having resulted from mental processes rather than from the formerly referred to "brain impulse" only.

The final impulse to act comes from passing the original sensory impulse through this intelligent, intellectual laboratory of the brain, so to speak. The interrelated "motor impulses" are then sent on to the muscles. The complete action that takes place is the result of what is called sensori-motor impulse, which means starting with or from a sense organ and ending in the muscles—in muscular movements. These impulses follow what are known as sensori-motor tracts or paths which will be discussed and defined later.

Many of the present-day psychologists attempt to analyze further the particular sense fields, such as the kinæsthetic or muscle sense mentioned, which, without doubt, are very much involved but, until lately, have quite generally gone unrecognized in such performances. Only in recent years have these come to be regarded as under the control of the subconscious mind, which also brings it under the meaning of the term we use here—subconscious control.

Others go to another extreme and credit these superspeed performances, and the various complicated shooting stunts and combinations, to the workings of what is referred to as the unconscious mind—unconscious control. We will now give that angle some consideration.

Due to our very intimate relations with this field of endeavor, we have never looked with favor upon the term "unconscious control" by, or of, an unconscious mind, or of performing particularly difficult and complicated shooting stunts through, or as a result of, any directed action of what may be termed "unconscious mind." Our experience with the subject in hand does not, for us, quite support such view, particularly the certain things, such as we are considering here, which from their very nature, as described, require great coördination of precision muscular movements, that must be exactly timed and very correctly controlled, so as to fit precisely into other relative movements and actions, which must be terminated at some very exact point of travel of each of several targets. Each of the several shots must be fired in very exact relation and accord of target and gun, one to the other, repeated at exactly the right instant for several successive instances in a very short period of time. The hands, arms, gun, sights, as one angle, and the targets as several separate angles, all move at the same time, under separate and independent impelling and governing influences, or motivating agencies.

Coördination of movement by the cerebellum is hardly a thing brought on by an **unconscious** state or condition, but rather the **subconscious.** I am of the belief that man does not **unconsciously** plan or accomplish any of the exceptionally skillful and accurately timed and governed movements and actions such as are required in the case under consideration. Hitting each one of several targets with one shot for each target fired from a revolver, when these targets are tossed in the air at approximately the same time, and which, due to natural causes as formerly pointed out, cannot remain in the air for any great length of time, cannot—in our opinion—be done unconsciously.

Nor can we place five or six shots in a can or other similar target, under similar conditions, in a similar period of time, in any such manner. The perfect coördination of muscular movements required cannot, we believe, result unconsciously; but can and should more reasonably result from subconscious control and kindred influence.

Positively directed effort requires that such ability or **directed** habit, if one wishes to call it such, must be built up and directed step by step by the conscious mind, until that part of our mental equipment regarded as the subconscious mind can and does assume control as a result of much and very oft-repeated performances, but must still be, to some extent— directed effort. Due to the ever changing and never exactly duplicated conditions, existing from one occasion to another, in which the targets are thrown, or are grouped, or separated, or scattered when thrown, on no two occasions being alike, each trial requires slight alterations in procedure. Unconscious movement or shooting by instinct could not exactly apply to this sort of performance, for the very good reason that instinctive movement is dependent on fixed conditions, relative location and proportion being the same in each case, something that is quite decidely **not** the case in these situations. If the shooting was dependent on instinctive movement, the changed relative position of the targets each time would defeat successful results.

A man may pull out his watch, look at the time, forget it again in an instant, and put the watch away again, while having his mind on something else and being greatly occupied by this other task, or he may take his handkerchief out of his hip pocket, wipe his nose or mouth, and not need to have his attention focused on the act, and perhaps not notice that he has done it, and promptly forget it. These are fixed conditions and fixed locations.

Many times I have been confronted with the argument that a person may shoot a shotgun at a flying bird and not have a conscious recollection of aiming the gun (which is only a small part of the combined effort), but have rather a sensation of just pointing the gun. My experience along this line leads me to believe that if one is any sort of a consistent shooter at all, he does the aiming subconsciously, through subconscious control developed by much practice connected with successful results, which made deliberate conscious aiming effort not noticeable as being separately applied to that particular part of the combined task. If such a person was not so trained, the hitting would—as results will usually show—be more the result of accident than positively controlled action, and I might mention that accidental results are not the most desirable things to have to depend on for success in exhibition shooting before mixed audiences.

On the other hand—too much deliberate and fully conscious control is not desirable. If a person should attempt to do this complicated aerial shooting we are discussing here, and control all the actions involved by the fully conscious mind and by deliberate consciously directed effort alone, he would not succeed, for the reason that with so many objects to be handled almost at once, and various other disturbing angles and incidents that are always present to prevent the fully conscious mind from concentrating separately on each item required, and the complete separation of all other items until that particular one on which the shooter has his attention, has been attended to, then the delays so resulting would prevent the completing of all of the necessary movements required within the prescribed time allowed, or possible to obtain, under the conditions as set forth. Here is an exact place where **taking time "to reflect, to deliberate, to choose"** motives or objects would be fatal to success.

I know from several years' experience in this line of effort, and from repetition of these certain combinations of conditions, that they require for successful completion certain combined movements, all of which, while performed with great speed, must be very accurately and positively directed. In other words, each shot that is fired is done in the face of very rapidly changing conditions, in no manner fixed. Such conditions cannot be met with and successfully mastered repeatedly, through or by any controlling influence or medium that we can find sufficiently supported by satisfactory evidence, other than what we refer to as "the subconscious control."

This is my honest opinion, well-supported by much experience. If I should be technically "just slightly in error," on some very fine point of deep scientific adjustment, I am still firm in my belief that I have defined it much more closely and clearly than has ever been done before, and it is the result of my search for a practical explanation, demonstrated actually and practically by a shooter, instead of theoretically, or a near scientific diagnosis by someone who never fired a shot at a flock of rapidly moving targets during his entire lifetime, the latter situation being quite often the case, and the general method by which many such things are considered settled, and quite definitely decided.

I will here submit a few definitions for comparison and the reader may then draw his own conclusions, for or against the matter as set forth.

Mental system—A complexly interrelated body of ideas and impulses, capable of functioning with relative independence and unity.

Mental-intelligent—Intellectual, as mental faculties; mental operations; mental exercises; mental impulses.

Mentally—In the mind; in mind; in thought; in idea.

Unconscious—Not conscious; (please note carefully) in a state unaccompanied by conscious experience, as a person in a swoon is unconscious; not capable of realizing; not appreciating; not being aware of; not known or apprehended by consciousness; not present in attention; not realized; not brought home to the intelligence; said of stimulations or processes which fail of their normal effect on consciousness.

Motives—The whole of that which moves, excites or invites the mind to volition, whether that be one thing singly, or many things conjunctively.

Impulse—Force so communicated as to produce motion suddenly or immediately. The effect of an impelling force; motion produced by a sudden or momentary force. An excitement of the mind, especially in the form of an abrupt and vivid suggestion, prompting some unpremeditated action or leading to unforeseen knowledge or insight. A spontaneous inclination arising either directly from the feelings or from some outer influence. Influence acting unexpectedly or temporarily on the mind. Impulsive force.

All of which is dependent for expression in action on nerve cells (or neurones, as they are more often termed) which may be classified as follows: (1) Sensory neurones (which connect a sense organ to the spinal cord or mid-brain), (2) motor neurones (which connect the spinal cord or mid-brain to muscles), and (3) connecting neurones (which connect all parts of the spinal cord, mid-brain and brain together). By, over, along and through these neurones, or nerve cells, is formed and developed what is called sensori-motor tracts in the nervous system, or sensori-motor arc, or path.

Sensori-motor arc—The entire path of a nervous impulse (consisting of a system of interconnected neurones) is sometimes referred to as a sensori-motor path, or arc. It is called sensory, because it has its origin in a sense organ (eye, ear, skin, touch, etc.). It is called motor because it ends in some muscle and is concerned in the movement of the muscle. The hyphen used in sensori-motor indicates that the entire structure from beginning to end is in reality one mechanism, and functions in a unitary way.

There are two ways in which newly organized sensori-motor tracts develop in the central nervous system: By the growing together of the branching processes of the neurones, so that new connections are made; by a reduction in the resistance offered by the synapses, which form the points of connection between the various neurones of any sensori-motor path. There is evidence that the synapse is crossed by the nervous impulse **more readily** (as a result of) the more frequently it has been used. To make it plain, the more often a performance is repeated, the more readily the nervous impulse traverses the entire sensori-motor tract, and the better organized, as a result, are the neurones that are included in that tract and **the more immediately the results follow.** It is by these processes that superspeed development, and rapid aerial target "group shooting," were made possible.

As a practical example of this, we will select a lot 100 feet square covered with snow a foot deep. In order to break a path through that snow following the outer edge of that lot and stopping to turn at each corner, the first trip around would involve difficulties that would require deliberate and determined effort. Each trip around thereafter would require less effort, less conscious attention, and could be done in a shorter period of time for each trial, until after many trials the trip could be made with little or no conscious effort, and very little conscious attention, finally practically coming under subconscious control, requiring no particular attention or deliberate effort to follow the path or to make the stops and turns. Also there would be no resistance from the snow, due to the fact that there was a well-worn path established over which travel was not resisted or hampered in any such way as was the case for the first trip over that particular route.

SECTION 13

CORRECTLY MEASURING SHORT PERIODS OF TIME RE-
QUIRED FOR HIGH SPEED REVOLVER SHOOTING STUNTS.
STOP-WATCH HANDLING BY TRAINED OPERATORS. NE-
CESSITY FOR ELECTRICAL AND MECHANICAL TIMING
MACHINES TO REPLACE AND AVOID "THE HUMAN ERROR."
TIME PERIODS AS INDICATED BY WORDS SPOKEN DURING
CONVERSATIONS, AND BY COMPARISON WITH WORD DE-
LIVERY OF LEADING RADIO ANNOUNCERS.

When attempting to secure absolutely correct results in the way of
recording time periods required for performing certain shooting stunts,
tests, and experiments that can be completed in one second, and lesser
divisions even below the half second mark, and also in writing of such
results after they have been secured, in a way that can be readily understood by the average reader who may not have a desire to study all the
technical points involved, I believe it would be helpful to more clearly
define some of the terms I will use while reviewing and explaining such
results, and the governing factors that enter into the methods employed
to secure them.

Instant; Moment; Second. These three terms will be used to indicate time periods of different lengths or duration as follows: Instant: A
portion of time too short to be estimated, emphasizing the idea of its
inappreciable duration. Instantly, Instantaneously—Without any per-
ceptable duration of time. Moment: Slightly longer continuance of time
than that which is understood as an instant. Momentary pause—A
slight hesitation, very brief. Second: One-sixtieth part of a minute of
time, first in order—for dividing time as we are accustomed to calculate
or to estimate it as it is divided and in general use today.

By the use of these terms, which are in general use, I hope to assist
others to separate and define time into three reasonably clear periods
of less than a second. The greater number of people usually regard
a second as a "flash or flicker of time" that has very little duration
which could be consciously realized. But the evidence presented here
will show that a second, though of very short duration, is still quite a period
of time when expressed in motion or movements and accomplishment of
human activity, particularly so when aided by, or in control of, various
types of mechanical as well as electrical devices and equipment such as
are used in the demonstrations herein described.

As a means of comparison of terms used here, we will employ for a
rather simple example, the established fact that some well-trained human

Fast and Fancy Revolver Shooting

TIMING ATTACHMENTS, ADJUSTED ON TRIGGER GUARDS

Picture shows the revolvers with electric timing contact mechanism connected up on the trigger guards, ready for the wires that operate the electric timing machines to be hooked on. These are the appliances that made it possible for us to get the correct fractions of a second required for doing the different rapid fire stunts. Notice that the contact points (where the arrow points) on each one are exactly like the breaker points on an automobile distributor. When trigger goes clear back at the instant hammer is released, the lever projection (inside the trigger guard) is pushed down by the lower part of trigger, which brings the platinum contact points together (at arrow) closing the electric circuit and causing the magnets on the various timing units to do the work that they have been specially adjusted to do, as explained in connection therewith.

MECHANICAL REVOLVER FIRING EQUIPMENT CONSTRUCTED FOR TESTING THE SUPERSPEED POSSIBILITIES OF DOUBLE-ACTION REVOLVERS

This hand-operated machine was built for the author some years ago which made it very evident at that time that the double-action revolver mechanism is much faster than any of our tests have been able to show that any man's hands can work them up to the present time at least.

It is the firm belief of the author that the revolver mechanism will function at least twice as fast as the fastest superspeed group shooting results have so far revealed man to be capable of. An electrically operated machine is under process of development to determine this important point in the near future.

Measuring Short Time Periods

hands can press the starting button on a stop watch, thus releasing and putting the split second hands in motion to measure time, then **instantly** press the button again, which will cause the watch hands to cease motion, and do these things in **one-twentieth** of a second. The movement of the split second hands in this case was of only momentary duration, all action from first to last occurring within the split fraction of the second as mentioned. The terms "instants," "moments," and "seconds" will be used by us here to signify different time lapse that may be later indicated correctly in very small fractions of seconds by the timing machines employed for that purpose.

These terms can be more readily understood and estimated for general descriptive purposes than fractional divisions of seconds, and may serve the purpose of enabling the reader to judge the time periods in his own mind by a sort of method that is more or less generally used and readily understood.

Having had more than twenty-five years of activity along this line of timing fast shooting, I know from experience that it is quite possible for some few persons to start and then instantly stop a "stop watch," with a period of time between the start and completion of the motions of only 1/20th of a second, which is just exactly five one-hundredths of a second. Our later stop watches have divisions of time marked on the dial of 1/10th second each, and these can be subdivided and clearly read with a magnifying glass, in divisions of 1/20th of a second and less. This is determined by the width of the upper part of the hand, which takes up and covers less than one-half of the 1/10th of a second space. As one-half of this space would be exactly 1/20th of a second, we have a good clear view of these divisions, which is not considered at all unusual in our experience with the watches.

But just to be reasonable about some of the arguments that arise in reference to errors claimed for hand timing—if it should (under normal conditions) take some operators even 1/10th of a second to start and then 1/10th of a second to stop a watch, it will be clearly seen that it takes—**under normal conditions**—the same mental control of muscular effort to stop the watch as it did to start it, making any lapse of time so occurring approximately even at both ends of the operation—start and stop—1/20th of a second each, or 1/10th of a second each, whichever it may be. When timing a performance requiring several seconds to complete, such starting and stopping motion time requirement would usually cause no material difference in results.

Much of the difficulty of correctly catching very small fractions of time in relation to movement, by trying to visualize the movement and to operate the stop watch at the same time, arises from the very evident fact that even fairly well-trained and experienced stop-watch

Fast and Fancy Revolver Shooting

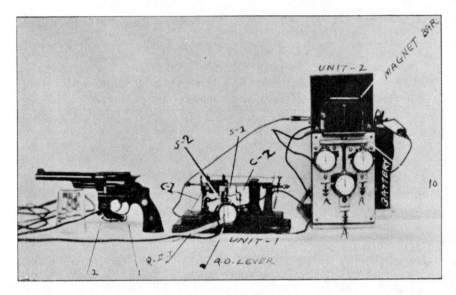

TIMING UNITS ONE AND TWO

Left to Right—Contact mechanism on trigger guard. Fig. 1 indicates lever that is forced down by the trigger as first shot is fired, which causes contact points to close at Fig. 2. This in turn causes striker bar on unit 1 to be drawn down instantly by the magnets. As a result the watch, which is located under striker bar, is instantly started.

While this lug which projects downward from the striker bar (indicated as S-1) is pressing down the stem of this first watch, a pin that projects outward from the side of this lug on the striker bar engages and closes another set of contacts indicated as C-1; which can be seen at left of the watch and just under the first striker bar lug S-1.

When the contact points indicated as C-1 are closed, the magnet bar on unit 2 is instantly drawn down so as to press the stems on the three watches located on the panel. All of the watches get going at the same instant, and the measuring of the time period begins.

As each shot is fired thereafter up to the fifth one the entire striker bar hammer unit, which has the two extended lugs attached to it, moves one space closer to the magnets or coils. When this part of the mechanism has been drawn down four times and again released to upper position the projecting lug marked S-2 comes into position to engage the watch stem and press it down again.

When the fifth and last shot is fired, at the same instant that the projecting lug presses the watch stem down, another projecting pin which is attached to the side of this lug indicated as S-2 engages and closes another set of contact points indicated as C-2. This immediately stops the three electrically controlled watches located on the panel of unit 2 and the time period for operating the revolver mechanism for firing five shots has been correctly measured.

If this contact attachment is connected with the timing drum of unit 4, the time periods can also be visibly recorded by the electrically controlled marking device indicated as unit 3 (page 197).

By this method the four watches, while working simultaneously, are still being checked against each other to a certain extent. The first watch in the special holder of unit 1 is checking against the three watches adjusted on the panel of unit 2. If any of these watches are allowed to get out of exact adjustment with the stem pressing portion of the equipment (10), as adjusted for each one, the error is immediately made apparent by the behavior of the particular watch so affected. If these adjustments are carefully checked the several

Measuring Short Time Periods

watches operate quite uniformly and in a very satisfactory manner. The three adjusting screws under the watches on unit 2 are indicated by the letter A.

The paper tape indicated as Q.D.T. is attached to an upright lever, which is visible in front of watch; the upper part of which, when the tape is pulled, engages the contact equipment visible just at the back of it. The paper tape can be looped around the little finger (or any finger preferred) of the drawing hand.

The first movement of hand towards the gun causes the Q.D. lever to make the contact, which starts the watches and begins the measurement of time. When the trigger contact mechanism is caused to operate by the firing of a shot from the revolver, the closing of the contacts causes unit 2 to stop the watches, thus ending the time measurement. This indicates the correct period required for the completed performance from first movement of hand towards gun to the firing of the shot, or of firing several shots as the case may be.

CAMERA HOOK-UP

Electric timer No. 2 connected up with two revolvers, a Colt and a Smith & Wesson .38 Special, operating special Ansco camera, having a shutter speed of 1/300 of a second. A spring motor built into side of camera (note construction) winds the film automatically each time an exposure is made. Electric contact mechanism on back of striker carrier can be set to operate camera shutter after last shot is fired, usually, although this can be adjusted to operate camera at any point desired during the series of shots, 1, 2, 3, 4, 5, etc. When in use the camera is mounted on a tripod in the regular way, and the electric attachment is held in position by a bracket fitted to the tripod for the purpose.

Note electrical contact mechanism on trigger guard of each gun. Timer bar shows striker carrier in position so that striker No. 1 is directly over the starting stud on the stop watch. You'll notice three small holes on the side of striker carrier between striker No. 1 and striker No. 2. These holes are where point of ratchet adjustment fits to regulate the contacts for the number of shots to be timed. Timer as shown is now set for five shots. The first shot forces striker down and starts watch. Each shot jumps striker carrier one space forward towards magnets. Shot No. 5 stops watch by forcing striker No. 2 against stop watch stud, the next pull on trigger of gun will operate the camera shutter, if set to do so. The contact parts that operate the camera can be switched on or off at will, without interfering with the rest of the equipment. Camera can be worked by hand in the usual way by simply disengaging the cable release from the clamp which holds it in place on the electrical attachment when it is being used.

operators require an average period of time, above one-tenth of a second for the combined operation of starting and immediately stopping the watch without having anything else on their mind. Many well-trained operators will require an average of three-twentieths of a second for the complete operation, yet for the reasons already stated relative to normally equal delay periods at both the start and stop, there is no cause for embarrassment or guilty feeling connected therewith when this is found to be the case—not at all. Such watch manipulators should, of course, confine their efforts to performances requiring time periods running into seconds instead of fractions of seconds.

To start and also stop a watch in as short a period of time as possible, requires five distinct muscular actions for impulse and control. Simplified it reads: (1) Down stroke of finger, (2) full stop of finger at bottom, (3) reverse and upward movement of finger (watch hand has started), (4) full stop of finger at top, (5) reverse and down stroke of finger to stop watch hand, shutting off movement. When this combination of movements has been completed in a total of one-twentieth (1/20th) of a second, as shown on dial of watch held in the hand (shown in photo), it means that each move and each stop has required approximately 1/100th of a second each.

When this is considered it will be evident that this represents a lot of movement in a very small amount of time, but the proof here submitted shows that it is at least occasionally possible; but we wish to state that it is not done with anything like monotonous regularity, and cannot be guaranteed as a **regular unfailing performance** any certain number of times out of any stated number of trials. Therefore it cannot be considered as a standard or fixed performance; for which reason we must leave it out of any possible "average performance," as we do not go below that one-twentieth second point often enough to offset the many times we go above it and show the longer periods that occur above the 1/20th second mark. Consequently we could not strike such a thing as a 1/20th second average continuously.

The reason and explanation is that if three watches are being operated by three persons at the same time, in an attempt to get a reasonable average for a guide, on some certain hand timed performance, or in the case of one person operating a stop watch three times in succession to determine his **average** required time period for such effort, we must recognize and adopt the middle course or period of time as the average time that has been so secured. For example, if a one-twentieth second average was to be decided, one watch would need to be stopped so as to show only one-fortieth of a second (not in any way a likely performance), the next watch would show one-twentieth, and the third watch must then necessarily show three-fortieths, the middle figure then being correctly

Measuring Short Time Periods

Mr. Frank Fish, the man who built and adjusted the various items of electric timing and recording equipment herewith described and illustrated, demonstrates the workings of the pens on the drum timer and shows just how the muscular efforts, and the periods of time required for them, when firing five shots from the double-action revolvers, can be visually recorded.

This new and much improved drum recording device was adopted to replace the former paper disc and its marking devices.

It is possible to get results of several trials, where two guns are used at once, recorded on the same paper covering of the drum, which is scaled off in divisional squares of one-tenth inch each.

The pens carry ink and make a plain line around drum when placed in contact with it. When in operation and a shot is fired from one of the guns the coils pull the bar holding the pen down, as visible by the black line; this line then continues at the lower level until the trigger contact is released, at which time the pen returns to the upper level again where it continues the marking until drawn down again by the coils as a result of the next contact, which occurs when the next shot is fired. Such movements continue in a similar order until all shots have been fired. When the trigger is released to go forward the pens always return to their original upper position. The period of time required for each forward, and for each backward, movement is quite clearly indicated and the fast ones and the slower ones can be compared and the cause and effect and the reasons for each can be analyzed. This equipment should produce much valuable data along such lines in future experiments. The time required for each revolution of the drum is checked by the watch panel, which is operated by the electric contact mechanism visible on the lower left of the drum, shown in the enlarged illustration on page 197. The pens and their controlling mechanism are also quite clearly visible in the same picture.

one-twentieth of a second. Three men handling stop watches could not possibly hope to do this.

For a one-tenth second average, the watches would show one-twentieth on the first watch, one-tenth on the second watch, and, necessarily, three-twentieths second on the third watch. Thus the average or middle figure would then be one-tenth of a second. From this it can readily be pointed out that the difficulty encountered by the three men would be somewhat disturbing, when attempting to watch the start and the finish of some specified movement, or series of movements, as executed by someone else (in our case the shooter), who may start when he pleases, perhaps without warning or signals of any kind to guide the watch handlers, proceed and conclude his performance, while the persons doing the timing endeavor to correctly check his movements during the elapsed time required, and be successful in finishing such test with a one-tenth second average. Such performance would constitute a situation which, to say the very least, would certainly prove to be a very difficult one, too difficult in fact to be successfully accomplished.

The fairly well-trained watch handler will not **average** 1/10 second results for starting and then immediately stopping a stop watch, for the reason that, with few exceptions, such operators will not get results below a tenth of a second for the completed movements often enough to offset the longer periods, so as to even up an average. A few trials will convince the most skeptical about this point and save much argument. Thus, if hand timing is done by attempting to watch the shooter's hand start its movement with the gun in it (which actually is giving him a head start), the timer's mental impulse must be formed and then transformed into action **after** he visualizes such movement; he must then get his muscles in action, realizing that the total time required is going to be very short. Such mental impulse, to be effective in such situations, **must** carry with it the inclination **to stop the watch at the earliest moment possible**; such urge to stop naturally grows out of much repetition and the association of ideas with results of many former similar trials.

Based on my own experience the method of procedure would be about as follows: The shooter's impulse is formed, his movement starts, the watch handler notices the movement and his mental impulse then forms to press the button and start the watch; all O. K., but at his best, in this case, the timer is behind the shooter at the start. **Bang!** Very soon after starting the watch **the disturbing effect of the shot shocks the watch operator's nerves,** thereby upsetting what would be the normal condition; he instantly reacts to the nerve shock and stops the watch—far faster than he was able to start it. The mental impulse to start the movement also carried, from constant association of the two operations, an accompanying and continued, but perhaps very slightly delayed, impulse to

Measuring Short Time Periods

TIMING UNITS THREE AND FOUR

This drum and the connected mechanism were constructed for the purpose of determining the variations in time periods for a series of similar muscular actions, reactions and efforts, as performed separately, and also when combined and continued over certain periods. Some examples of such performances with double-action revolver mechanism have been produced and have proven quite enlightening in several ways.

stop it. The second or stopping action, in this case due to nerve shock, might come quicker than the first or starting one did, and, under such conditions, what would be for example a three-fifth second stunt, could very easily be timed by the hand method at around ½ or 2/5ths of a second, due to the slow start and the disturbing nervous shock from the shot, resulting in a very quick stop.

If the watch operator has not had plenty of actual training and much experience, he will, under the urge of necessity for extremely short timing periods, and the disturbing effects usually attendant thereto, succeed in timing only his own bewilderment, and will not be successful in securing accurately the actual time required for starting and completing any particularly short time-period performance.

The misleading results secured and the difficulties encountered by us during many tests in our earlier attempts at measuring short-time periods by hand-operated watches, were the active agents that **forced us to develop the electric timing devices** for use in connection with such tests and experiments. Necessity was most certainly the "mother of invention" in this particular instance. I have been very active with such timing attempts for many years and, as a result, by special arrangement, the dials on all of our later watches, as used in the electric timing machines, are divided into tenths of seconds, and, as stated, the specially slender end of the hand on each one occupies less than one-half of the tenth of a second space, thus the time can be very clearly read in twentieths of a second or slightly less when necessary. **The drum timer,** with its several marking and recording units, also electrically controlled, can readily be adjusted to take care of all other fractions of seconds. This device can be adjusted to catch the time of two guns, being operated at the same time. By these methods we have determined clearly some of the things that we cannot do **by hand** with the stop watches, as well as the many things that we can do with them when **electrically controlled.**

Starting and then immediately stopping the watch by hand, as shown, in a period of one-twentieth of a second, does not allow for any prolonged conversation when issuing signals or for any observation of any kind of movement that may be executed by another person, and we would also add, in an effort to make it clear, that operating it in the tenth or fifth of a second period has the same limitations, as regards observing and accurately recording any movement or action of others while concentrating on operating the watch in any such periods as mentioned. Our experience in this field of endeavor has led us to discontinue any such attempts.

The same mental impulses, muscular reactions, and timing rhythm are continued and carried out to conclusion; producing practically the same

Measuring Short Time Periods

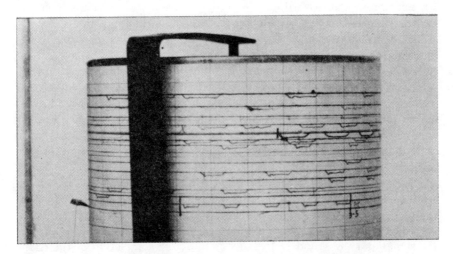

This view of the drum timer unit, which is known as No. 4, in connection with the marking unit No. 3 serves to make a visible record of the muscular actions and their average spacings, which are required to shoot five shots in various time periods.

The lower group of five shots as recorded hereon and checked by the watches at the same time required a time period of three-fifths second for the performance.

results, as concerns success, when working with the revolvers in the field of activity described as **"the quick draw in response to signals."** The similarity of reaction and effect can be easily recognized in the reports of the following series of demonstrations.

On the evening of January 18, 1934, at the American Legion Hall, Lewistown, Montana, a demonstration of these points was carried out for the entertainment of the members of the Legion who were present, and whose names are signed on the 9/20ths second electrically timed target of that date. My attention was called to the many instances that occur in Western history, and in Western stories quite generally, wherein the six-gun wizard, as the hero of the story and usually described as a superspeed expert on the draw, has a habit of making a speech, either just before, or possibly **during,** the time he is performing his lightning draw; or else while his opponent (who may be almost, if not fully his equal) is "going for his gun" in a futile attempt to perform his own fast draw under the urge of protecting his life. These stories, as usually written, would be very interesting indeed **if the facts could be overlooked** as regards the time periods which would actually enter. For instance, many of the draws as done by me on the date mentioned were started from various signals, the nature of which were announced beforehand.

Various persons present were asked to assist in these tests by getting ready for the signal in the same manner as the quick-draw demonstrator (myself) was ready, and, in response to the agreed-on signal, some of them were to clap their hands as many times as possible between the signal and the sound of the shot fired at the completion of the draw, and others were asked to call out as many numbers as possible; while still others were asked to say as many words as possible, from the supposed familiar phrases of the "early day" gun slingers, such as "Go for your gun," "Fill your hand," "Turn your wolf loose," "Slap leather," etc.

The draws during this particular demonstration were made with .38 calibre double-action Smith & Wesson guns, one having a barrel four inches long and one with a barrel two and seven-eighths inches. When the short gun was used for the cross draw with the short slanting holster (see page 267) hung at the left of center and drawn by twisting the body to assist in releasing the gun from holster and then firing with arm across the stomach at just about the level of the top of the belt, the time period required was usually around a half second.

During these trials the members did not seem to be able to get farther than—one, two, or the second clap of hands. When four-inch and five-inch barreled guns were drawn from a low hung hip holster below the right hip, and draw was made with an upward sweep of the hand and fired about on a level with the belt, the time was also short enough so that the hand

Measuring Short Time Periods

Stop watch, with tenth of second divisions, operated by hand by the author was started and stopped in one-twentieth of a second as formerly mentioned. Photo also shows how such smaller fractions of such divisions can be read clearly with magnifier.

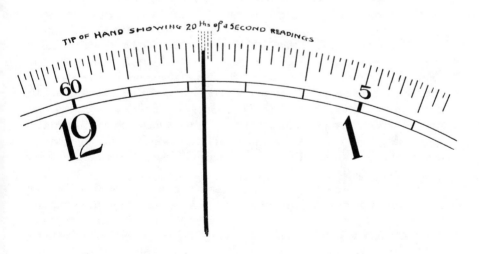

TIP OF HAND SHOWING 20 ths of a SECOND READINGS

clapping and counting and talking seemed to be interrupted by the shot in almost as short a time as the other trials. In other words, as a result of actual tests, the talking, etc., would consist of—one, two, clap, clap, or "Fill yu—, Go fer— (gopher), Turn yu—," or more plainly expressed, a person could just about say, "Stop!" "Don't!" "Whoa!" "Hold!" He couldn't quite say, "in a voice like ice" (as usually written), "Jim Smith, I'm a-goin' to kill you, go for your gun, there hain't room enough for you and me in this town," etc. A whole gang battle could be completed during that much talking.

If a trained quick-draw man knew that the other super gun artist— the hero—was looking for him with the avowed intent of killing him, the (No. 1) super gun artist with all the "gab" would just about get as far as "Jim Sm—" if he didn't drawl the words out too long; then this same No. 1 super gunman, while the smoke was clearing away, would probably be addressing the rest of his speech to "Saint Peter" because if super gunman No. 1 (the hero) showed any signs of an intention to draw, by exhibiting any fancy crouching motions or other recognized gun jugglers' gymnastics, gunman No. 2, James Smith, could draw and shoot him in just about the same amount of time as that in which he unburdened himself of the words "Jim Sm—." If both men were equally fast they should both be hit at just about the same time and "Jim Sm—" would be about all the talking that would be done.

The mental impulse required for the quick-draw demonstrator, who in this particular instance, at the Legion meeting, happened to be myself, to draw and shoot, was just about similar in nature to the mental impulse that was required by the other Legion members to clap hands, call numbers, or start to voice the words agreed on. The quick-draw training and subconscious control built up by much practice enabled me to catch the signal and to act in response thereto in the short space of time indicated by the efforts of the various persons to clap hands, call numbers or to pronounce words. As everyone is familiar with these movements and with average speech, the time period so indicated will be more clearly understood by many persons than small fractions of seconds, as they are indicated and quoted from the stop watches.

One-half of a second for a draw allows not more than two words by the very fastest speaker. Five words a second would mean **three hundred words** a minute, 4,500 words in fifteen minutes (note this), or one word for every fifth of a second that passes. Floyd Gibbons, one of our most famous and fastest radio talkers, is credited with being capable of speaking around 275 words a minute for fifteen minutes, or slightly less than one word for each fifth of a second. The words would, of course, be fewer if figured out along the lines of how many words the average man could deliver during a fast draw, keeping in mind that a quarter second equals two and a

Measuring Short Time Periods

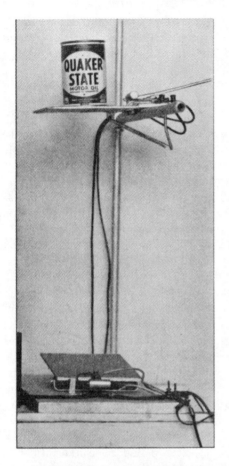

Drop Meter

Here is shown what we have been pleased to call the drop meter. An electric arrangement for timing dropped targets. When catch is released the upper platform springs away from the can or other object to be timed; when the release of the shelf occurs an electric contact is instantly made which starts the timing, and when the can or coin or other object strikes the lower platform the second electric contact is instantly formed which stops the timing and shows the total elapsed time required by the object to travel from the one contact point to the other.

Various objects can be timed by this arrangement while dropping various distances. The present arrangement is capable of a 7-foot drop. Another rod attachment extends the drop to 20 feet. Various other arrangements can be made quite easily if desired.

Frank Fish supervising the timing equipment while Walter Groff of Philadelphia does some fast double-action shooting on the bull's-eye placed on the Olympic target. The results of these and similar tests will be found in Section 10 under title of Double-Action Shooting.

half tenths of a second (or 1/5 and 1/20). Two-fifths of a second equals four-tenths of a second. Gibbons' time requirement averages around two and a fifth tenths (or 1/5 and 1/50) of a second per word; just a little over a fifth of a second per word, or perhaps two words spoken just a little ahead of a half second draw. What is the answer to the conversation before the draw and after making known an intention to do so against an equally fast opponent?

Reviewing an incident in a so-labeled fact article recently, relating to a supposed meeting between Clay Allison and Wyatt Earp, we find suitable material for comparison.

Clay Allison, who has been termed by the author of the article "The deadly Texas wolf," is credited with going to Dodge City for the express purpose of killing Wyatt Earp. According to the story they met at the corner of the Long Branch Saloon. Clay Allison asks, "You Wyatt Earp?" (three words) "I am," Earp answers. "I'm looking for you," Allison grated. (four words) By now, his body against Wyatt, Allison twisted his body slightly so as to cover his draw. His right hand dropped. **Like a flash** his Colt leaped(?) **half free** (note this) of its holster, then he froze stiff. Wyatt's .45 **was** (already) **poked** deep in his middle. **A full minute the two stood,** then slowly Allison began to back away. His hands lifted into the air. "I'll be moving," he said. If both of these men were fast on the draw, what delayed action long enough to allow so much time consuming conversation? "Are you Wyatt Earp?" were all the words, and time, also, that should have been necessary to start and finish the quick-draw battle with perhaps both men dead; that is, if Clay Allison really meant to **kill** Earp, and particularly so if Earp knew about it beforehand and had no desire to be killed. Both of these men were outstanding Western characters. According to the time period measurements, per word, etc., what is the answer? What would be their actual drawing time, and what would "the halfway out of the holster" time be during which Earp is supposed to have completed his own draw and poked his gun barrel into Allison's middle? Allison's mental impulse as we are given to understand started, then checked his draw halfway finished only. Earp's mental impulse to draw and shoot if necessary must have started after Allison's draw was under way. What stopped Allison if both men were equally fast? What stopped Earp from completing his draw by firing the shot, as under such circumstances he very naturally would have done, urged on by the law of self-preservation if nothing else? How could Earp know that Allison was not going to finish his draw and fire a shot?

Superspeed drawing movements in the face of death were not usually interrupted or abandoned in mid-air on account of any disturbing influence short of paralyzing shock or instantaneous death. One gun slinger, as described here, did not, or at least should not, consistently succeed in doubling up on the speed of another equally fast opponent who, as stated in this case, already had the start on impulse, intention, and movement; in fact already "in action." "The Pronto Bug, "as we sometimes call such instances, was already taking Allison places on the high jump. For him to slow, or entirely halt, his draw would have been a practical impossibility. For Earp to "beat him to it" to the extent stated would have required a mild sort of miracle.

The trouble is not in the possible ability that these outstanding frontier characters may have possessed, but is due almost entirely to the narrators and their entire lack of knowledge of the controlling factors that govern such actions, and the reactions that would and did take effect on the men concerned in such situations. When we remove this angle of misinformation from the work of the early day experts, while making an effort to compare it with the work of the present day along somewhat similar lines, we can without doubt reach at least reasonable conclusions.

From this point we very naturally should step over and into the present-day methods of developing proficiency in "hip shooting" and its close relative, the "quick draw," with the sure hitting methods of procedure that have been developed along these lines. The trained mind, controlling the correspondingly trained hand, can get some surprising results in the way of accurate and positively controlled movements, when performing such and similar gun handling operations repeatedly.

This fast shooting, fast gun drawing and flying target shooting with revolvers, and the accompanying accurate recording of results, demands precision movements, timing rhythm in execution, and perfect and complete coördination, in and throughout each and every part of such a program of activities. To correctly register the results of these various performances also requires the use of some sort of dependable instruments similar to, or at least somewhat on the order of, the electrically controlled equipment shown and described in the preceding pages. This conclusion is based on our own extensive experience and efforts in this field of endeavor

However, there is no intention here or elsewhere to discredit the purposes or the results of carefully conducted hand-operated, stop-watch tests for the purpose of forming reasonably close estimates of the average time periods required for certain fast gun handling performances. Thousands of such tests were conducted by us with reasonably satisfactory results before we were able to secure the more reliable equipment that was later developed through necessity for more definite results.

As an added assurance of the correctness of the timing results herein set forth, it may be well to call attention to the fact that The Pastor Stop Watch Company, 43 East Main Street, Waterbury, Conn., from whom all of our high-grade split second watches are purchased, makes a practice of checking them over carefully for absolutely correct performance before sending them on to us for use in the electrically controlled timing equipment.

While at Washington, D. C., in December, 1936, I dropped in on Mr. R. E. Gould, of the U. S. Bureau of Standards, and he checked several watches for me and found them to be correct. Using several watches, all operating at the same time under control of the electrically operated timing mechanism, guarantees accurate results.

SECTION 14

HIP SHOOTING WITH REVOLVERS. ITS RELATION AND VALUE TO QUICK-DRAW SHOOTING.

A very interesting and important feature of romantic Western history that has been handed down to us with much fancy trimming, comes under the head of "Hip Shooting." This type of shooting derived its name from the fact that the revolvers are shot from a position in the vicinity of the hip, or, generally, just around or slightly below the waist line. Contrary to general belief, the gun is seldom if ever held at the exact location of the hip. This has always been a very much discussed style of shooting, and is still a very active and interesting topic wherever revolver shooters gather and swap yarns. As is usually the case with all other shooting topics, opinions differ greatly, and quite often reach extremes on both sides of the argument, for and against the usefulness or practicability of such methods of handling firearms. However, contrary to all arguments of an opposite nature, very satisfactory results can be secured by this method of shooting revolvers.

I have done and also witnessed some very good work by others with the single-action Colt revolvers when used under these conditions. Attention should be called to the fact that all of the fancy gun fighters' stunts, so elaborately embellished in the flowery language of the writers of Western history, both fact and fiction, depend for romantic appeal on the various assortment of shooting feats that have their foundation in, and are built up from, this particular hip shooting accomplishment.

Many of these writers overlook the fact that the range of its effectiveness is controlled by the limitations that the very nature of its performance would quite naturally place upon it. Other writers, perhaps through lack of knowledge, ignore these points and set forth very awe-inspiring stories of the things that **have been done**—not can be done—by this method of procedure. In my account of it here I will endeavor to set forth some facts which are supported by evidence resulting from actual test and experience.

It is well to remember that the most famous stunt of all, and the one most generally misunderstood of all of the early West's gun handling magic which absolutely depended on hip shooting for success, is known as "fanning the hammer" (elsewhere described in detail). There are several other stunts, such as "thumb whipping," "slip shooting," firing from swivel holsters, shots released just as barrel clears lip of holster, and all very fast draws as done from hip holsters, with one gun or two guns. All are and **must be,** by their very nature, performed while the guns are in the vicinity of the hip.

The necessary quick firing of guns on account of the extremely short

Fast and Fancy Revolver Shooting

HIP SHOOTING

Walter Groff demonstrating well-balanced position for two-handed hip shooting.

HIP SHOOTING

Walter Groff demonstrating two-handed hip shooting at several objects in rotation.

time periods involved, compel the use of such position and procedure. All of these variously named shooting performances and gun positions are quite clearly shown by photographs. A reasonably close study of these will make many points clear. In many of these pictures, as well as in the quick-draw pictures, the targets are arranged close to the shooter in order to show the shooter, target, and gun positions as well as possible. This explanation by me is here offered for clarification only—not as apology to the critics. Please understand it that way.

The greatest difficulty in relation to a clear understanding of the value of hip shooting by that portion of the public that may be interested is due to the fact that many persons have a desire to start hip shooting demonstrations before they have developed enough shooting ability by any other regulation methods to even hit the proverbial "barn door," and as a result hip shooting and all of its various angles of influence are very thoroughly condemned, all of which may appear to be in direct opposition to the here fairly well-established fact, that such system of handling guns is a most valuable foundation for all ultra-fast draws and kindred superspeed performances.

The hip shooting student has no right or place in any beginners' class. He should be, and rightfully belongs, in the post-graduate class and only after he has developed proficiency in the several branches of accurate revolver shooting and rapid fire practice in stipulated time periods. This development does not have to be carried out on paper targets exactly, but it must be positively established by some such similar training, by concentrated practice on some specified objects of **definite size** and proportions.

I have taught hip shooting to quite a large number of persons by the above-recommended system and have secured excellent results. Practice and study can and will develop surprising skill in this style of revolver shooting, just as it does in the various other lines. A few practical demonstrations of this type of shooting is contained on and described in connection with reproductions of twenty or more witnessed targets, which in this particular case were shot from a distance of fifteen feet. Several hip shooting positions are also illustrated in connection with these targets.

Close inspection of these targets will disclose one or two groups that can be covered with a dime. Nevertheless this type of shooting is not generally made use of for attempting to hit a dime at a thousand-yard range, regardless of the fact that the **"Puzzle Putters,"** who usually hang around shooting ranges, may request you to try it, just to show up your **lack of ability** or the faultiness of any theory regarding its effectiveness. Such folks are usually very liberal when specifying distances and difficulties for others, but usually are great whiners when it comes their turn to make good—on anything.

Hip shooting, as herein illustrated, follows very naturally in line after

Fast and Fancy Revolver Shooting

HIP SHOOTING

The author demonstrating excellent hip shooting position when using one hand only.

The position here shown is with the arm firmly pressed against the body from which hip shooting is generally done with all types of revolvers. This is also the most convenient position from which to do hip shooting when using two revolvers at the same time. It is also the quickest position from which to get into action that is adaptable to all styles and positions of holsters, where bullets are to be delivered out in front of the shooter; it also gives the widest range for body movement and a clearer view for the performer.

This is the foundation for all hip shooting positions—plain and fancy. Special positions for special hip shooting performances, using either one or two guns, can be worked out after reasonable skill has been developed by this method.

Attention is called to the fact that the author does not refer to any of his recommended positions or methods advanced for any of the performances described herein, as the CORRECT or PROPER position, etc. Whether such positions and methods are correct or proper, depends to a great extent on the individual make-up and peculiarities of the performer, much more so than on anyone's personal opinion. By this method the author has been fortunate in avoiding much argument. Respect for the opinions of others lies behind this attitude.

Note that the success of all very fast, quick-draw shooting, fanning, slip-shooting and much of the two-gun work depends greatly on the degree of skill developed in handling revolvers from what is generally referred to as hip shooting positions. It is quite important that such positions and such shooting be studied carefully and practiced persistently if success is de-

Hip Shooting

sired in this branch of the shooting game. It will be noticed in the various positions illustrated that widespread legs and tense, strained positions are entirely absent. The effect produced by such things is to generally interfere with maintaining the required balance and free movement of the body necessary for overcoming the disturbing effect of recoil and immediate readjustment of pointing control. Body weave forward and backward as well as from side to side is the enemy of good bullet control. Too much tenseness in one angle of body position usually exaggerates the body weave from some other angle. The happy medium is the desired condition being sought. Try not to overtense any part of body or limbs. There are usually no beneficial effects to be derived from so doing.

DEMONSTRATING POSITION FOR ACCURATE HIP SHOOTING

Hip shooting position with gun carried over to extreme left as demonstrated by Captain William H. Sweet, U. S. Army, and Captain James W. Baldwin, U. S. Navy. The photos and descriptive details appeared in *American Rifleman* of May, 1930, and also in the recent issue of *Burning Powder* compiled by Lieut. Colonel D. B. Wesson.

Courtesy of *American Rifleman*

developing control of the guns through the sense of feel and balance that comes from actually **knowing** when the guns are pointed just right. This feeling is developed, as formerly made clear, by experience with them when sighting over them, and subconsciously realizing just how they felt in your hands when you knew absolutely that they **were pointed** for a **sure hit.**

To attempt to shoot from the hip and register **sure hits** in a reasonably short space of time before becoming proficient in the regulation ways of shooting a revolver, by sighting, holding and squeezing, would be a rather absurd way of trying to perfect a very difficult stunt. The **sure hit** ability must be developed by deliberate holding experience first, then a good degree of speed by standard target methods of rapid fire must be developed next, then the actions necessary to control gun muzzle movements within a certain area will require attention.

The muscular effort necessary to move the muzzle a certain distance must be carefully studied and practiced until confidence in such control is firmly established, then the greatest factor for correctly directing hip shooting groups will be mastered. The time spent in studying this correct feel and balance of the gun in your hand and the ammunition used in developing the correct distance control, combined with proper direction control, will pay very good dividends by improving your gun control in all branches of the shooting game.

My method of coaching the student in hip shooting is carried out along the following lines: When some suitable paper targets or other convenient objects have been selected and placed a short distance away (perhaps fifteen feet if convenient) you may assume any one of the hip shooting positions (pages 208, 210, 211, 213) that you may prefer, and remember that you can change the point of impact of your bullet groups the desired amount by just moving your left foot slightly backward and forward various distances ahead or behind your right foot, which action twists the body a small amount each time, and by this method you can eventually find your own individual "correct position." When you do find it, mark out where your feet were, and practice getting into that position regularly and quickly—and often. Body weave can be controlled and often practically eliminated by foot position.

Do not spread the feet too much—about ten to eighteen inches, depending on your build. Study it out carefully and carry most of the weight on your right foot, which usually with most shooters will be slightly in front, a fact that has coined the term for us in our training classes as "standing on your front foot," while using your "hind foot" (left) for stabilizer. Left-handed shooters should reverse these instructions. Many right-handed shooters also reverse the foot position, but still carry most of the weight on the right foot, moving the left foot backward or forward as the need is indicated by where the bullets may be grouping.

Hip Shooting

HIP SHOOTING, USING TWO HANDS

Left—A more complicated but exceptionally steady and effective method of hip shooting. Holding one gun with two hands while keeping both arms well supported against the body. Surprising results can be secured by persistent practice with this method of handling a revolver, and while not adaptable to any of the two-gun performances, it is a necessary part of the usual methods employed for most of the fast and fancy performances when using single-action Colt and similar revolvers.

Right—This hip shooting position with the arm resting more across the body gives very firm support for the right arm as a result of more contact against the body, and is productive of very good results.

This is also the position which is quite generally used when trying for top speed cross-draw performance, where only one hand contacts the gun, but the right arm is used with very much the same firm position against the body, as shown here. All shots following the first one can be accurately controlled by this method.

Fast and Fancy Revolver Shooting

The foot movements simplify matters greatly, as you'll find by actual practice along this line. The importance of correct foot movements cannot be over-emphasized in this and all other branches of fast and fancy, as well as what we term practical, revolver shooting. Study these foot positions carefully—they are liberally illustrated in this connection for that very purpose.

At this point I will make it clear that hip shooting proficiency cannot be built up for consistent results by any manner of free-hand gun control. The arm and hand should be supported by firm contact with the body. The wrist, if extended, should be held fairly firm in line with arm and not bent or moved separately or independent of the arm. The hand holding the gun should not be moved at all, only for trigger action and for making slight alterations in pointing and leveling gun—before firing the first shot.

Any and all movements for changing point of impact of bullets, after that, must be made by movement of the body. Shifting gun from one target to another must be done by moving the body. Any corrections in case of a miss must be made by movement of the body. If shots are regularly grouping too far to right, move left foot back till this is corrected. If bullets are going regularly too far to the left, move left foot forward gradually until corrected. Leaning upper body forward lowers the bullet grouping; while leaning backward will raise it. Wabbling the hands around free of arm and body control will simply ruin the grouping, and bewilder the shooter, with no resulting benefit to anyone.

The next question up for attention concerns guns to be used. For my own shooting and for training all members of my shooting classes, I use and recommend the high-grade double-action revolvers now available in various models. Several of these models, as illustrated herein, are particularly well-adapted to, and also very necessary for, the class of shooting I am featuring in this book. If the student will study the two sections devoted to double-action shooting and trigger control, he will find detailed instructions for this method of operating the revolvers, and, if these instructions are followed, successful results will follow right from the beginning of such training as we are here going into.

With targets all arranged, and some knowledge of the smooth operation of the double-action mechanism of the revolver, we are ready to "start firing!"

The style of hip shooting (one handed or two) that appeals to the student, and the preferred position having been decided upon, the loaded gun should be placed in the hand, and an effort made to hold it, as near as possible, to the way it is held for deliberate target shooting. Make such necessary adjustments and slight changes as are necessary, for a comfortable feeling in the hand, while holding the gun, then place the forearm rather firmly against the body (pages 208, 210, 211, 213). Then when the gun

Hip Shooting

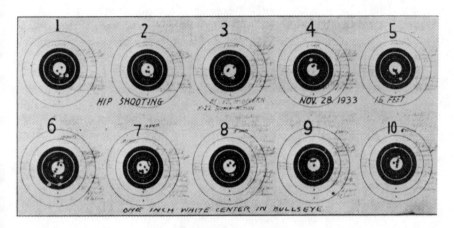

HIP SHOOTING BY THE AUTHOR

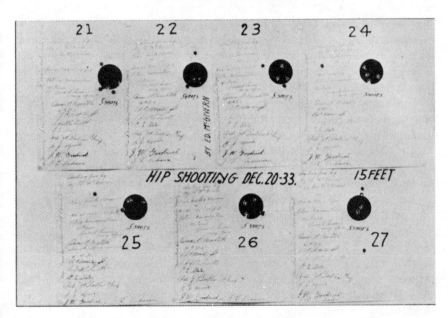

HIP SHOOTING BY THE AUTHOR

seems to feel right in the hand, direct your attention to the number one target, and **while watching intently line up the gun** as well as you can, so that you feel that you are pointing exactly at a center line running up and down on that particular target. At this time take one more careful look at gun barrel for line-up with target and try to figure out the correct elevation also, judging the elevation by the way it feels in your hand.

Next thing necessary now is to follow the instructions found in the double-action training methods. Start carefully squeezing the trigger until the shot is fired, then without allowing any movement to disturb your gun or hand carefully check where your bullet hit. If you scored a miss, judge as well as you can just about how much gun muzzle movement will be needed to correct your pointing, and in what exact direction and what exact distance the muzzle of the gun should be moved to register a hit. When you have determined these points as well as your judgment will permit, move the gun by body motion, not with your arm or hand. A slight body movement makes much difference out where the bullet strikes. If your first shot is a hit, move on to the next target and go through the same movements. Study the effect of each movement by the results of each shot. It will be surprising what rapid progress can be made.

Don't be haphazard in your methods at any time or about anything. Cultivate the habit of arranging the targets at certain regulation distances apart; at first on a straight line from left to right, separating them ten inches to a foot to make room for wild shots. This is a good arrangement for starting practice. As success comes, changes can be made and the objects can be worked out to make certain designs. More objects up to ten (for two guns) can be added if desired.

Practice shooting from the hip from any of the positions desired, or selected from those shown in photos, and keep at it. Select the range, short at first. Don't change it until sure hits begin to get monotonous. Reduce size of targets gradually, increase the distances gradually. For breakable targets start with clay pigeons which are four and a quarter inches in diameter. Peters Cartridge Company's Duvrock clay pigeons can be used later. These are three inches in diameter. The Van-aumatic Duster targets come next, one and five-eighths inches in diameter. These come in black, red, orange and light yellow in color and are supplied by The Fred Goat Company, Inc., 314 Dean Street, Brooklyn, New York. I use them in my police training.

To perfect yourself in hip shooting, when using a series of targets as outlined, and endeavoring to break them in rotation, try the following training methods:

Secure large sheets of paper and practice making a row of bullet holes straight across the center of the paper, say, for instance, six inches apart. When this can be accomplished with fair regularity, try a row of bullet

Hip Shooting

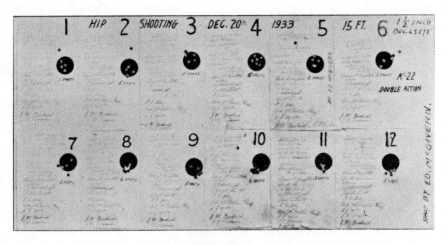

<small>HIP SHOOTING BY THE AUTHOR</small>

<small>HIP SHOOTING BY THE AUTHOR</small>

holes straight up and down in the center of paper, same spacing. Next, starting at lower left-hand corner, move the gun so the bullet holes are running in a line towards upper right-hand corner. Next, run a line of bullet holes from upper left corner, slanting across and down towards lower right-hand corner. This is the secret for accurately moving gun in the various directions and the proper distances to direct your bullets on the targets. Changing the training occasionally so that you separate the bullets four inches, then three inches, and later two inches apart for a series of paper target trials, will make you a thorough master of hip shooting judgment and accuracy in bullet placing ability.

Now the secret—never move the hand independent of the body and arm—never move the arm independent of the body. Keep these points in mind and the mystery of hip shooting will be "Gone with the Wind," and the "can't be done" gentry get another punch in the solar plexus. All that is needed to master any of these shooting performances is a good supply of ammunition, a good double-action revolver, or two, and a liberal supply of common sense and a willingness to make good use of it.

The mystery of doing these things with two guns is very simple. Train each hand separately and well; later, combine them and stay on the job. Follow the advice contained in the story about tomatoes when the farmer said, "We eat all we can, and what we can't eat we can." Just can the "can't" and go on with your shooting—there is no "can't" in this game. Don't waste time looking for artificial aids—you won't need them. Everything that is needed for success is contained right within one's self.

The draw can be added at any time or at any part of any of these performances. Hip shooting, lightning quick draws, ultra-speed group shooting, are all closely related, sort of like the "in-laws" in human relationship.

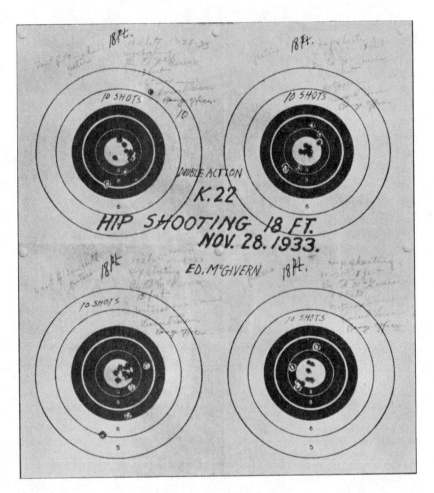

Hip Shooting by the Author

Fast and Fancy Revolver Shooting

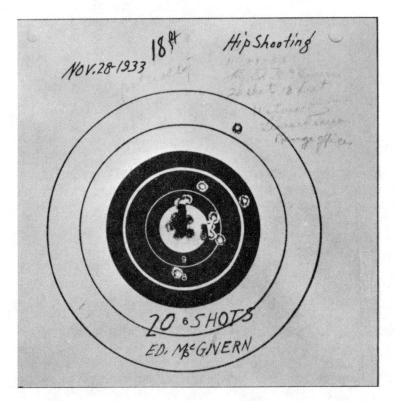

HIP SHOOTING BY THE AUTHOR

The four spotting shots, which are the first shots fired after pointing the gun, are easily identified by being located away from the main group. These first locating shots are generally noticeable as such on most of such hip shooting targets.

In offering the reproduction of the targets showing the results secured by what is generally known as hip shooting, attention is called to the fact that preparations are always made beforehand for conducting any demonstration of any particular shooting performances for determining the probable results that can be expected to be produced.

In preparation for the 35 or more targets constituting the various groups shot under the conditions set forth in connection with the targets offered, consisting of many five-shot groups, several six-shot groups, also some ten-shot groups and one twenty-shot group, as shot by the author, it should be made known that a total of 3,500 shots were fired on various occasions immediately preceding the dates on which the listed trials took place, consequently the results should give a fair idea of what can be expected after a fair amount of practice.

It is the author's belief that no worth-while experiments can be conducted to determine reasonable probabilities without a series of trials continued over a reasonable period of time and the use of a fairly liberal quantity of ammunition. A few trials with a few cartridges can seldom determine any important point in relation to such matters.

The first shot, generally referred to by us as the spotting shot or locating shot, is the most important item. Careful control over the movement of the gun thereafter will usually give fair groups. These spotting shots are generally very easy to locate on hip shooting, slip shooting and fanning targets as all such shooting depends for results on the same manner of body movement and balance and the ability to overcome the disturbing effect of recoil whether large or small caliber guns are used.

SECTION 15

THE QUICK DRAW. DROPPING COINS FROM SHOULDER
HEIGHT. MENTALLY ESTIMATING SMALL TIME PERIODS.
DEVELOPING TIME PERIOD JUDGMENT.

The "quick draw," as here outlined, means reaching for and producing
a revolver or pistol from some sort of a holster, scabbard, pouch or similar
receptacle carried, hung, or secured somewhere on the person for the purpose of carrying and keeping such gun or pistol within convenient and
easy reach of the hand of the wearer when wanted, or, by conditions or
force of circumstances, urgently required for immediate use. The completed gesture, of course, includes firing the shot from the quickly produced
gun at some object, either selected by the shooter at the time, as in a gun
fight, or designated beforehand and agreed upon by the persons interested
in the result of the test, or demonstration, as the case may be.

If the subject is to be thoroughly covered it is necessary to go back to
and include the early day killers when the lives of famous law officers, as
well as those of other famous, or perhaps infamous, early day characters
depended entirely on their success or failure.

In situations such as these the only angle of safety lay in refraining
from any motions that would indicate an intention of starting a draw,
but when once the motions generally regarded as incidental to the draw,
or to an intention of drawing were started, the very seriousness of the
matter made it absolutely necessary to follow through to completion, in
the shortest time and by the most direct method possible.

In those days guns were worn openly and within easy and **very convenient** reach, and when demonstrating such draws and the various gun slinging
and gun fighters' tricks and stunts, the same sort of gun harness and ways
of wearing and adjusting it should be made use of. Such belts, holsters,
and combination of rigs were generally regarded, at that time, as the best
suited and most conveniently adapted to fast gun handling methods.

When we step up to present-day conditions, where the majority of our
law enforcement officers, under modern custom and usage, must keep their
guns concealed but still available and readily accessible for immediate
use when an occasion demands it, we must make use of and deal with such
equipment as can be suitably adapted to such purpose; later on comparisons can be made and conclusions reached on a sensible sort of basis instead of theory or romance.

AUTHOR'S NOTE: Parts of the following material as set forth here by the writer, covering
quick-draw results, were taken from this chapter, and appeared in February, 1935, issue of
Sports Afield, under title of "Quick Draw."

Fast and Fancy Revolver Shooting

"THE HIP POCKET DRAW" FROM THE BAKER HIP POCKET HOLSTER

Upper Left—"The hip pocket draw" from a very fine holster for the purpose, designed and used by former Chief of Police Baker of Lewistown. Note that the holster is fastened to the belt and also to the pocket, as the illustrations show; it STAYS firmly anchored during all of the necessary movements of getting the gun out. An excellent dress-up gun rig and is comfortable, convenient, and not troublesome during an officer's usual activities.

Upper Right—This shows the method of grasping the gun grip when using this gun rig. Note the grip is quite conveniently placed and in a good position for hand to engage it quickly, and gun comes out and forward with a reasonably small amount of effort.

Lower Left—This shows the gun grasped and partly released. At this point as the gun clears holster the wrist can be turned slightly to the right and the gun pushed out in front just grazing the side of the body and the man out in front can be covered before fully realizing what he is looking into or at, and here again the ability to shoot fairly well from the hip position will pay added dividends in the way of time saving, by reducing the amount of hand movement required for completing the performance.

The Quick Draw

When the draw is to be accomplished with more than one shot being fired after drawing (and these to be included in the time period with the drawing movements), such trials must be termed "draw and fire five shot groups," etc., dependent on the number of shots, more than one and up to five, that are to be included.

As the old custom was to carry only five loaded cartridges in the revolvers, with an empty shell, or unloaded chamber under the hammer, for safety or accident insurance, we will continue such practice here and conduct tests and demonstrations and make comparisons on that basis, five shots from one gun, and ten shots from two guns in all two-gun tests. Attention should also be called to the fact that most of our target shooting contests are conducted on the basis of five shot strings and usually continued in that manner until the total number of shots required have been fired.

Under this kind of program a great variety of gun producing methods must necessarily be covered, with some sort of outline of the necessary equipment, and the various ways and means employed to increase speed and to save time, and fundamentally to cut down movement to the smallest amount with which the work can be done.

Speed, or rapidity of movement, is the result of practice and training which finally brings all movement under subconscious control. Time cannot be gained—time must be saved, by the systematic study of the various inter-related movements absolutely necessary for the performance of the particular style and kind of draw that is being developed. All movements must be cut down to the smallest number and to the shortest possible travel of arm, hand and gun. This is vitally important before the gun is drawn, and of equally as great importance after the gun is clear of the holster, or whatever carrying device is used.

Here the time factor enters and really is the most important thing to be considered in connection with the exact relation of the word "quick" to the various draws and gun producing methods generally referred to by that very romantic but broad term **"quick draw"** as handed down to us through Western frontier history. Fact and fiction alike make free and unlimited use of this term. Just where and how does this word "quick" fit in, and just exactly what does it signify and correctly indicate? What are its limitations in this connection?

The usual method of timing the so regarded quick draws of the early days was "faster than the eye could follow," and from this method of observation comes the magic implying term **"quick draw."**

To the best of my knowledge supported by diligent search, no accurate system of timing or definite classification was ever worked out to properly arrange the various draws in their correct relation to time periods, which would be vitally affected by, and be dependent on, conditions under which they were done, or were to be attempted, and the results that could

SUSPENDER HOLSTER DRAW

Left—The author explaining the "suspender holster draw." This is a short movement draw which can be and usually is fast, from a convenient and comfortable "dress up" gun carrying combination.

This is usually a more convenient gun arrangement for a short, stout person than the average shoulder holster, and as a rule can be adjusted very favorably for fast work. It is a close re lation and also a close competitor to the short cross draw. A very slight body twist is usually used to assist in the gun clearing the holster movements.

This type of holster is firmly anchored at the lower part by the spread leather suspender attachments that are passed through loops on holster and then fastened to the waist band.

Right—The finish of the draw indicates rather clearly the small amount of movement which is necessary for the entire performance, and does it look as if that slug would connect with the target, that, in this case, would be the camera. The camera operator was a little inclined to believe that it would.

The Quick Draw

with any certainty be secured under such conditions. This is the under-lying and undiscovered (or at least unconsidered) angle that regulates and controls the amount of **quickness** that can be **regularly,** and, **with certainty,** secured under such specified conditions.

Next to the time factor these specified conditions assume great impor-tance, so much so, in fact, that the entire relative results of any one, or of a series of tests, can be changed completely with sometimes amazing develop-ments. From this angle I have developed a classification for convenience in handling the various draws, as influenced by the various conditions, that I will set forth as superspeed draws, fast draws, average draws, medium draws and deliberate draws, of which the slowest are, and would be, classed as "mighty quick," at least so far as the eyes alone could gauge or judge the time.

As stated on various former occasions the actual accurate timing of the various draws has resulted in **some very surprising** results, as conducted with, by and from the large assortment of greatly varying types of holsters at the present time available, which are made to be worn, fastened, hung from and in, or attached to, all sorts of rigs and contraptions, belts, straps, strings and springs, that have been suggested, recommended, and sup-posedly carefully figured out as right, and otherwise advantageous, by various well-informed persons (and others), and also by some evidently misinformed individuals who were, and perchance still are, interested.

The timing of all such tests to be of any value as a method of com-parison to past, present, or future performances, must begin at such signals as have been agreed upon beforehand, as the starting point, and must be continued on to the point at which the particular shot is fired that has previously been decided on as concluding the performance. A normal quick-draw test against time requires the firing of one shot only, as a com-pleted test. Firing five shot groups after the draw is another branch of superspeed performance.

Conforming with these rules while conducting such experiments the action of the shooter is started by a sense impulse such as sight, hearing, touch, etc., in response to a flash of light signal, various sound signals, or by contact with some person or with some object designated here as touch signals. As classified, the light signals are instantaneous in starting action and very uniform in results. Sound signals are slower by varying degrees, differing somewhat in effect on individual reaction. Touch or contact signals differ still more, but electric contact on flesh—very short shock— seems to produce very quick response. It may be very similar, no doubt, to the so-called electrifying effect of the "danger sign" supposed to be apparent just before the starting of the man-to-man gun fight, which is generally credited with having the effect of starting "the hand-towards-gun movement" almost instantly.

Fast and Fancy Revolver Shooting

DRAWLESS HOLSTERS   FREEING HOLSTERS FROM BELT

Left—The guns are fastened securely in these holsters, the end of barrel projects out of end of holster as here shown; they are just flipped up on swivels into firing position. Very fast and effective double-action hip shooting can be done with this outfit. The holsters are ventilated and so constructed that the guns operate freely without any drag or binding of any kind, and the shots can be fired out through the bottom of holsters without doing any damage to the equipment. This constitutes a very fast combination for top speed performance.

Right—Showing how, if and when the guns are wanted for use, they may be detached and freed from the belt. The guns and holsters combined are, when leveled, just flipped back about three-quarters of an inch and, as clearly visible, are entirely free of any attachment or fastening of any kind. They can then be used just as freely as any other guns and the surprise comes when it is made apparent that the holsters are so fitted that target sights can be used and clearly seen.

The only extra requirement for these guns when used for this particular purpose is to be equipped with both front and rear sights about one-eighth of an inch higher than regular. When so arranged the sights are as clearly visible on these guns as when guns are entirely uncovered.

The Quick Draw

Most assuredly here is plenty of food for thought, and likewise plenty of material and room for argument. Personally I do not like arguments about guns and shooting, so I'll offer a few results of my observations, covering a period of years and the witnessing of, as well as taking an active part in, many trials and demonstrations. Time periods required by various persons for what is generally termed "quick draws," range from right around the quarter of a second mark up to one and three-fifths seconds, and all divisions and fractions of time that may be indicated in between, depending on the system used and the conditions existing at the time.

It is important that at this time special attention be called to the fact that it should be, and in all probability may be, pretty generally understood by interested persons that quick-draw shooting and hip shooting with revolvers are very closely related, and that each is dependent for success on pretty much the same principles and methods of control, particularly so in the various attempts for high speed performance. It is also a recognized fact that, with few exceptions, "quick draw" and kindred activities are not now, and never were, successfully performed at any very long ranges. Both styles of shooting, either separately or together, are, by the very nature of the principles involved, limited for successful results to the shorter ranges, particularly so where the time limit enters for serious consideration.

Even the best performers of the early days were very careful about such things, particularly so in regard to the distance that separated them from an opponent, less than fifteen feet being the range more often selected, and there were plenty of misses made on live men targets at distances much less than that.

In the training course which I have worked out for law enforcement officers I do not recommend carrying any sort of draw and shoot instruction beyond fifty yards when using the Captain Ed Langrish limbless man target, which I favor and have adopted for all such training. Such decision on my part is due to the necessary increase in time periods required for the sure hit results on account of the increased distance between target and shooter.

Drawing a revolver from any sort of a convenient holster, and scoring a sure and well-placed hit on a Langrish upper man target at fifty yards in two seconds, is considered an excellent and very satisfactory performance. Although much better time results have been and can be secured by continued practice, it is not a good idea at this time to offer anything faster than the two seconds result as a probable average for comparison with the work of the average performer. Well-placed hits in time periods between two and three seconds will not grow monotonous through too frequent occurrence.

Comparing the draw and shoot performances by separating them into five classes—**superspeed, fast draw, average draw, medium draw,** and

Fast and Fancy Revolver Shooting

DRAWLESS HOLSTERS REMAIN ON GUNS

Showing these guns and holsters free of belt and in the usual fast two-gun front position. These guns and holsters can be handled from here on just like any guns that are drawn entirely free of holsters. The specially arranged sights when attached are as clearly visible over the tops of these holsters as on any of the guns without holsters, and when guns are extended and raised to eye level, deliberate sighting can be done, and even some aerial target shooting can be added to the program. An interesting experiment consists of having an assistant place a can on the ground in front of shooter, then at a signal toss another target in the air. As the target goes into the air, the can on the ground is shot by swiveling the gun and shooting from the hip. When that shot has been fired the holster and gun are flipped loose from the swivel on the belt (see page 226) and the gun is fully raised, extended and sighted at the aerial target, in the regulation way of doing such shooting with any other gun. This sort of shooting performance combines the old timers' swivel gun feature with the later developed aerial target shooting, sort of blending two extremes. Of course various stationary targets placed in several positions will answer the same purpose as aerial targets.

deliberate draw—furnishes us a fairly satisfactory basis on which to work. The title of each draw carries with it a fair indication as to its time requirements.

From this effort towards analysis of time results it would appear that when working at the shorter ranges, around fifteen feet, a quarter of a second for a draw and one shot, which is plenty fast, is entitled to **hold first place for the superspeed draw,** while the other apparent extreme of two seconds seems to be about the period of time actually necessary for a fairly well-trained performer to complete a draw and score a hit on an upper man target at a distance of fifty yards.

What is generally considered by experts as constituting **the fast draw,** and firing of one shot, usually requires a time period of approximately a half second. **The average draw,** as done by trained performers, will usually range around three-fifths to nine-tenths of a second, while what is termed **the medium draw,** with gun raised enough to come into line with the eye, as is very generally done, should be completed in a period of time from nine-tenths of a second to around one and three-fifths of a second, and, what we shall term **the deliberate draw**, where the shooter looks over his sights to aid him in placing the shot correctly at the increased distances, will usually require around one and three-fifths to two seconds, often requiring three seconds, depending, of course, on conditions. A well-placed hit at fifty yards in three seconds is really a very good performance.

Many things enter into the successful performance of the various styles of "sure hit" draws, and naturally the question arises: What causes such a great difference in time periods for the performance of these, as it is generally considered, **very similar series of movements?** Why does it require less than one-half of a second (bordering quite often on a quarter second) for the "superspeed" draw at the closer range of around fifteen feet, and a period of time around two seconds or over, for the draw and one sure-hit shot, as described, when done at a distance of fifty yards? The answer seems to involve, to a great extent, the very important factor of distance, an item that is of much importance in all branches of the shooting game, fast or slow. Actual **experience** forces many of these points to be rather clearly recognized, while they can be, and quite often are, entirely overlooked when conclusions may be based on, and built up by, theory alone.

The superspeed draws mentioned as possible to complete in periods of time bordering closely on a quarter of a second occur only occasionally, and at such times are performed under the most favorable conditions possible, when all influences, mental and physical, happen to be exactly right, aided by plenty of practice and experience, and further assisted by the favorably arranged and correctly adjusted equipment in the way of holster, gun, etc., all conditions being just right in every detail at the time.

No man can ever be absolutely sure of any such performance being

THE CROSS DRAW

Upper Left—"Teaching the quick draw." Walter Groff "waiting for the signal." Notice the feet in relation to the boxed-in area.

Upper Right—"The hand to gun movement." No wide spread leg position necessary.

Lower Left—"The finished draw." Notice the direction of gun pointing in relation to the boxed-in area. Note the body position. This draw IS fast, with a minimum of movement.

mastered to the extent of becoming a regular and consistent result that he could guarantee to perform at any time called upon.

It must be remembered, in connection with what we term here a super-speed performance, that, in order to do a quarter second draw the performer would have to be able (without any hesitation between) to perform the complete movements involved four times within a one second period of time, likewise five times for a one-fifth second draw and ten times for a tenth of a second draw.

The controlling factors are fully described a little later on in descriptive matter relating to the cross draw, etc.

The fast draw mentioned is the one that is usually regarded as the lightning draw and is done by leveling, pointing, and firing the revolver at the instant that it clears the holster from somewhere around the belt level without making any move towards raising or extending gun towards target after drawing. Plenty of training in what is generally termed hip shooting is a very valuable help with this type of draw. Many performers among my pupils get fairly good results with this system up to and around twelve yards.

The average draw is taught to and very generally used by trained men in all branches of law enforcement and kindred occupations.

The medium draw is done by drawing the revolver from any holster that may be favored by the person active in the performance, and then, while leveling and pointing the gun, it is raised to about eye level while being extended towards the target as the shot is being fired. This is an excellent system of getting sure hits at various short and medium ranges. The extra time indicated by the timing results as being required for the extra movements necessary, is time very well used, as it will enable the **average** performer, who has had a reasonable amount of training and experience, to very consistently score all hits on a medium-sized target up to and including 20 and 25 yards. Reproduction of many of the targets shot by law enforcement officers, under my instruction in this system of drawing and delivering the shot (or several shots fired after the draw), will show very surprising results, much above the average generally expected. This is a very practical, effective, and reasonably fast draw. The difference in time requirements should be quite easily understood.

The deliberate draw is next up for attention, and due to the many angles entering into it, the time period must, of necessity, be prolonged, due to the much greater amount of movement and careful, deliberate aiming that is absolutely necessary for delivering a well-placed hit on a Langrish target placed fifty yards from the shooter. The preliminary movements in all of these draws are fundamentally the same, but just as soon as the gun begins to move away from the body the extra and later added movements require time, which is consumed in direct proportion to the amount of speed

TWO-GUN DRAW

Left—"Teaching the quick draw." Walter Groff with thumbs hooked in gun belt watching for signal from the author. Note foot position relative to boxed-in area. No sprawling or awkward strained positions necessary.

Right—"Hand to gun movements."

with which such movements will follow the original drawing movements. Up to the time the gun leaves the holster and is leveled the drawing movements are the same, and the time periods also should be the same, and in all probability are, but the added movement following in the two later draws mentioned extend the time. The necessity for the added deliberation required for more careful holding and sighting at the longer ranges, requires still additional time, which accounts for the one-fourth second to two second variation.

Distance works with the time factor to cause delay and interfere with successful sure hit results. Almost any fairly well-trained quick-draw performer can make as fast a draw as he is capable of, and snap a shot into a Langrish man target at fifteen feet with fair regularity, yet surprisingly few, if any, could snap a shot away in the same manner and in the same amount of time and be successful in hitting the same target at fifty yards, except perhaps by accident. The best method of securing convincing results is to try out these various situations a number of times. The enlightenment will be worth the trouble.

Analyzing quick draws in sections from the "impulse" to the time that the hand comes into contact with the gun grip, the gripping of the gun, the drawing of the gun from the holster, and the firing of the first shot and scoring a hit, runs along **approximately** as outlined in the following:

The average quick-draw performer divides his activities from start to finish into three sections or periods of time of about equal proportion. It takes him practically one-third of the time from the starting impulse to get into action and get his hand to the gun, then the next third of the time is required for the necessary gripping and drawing from holster movements, and the last third of the time is used for pointing the gun at the target, and at the same time performing the finger movements necessary for firing the shot just as the pointing movements are completed. There may be slight variations with different persons, but this outline will be found to be a fairly good general average rule, and helpful in gauging how the time periods for such actions are divided. It will also be found that the one-third time period mentioned as being required for combining the pointing and firing of the shot will prove to be just about the amount of time that will elapse between any two shots fired thereafter, from the first one to the last.

For instance, a one second draw with a double-action gun is usually divided—one-third second from the signal until the hand closes on the gun grip, one-third second for drawing gun, one-third second for pointing it at the target and doing the finger movement necessary for firing the shot. Following this rule of averages we add an extra one-third of the total time period required for completing the draw stunt, thus making four periods, so as to get as near the correct time as possible, that should be needed to

Two-Gun Draw

Left—"All set to squeeze 'em off and release the shots." Note foot position and also gun position relative to boxed-in area. There was no necessity for changing foot position and the guns are accurately lined up and correctly pointed for effective results.

Right—"The completed draw." Side view of the completed draw. Note perfect line-up and elevation of both guns.

fire five shots only, double action, with the four spaces of time between them, and we reach the conclusion that this operator should be able to shoot five fairly well-directed shots from a double-action revolver, separate and apart from the draw, in one and a third seconds. He should also be able to complete a draw combined with five shots to follow instead of one, with the four extra time spaces between shots added and complete the performance within seven-thirds of a second, or a total of two and one-third seconds.

A half second draw would measure approximately, of course, one-sixth second from signal, until the hand closes on grip, one-sixth second for drawing the gun, and one-sixth second for pointing it at the target and doing the finger movement necessary for firing the shot. Following the same rule and adding an extra one-third of the total time in this case, and we reach the decision that this half second draw operator should be able to fire five shots from a double-action revolver, separate and apart from the draw, in four-sixths, or two-thirds of a second, and complete a performance combining the draw with five shots following it, in seven-sixths of a second, or one and one-sixth seconds.

The quarter second draw, on the same basis, would give one-twelfth second for reaching gun, one-twelfth second for drawing gun, and one-twelfth second for pointing and finger movement necessary to operate trigger mechanism to fire shot, then, as we have been doing it heretofore, we add an extra third of the total time and we have four-twelfths of a second indicated as the time that should be required, separate and apart from the draw, for firing five shots double action, which, in plain figures, means one-third of a second. This man should complete the performance of combining the draw and five shots on a target in seven-twelfths, or not quite two-thirds, of a second.

A fifth of a second draw would be twenty-hundredths of a second, one-third of that time for gun reach would be one-fifteenth of a second, one-third for drawing gun would be another fifteenth of a second, and one-third for the pointing and finger movement necessary for firing the double-action shot, gives three-fifteenths total time for completing the draw and firing one shot. Now to conform with the rule we will add an extra one-third of the total, which will give us four-fifteenths of a second, and we can thus determine that any gun operator who can complete the quick-draw stunt in one-fifth second should be able to shoot five shots double action, separate and apart from the draw, in four-fifteenths of a second, which really is just a little more than a quarter of a second. He should also be able to combine the draw with five shots following it, in seven-fifteenths of a second, just slightly less than one-half second.

Bringing these comparisons down to the one-tenth second draw, if such a thing is possible, would require gun reaching time of one-thirtieth of a second, drawing time of another one-thirtieth of a second, pointing and

Fast and Fancy Revolver Shooting

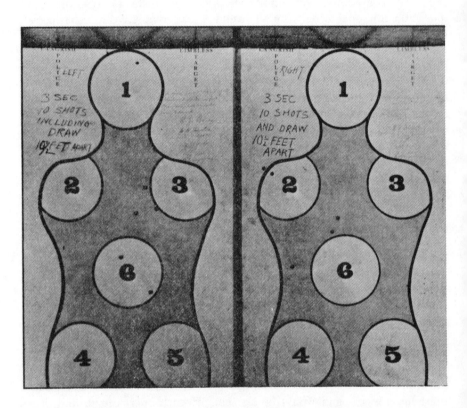

DEMONSTRATION BY THE AUTHOR

Drawing two guns from Myres Buscadero belt holsters, firing 5 shots from each gun at two Langrish targets placed 10½ feet apart. This performance was completed in three seconds. Shot July, 1934. Witnessed by Ellery Knowles and party from Grand Forks, Minn.

Witnesses' signatures on upper right of each target.

The Quick Draw

finger movement necessary for operating double-action trigger to fire the shot requires another one-thirtieth of a second, total, three-thirtieths. According to the rule, we now add the other extra one-thirtieth of a second, making four-thirtieths of a second, just a little over one-eighth of a second indicated as the time that should be required by this operator to fire five shots from a double-action revolver, separate and apart from the draw, and for combining the draw with the five shots to follow it should require seven-thirtieths of a second, or slightly less than one-quarter of a second, a feat that is not at all probable of accomplishment.

Based on experience gained while conducting experiments in attempts to secure superspeed results, through repeated quick-draw trials with various performers, the time required after the gun has been drawn to point it and release the shot, which we here term the pointing time and the finger movement time, which is necessary for working the double-action trigger to get the shot away during such attempts for speed, is usually directed by the mind of the shooter so that they are smoothly combined, both being performed at the same time and both being completed at the same instant.

This combined pointing and finger movement usually consumes about one-third of the total time required to issue the impulse to act and complete the draw by firing the shot. Therefore, if we multiply this by four we have the necessary time for the finger movement required during the four intervals or spaces of time between five shots. To secure this necessary time for such **continued firing movement** we add one-third of the quick-draw performer's total time to the full time he required to complete his draw and one shot performance, which will give us four-thirds instead of three, as the total time that should be, and usually is, required for an expert performer to shoot five shots double action when following a draw, the finger movement for the first shot having already been counted in with the draw the time for the four shots following the first one is fully accounted for by the four time intervals mentioned.

In other words (and it's a reasonable conclusion), the time period required by him to fire his one shot in connection with the draw should be plenty of time for him to fire any one shot of the five-shot string; when not hampered in any way by other conflicting movements such as are present when doing the draw, and by adding four such periods of time to the total draw time we have the correct answer for a draw and five shots combined. The basis of this reasoning lies in the fact that the average performer can fire a shot by the double-action method usually in slightly less than one-third of the total time required for completing the draw and first shot. This rule of averages usually works out very well with most performers and quite uniformly with persons who have had some such training.

While discussing five-shot groups attention should be directed to the

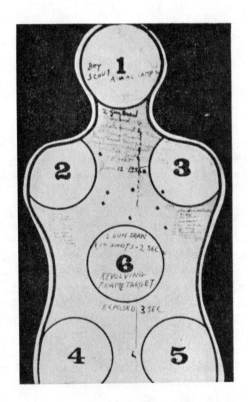

TWO-GUN DRAW BY THE AUTHOR

Includes 5 shots fired from each gun on a revolving frame target which faces the shooter for three seconds. Shot at Kiwanis Boy Scout Camp, June 12, 1935.

This performance was completed in two seconds.

Note witnesses' signatures.

The Quick Draw

fact that by **the very generally employed method of timing** there are only four time spaces occurring during the firing of five shots. The preliminary finger movements ahead of the first shot are not usually registered, but in the present situation they have been included in the total draw time and ahead of the first shot. On the few occasions where such preliminary movements are included the fact is generally clearly stated. It has been quite generally known and very clearly understood that, by the system of timing in general use, it is the custom to start the timing with the release of the first shot (not ahead of it) and end it with the release of the last shot. The time spacing runs 1*2*3*4*5; thus it can be readily realized that the division of time made use of here, and the adding of the extra third of the total draw performance time period, constitute a pretty good basis for the conclusions regarding the probable time that would be required for the firing of five shots in connection with the draw, as the timing systems formerly mentioned would only time the four intervals following the first shot, regardless of whether the five shots were fired in connection with the draw, or entirely separate and apart.

In order to avoid misunderstanding or the appearance of any intent to mislead, it is here necessary to explain that if the time period is desired to cover and include the response to a signal and the issuing of a mental impulse to start action, and the preliminary finger movement for firing the first shot is also to be added to the period of time from release of first shot to the release of the last shot (without the draw), then all that is necessary to do is to add another one-third of the total quick-draw time period and you have five-thirds, with time spaced like this *1*2*3*4*5, instead of 1*2*3*4*5, or five trigger finger movements complete (indicated by stars), instead of the customary four. The movement indicated by the star ahead of the first shot is counted in this case, which would then constitute the extreme time period that should be required, including reaction to the signal and the full impulse time and the full five-shot firing period complete.

By this method of timing the one second draw artist would require five-thirds of a second or one and two-thirds seconds for completing the five-shot test only, without the draw. The time starting from signal includes impulse and each of the five shots. The half second draw artist would require five-sixths of a second for the same test; the quarter second draw artist would require five-twelfths of a second; the one-fifth second draw artist would require five-fifteenths, or one-third second; the one-tenth second draw artist would require five-thirtieths, or one-sixth of a second, and all that is needed to determine time for combining the draw and the extreme limit of such five-shot performance is to add the time together. Add two more of the same fractions of a second for the reach and draw to the five fractions for the finger movements later given for each separate draw artist, and you have seven instead of five fractions for the combined

THE HIP DRAW

Left—Walter Groff, the author's understudy, demonstrating the quick draw with a short upward movement for gun pointing. A three-fifths second combination. "Hand hooked in belt."

Right—"Hand contacts gun grip."

answer in each case. The combined total remains the same for draw and five shots by either method of figuring, as the pointing movement is combined with the first shot finger movement in either case.

One-third of any quick-draw time will usually give you approximately your firing time period per shot. Two-thirds of your total draw time will be consumed with the initial reaching for gun and drawing from holster movements without the shot being fired, then one-third of the total time for releasing the shot. In fact, it takes a period of time equal to one-third for each shot—first, second, third, fourth, fifth—which will make a total of seven-thirds of your draw and one-shot time. Added together this will give a reasonable basis on which to figure the results that should be expected from any performer whose average time for a draw and one-shot performance has been determined.

It would be somewhat nonsensical to expect to draw a gun and fire a sure hitting shot in connection with the draw in much less than three times the time period that it takes to double action a gun for the firing of **each one** of five shots with sure hits in a five-shot string. In plain terms, if the time space between any two shots so fired in tests for speed, by the same person who is attempting the quick draw, is regularly greater than the time claimed for the draw and shot combined, there is a grave error some place in the timing system which should be corrected.

For an illustration, if it takes two seconds or ten-fifths of a second to fire five shots, which allows two-fifths of a second per shot, a person could hardly hope to add the drawing motions also to the shooting movements and complete the draw and firing of one-shot performance in less than three times the two-fifths second time period that the shooting movement for one of the shots required, or, to be exact, six-fifths of a second (1-1/5 seconds). Careful analysis of quick-draw reports will show that this error in figuring has occurred on several occasions in the past and is only misleading information.

To cover some of such possible errors of calculation that might occur we have here figured out in careful detail the one-fifth second, as well as one-tenth second, draws as a convenient method of comparison for even such visionary possibilities. This may be crowding the time limit pretty close to the vanishing point, but during our research and experiment we have heard considerable talk about it being within the range of possibility for some to accomplish, although personally I must admit that the results on the timing machines have never brought me quite within the danger zone of the blank space, or the vanishing point, as yet.

The foregoing figures should help to answer many questions that occasionally arise concerning quick-draw and superspeed double-action revolver shooting, either separately or combined.

When preparations are being made for timing such quick-draw demon-

THE HIP DRAW

Left—"On the way."

Right—"Finish of the draw." Note Myres holster. Note foot position. As a general rule, the higher in front of the shooter that gun is raised the more time will be required for the completed performance.

strations, etc., with the use of the electric contact equipment formerly mentioned, certain methods of procedure are necessary to adapt it to the special nature of the stunt under consideration at the time. These vary somewhat in accordance with the nature of the experiment.

For determining the time period required for a person to react to a signal, and get into action after such signal, the usual method is as follows: a light switch is conveniently arranged to connect with the striker bar of the timing machine. The person operating the machine, when all is ready, pushes the switch or strikes down the timer bar, as preferred, causing a flash of light which signals the shooter to start his draw and at that exact instant the hands of the several watches are set in motion. When the shot is fired, the electric contact at the trigger (shown in pictures) stops the hands of these watches at the precise position they occupy as the contact is made. This method is absolutely reliable and gives a perfect check-up. The ratchet bar of the timer is adjustable from two contacts to ten contacts. When set at two, it starts and stops the hands of the various watches with the first two motions as described.

When timing a draw and the firing of five shots (six items to be registered) the electric timer is set in the same manner as for the recording of six shots. First, striking down the timer bar makes the light flash, giving the signal to start the draw. The shots follow, *1*2*3*4*5; the first shot in this case has the time period indicated ahead of it by the cross or star; the fifth shot shuts off the timing at that point. As stated, the light flash signal is faster than vocal or other sound signals. The self-issued "Mental Impulse," which results in the fastest draw of all, can be timed only through and by direct connection with the reaction of the shooter himself.

A very excellent method for timing the self-released Mental Impulse (without signals) is with a small paper tape looped over the little finger of the gun hand, the other end of the tape being connected with the timer. At the first move of the drawing hand an electric contact is formed by the action of a connecting lever before this small paper tape can break from the pulling strain exerted on it, as the drawing hand is moving towards the holster. This tape-governed contact starts the timing mechanism at the very first move of the hand, and the trigger contact, formed by firing the first shot, again operates the mechanism which stops the hands of the watches and also marks the paper record on the drum timer, if desired, when so connected, thus showing the elapsed time from the impulse to act to the finished muscular action required for the completed performance.

When it is desired to time the two gun draw and one shot from each gun, or the two gun draw followed by any number of shots up to five from each gun, each hand can be connected up separately with the drum timer mechanism and the other registering devices by means of the paper tapes.

SHOULDER HOLSTER DRAW

Upper Left—Joe Young performing quick draw from Clark shoulder holster under instruction of the author. This view shows a very good position of hand on gun grip when starting the draw from this sort of gun-carrying equipment.

Upper Right—Gun is freed from spring clip and by moving hand down slightly and at the same time away from holster, the gun is —

Lower Left—Entirely freed from holster and by a slight wrist movement it is pointed forward and into —

The Quick Draw

The first move of either hand against the tape forms the electric contact and starts the timing mechanism connected with that particular gun. Both hands may start at the same time and finish at the same time, or one hand may start earlier and finish later, and the timing will be so recorded. The selection of signals and the methods of conducting the tests is a matter of the desires of the various persons interested, depending on what points seem to be the more important.

Electrically timing this sort of self-starting impulse also helps to explain some of the angles connected with the "Unbeatable Quick-Draw Stars" of the Old Days. They generally decided and issued their own signals, and promptly formed their own mental impulse, to move. They were usually all ready, very willing, and, as quite generally known, started first—all of which formed a combination that was very hard to compete with.

These so-called unbeatable quick-draw artists on the wrong side of the law were willing and usually anxious killers. The opponents of these men were generally reluctant to kill, and, as a general thing, had to be forced into it, which usually caused them to hold back the starting of their draw until sometimes too late to be effective. This was really more the cause of the other fellow beating them to the draw and first shot, than the actual phenomenal speed which these opposite the law characters were supposed to be capable of and consequently credited with.

When equally proficient law enforcement officers took a hand in the game, conditions were changed immediately. The ruthless quick-draw killers faded out of the picture of those days, much the same as the Dillingers, the Barrows, and the "Pretty Boy" Floyds of today "faded out" under similar treatment by the G-Men. Law officers, well-trained and proficient in the use of firearms, handled these situations successfully in the Old Days, and by the same method can handle all such situations that may arise at the present time; if they are permitted to **issue and follow their own self-starting signals and the mental impulse** to get going and act immediately, instead of waiting till the last instant on the other fellow. These timing experiments show clearly that this waiting for a signal is the important point, and that in this regard, at least, many of the early-day conditions were very similar to those of the present day; the results in all cases, then and now, depending largely on who first issues the signal (mental, visible, or otherwise) and first directs the impulse to act. The next important item is the ability to score sure hits with the **first shot** and the following ones also, if more shots are necessary, in the shortest possible time in which they can be accurately directed.

It is here necessary to mention some of the essential features that enter into quick-draw work, and later described superspeed shooting, which are closely related. Body balance is one of the vital factors governing well-placed hits in quick-draw shooting. Stiff, cramped, awkward

Fast and Fancy Revolver Shooting

Left—Shooting position ready for any emergency, or —

Right—Raised up level with the eye, from which position any sort of accurate pointing that may be required can be successfully controlled, and good shooting performance, at somewhat more extended ranges due to the opportunity thus afforded for looking over the sights, should be the result.

SHOULDER HOLSTER EMERGENCY DRAW

Under pressure of emergency and position the gun can be quickly drawn from this type of holster with the left hand (as shown) just as easily as it can be done with the right hand. Herein again the value of two-handed training is made evident.

The Quick Draw

poses and strained positions of body, legs, and hands are not productive of any fine degree of sure hitting results. I am fully aware that this is contrary to the heavy "chatter" of many of our Western writers on the subject, who delight in such expressions as "gunman's crouch" and "clawlike hands" held over holstered gun butts, etc. Outside of the fact that such actions will telegraph your intentions to your opponent, you are very materially slowing up your own movements when making use of such tactics.

Dancers, tennis players, and boxers give the quick-draw student a very good example of this vitally important matter of body balance. What could any of them do in the way of performing and controlling the various movements necessary for success in their chosen field of endeavor, if they disregarded this matter of balance and control? Absolute freedom of body and leg movements and their skillful control enter into the quick-draw problem to an amazing degree. The problem of shifting hands around in rapid manner is only a very small part of the movements that constitute speed acquiring technique in connection with regularity of performance, as regards sure hitting ability and certainty of placing the shots on or close to the spot where it was intended that they should be put.

Hurried, fluttering, aimlessly directed motions of hands and arms, which may appear very mystifying to the inexperienced, are not helpful to the shooter who desires to excel in this branch of revolver manipulation. The ability to secure consistent accuracy in quick-draw shooting depends to an astonishing degree upon the way the gun is handled **an instant before and just after it leaves the holster.** The quick-draw artist to be successful **must be able to grasp his gun in such a way that it lays and balances in his hand when it leaves the holster in practically the same relative position that it assumes when he is doing deliberate shooting in his normal shooting position,** otherwise his quick-draw shots will be even more widely scattered than they would be on the target, when the position of the hand on the grip is changed between each shot fired. This is a proven result on targets and will be just as positive a result in quick-draw shooting, if the grasping of the revolver grip with the hand is not done in a regular and uniform manner, and thoroughly mastered, until it becomes a positively controlled and correctly directed action, that will regularly secure the above-described normal "shooting hold" position on the grip.

Close grouping of the bullets on the target at a certain designated spot selected beforehand, cannot be accomplished until the correct "grip grabbing" motions have been mastered as directed above. After the grip grasping motions have been successfully worked out and can be uniformly executed, surprisingly close groups can be secured over quite a long continued series of shots, either when drawing for one shot only to be delivered, or when drawing with the intention of delivering five shots.

DRAWING STRAPPED-IN GUN FROM A MODERN HOLSTER

Left—Demonstrating the new top flip-off safety strap as worked out by the author for the Montana State Highway Patrol officers' holsters. Patterned after his own assorted holster combinations. Getting the gun grip, then, with thumb engaging extended lip of the safety strap, which is here clearly visible. —

GUN IS FREE

Right—Strap is flipped loose with the end of the thumb while closing the hand over the grip. The draw is started in this way just about as quickly as from an open top holster; no fumbling and no binding or hanging. (See page 250.)

The Quick Draw

Getting your hand to the gun in a hurry, while being quite important, is only a small part of the job. Just how you get your hand on the grip—and just how and in what position you get your hand closed around that grip (see illustrations), is the key to your success or failure with the shots that follow your draw. If the gripping of the gun before drawing is done properly, the pointing and directing of the gun after drawing is then a fairly simple matter. Scoring hits is a rather easy thing to do with a gun that has been properly grasped and drawn in such a way that it fits into your hand in the regular position in which you are accustomed to hold it when shooting normally. When this part of the quick draw has been properly mastered the problem is solved; results are then reasonably sure. But, until that part of the draw is learned correctly, the hitting percentage is very much a matter of luck instead of deliberate intent.

In speaking of the quick draw in these terms, I am referring to making sure hits with every shot on a certain sized target at certain specified distances, the size of the target, of course, being regulated by the distance it is placed from the quick-draw performer.

As clearly demonstrated by reproductions of targets in connection herewith, sure hitting and close grouping of shots is possible in quick-draw shooting in much the same way as similar results are possible in other styles of shooting, and will come to you through careful study of the various relative movements required. Equally important also is a close study of the movements that are **not** required. Persistent practice is a very necessary part of the program if you wish to become fast and positive in your movements. Rapid movement of the hands, as stated, is only a small part of successful quick-draw shooting, but it is the part that a great many not so well-informed persons really believe is the solution to the whole program; it is this idea that keeps many persons from mastering some of the apparently simple but actually much more important things that will assure success.

To the majority of persons who are actively interested in quick-draw and speedy gun handling methods, the important questions seem to be, "What is the best type of quick-draw holster and gun, just where is the 'best place,' the 'best position,' and the 'best' or 'proper slant,' etc., to wear a belt, a holster, and a gun?" These questions, as yet, have never been satisfactorily answered. The various arguments arising from these questions have never been settled. I make no rash promises here about settling the arguments, or answering the questions in a manner that will be satisfactory to everybody. Such a task would be difficult indeed, as chest measurements, waist measurements, and length of arms differ so greatly, and the height of persons from shoulder to hips vary to a still greater degree. The man who will attempt to establish any certain "correct" or "proper" or "best" position of belt, holster or gun, for such a

Fast and Fancy Revolver Shooting

VIEW TWO   VIEW ONE

THE HIP TWIST   THE BODY TWIST

Left—While slightly twisting the left hip to the rear the gun is instantly cleared from the holster by a very short drawing movement and can be quite accurately fired from the position here illustrated. This holster and adjustment is a safe and dependable piece of gun carrying equipment for an officer.

Right—"The cross draw twist or instant reverse." A valuable gun trick for officers. Note that this is done with and by the body; the right foot is still in the same position, while the left foot or stabilizer, as formerly referred to, is used to start, to stop, and to accurately control the correct amount of body movement. Demonstrated by Joe Young of the Montana State Highway Patrol, pupil of the author. (See page 252)

vast assortment of persons of such varied measurements and proportions, would most certainly find himself in a maze of argument that could never be satisfactorily settled. We will, therefore, try to avoid such a situation.

There is no **one** certain "best" or "correct" position for gun and holster that will apply to all persons and give satisfactory results. This has been definitely settled in my mind for many years; also that the terms "proper" position or "correct" position, etc., are very much overworked figures of speech, representing in most cases simply one man's idea. There is no such position that can **correctly** apply to everyone. This is one of the most important points to be considered when studying the various angles of quick draw and the necessarily connected speed development, something that must be carefully worked out to conform with the individual's physical proportions and mental reactions.

The most proficient men in all lines and branches of the shooting game are, and always have been, originators—not imitators. Naturally, to be successful, they must study the rules of cause and effect, study the advantages and disadvantages of certain lines of conduct and general behavior. After that they study special behavior and specially directed effort. They study methods of securing particular results and eliminate everything that is not actually and positively necessary. The most important subject to be studied in connection with all of this superspeed and positive movement proficiency is **yourself.** Your individual peculiarities need special study and plenty of it.

There is absolutely no type of so-called quick-draw holster that can make a quick-draw artist of you just because it is hung somewhere on your person with a gun in it. Such holsters are only tools that may be of assistance to you in your work, provided that you are well-informed in relation to the various principles involved and well-trained and proficient in the movements necessary—all of which must be developed within yourself and which cannot be purchased ready at hand and incorporated in any holster, regardless of who the maker of the holster may be, how much money you may pay for it, or what fancy name may be attached to it.

A much favored and somewhat standardized position for a quick draw, with one gun or two, at an unexpected signal, is the reasonably low hung (not too low) hip holster which allows the hand to draw the gun with a slightly upward sweeping motion and point it front with little effort. This is a modified form of the well-known hip draw featured so much in Western stories, and seems to be productive of good results for the average person. If the gun is to be concealed, of course the holster will need to be hung about level with the waist line so as to be concealed by a coat or other garment.

One of the most satisfactory condensed movement draws that I am particularly fond of teaching to law enforcement officers on account of

Fast and Fancy Revolver Shooting

"Reversing Positions." The Author Demonstrating with Aerial Target.

In learning the so-called correct firing position for practical defensive shooting, be sure that, if necessary, you can turn the body completely around, so as to place a "sure hit" shot directly to the rear, in case some bold, bad one sneaks up behind you. This target was thrown over the left shoulder with the left hand; shooter turns to the right, shooting directly behind the body, as shown. If you spread yourself all over the lot, with feet wide apart, you can't do these stunts, and they really are very handy tricks for officers. A quick-draw shot can be done the same way. Notice feet still point to the front though upper body is turned sufficiently to shoot towards the rear. Notice that the position of feet in both views of the body twist (page 250), and the position of the feet in this picture, are very similar. The operating principle is the same in each situation.

its superspeed possibilities, and surprisingly effective results at the shorter ranges, is made from a cross-draw holster. This is not a beginner's simplified draw by any means; it is, instead, a draw for the post-graduate branch of the game. My favorite position for placing this holster, whether worn inside the waistband of trousers or outside (excellent holsters for each being available), is just slightly left of center in front, top of holster about even with the top of the belt, slanting so that the gun points somewhat quartering across body to the left and down. The butt of the gun is turned toward and also leans to the right. In this draw the hand grasps the gun and the body is instantly twisted to the left by a movement of the hips. This movement should be enough to draw the holster more than halfway off from a gun with a six-inch barrel, and almost completely off from a three and one-half or four inch barrel. The slight additional hand movement required to point the gun in connection with this twist makes this draw very fast—in fact, it is one of the fastest on the entire list. This draw can be done equally as well with the left hand, when position of gun, angle, and slant is reversed. This draw can be done nicely while wearing a coat, which, of course, must not be buttoned at the time the draw is to be made.

The first shot is usually fired with the arm pressed or resting against the body above the line of the belt, as a rule, but it takes only the merest fraction additional time to point the gun straight out in front, if so desired. This particular draw is also excellently adapted to the new suspender holster which, as shown on page 224, places the gun a little more forward than the shoulder holster does. Shoulder holsters are not so good for stout, full-chested persons who may also be handicapped with short arms, like mine. My gun must be in a more forward position than the usual shoulder holster puts it. In a special shoulder holster made to my order this difficulty has been remedied to a great extent.

The draw from either Captain Hardy's, Sam Myres', or E. E. Clark's shoulder holsters can be done by the **average person** with quite a little saving in hand movement; some of my pupils are very expert at it. The grip is caught, the gun freed from the clip with a downward movement, and the body twisted to the left to help clear the gun, which is then quickly leveled with very little effort and shot while pointed across the body about midway between side and front. The body twist is important and very helpful in all of these draws and particularly so in the behind-the-back draw.

This behind-the-back draw is carried out on the same principle as the left side cross draw. The left side of shooter's body is towards the target. The holster, **a left-hand one** in this case, is hung at the right hip and the gun butt is, of course, turned forward. (The gun can be hung at the hip in the regular right-hand manner if desired.) The gun is grasped, drawn,

THE ROAD AGENT'S SPIN

Left—Demonstrating what is known as "the road agent's spin," using an aerial target to make evident the short space of time in which the spin can be made and the shot can be fired.

The revolver is turned in attitude of surrender to arresting officer. The target is placed on the curve of grip back of trigger guard and, as can be seen in the next view, —

Right—The target is tossed in the air with the movement of the gun, not with the hand, and while doing so the trigger finger is slipped into place and the gun is flipped forward and, as evident in the next view, —

raised, and leveled and the body is twisted just at the instant of the draw, keeping the right hip farther back than other parts of the body, allowing the shot to be fired across the back in approximately the same way as when firing across the stomach.

I demonstrated this behind-the-back shooting for Col. D. B. Wesson and Ernie Miller and friends at the latter's dude ranch near the west entrance to Yellowstone Park on October 9, 1935, just after their return from the Colonel's very successful big game hunting trip with the S. & W. .357 Magnum revolver. The object used as a target was a gallon can which had originally been filled with pie fruit. The distance was twenty feet and the five shots from a .38 Special S. & W. revolver fired double action, of course, made a group less than the size of the palm of a man's hand. The Colonel was greatly interested and very much pleased. I, too, was pleased with results until my shooting pal, Mrs. McGivern, called my attention to the fact that I had burned some very nice holes in the back of my much prized shooting coat.

This same position of holster, as described above, will also allow a very quick draw with the right hand when the body is in a position facing toward the target. The right-hand gun is in a left-hand holster, hung on the right side, with the butt to the front, as above described, and it is drawn without the body twist, but the gun is turned **up and over** along side of the body and pointed by motion of the wrist directly toward the front. This could be a good surprise draw, as an opponent would be looking for the left hand to make a cross draw which, of course, could also be done very neatly under these conditions, if desired, by simply shifting the body to the left and pointing gun across the body with the right side towards the target. By using a body twist, in this case to the right, as the gun clears the holster, thus turning the left side of body to target, the gun will naturally come around so as to be held in line with the target by extending the arm at almost any pointing angle desired. Plenty of careful practice will make this, or any of the other described draws, very fast. Persistent study and practice is the real secret behind successful quick-draw shooting.

The same position of gun and holster, moved slightly forward if necessary, can also be used for the left hand when doing the **two-gun** cross draw. Various similar arrangements of both right and left hand holsters, spaced conveniently, anywhere from near center line of body in front, to any desired position around toward the hips that may suit the person wearing them, can be used for a variety of these two-gun cross draws. Variations in holster positions, and ways of wearing them, include the use of double draw suspender holsters, as well as two-gun draws from various styles of shoulder holsters, hip-pocket holsters, waistband holsters, etc. The details of arranging them are determined by the physical proportions and

THE ROAD AGENT'S SPIN

Left—The right thumb is hooked over the top of the grip and the spin is completed and the remaining three fingers are drawn towards the under part of the grip and during all of these movements the muzzle of the gun is traveling towards the target. —

Right—This view shows the hand closing on the grip and correct pointing control is now being made possible and —

personal peculiarities and preferences of the person who is going to use them. Any one-gun draw can be developed into a two-gun draw by training each hand and learning to work them together. There is no mystery about it.

The front and back cross fire **two-gun** draw follows very closely the holster arrangement mentioned. The left-hand draw in this instance is made from a left-hand holster with gun in normal position and is done in the regular way. Gun is then leveled across the body towards the right with arm resting across and against the stomach well above the belt. The shot from this gun is fired at a Langrish upper man target located on the right side of the shooter. The gun on right-hand side, placed in a left-hand holster, with butt pointing towards the front, is drawn with the right hand reversed (back of hand towards body) so that the gun when clear of holster can be leveled with the arm resting against the back, in a manner similar to the one across the front.

The shot from the right-hand gun is fired at the Langrish target located on the left side of the shooter. In practice both guns are drawn and fired close together. When all goes well and as intended, both targets are hit at the same time although placed on opposite sides of the shooter. The absolutely correct construction of the gun harness used in such stunts as these is a most important matter. Our deep appreciation of the skillful workmanship of the makers of this equipment, as expressed elsewhere, is well-deserved. One of the Buscadero belts made by Sam Myres for this demonstration is shown with two left-hand holsters attached. The successful performance of this stunt is, I believe, original with us. It should, of course, be kept in mind that fancy and complicated two-gun draws are made use of these days mostly for exhibition purposes and entertainment. This also applies to a great part of the other fast and fancy gun-handling accomplishments.

THE LAW ENFORCEMENT OFFICER AND THE QUICK DRAW

Do not assume sprawling positions that require various preliminary movements and gestures before you can get started into action with your revolver. Do not indulge in unnecessary gestures or suspicious movements which may warn your opponent of your intentions towards starting the draw.

The less fluttering and fancy movements connected with quick-draw practice the better the results will be under all conditions.

The author's instructions to all enforcement officers when under his training: If you find it necessary to resort to the quick draw to get out of a tight spot and you are risking everything on the successful outcome of the

THE ROAD AGENT'S SPIN
The Concluding Gesture

Here the gun is under perfect control and pointed at the target with the hammer almost ready to fire the shot. The short amount of time consumed by these combined movements can be easily estimated and furnishes a good idea of just about how much time the officer would have in which to work out his own salvation when confronted with such a situation.

attempt, watch exactly what the other fellow is doing, also watch his every reaction in response to what you do. In other words, study your opponent without (if possible) giving him any outward evidence of any emotion or intention on your part. Study closely just how he reacts to certain behavior on your part and try to foresee, so far as possible, his next move in order to forestall it. Keep your mental impulse to act quickly keyed up to the highest tension under which you can still keep it firmly under control.

Remember at all times that the degree to which you can consistently perform any of these quick-draw shooting performances, depends to a very great extent on just how persistently you study and practice.

THE TWO-GUN CROSS DRAW

Left—Waiting for the signal or the "external stimulus," as formerly explained in Psychology section, to start action.

Right—"Hand to gun movements." Action under way. Hands on gun grips. If right-handed, the right arm is usually placed over the left arm and the reverse for left-handed persons, when performing this particular type of cross draw.

THE TWO-GUN CROSS DRAW

Left—"Right gun out. Left gun on the way." When using this sort of two-gun rig, the right hand usually brings out the gun hung on left side first. It is then usually moved far enough forward to allow the left hand room for action. There are various ways for cross draw artists to start their guns "on the way out" of the holsters. This view shows a smooth, fast action and positive pointing combination.

Right—"Ready to cut loose with the lead." This positive control system of two-gun pointing is the usual position to which all of the various combinations of two-gun manipulation leads. The variations can be added at any point just before or just after this position is assumed.

THE ONE-GUN CROSS DRAW

In this series of views, showing the changes in the positions and movements of the gun after it leaves the holster, one-fifth of a second will be added for each one of such changes, for the purpose of establishing a simple means of showing the influence of the time factor and how and where the time is used, and why it is used. The importance of the immediate trigger finger contact at the start of the draw and at the instant of contacting the gun grip, has been explained in detail elsewhere. This view shows it quite clearly. It is the author's opinion that this is of much importance. At this point the draw can be materially assisted, and as a result the time period required to complete it will be shortened by twisting the left hip slightly away from the gun as "the hand on gun movement" starts action to free the gun from the holster.

The Quick Draw

THE ONE-GUN CROSS DRAW

Left—"The hip twist." This view shows the left hip twisted back slightly and as a result the gun is leaving the holster. Only a very short additional hand movement is now required for the end of the barrel to clear the top of the holster. This twisting motion has had the effect of lifting the holster away from the hip and in position for a straight back move of drawing hand, which will quickly bring the gun out, so that the hand will be in a position just above the belt buckle, as clearly shown in the short gun cross draw (page 267). If the shot was fired at the instant that the gun cleared the holster, the time period for the draw would be in the close neighborhood of two-fifths of a second. To illustrate time consuming actions from here on we will start with and assume that the draw up to the point mentioned did require exactly two-fifths of a second.

Right—"Turning gun away from body." This view shows the gun leveled quartering across the body and this slight puttering around has cost extra time, of course, so we will crowd our time limit just a little and call this a three-fifths second draw, if the shot is fired at the instant that this gun was at this stage of being pointed and leveled.

THE ONE-GUN CROSS DRAW

Left—"Moving gun forward." This view shows just a little more deliberation, also a little more gun movement and some extra careful pointing effort, so this draw will be classified as a four-fifths second performance providing, of course, that the shot is fired at exactly this point of maneuvering without any more puttering around.

Right—"Extending gun for lining up." This view shows still more deliberation, more pointing effort, more hand movement, more hesitation and, as a consequence, more delay. In consideration of which we will be compelled to add at least another fifth of a second, and as a result a full second would in all probability be consumed before the shot would be fired which required so much deliberation.

The Quick Draw

THE ONE-GUN CROSS DRAW

Deliberate Sighting

This view shows the generally adopted position and method of procedure usually employed when attempting to teach and develop the average pupil in quick-draw shooting. This sort of deliberate pointing effort with which is combined careful sighting, careful holding, single-action cocking of the hammer and cautious squeezing of the trigger will usually require from around one and a tenth seconds for an unusually fast performer up to one and three-fifths seconds for an average performer at the shorter ranges of around six or seven yards. When the range is extended up to and around ten to twenty yards the time stretches out to around two, to two and two-fifths seconds, and when carried out beyond that to twenty-five yards, and again out to an occasional fifty yards, the quick draw and hit combined often requires an extension of time that is somewhat surprising.

The performer who can get a gun from a holster and register a hit on the upper body part of a man target, such as the Langrish or Colt targets, placed at a distance of twenty-five yards from him in a period of time just a fraction below two seconds and do it consistently, is a very proficient quick-draw artist. At fifty yards the difficulty is increased in almost direct proportion to the increase in distance. The time requirements seem to be affected more or less directly by these various changes.

The exceptional performer must always be taken into consideration, however, and no hard and fast or fixed rules can be worked out that will correctly apply to all persons and to all situations. The more complicated movements there are involved, the more time will be required for completing them.

Soft leather holsters are not satisfactory for quick-draw practice or for continuous use. Holsters which are shaped and moulded to fit the particular model of gun, used and made of saddle-skirting leather, will stand much use and will seldom give trouble. Occasionally a

(Continued on page 266)

Fast and Fancy Revolver Shooting

(Continued from page 265)

sharp cornered front sight or a sight with a thin and somewhat sharp top may cause unusual wear to occur on the inside of the holster and may need attention. This is somewhat provided for in the better grade holsters by having a firm support for the lower frame and trigger guard of the revolver to rest on when gun is being carried in the holster.

Hair triggers, so-called, and various other visionary superspeed trigger adjustments are not at all necessary nor desirable. A normally adjusted standard weight trigger pull is safer, surer and productive of much better results and more consistent "sure hits" than any of the freak combinations so often mentioned as marvelous alterations for man-stopping purposes. Lack of knowledge and actual experience are the cause of advancing most of these fantastic theories regarding the great advantages supposed to be derived from the usually suggested freak alterations.

"Well-greased holsters" so often read about are also on the list of don'ts. These are not necessary, not an advantage and certainly not desirable for handling or wearing or for actual use. The less grease there is on the outside of the gun the better for all concerned. Handling a greasy gun when attempting to perform with speed and precision does not as a rule work out well in the way of securing positive and satisfactory results. No such artificial aids, alterations or freak adjustments can ever take the place of persistent practice. There is no artificial substitute for skill and experience that can be depended on in emergency situations. Standard guns, standard ammunition and a standard quality of dependable holsters and equipment, as turned out by reputable makers, will work out a successful solution for all of the problems involved in this branch of revolver shooting.

THE ONE-GUN CROSS DRAW

These six selected views from slow motion moving pictures rather clearly show the cross draw with the gun being extended out in front of shooter instead of being shot across the body as usually done in fast cross draws. The extra movement necessary to extend gun out in front of shooter requires slightly more time but generally insures somewhat better pointing. This series of views represents the usual behavior for the more deliberate cross draw. It is possible to reduce the time somewhat by reducing pointing movements. Note that the gun, although extended fairly well out, has not been raised to eye level. This gun could have been effectively pointed and fired from position four by twisting the body to the right. Note that there is no sprawling, no widespread leg positions, no "Gunman's Crouch" evident in any of these quick-draw illustrations.

The Quick Draw

THE SHORT GUN CROSS DRAW
A Fast Combination

Left—Showing a very fast method for performing what is often termed the "short cross draw." The small amount of drawing movement needed to free this gun from the holster is aided by twisting the hip slightly to the left. This combined movement serves to get this short gun out of the holster almost instantly. The arm is then immediately brought into firm contact with the body. In this instance it will be noted that hand is just above the belt buckle when the gun comes free of holster.

Right—The wrist instantly elevates gun to firing position, hand is still just above belt buckle. The hand requires no further movement except the slight wrist action necessary to elevate gun muzzle. The shot can be effectively delivered from this position and follow-up shots can also be well controlled.

This is the draw that has the possibilities to hover around the quarter second and the two-fifths second marks. The shooting is done by the double-action method and a proficient performer really controls one of the most valuable trumps in the quick-draw game. This is a condensed movement (superspeed draw) which usually produces effective results.

Fast and Fancy Revolver Shooting

The Hip Holster Draw

Eight reproductions from slow motion moving pictures of the regulation from hip holster draw. This draw is usually started from position of having the thumb of the right hand hooked over the top of belt in front. The successive movements clearly visible here represent the usual quick-draw performance. Note that gun is almost level with the eye in this particular demonstration.

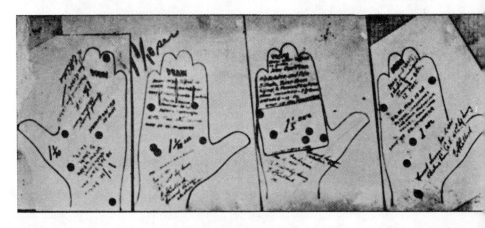

Drawing revolver from holster and firing five shots double-action. Shot January 18, 1934, at Armory of Company K, 163rd Infantry.

The Quick Draw

Left—This shows what we termed the "behind-the-back draw" and is the foundation from which was developed all of the later behind-the-back fancy shooting combinations herein referred to.

Right—The Sam Myres two-gun Buscadero belt (Spanish — *buscar*, to hunt; *dero*, he who is or does) with two left-hand drop holsters, as used for the two-gun draw, back and front cross fire, at Langrish targets placed one on each side of shooter, combining the front and back draw and firing across body, as described. This outfit is fast, perfectly constructed and properly balanced for the purpose.

Fast and Fancy Revolver Shooting

Front view of the two-gun draw and cross fire, shooting both back and front guns across the body at targets placed on each side of the shooter, as shown.

Rear view of the two-gun draw back and front cross fire. Both guns are usually fired at about the same time.

The Quick Draw

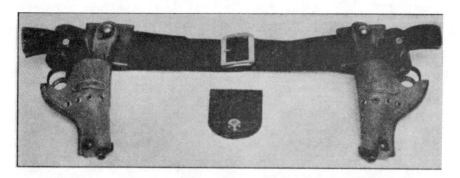

THE McGIVERN DRAWLESS HOLSTERS
(Made by Sam Myres)

These holsters and swivels as at present arranged are for entertainment and demonstration purposes only. If it is desired to wear and use guns regularly with such holsters, the metal swivel button should be on the upper part of belt block and a forked spring attached to the upper shank of holster or the reversed order if preferred. Then the guns could not become disconnected from belt except when intentionally done, but when so desired could be instantly removed by raising to horizontal position and flipping back slightly to disengage spring. The leather belt block just below the buckle shows the type of metal stud that is suitable for such arrangement. The upper shank of these holsters has a metal reinforcement sewed between the two layers of leather. The long shank is necessary to keep the short barrel guns from tipping backward too much.

SHORT GUNS FOR FAST HANDLING

The four-inch barrel guns are used in the drawless holsters. Also used in the cross-draw holsters. The two-inch barrel gun at left is ideal for the short cross draw and fire across body, as illustrated in the Short Gun Cross Draw (page 267).

Fast and Fancy Revolver Shooting

OFFICERS' PRACTICAL HOLSTER REVOLVERS

Nos. 11 and 12.   McGivern Model Smith & Wesson target revolvers, .38 Special caliber. McGivern front sights and standard equipment in every way.   Extremely fast and accurate, sturdy, dependable in operation.   Have everything in the way of reliability that can be built into a gun.   Have protected cylinder pins.   Can be used by an officer for a club in an emergency without fear of damage.   In the writer's opinion it is an excellent all-around general purpose gun.

No. 12 is equipped with Smith & Wesson standard grip adapter for larger hands.   A neat, reliable, well made gadget for the purpose.   The Smith & Wesson new Magna grip is also available.   These guns are nicely balanced for two-gun quick-draw work, and for general fast and fancy shooting.   They will stand a long siege of the hardest kind of double-action shooting.   The writer has not had one falter or fail to function in any way whatever during the most severe, prolonged tests.

No. 13.   Standard Smith & Wesson M. & P. .38 Special double-action revolver, 4-inch barrel, target sights, McGivern gold bead front sight.   An excellent all-around officers' gun of medium weight, fast and accurate.   Excellent cross-draw or shoulder holster gun, convenient size, heavy enough for heavy special police loads, not too heavy for comfortable carrying, well balanced, fast and reliable.

No. 14.   Smith & Wesson .38 Regulation Police 4-inch barrel, McGivern gold bead front sight.   This gun is an ideal, light weight, fast and accurate, dependable revolver for general protection purposes.   The writer often carries this one in a suspender holster.   The small bulk makes it convenient and comfortable to carry when wearing your "all dressed up."

No. 15.   Smith & Wesson Regulation, military sighted, knock-around gun, that has seen lots of service, been much abused, but is still fast, accurate and dependable.

The Quick Draw

Nos. 16 and 18.   Smith & Wesson .45 caliber double-action revolvers.   No. 18 has interchangeable cylinder (No. 19) for .45 Auto. cartridge and .45 Auto. rim cartridge.   The regular cylinder handles the regulation .45 Colt revolver cartridge.   This gun has a 6½-inch barrel, target sights, McGivern front sight.   It has a very fast double-action mechanism.

No. 16.   The 1917 Army model equipped with target sights, McGivern front sight, 5½-inch barrel, handling .45 Auto. pistol and .45 Auto. rim cartridges with metal-cased or plain lead bullets (latter preferred by writer).   This gun is fast, accurate, and nicely balanced. These two guns, besides being accurate, are real "go-getters" and effective man-stoppers for law enforcement officers' use, effective and most dependable for the purpose.

"Hide-out Guns," "Sneak Guns," "Stingy Guns"

No. 1.   Smith & Wesson .38 Special, 2⅞-inch barrel, round butt, specially remodeled for the author.   A very fine reduced length barrel, standard in every other way.   A very fast gun and accurate to a surprising degree.   A sturdy, reliable defense gun that has no superior.

No. 2.   Smith & Wesson .38 Safety Hammerless, 2-inch barrel, McGivern front sight, fast, handy and plenty accurate, and a hard hitter.   By using an interchangeable cylinder in this gun we can also shoot .38 Special wad cutter bullet cartridges.   This is a special feature, not supplied by the factory.

Nos. 3 and 4.   Remington Derringers, for .41 rim fire cartridges.   We have fitted gold beads in the front sights of these guns and find that very good shooting at average defense ranges (15 to 25 feet) can be done with these two guns.   This may be contrary to general belief, but is no less a fact.

No. 5.   Colt Detective Special .38 caliber, 2-inch barrel.   An excellent pocket revolver for defense purposes.

SECTION 16

TEACHING THE QUICK DRAW. SUITABLE GRIPS. SPECIAL GRIPS.

When teaching any of my pupils the quick-draw and other fast gun-manipulating methods I do not—in the beginning, as is generally done —teach him to stand with his body in any certain position, or to have his hands or feet in any predetermined fixed position; particularly do I avoid letting him assume any position of body and legs romantically known as "the gunman's crouch," such as is usually described by writers of Western stories as along the following lines: "Leaning forward, with body tensed on widespread legs, with hands poised above gun butts, and with clawlike fingers ready to stab with the lightning movements of a striking snake, for his guns, that seem to literally jump into his hands without any perceptible movement of those hands, just a blur of speed in response to the first inclination of his will to get into action," etc., etc. A very nice sounding yarn, if there was any sense to it or any probability that such things as guns, jumping into hands, without any perceptible movement of said hands, could happen.

Let us analyze such a situation and see just what should happen and why. In the first place any man assuming such a posture, in a tense situation, would simply be committing suicide by inviting instant death from a well-trained opponent, as a close study of drawing time and condensed drawing movements makes quite evident. The less warning that is given, by the preparations entered into, before attempting a draw, the better. If a person is trained to follow only his own usual and natural movements to get into the most convenient position (for him) for the top form speed movements required to complete a fast, sure hitting draw, his actions will not arouse any suspicion until he is in a position for immediate action, and then it is too late for any opponent to do anything about it by any fancy system of "gunman crouching" or "clawing movements" of any kind whatever.

Realizing these facts and being in earnest about preparing our law enforcement officer pupils for just such emergencies, we start our training with a foundation based on this knowledge. First, we are confronted with the fact that each person's physical make-up and proportions are quite generally different from those of his closest relative, and decidedly different from most other persons. This fact alone should make his muscular reactions and responses, particularly any hurried movements, somewhat, if not decidedly, different from those of any other **individual,** and instead of setting him up in some sort of **standard position** that may

Teaching the Quick Draw

SPECIAL GRIPS AND ADAPTERS

PACHMAYR ADAPTER   SMITH & WESSON ADAPTER

Left—The Pachmayr adapter fitted to the Colt Shooting Master. This attachment is considered quite helpful by many shooters. Made in several sizes and for all models of revolvers.

Right—The Smith & Wesson adapter is constructed on metal side plates. The composition filler block back of trigger guard is held firmly in place by a screw. A practical, well-made attachment of real value to revolver shooters.

SMITH & WESSON NEW MAGNA GRIP

The steadiest and most comfortable standard grips so far designed by anyone and excellently proportioned and well suited for fast double-action shooting and also quick-draw shooting. These grips are standard equipment on the .357 Magnum revolvers and can be furnished on all Outdoorsman models and the K-.22 and K-.38 Military and Police models.

have been inspired by the fond dreams of someone who may be an enthusiast about certain forms and features, envisioned by him as "classy and ideal," and as a result try to force the pupil to perform various forms of contortions and gymnastic stunts in order to get his gun out of a holster and attempt to hurriedly place a shot on some designated spot, by a series of starts and jerks combined, to some extent perhaps, with other slightly painful movements. Suppose that we suggest that he be allowed to naturally and gradually determine, by his own natural movements and muscular reactions, just about what position would be the more comfortable, convenient, and agreeable to his personal make-up, and from which he could make his most uniform and more positive movements.

Instead of attempting to force our pupil to adopt "Johnny Sure Shot's" position and technique, just suppose that we at first let him assume any natural, comfortable, and generally agreeable position that may appeal to him, and then ask him to draw his gun with a reasonable urge for speed and place a shot somewhere in the general direction and location of the selected target, where his bullets are expected to eventually be grouped. If our pupil stands normally and naturally in response to his own inclinations, he may not place any of his first shots on or even very close to the designated spot that should later on be the grouping point.

We will here christen our pupil "Jimmie" and we'll instruct him to go through the same series of natural movements as before and fire another string of shots in the same manner as he did his first ones. If Jimmie is following his natural impulse and has been making natural movements, caused by his natural reactions and controlled and directed by his own natural physical proportions, we will, after several attempts, secure a group of bullet holes that will show much more clearly than any other method, just where Jimmie's natural physical reactions would normally place his shots, and it matters not at all whether they are on the spot or two or more feet away from it. We have determined Jimmie's natural registering point where his normal muscular actions will place the majority of his shots, when he follows his natural inclinations, and we have secured the most valuable data from which to develop Jimmie's quick-draw proficiency that could ever be secured by any known method.

At this stage of development we will have Jimmie continue his shooting, naturally, freely, and entirely in his own particular style and manner. A little coaching at this point may help him to shorten the up and down distribution of his group of shots and quite possibly he can reduce the width of the grouping also, and in a very short time control all of his shots so as to strike within a certain area or a certain limited amount of space.

When this occurs the greatest catch in the problem has been solved. We now suggest certain changes in Jimmie's relative foot positions and

Teaching the Quick Draw

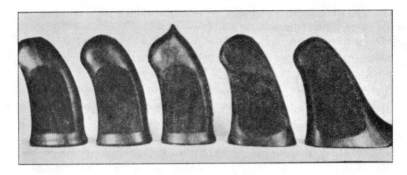

HARRINGTON AND RICHARDSON GRIPS

Five special grips put out as standard equipment on their sportsman revolvers and single-shot pistols, which have done wonders for many shooters and have improved their scores as a result of the fact that with slight alterations some one of these grips can be adapted to exactly suit the shooter's individual peculiarities.

TEN-POINT GRIP

This grip is made of a material that can very easily be worked over, and all slight alterations necessary to make a perfect fit for his individual peculiarities can be made easily by the shooter. It can be secured from Fray-Mershon, Inc., 340 South Vermont Ave., Los Angeles, California.

by moving the left foot backward and forward a little at a time, during trial shots, and also making slight changes in his body posture, such as leaning slightly forward or backward so as to consequently lower or raise the point of impact or grouping point of his bullets, we should be able to cause him to place his bullets on the desired spot and all of it can be done without causing Jimmie (or any other pupil) any physical inconvenience or strain of any kind.

Instead of attempting the reconstruction of Jimmie's physical make-up, we simply direct his natural muscular movements and reactions in a sensible manner until his point of bullet impact will register on the designated spot, and the gradual, but carefully studied, slight changes in posture and foot positions will cause his naturally controlled movements to be consistent and uniform, and the quick-draw bullet grouping will be correspondingly uniform and remain so, once the successful position has been established by natural means, instead of unnatural and mechanical effort.

It is a mistake to adopt certain body and foot positions first, and then force the development of bullet placing control afterwards. The more use that is made of the pupil's natural movements as resulting from, and controlled by, his physical proportions, the faster and the more positively will his ability be developed and the more consistently will results continue to improve until the desired results have become accomplished facts. This sort of quick-draw performer, when his training is completed, does not give widespread warning by any strained or unnatural gestures occurring before he can get into action. Instead, this sort of trained performer gets into action easily and instantly without any unusual or betraying movement preceding the start of his gun-producing activities, and the movements that follow the starting actions are usually uniformly sure and positive.

The fastest and smoothest draws, combined with uniformly well-placed hits coming under my observation and experience, are quite generally started with the hands just opened naturally and in a normally relaxed condition. In many cases the conditions call for the draw to be started at a signal that may occur at any time while the hands are roaming around, in and out of vest pockets, etc., in apparent search of matches, coins, or other objects, or while toying with pencils, watch chain, or adjusting the necktie, etc., etc., following the usual routine of movement generally performed by the hands of any normal person.

These random movements are continued up to the instant that the mental impulse starts action to reach for the gun in response to the signal, which may occur at any moment that may be selected by the instructor. Stiff, strained tenseness, clawlike hand positions, all clawing motions, warning poses and attitudes must be left entirely out of such training performances. Deliberately assumed widespread leg positions will greatly

SPECIAL GRIP

A built-in filler block back of trigger guard, showing how Walter Roper's special grips are fitted to the S. & W. revolver, extending up on the frame and also down below end of metal and giving a longer and more roomy hand hold, which is required by many shooters. Any type of grip will be made to your order.

interfere with freedom of fast movement in any of these quick-draw and fast gun action situations. The much overstressed and quite unnecessary "gunman's crouch" will quite generally, for most persons, prove detrimental to the development of quick-action proficiency in the various situations.

It is my candid opinion that a minimum of motion and a maximum of speed can be combined by moving the open hand towards the gun so as to make contact with it on the side in such a manner that the hand will need to be drawn slightly back in a movement parallel with the gun, and traveling perhaps one to one and a half inches back towards the grip, as the hand passes along the side of and over the stock. The lower part of the fingers are closed under the lower part of the grip as the palm comes in contact with, and closes over, the side and top, while the thumb and upper part of the hand naturally cuddles around the back strap and left side of the stock, and the end of the trigger finger slips easily into place in readiness to fire the shot, either double action or single action, as the case may be. The thumb, as a result of practice, will naturally engage the hammer spur as the gun starts to leave the holster, and the hammer lifting motion, which is essentially a part of the single-action draw movement, will materially assist in bringing the gun from the holster, and will also prove a protection against the hammer spur catching on clothing of any kind as the gun comes clear. If the double-action method of operating the gun (which is the most favored by us) is made use of to fire the shot, the thumb is easily and quite naturally shifted over to the side and out of the way of the hammer spur by the same motions as are shown in the combined photos (page 108) of slip shooting with single-action guns, and for rapidly cocking double-action guns, for fast single-action shooting.

In response to many inquiries regarding my own particular method of operating the triggers of double-action revolvers, I engage the trigger with the tip end of the trigger finger only, and ahead of the first joint always—never on or back of the first joint at any time. Practice has developed this part of the trigger finger so that it has much more strength and power than is ever needed to operate the heaviest and hardest working double-action mechanism so far encountered, and, as can be quite readily realized, it gives a fast, positive, and straight-back trigger operating action. Extending the trigger finger through the guard until the upper joint of the thumb can be touched with the tip of said finger, is not at all necessary for the rapid operation of double-action revolver mechanism. The finger position which I use has proven to be, for me, the best one of a great many that were tried out during a prolonged session of experimenting, and the detailed description of it is here offered for the benefit of others. For all attempts at fast shooting, of whatever nature it may be, I hold my thumb down in contact with my second finger as it curls around the

SPECIAL GRIP

Side view of Walter Roper's special grip fitted to Smith & Wesson M. & P. target revolver. As can be seen this has the filled-in block integral with the stock to occupy the space between forward part of metal strap and back of trigger guard, a much better arrangement than a stuck-on adapter.

The wide and very comfortable feeling hammer spur was put on this gun by R. F. Sedgley of 2311 North 16th St., Philadelphia, Penn., who is also responsible for the adjustable trigger stop plainly visible as attached to the trigger.

grip (as shown in photos, pages 46 and 47).   For all slower and more deliberate single-action shooting I hold my thumb along the side of the frame of the revolver, but in either case the trigger finger position remains the same.

While wishing to maintain an attitude of fairness towards all persons and opinions and products, personally and for my pupils' use and for instruction purposes, I do not favor holsters that are so constructed that it is necessary to get the revolver part way out of the holster, in any direction, or by any method, before the trigger finger can come into contact with the trigger, others entitled to their preferences notwithstanding. I prefer to have my trigger finger come into immediate contact with the trigger before any drawing from holster movement begins, and at the exact instant that the palm and the rest of the hand comes in contact with the gun grip. This system of grasping the gun does away with much of the fumbling and troublesome uncertainty that has proven so annoying to many persons who make frantic attempts to grasp the trigger after the drawing movements have been partially performed.

The best time to make sure and positive contact with the trigger is when the hand first contacts the gun grip. Persistent practice of this par-ticular detail will develop superspeed performance possibilities and build up a positive gun gripping position of the hand, which will help a great deal to keep the gun from getting twisted off center and shifted to one side or the other.

A persistently practiced and positively developed uniform finger contact on trigger, when hand first contacts the gun grip, will develop positive central line-up of barrel and uniform pointing of the gun each time the quick-draw movements are completed. Without the guidance of the trigger finger contact it becomes a very easy matter to let the grip assume an unnoticed but slightly twisted position in the hand, which will cause the bullets to be placed first to one side of center alignment and then to the other.   Careful training and close attention to trigger finger contact position helps greatly to eliminate this very common error. Even when using single-action guns with tied-back triggers for quick-draw work, the accurately placed trigger finger contact helps greatly in controlling the point of impact of the bullets fired from the various types of slip hammer guns. The trigger finger in such instance is used in much the same manner as though required for firing the shot. These positive trigger finger positions and contact habits in themselves will help very materially in positive and uniform pointing control of the revolvers.

It is on these very important points that the statement is based that the sure-hit quick-draw artist assumes control over where his bullets will hit, at the instant that his hand is placed on his gun, and his hits or misses are caused by the result of his hand and finger position just at the instant that the gun starts from the holster. This seems to be a very important

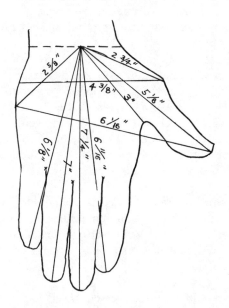

Diagram of the Author's Hand, with Detailed Measurements, in Response to Numerous Requests

point of control that appears to have a great influence on the success of the whole performance, more so perhaps than many of the things that are usually done after the gun leaves the holster. Much of the effect of such influence has been cheerfully overlooked, or else it has not been fully realized.

When this portion of quick-draw technique has been mastered, progress and expansion can be made by following the instructions for hip shooting and the various kindred subjects.

The next most important thing to correct relative position of trigger finger contact concerns the shape, the style, and the general dimensions of the stocks or grips as fitted on the revolvers to be used for quick-draw shooting and other fast shooting performances from the various positions herein described.

In order to secure positive pointing control of a revolver by the feel of the revolver in the hand, as based on former shooting experience with it, some sort of properly proportioned grip adapted to, and suitable for, the size and general dimensions of the hand of the individual who is doing the shooting should be used. It would be absurd to expect to have the correct feel of the gun in the hand so as to direct the pointing of the gun properly while using a round or sort of baseball bat pattern of grip. No amount of practice would develop the positive pointing feel of any gun with such a grip.

Every person's hand has certain characteristics and individual proportions that require certain dimensions for upper and lower portions of the revolver grip that will feel comfortable in the hand and produce the feeling of confidence relative to general pointing accuracy that will be realized, almost instantly, when the hand is closed over a grip properly proportioned for that particular hand.

When attempting to perfect one's self in quick-draw, hip, and super-speed shooting, it is not a very difficult matter to figure out the necessary changes required for making revolver grips just a little more adapted to the slight peculiarities and variations occurring in the hands of average persons. Careful study of some of the more common things that lead to poor performance, and the more or less generally unsatisfactory results which are usually encountered in the beginning of such training, will often make it possible to determine definitely that the trouble lies in great part in the grips, in relation to the proportions of the hand, somewhat along the following lines:

1. Grip too thick at the bottom, not suitable for an individual with short third and fourth fingers, causing gun to be twisted to right as a result of the effort to reach around such a grip.

2. Grip too thick at the top; not suitable for short thumb and trigger finger, same twisting result, and similar inaccurate pointing, as in number one.

Teaching the Quick Draw

3. Grip too round or too square, not flat enough to give a feeling of definite direction or correct pointing alignment in relation to wrist and forearm. Pointing direction will vary—first to one side, then to the other.

4. Grip too flat on the sides and too thin at the back; not, as a rule, a comfortable shooting grip, and usually induces poor pointing and a strong tendency towards twisting the gun sideways, thus causing poor alignment, and a general lack of control over the grouping of bullets, when attempting any sort of fast shooting. The discomfort resulting from recoil when using this type of grip will soon cause flinching, due to punishment such grips usually inflict on the hand. A reasonably wide and rounding surface, where thumb and finger span the back strap and upper rear part of frame, will be found to be very helpful in avoiding the development of the flinching habit. If gun is padded slightly at this point, it will usually prove very helpful in avoiding, or, at least, assist in overcoming, such habit early in its development. A reasonably heavy trigger pull and a grip that fits the hand comfortably will quite often help very materially in overcoming the flinching habit. I have used this method successfully on a number of my pupils.

5. Grip too short at the top, not extending high enough up on frame of revolver to protect that part of the hand between finger and thumb from punishment by recoil.

6. Grip too short at the bottom to give a comfortable feeling to the lower part of the palm and the third and little fingers for a person with a fairly wide hand. Usually causing serious variation in elevation and general lack of confidence in determining the correct pointing feel of the gun in the hand.

7. Grip too wide from side to side, not suitable for any person with a short hand, causing twisting of gun sideways in hand, making a positive feeling of pointing certainty, impossible of development.

8. Grip too wide from back to front gives same result, usually causing twisting of gun out of line, quite generally to the right, due to the effort required to reach around the grip and make proper contact with trigger.

9. Grip too narrow from side to side, also too narrow from back to front. Not suitable for a long fingered hand and generally having a reverse effect to that mentioned in No. 8. Usually causing twisting of the gun to the left, which is also further aggravated by the recoil.

10. Grip with too much bend or curve or too much hook shaped for a hand with long fingers, usually has the effect of twisting the gun to one side, then to the other, which effect is also generally increased somewhat by the recoil. This sort of grip is usually not productive of uniform results.

11. Grip too near straight will not give uniform nor comfortable wrist position. Grips should be curved enough or slanted properly to hang naturally and comfortably in a straight-ahead fairly level pointing position.

12. Grips with built-in elevating blocks, or adapters made of some suitable material for filling the curved place at the bottom of frame just ahead of front strap and back of trigger guard, will be found to be very helpful to many persons, while many others can be helped greatly in more firmly controlling their revolver pointing by the addition of thumb rests of various proportions, slants, curves, and groove widths.

Fast and Fancy Revolver Shooting

All of these requirements and correcting adjustments can be quite easily determined and carried out to satisfactory conclusions by a reasonable amount of study and experiment, conducted along the old reliable trial and error method.

The individual who is willing to conduct a little research work can quite readily remedy any slight variations and irregularities or personal peculiarities that may exist in the proportions of either one or more fingers, or thumb, or in either hand generally. When such corrections are made in the grips and suitable proportions are finally secured, the person with grips so fitted and adjusted will soon forget his troubles and settle down to consistent progress and his performances will soon become positive and satisfactory.

Special grips, with the filler block additions built into them, can be secured on special order with all necessary and correct proportions worked out to exactly fit the individual hand.

Much of the unusually successful results secured with Harrington and Richardson .22 caliber Sportsman revolvers and target pistols were undoubtedly to a great extent the result of the fact that this firm was one of the first to supply a variety of grip patterns adaptable to the peculiarities of the hands of their customers who would purchase and use their target arms. Several patterns of these grips are herewith shown and with usually slight alterations some one of these grips can be adjusted to fit any average hand.

Much time and money has been spent on special target grips to correct faults both real and imaginary. Many of these special grips are very sensible, while many others are somewhat freakish, but all of them are designed for the purpose of gaining higher points and more credit or fame for the user.

Yet, the general custom still seems to be very actively in favor of having our law enforcement officers risk their lives on the generally unsatisfactory performance of guns that are in no way adapted to or equipped for quick pointing accuracy or fast handling. Little or no attention is paid to the proper kind of correctly fitting grips suitable for, or in any way adapted to, fast action or quick-draw shooting or other fast and effective shooting of any sort, such as an officer should be able to do when occasion may demand it.

Why this situation exists is very difficult to either understand or explain. Just why an officer's life is held more lightly and of less comparative value than a hole in a paper target that at best can add only a few points to the score and perhaps a little more flattering acclaim to the performer who did the shooting is beyond my understanding, but the facts seem to indicate that this really is the case. Expensive equipment seems to be both necessary and desirable for plugging paper target scores. But, in the situations involving the lives and welfare of officers and their families, almost any old kind of junk in the way of guns and equipment seems to be considered satisfactory, on a sort of "good enough" basis.

Personally, I can never be in accord with such an attitude. In my estimation, there is nothing too good or too expensive for the protection and welfare of our law enforcement officers.

In so far as my personal requirements are concerned, I have had very little trouble about grips or special fittings. My hand has been well-suited with the standard regulation grips on Smith & Wesson Military and Police revolvers and the larger framed revolvers as well. The only alteration I ever actually needed was to attach a small piece of sponge rubber at the upper part of the back strap and bind it in place with electrician's tape when I planned on indulging in prolonged rapid fire experiments. (Photo of S. & W. gun No. 286600 shows this arrangement in place, page 140.)

Later on when the S. & W. Magna pattern of wood grips was brought out I switched to it on many of the guns and by reducing the general thickness and proportions just slightly I have been getting very satisfactory results. The dimensions of these grips as I use them are—one and a sixteenth inches in thickness from side to side at the upper part, which extends up on the frame, and the thickness at the bottom is one and seven thirty-seconds. The circumference at the top on a line passing just under the frame is three and seven-eighths inches. The circumference at the bottom measures five and a quarter inches.

On the Colt Officer's Model, both .22 and .38, the smaller pattern of wood grips supplied by the factory suits my hand very well. The .38 Shooting Master grips were also quite satisfactory.

The detailed dimensions of my hand are herewith given in a line drawing with the various measurements indicated from the wrist to finger tips and tip of thumb also. This is offered for the purpose of making comparative measurements in relation to grip proportions as herewith given, and it may also perhaps serve as a guide for others who may be interested in grip proportion problems. Most of such problems will need to be worked out by the shooter himself by the old "cut and try" method.

Perhaps the shooter may wish to refer his special grip problems to a specialist and if such is the case I can recommend Walter F. Roper, 458 Bridge Street, Springfield, Mass., also Kearsarge Woodcrafts Co., Warner, N. H.

R. F. Sedgeley of 2311 North Sixteenth Street, Philadelphia, Penn., is also equipped for taking care of your needs along the special grip line. Mr. Sedgeley can also handle any and all special remodeling, repairing, rebuilding, and adjustment work that may be needed on any and all types of guns, revolvers, and pistols. Mr. Sedgeley has done a great deal of such very satisfactory work for me.

Sending a drawing of the hand along with the order, and some explanation regarding any peculiarities that may exist, will help greatly in getting an exact fitting grip.

SECTION 17

COMBINING QUICK DRAWS WITH AERIAL TARGET SHOOTING. VALUABLE POINTS FOR POLICE.

As a means of checking up on your quick-draw movements when you feel that you have them under perfect control, try combining them with aerial target shooting. Stand twelve or fifteen feet from a mark or spot, with gun in cross draw holster at left of front, toss a fair-sized target with the right hand and draw the gun with same hand. A shot can be fired and hit scored before the target reaches the mark. The complete throw, draw, shoot, and hit can be done in around three-fifths of a second, but is not by any means the rule. It usually takes just about half of the total time for the impulse to set the muscles in motion, and for throwing the target. The balance of the time is used for drawing and pointing, and for firing and scoring a hit.

The sense of direction is already established by the motion of tossing the target. The drawing of the gun is done by continuing the circular motion of the hand used in throwing. The gun is drawn just as the hand makes the second upward curve, bringing the gun out freely without stops, stuttering, or hesitation. The movements required, being circular, are materially less than in the usual procedure followed when drawing from a low hung hip holster. There are no sharp corners to turn, no stops made that require renewal of movement, no forward or backward movements with the usual full stop between.

Only one mental impulse to act is necessary to start motion and continue it to the conclusion of the performance by firing the shot at the target. When the target is tossed, the drawing hand is already in circular motion for the draw. When the target is released the circular motion in use brings the hand around to the gun which comes right along with the hand as the motion is continued upward, and by the same circular motion the gun is turned out from the body and pointed at the target. By practice the gun is so controlled that it follows the flight of the target with very little apparent effort. Thus, through practice, the subconscious mind soon assumes control over the combined movements, and reduces the process to one mental impulse to act. The combined movements follow in a continued unbroken series until the full stop point is reached, which occurs at the instant the shot is fired.

This is one of the fastest "combined movement draws" on the list of fast gun action. As a combined flying target and quick-draw demonstration it has everything crowded into a small amount of time, and is really a very fine course of training to develop the skillful handling of revolvers

Combining Draws with Aerial Targets

Combining Aerial Target Shooting with the Quick Draw

1—Ready to toss the target

COMBINING AERIAL TARGET SHOOTING WITH THE QUICK DRAW

2—Target tossed and gun being drawn. Target about three feet from thrower.

Combining Draws with Aerial Targets

COMBINING AERIAL TARGET SHOOTING WITH THE QUICK DRAW

3—Gun drawn, pointed and fired. Target broken less than seven feet from shooter. Time can be judged by tossing an object a distance of seven feet.

by combining accuracy with speed. (See photos illustrating the several stages of this combined movement stunt.)

Another very fine training activity which is also an interesting exhibition stunt, combining aerial targets and quick-draw proficiency, is performed by having the assistant, who is to do the throwing, concealed behind a fence or other convenient, or perhaps purposely arranged, medium height obstruction which will conceal him from view. Arrange to have him toss targets in the air in response to certain signals which have been agreed on beforehand and to be issued at certain intervals. Gun is not to be drawn from holster until target appears above the fence or other barrier used.

The post-graduate course in this field of activity comes at a little later period when the shooter feels confident that he has the situation well in hand. When this stage of development is reached the assistant is allowed to send the target up in the air without any warning whatever and the quick-draw artist's only signal for immediate action is the appearance of the rapidly moving object within his field of vision. His external stimulus to action comes from the eye, it being the sense organ that, in this case, issues the sensory-motor impulse which, as a result of training, will continue with all necessary movements to the conclusion of the situation, which is at the instant when the shot has been fired.

A very valuable training angle may be added to this situation when a miss occurs, by immediately firing another shot, and if the second one fails to connect, try a third. It will be surprising how much help this sort of practice will be in building up skill to later handle several aerial targets tossed at the same time. This system of follow-up shooting can, of course, be applied to any part of the aerial target practice with equally as good results as when combined with quick draw.

We have gradually advanced to the stage of progress where we have combined hip shooting, quick draws, aerial targets and close group shooting against time limits. All of these things rightfully belong together and are very much interrelated in the study of fast and fancy revolver shooting. Proficiency in this combination will prove a very valuable addition to any shooter's accomplishment.

This mixed branch of revolver shooting will also be found important and very valuable in the training of all law officers. If such training would become general, the efficiency of our officers would be so much improved that the glaring headlines in the daily news sheets would tell an entirely different story than the usual ones that attract our attention at the present time. If an officer were properly trained in this mixed branch of revolver work, he would be capable of hitting the gun hand of the criminal or, if only the head or arm or part of a leg of a gunman was exposed to the officer's view, he would in all probability be able to register a hit with the

Combining Draws with Aerial Targets

1—Throw

LEFT-HAND DRAW ON AERIAL TARGET WHICH IS TOSSED WITH THE RIGHT HAND

1—As target is tossed left hand reaches for holstered gun —

2—Draw   *3—Shift*

2—Which is drawn with left hand and tossed to the right hand, and —

3—When gun reaches the right hand it is immediately fired at the aerial target.

Combining Draws with Aerial Targets

first shot at any reasonable distance at which revolver battles are generally carried on, particularly so within the average store or bank lobby, etc. With this sort of training an officer's shooting ability could be developed to the point where he could hit a bank bandit, or other criminal, on some part of the body above or below a bullet-proof vest, and just about where he wanted to hit him, with a bullet fired from his revolver in an amazingly short space of time, without danger to the spectators or others in the immediate vicinity of the person who is being shot at. These statements are well-supported by actual results developed by such training.

Let us hope that the effort put forth in developing these various branches of what we may be allowed to term "Practical Revolver Shooting" and the information relative thereto, as contained herein, may prove of some value to our many friends among the law enforcement officers who, in these so-called modern times, are often called upon to risk their lives in performance of their duty.

I would like to call attention at this time to one of the cleverest devices that has yet come to my notice for quick-draw practice. This is a supplementary chamber for use in the .38 Officer's Model Colt or Smith & Wesson M. & P. revolver. It consists of a rifled tube made in the shape of an extra long cartridge—being flush with the end of the cylinder and having a rimmed head similar to the .38 Special cartridge. The head holds it in proper firing position in the chamber of the cylinder. This tube is chambered for the 4 mm. center-fire practice ammunition, Model 1920, with round lead bullets. The accuracy of these is very good up to twenty feet. For quick-draw practice indoors, or in the basement or attic, this combination is very serviceable, giving about the cheapest yet satisfactory ammunition for the purpose, and allowing the use of your pet gun in actual operation. I believe that these supplementary chambers can be had to fit any size revolver. The price for the one fitting the .38 Special is $1.50. The 4 mm. B.B. caps run about 60 cents a hundred. This little accessory was brought out by Mr. R. E. Davis for his own use originally, but can be had from the Davis Engineering Works, 304 Second Street, Grand Island, Neb. I can recommend this combination for economical quick-draw instruction and practice.

SECTION 18

REVIEWING QUICK DRAWS AND TIMING METHODS OF THE EARLY DAYS.

Many wonderful stories come to us about the amazing speed and accuracy of some performers of the early days with various combinations of guns and holsters, and the general trend is to belittle our present-day gun handling experts in general, but we must remember that the method by which all such things were timed in the early days was by the simple rule of "faster than the eye could follow," and the observations were usually made by persons wholly untrained in any form of speed tests or demonstrations.

The eye alone, under such conditions, is not an accurate instrument with which to measure movements that occur in fractions of a second. The fact of the matter is that the average person's eye cannot distinguish the actual difference between a half second draw and one that requires a full second for being completed, nor can the average eye accurately gauge any of the varying periods that exist between two similar stunts, such as tossing a target with the right hand, then drawing a gun from holster with that same hand and hitting the target with the first shot. If one trial covers a time period of one and one-fifth seconds and the other requires three-fifths of a second, or any of the other periods of time possible between the two, both will quite generally appear to the **eye of the average person** as being of about equal duration.

Many tests conducted for determining several of these points were made at various times and places and were participated in by many persons, pupils, and spectators alike, and the results verified these conclusions on numerous occasions. The more experienced well-trained members of the shooting classes who had been studying such things for some time, backed by practical experience in the work, could often make reasonably close estimates, while the untrained ones had no conception whatever of the time periods.

The close-time estimating ability of the more experienced persons, who had been in close touch with timing activities, and had been attentive witnesses to many timed tests and experiments, can be accounted for by the results of our own research and investigation. Through close application and study, subconscious response can be built up in relation to certain sounds, signals, actions, and movements, in such a way that a certain sort of vibration is aroused, which is put into action within our nervous system, and registers the duration of certain impressions or sensations affecting our mental reactions in such a way that we have a very clear and lasting impression of certain things with which we have grown familiar by re-occurrence, or intentional repetition, even though of only momentary duration.

When we have many times watched and listened to a long continued series of trials, the time for each one of which, as soon as completed, has been impressed on our mind by being promptly announced, etc., we become highly sensative to the duration of the impressions on our two senses— sight and hearing—and through the workings of what we may here, for convenience, refer to as memory (meaning the medium that brings past experiences promptly to mind for comparison), we can easily recall some such similar experience, or perhaps we may even feel that it is an absolutely identical experience, of time sensation that was correctly measured as exactly one-half, three-fifths, or one second, as the case may have been. Thus, by frequent repetition of such experiences, and their accompanying reactions having been promptly and correctly timed, and the results made known to us at once while the sensation experienced in connection therewith was being actively impressed on our subconscious mind, we can learn to estimate time in fractions of seconds to a quite surprisingly close margin, due to the acute sense organs, eyes and ears having been trained to work together on the problem.

This above-outlined system of training, wherein the two very alert senses of sight and hearing are combined in concentrated and co-ordinated effort to register the effect of certain signals and sounds on our movements, and the effect certain movements have on our concentrated effort towards a definite goal, furnishes the foundation on which was developed the super-speed group shooting which, as shown by reproductions of witnessed targets, can very consistently be done in connection with the quick draw. The progress that was made which embodied the steady improvement in super-speed development not connected with the draw, with pretty regularly maintained accuracy, is also very much in evidence, equally well-verified and similarly illustrated, the time periods ranging from one and two-fifths seconds for five shots down to two-fifths of a second for the five shots with well-controlled bullet grouping.

Superspeed in either line, separated from or combined with quick-draw trials, must be developed by consistent training with some sort of dependable timing equipment—not by "haphazard" or "just guessing at it" methods. By comparing notes we can very easily determine that the old methods of figuring out speed of movement—at least, such as have been revealed to us—does not quite qualify with the later much more exact methods now in use. "Quicker than the untrained eye can follow" was not, and still is not, a very accurate or reliable method of measurement.

The training required in order to become proficient in estimating small periods of time correctly, as outlined here, would in all probability require a greater number of trials, tests, and experiments than all of the widely scattered quick-draw killings of the Old West combined. Who could possibly have been in a proper position at all of such happenings to correctly check up or correctly estimate the time factor that entered into the famous draws of "Ye Olden Days"? Who, at that time, had this actually necessary time demonstration training? Who had the suitable timing equipment? Who can actually give us the absolutely correct time of the Old Timers' fast draws to assist us in making comparisons with the correct timing that is now possible on the quick draws and various other superspeed revolver shooting stunts of today?

The romantic aspect of the "quick draw" still holds the attention of many shooters. The romantic interest of the younger generation, in this subject, no doubt growing out of the stories of the Early Day gunmen and the heroes of the Old West, is still very active. At this point we might be allowed to explain that fancy empty gun juggling and similar gun gymnastics do not constitute quick-draw proficiency, the all-important part of all quick-draw training—the firing of the shot and scoring a hit having been left out entirely.

It can, of course, be very clearly seen that actually hitting what you are supposed to be shooting at with the firing of the first shot is really the boiled-down essence of the whole quick-draw situation. The time in which this can be done is actually secondary in importance, and not first as usually considered. Speed without fairly consistent accuracy of control means nothing whatever as a life-saving agency to an officer engaged in a gun battle. Successfully combining both is the winning combination.

An amusing incident comes to mind here as an illustration of speed timing methods by observation and recounting from memory, no doubt slightly hazy at times. Most of us have heard, and many of us, including myself, have read several flattering accounts about Harvey Logan and several others. Perhaps it was written about many others also, depending on what hero the writer happens to admire the most. As the story goes about Logan he was so fast that he could hold a coin or poker chip, when it was handy, on his wrist, arm straight out from the shoulder, then by turning the wrist the coin would slide off and start for the floor or ground. Immediately upon the departure of the coin from the wrist the person doing the trick would get into action. As the report is handed out, he would draw a single-action revolver (note this carefully) from a holster and fire three, and quite often four, shots out of the gun by the time the coin or chip would hit the floor—as told by some it would be **before** the coin hit the floor. This was, no doubt, told in an attempt to accent speed and specify some certain amount of time in which the stunt could be done.

Another similar account of a speed artist that interested me was as follows: "He was facing a huge dead cottonwood. Low on his thighs were two Colts (presumably single-action) tied down. He would stand erect, place a silver dollar on the wrist of his outstretched right arm, then suddenly streak for his gun. His Colts would be empty before the dollar hit the ground, and then he would walk over to the cottonwood and see how his slugs were grouped. Time after time, patiently, doggedly, he did it, until it seemed to the man watching him that he was satisfied."

A little further diagnosis calls to our attention the following points: If a man is six feet tall and holds his hand out straight from his shoulder, the coin, when released, will drop from his shoulder to the ground or floor in a period of time of approximately two-fifths of a second. A careful study of the very fastest drawing time mentioned in these pages as probable for single-action guns being around three-tenths to one-half second, it will come in handy for comparison here. A coin will drop approximately sixteen feet a second. This should give us around one-third second for the coin's drop. Of course, the first part of the sixteen-foot drop should be the slowest part of the drop, thus two-fifths of a second is a reasonable allowance of time in this estimate. (See photo of electrically controlled drop meter, for timing falling objects, page 197.)

While the attraction force of gravity exerted on falling objects is generally regarded as constant, the effect of air resistance enters into the situation when dealing with light articles such as handkerchiefs and other light and bulky objects, but in the case of coins and similar material, the air resistance need not be considered. The closing detail that attention should now be directed to is the fact that this drawing and "superspeed" shooting, as outlined in the Logan and other performances, was supposed to be done with the single-action, or thumb-cocking, style of revolver, this also being the type of revolver more generally used in most of the other high speed performances handed down to us from the early days of the West, etc.

Accurately timed tests of the various methods of operating single-action revolvers for superspeed results are quite clearly explained, the time periods also given, and photos of results are shown in connection with full descriptions of such methods.

The outstanding fact of the matter is that there is no method known whereby any single-action revolver can be hand-operated at a speed of four shots in two-fifths of a second, which is a more simple task than making a quick draw and firing four shots in the two-fifths second period. We spent a great deal of time and used many thousands of cartridges in attempts to solve this and similar problems with single-action revolvers, having all sorts of special adjustments and favorable alterations and built-in timing attachments.

After forty years of experiment and study I finally was successful in firing five shots in two-fifths of a second, **without the draw,** from a Smith & Wesson .38 caliber double-action revolver, but, when this five shots in two-fifths of a second well-grouped on the target was first made public, and the well-supported detailed reports were submitted to our interested friends and the writers and shooting authorities, who, by the way, were also our very loyal supporters, it created a sort of attitude of uncertainty that at times bordered very closely on disbelief.

If we had not taken care to have the timing equipment and everything connected with the performance properly verified with signatures of the very reliable witnesses placed on the **original** dated target right at the time and place where it was done, as well as securing signed statements and photos of the witnesses to support the targets and published reports that appeared later in connection with such targets, we certainly would have been regarded as one well-defined bunch of liars. Yet our dear friends, the general public, very gladly and willingly accepts the unsupported statements such as the Logan draw and four-shot stunts, and many, in fact, almost any, similar statements or reports about such things that may be handed out to them, without ever questioning the reliability of the information, or even the possibility of such performances being successfully accomplished.

On this basis we make our comparison of the, no doubt, honestly intended timing attempts made by the observers who attempted to check up on the various movements mentioned in the Logan report, by the use of the eyes only, and a falling coin. Possibly the now very apparent error was due to the overzealousness of those who reported the performance, which might perhaps have been more liberally flavored with "hero worship" than with actual knowledge of gun mechanism and accurate time periods.

The figures that are involved give our hero approximately two-fifths of a second in which to complete his task—(and task it would be indeed). The draw would require at least three-tenths of a second; added to this would be the lowest single-action fanning time secured by my tests, which measured three-quarters second for the extra three shots after the original draw shot. The superspeed possibility checked accordingly gives slightly more than a second, or more than two and a half times the longest possible period of time the falling coin would be in the air. Fanning the hammer of a single-action revolver is the fastest possible method of firing the shots from such guns by hand. The shortest time periods are given elsewhere in detail under the heading, "Fanning."

When such reports as we are here discussing are coupled with the romantic characters of the Old West they are accepted as quite O. K. and beyond any reasonable doubt. This situation is, of course, a psychological problem that is very hard to explain. These are just a few of the peculiar angles we have had to contend with, and which will have to be dealt with in a fair and open manner during treatment of this subject. It is necessary to treat all of these things openly and present them as convincingly as possible, supported by the very reliable evidence we have at hand.

Reviewing Early Day Draws

Left—Left to right, Burt Bell, Joe McClintock, Mr. McGahey, Ed McGivern, on lawn of the Adams Memorial at Deadwood, South Dakota, August, 1932. Mr. McClintock is holding the author's modern S. & W. .38 double-action gun, with electric timer attachment connected with the timing machine resting on the table. Mr. McGahey is holding the Smith & Wesson gun originally belonging to Seth Bullock, Deadwood's first sheriff, which is now in the custody of the Adams Memorial. Mr. McGahey is the superintendent of the Memorial.

Burt Bell was the secretary and manager of the Days of '76, Deadwood's Frontier Days celebration.

Mr. McClintock is an old pioneer and was a stage driver during Wild Bill's time in Deadwood. He has a reputation for reliability and truthfulness in relation to all the happenings of early days in Deadwood of which he has unlimited first-hand information from actual contact and experience.

Right—The author standing by the statue of Wild Bill Hickok at Deadwood, South Dakota, August, 1932. This statue was generally credited with being a correctly proportioned and exact likeness of Wild Bill Hickok.

So long as we cannot secure absolutely accurate information regarding the time in which the star gun handlers of "Ye Olden Days" could do the draws and other fancy stunts, we must make for our own guidance such comparisons as above.

The 1934 performance of firing five shots from a double-action revolver in two-fifths of a second, the one with which the Logan and similar performances are being compared, has been quite generally established by very painstaking research as the fastest, correctly timed revolver shooting of which there is any properly supported evidence available, and, as mentioned, required years of research and experiment.

Fast and Fancy Revolver Shooting

INFORMATION ABOUT ONE OF WILD BILL'S GUNS.

Much has been written about Wild Bill's guns and if they could all be traced it would be proven that there must be, at least, fifty or more of them. During August, 1932, I visited Deadwood, South Dakota, in order to find out just how much information relative to his guns could be secured. One of his guns, a Smith & Wesson, is in possession of Mrs. Emil Willoth (née Hazel Fishel). This was the only gun we could locate during our visit, except the one taken from his casket.

An old-timer, Mr. Joe McClintock, has authentic information regarding Wild Bill, and was there at the time Bill was shot. He said that Bill was buried in the old cemetery in August, 1876, but was exhumed in August, 1879 (three years later), and buried where he now lies. A small gun, a "hide out," was reported as being found in the casket at the time, and is now in the Adams Memorial Hall at Deadwood. Bill's latest statue was erected in 1892. It was carved by James H. Riordan of New York. The first statue was destroyed by souvenir hunters.

Later correspondence produced the following information: "Mrs. Willoth has Wild Bill's gun sealed up in a case just as her husband left it when he died, and she won't allow it to be taken out." The gun was given to Mr. Willoth by Seth Bullock, Lawrence County's first sheriff. The number of the gun was not visible. There is another gun in the Adams Memorial Hall, loaned by Mrs. Lillian Casey, which was found buried with Wild Bill when his body was disinterred from the old cemetery and buried in Mt. Moriah. This gun is a "pepperbox" gun but Mr. McGahey could find no date on it, as it was rusted and corroded. It came into possession of Mr. Casey at the time.

Mr. McClintock is still living (Nov. 30, 1937). He was born January 15, 1847.

Wild Bill is generally credited with using two cap and ball Colt revolvers, but there does not seem to be any very accurate information available about just exactly how he carried his guns or just how he manipulated them. Of course there has been plenty of "chatter" but no definite proof. However, there can be little doubt about his proficiency with his pistols. He certainly could not have survived all of the gun battles chalked up to his credit if he had not been a more than average expert in the handling of his guns.

When killed in Deadwood it is reliably reported that he was wearing a large caliber Smith & Wesson revolver, which his close friend, Charlie Utter, took from his body and kept for his own use. (Page 11*)

* "Wild Bill Hickok" by Frank J. Wilstach. Doubleday, Page & Co. 1926.

Reviewing Early Day Draws

Mr. McGahey of the Adams Memorial at Deadwood, South Dakota, holding the Smith & Wesson gun formerly owned by Seth Bullock, Deadwood's first sheriff. This gun is exactly like the gun in the possession of Mrs. Emil Willoth (née Hazel Fishel).

The Willoth gun is quite generally established as being one of Wild Bill's guns, and all reports seem to support such claim quite convincingly.

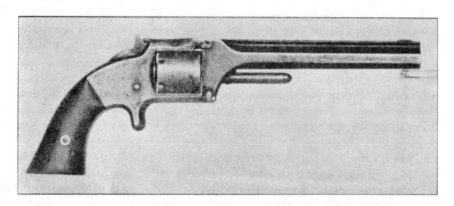

This is the same model of gun that is in possession of Mrs. Emil Willoth of Deadwood, South Dakota, which formerly belonged to Wild Bill Hickok—a Smith & Wesson Model No. 2. The hammer when it starts to raise releases the cylinder lock and the gun opens upwards; the cylinder is taken out and the shells are ejected by slipping the chambers over the pin extending along under the barrel. The cylinder is then loaded with new cartridges, and placed back in position; the gun is then closed and all is ready to go. The gun formerly owned by Seth Bullock in the Adams Memorial and the gun now owned by Mrs. Emil Willoth are the same type and model of Smith & Wesson rim fire single-action revolvers.

SECTION 19

MUTILATING GUNS AS AN AID TO SPEED. TARGET-SIGHTED REVOLVERS AS HOLSTER GUNS.

Having reached the point where aerial target shooting, superspeed double-action group shooting, hip shooting, quick-draw shooting, and combinations of the several types of such shooting have been covered, along with an outline of various two-gun combinations and training methods, the next section will contain recommendations for adapting the foregoing types of shooting to the training and use of law enforcement officers, whose very life, on many occasions, may depend on the perfect operation of his revolver, or one supplied him in an emergency by a brother officer. It seems quite important to make some definite statements, based on experience, regarding the mutilation of revolvers, with the idea, that by making such radical changes, much more speedy performance will be possible.

I am quite firm in the belief at this time that such mutilation is not as generally beneficial as some usually hastily arrived-at conclusions by some writers would seem to indicate, or at least would have a tendency to lead the readers to believe. One of the much featured and urgently recommended mutilations consists of cutting away the front part of the trigger guard, which is claimed by some to be a great help towards superspeed, and also an aid in doing away with fumbling on the draw. I do not wish to argue the point to any great length, but personally I unreservedly condemn it. I have not been able to find any sensible reason for having any such changes made in any of the guns used for such purposes. I have never experienced any trouble from the trigger guard interfering with fast movement, nor has it, in my experience, been the cause of fumbling the draws. After a reasonable amount of study, training and practice, all such trouble was also eliminated from the quick-draw performance of my pupils.

I have not, as yet, found it necessary to cut up, or otherwise mutilate the double-action guns in any way, in order to develop speed. I first developed the speed by persistent study and practice for developing hand and finger control, after which I found that the guns were not in need of alterations, and as a result I was able to successfully handle some eighty assorted, standard models of revolvers, just as issued from the factory, which had no alterations except sight adjustments suitable for the various programs of mixed performances listed later.

I do not weaken the mainsprings, or the trigger springs, change the weight of the hammers, or make any other alterations in the mechanism of any of these guns for any kind of fast work, for the simple reason that such changes are, more often than not, the cause of endless trouble with few, if any, advantages to offset the trouble so caused. I have never felt the need for such changes. Weakened mainsprings lead to misfires or hangfires, with a tendency toward slow and faulty ignition generally, all of which can be very dangerous in any kind of fast shooting.

When a gun fails to fire the cartridges properly, and the bullets, as a consequence fail to leave the gun and be placed somewhere on the target, the very fastest possible gun handling is just so much wasted effort. No matter how fast the gun may be operated it accomplishes nothing worth while if it does not fire the cartridges regularly, and it should be quite clear to anyone that if the cartridges are not fired regularly, the performance is nothing more than empty gun juggling. Fancy fluttering gestures with empty guns, while quite popular with some, have never been of any interest to me and I believe would be of little value to my readers, therefore I do not display any guns designed, weakened, butchered, or adjusted for such purposes, nor am I willing to support the false impression that anyone's practical shooting speed may require such drastic alterations. If such alterations were considered necessary or practical, the two leading revolver factories would undoubtedly be manufacturing the guns that way.

Attention is called to the fact that the Frontier model of single-action Colt guns were used for an amazing amount of life or death quick-draw work. It is well-known that these guns have a very small amount of room inside of the trigger guard, much less than the average double-action revolver has, yet very seldom did we hear of anyone cutting away the trigger guards on these guns. If a cut-away trigger guard should get bent upward only slightly, a thing that is very easily done without being noticed until too late, the gun is hopelessly out of commission for immediate use. If the first attempt to place the finger on the trigger, while drawing a regulation revolver, should not be entirely successful, the next slight move, only a very small fraction of a second later, will set it off O. K., but with the unexpectedly bent trigger guard the gun is out of the game altogether, and the owner would be, also, under certain conditions.

Another very important angle in relation to cut-away trigger guards, is the many chances of accidental discharge possible from various causes, such as when hurriedly putting the gun in a holster, pocket, or other similar receptacle, the probability being that such accidents may and can happen, in all sorts of unexpected places, and under all sorts of unexpected conditions. It is my honest opinion that the protection of the trigger guard on double-action guns is worth very much more to anyone than any advantage, real or imaginary, that can come from mutilating it by cutting it off for any purpose whatever. Enlarging the forward part of the trigger guard, which was done as an experiment only, on one of my guns, to accommodate unusually long or larger trigger fingers, is, in my opinion, based on my experience, a much more sensible alteration than cutting it away. The alteration on this particular revolver, as pictured, was done by Mr. W. A. Sukalle, of Phoenix, Arizona, who is an excellent workman (page 311).

To avoid all such annoyances as mentioned, I use the standard double-action revolvers, both Colt and Smith & Wesson, just as they are sent out by the factory for distribution to the retail trade. I do not try to improve on the work of the factory experts in whose hands the guns have been properly assembled, adjusted, and inspected. I used one such gun, a .38 M & P., Smith & Wesson No. 286600, steadily and regularly for more than eight years without experiencing any failures, and without making any repairs. Col. Douglas B. Wesson now has this revolver, still in its original condition, just as I presented it to him some time ago. As a result of this attitude toward guns, I have never had trouble with misfires, hangfires or balks of any kind, when using any of the standard factory loaded cartridges.

Some of my special single-action guns herein illustrated have been adjusted and altered somewhat by the late J. D. O'Meara, of Lead, South Dakota, who was an expert, and a very fine workman. He certainly could and did fit them properly for the particular kind of shooting for which they were to be used. I had very good reason for having this work done, as pictures and descriptive matter explain. For these single-action guns the holsters were also properly fitted so that the target sights did not bind or drag on the leather or interfere in any way.

I do not, and cannot, view with favor the weakening of any functioning part of a revolver with the idea of gaining speed. Steady practice and exercise will train and strengthen your hands so that your movements may be properly controlled and sure and positive in results. Altering the double-action guns to any great extent will then be found quite unnecessary.

For years I have been deluged with arguments and discussions, between the careful holding, very deliberate target shooters, on one side, and the somewhat faster and generally referred to as "practical shooters" on the other side. Here we find the so-called practical (or defense) shooters poking fun at the slower, deliberate fire, close grouping target shots, and, in their turn, the deliberate fire enthusiasts poke fun at the "Slam! Bang!" crowd, as they sometimes like to call those generally referred to as the "practical shooters."

There is really no sensible reason for this attitude, for, actually, the better performers on either side are not so widely separated. One style of shooting is just as important as the other, and each has its own very valuable place in that particular field of endeavor where it is needed to secure the desired result. Personally, I find, after being active in the game for some time, that all of it is very interesting, and I admire the leaders in each class of pistol and revolver shooting.

My candid opinion, formed as the result of such experience, is that all revolver shooters would profit materially if they would try to be a little more broad-minded, and study the whys and wherefores of the different branches of the game. They should strive to become reasonably proficient in each branch, even though still slightly favoring their own "preferred brand" as being the most important. Several of our more brilliant revolver shooting stars have done just that, and have been very well-pleased with the result of their efforts. Dr. F. R. Calkins of Springfield, Massachusetts, is an outstanding example of such conduct. It is well-known that he is considered one of the finest pistol and revolver shots in the world and is one of the very few champions in any line who has retained his standing for over thirty consecutive years.

Some of our friends among the "practical shots" have apparently created a false impression by seeming to favor a complete remodeling of all revolvers for defensive purposes. Some have treated their guns to a very thorough overhauling, with such crude tools at times as a hacksaw, a pipe wrench, and a good coarse rasp, until those same guns are mutilated beyond any possible recognition as to their original form, and are practically useless for anything but the empty gun gymnastics mentioned. This practice was, and still is, responsible for more or less severe criticism. Personally, I have never felt the need for any such vicious and misguided alterations.

Acting on this same advice which I so freely pass out to others, I assigned to myself the very interesting task, which later I found was also a very agreeable one, of combining much of the superaccuracy possible with standard, as issued (in no way changed), target revolvers with the much talked-of "practical speed," some of which I seemed to have developed. The object was, of course, to get as much uniform "sure hit" results as plenty of practice, combined with a close study of the subject, would develop, while using standard target-sighted revolvers.

As the work progressed, the results obtained became increasingly satisfactory. I found that I was combining speed and accuracy sufficiently to score hits on moving objects in rapid succession, as well as small groups on stationary targets. It didn't seem so difficult after all. Combining the technique of the stationary target shooter with that of the flying target shooter resulted in some ultra-rapid fire bullet grouping on small stationary targets, which was pleasantly surprising, and the shortness of the time required to make these groups was also surprising. Once accustomed to the target shooter's tools, I saw no good reason for making radical changes, a fact which explains in a measure just why target revolvers were used for all of the fastest work, and for the quick draw. I use exactly the same kind of guns for speed work that are used for slow, deliberate target shooting.

The formerly somewhat commonly held opinion that a very fast draw with a sure hit shot, or a fast draw and five sure hits after the draw, could not be done with fully target-sighted revolvers, is erroneous, as we have quite clearly proven. In our experience this idea seems to be somewhat permanently offset by the results obtained with standard target arms and properly fitted holsters, several photos of which are herewith submitted. I take the liberty to express an opinion that these results will not suffer by, or in, comparison with the results obtained by use of the quite widely written-up type of specially remodeled guns, that have been worked over under the label of—"for defense purposes."

Remember, the first and most important thing in all revolver shooting is to be able to score hits. It is not a good idea to try to do fancy stunts before one can do accurate shooting in the regulation way. **This qualification is very necessary indeed.** Mutilating guns will not aid anyone in becoming more proficient. Your own speed and proficiency cannot be built into guns by eccentric alterations of any kind. Such things must be built up and developed within yourself by study and practice. When anyone has mastered the fundamental principles of the speed movements, his progress is assured and the ability to score hits will very soon become an actual realization, instead of a theory or a dream.

The writer feels (and, I believe is justified) that it would be a very interesting fact to **know definitely** as determined by **correctly timed tests,** instead of **just theoretically,** as it very generally stands at the present time, just how many hundredths, or even thousandths, of a second can be **actually saved** by an expert performer, as well as by various other persons not so expert, who may favor the abbreviated trigger guard, during the performance of a quick draw or other quick gun producing method, from any favored position, and from any favored holster, pocket or other receptacle, coupled with the firing of one **sure hit shot,** using any of the various factory loaded cartridges, in any of the .38 Special caliber double-action revolvers or .45 caliber revolvers, if preferred, having a cut-away trigger guard. Also the actual saving for the same sort of draw, etc., followed by five **sure hit shots** at the highest speed that the expert and various other persons are capable of, the determining comparisons to consist of the same sort of **correctly timed** performances by the same experts and other persons, whoever they may be, while using regulation, factory issued, revolvers of the same weight and exact dimensions in every way, with the one exception—that the regulation trigger guard is not to be altered or molested in any way whatever.

During such trials conducted by the writer with the remodeled—by W. A. Sukalee—.45 Smith & Wesson revolver (as shown in the several

Mutilating Guns

Cutaway Trigger Guards

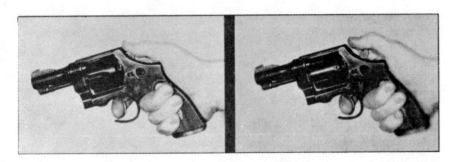

Left—To shoot the above type of remodeled guns, it is necessary as a safety measure to hold thumb back of hammer to avoid accidental discharge when cocking the gun for firing a carefully aimed and deliberate shot at a target or other object, by the single-action method.

Right—When starting hammer back hold thumb over firing pin for safety.

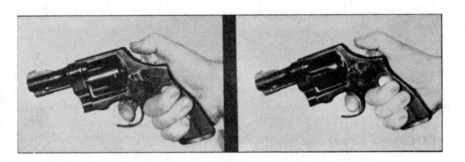

Left—When halfway back the thumb gradually slides to left and —

Right—When full cock position is reached the thumb is twisted to left.

photos), which is an exceptionally fine and smooth working gun for the purpose, there was no consistent saving of time on the first shot, over a series of trials made in comparison with the standard, in every way, similar gun, belonging to the writer. But, when trying for top speed performance for five fast shots with close grouping of bullets, there was a sort of annoying balk often occurring at the end of the forward trigger move-

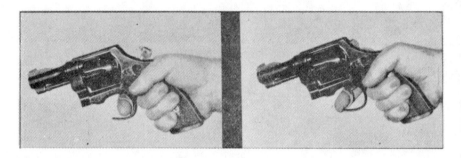

Left—Thumb is back in place ready to fire shot.   Thumb can also be held high on frame if desired.

Right—But, when attempting to deliver a fast string of shots the trigger finger can easily become caught on the forward end of any cutaway and shortened trigger guard, thereby balking the shooter in his attempt to quickly double-action the gun and get the next shot away.   There are more dangerous angles and probable delays, often causing complete failure to operate, connected with cutaway trigger guards than when original trigger guard is left unchanged.   Such at least is the opinion of the author after various experiments and experiences with several guns which underwent alterations, such as are on the gun above shown. The alterations and special features were handled by W. A. Sukalle of 1120 East Washington St., Phœnix, Arizona, and show very fine workmanship.

ment (as shown in photo) which was slightly detrimental to the superspeed group shooting time, for the several shots following the draw. In these instances the mutilated guard seemed more of a hindrance than a help, and which, as I wish to call attention to, would be entirely absent when using normal trigger guards.

Of course, in the opinion of some, I may have been slightly handicapped by being so situated that I could not supervise or take part in any experimental man killing to satisfy the more serious minded. I was compelled to rely on inanimate targets only for my experiments (in this case) from which to draw my conclusions, but, which I might add, were very satisfactory to me. I also wish to add that when I find any sensible alteration which is really an improvement, not simply a theoretical change, that will even in the slightest way add to or improve efficiency, develop more skill,

Mutilating Guns

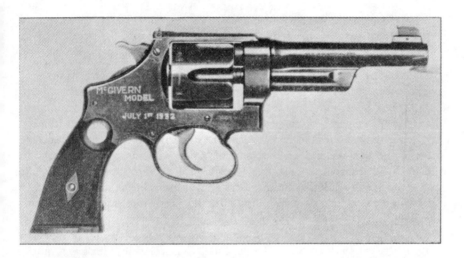

A somewhat sensible trigger guard alteration suggested by the author instead of the more dangerous cutaway type. This provides more room for trigger finger if it is absolutely necessary for certain peculiarities in the proportions of certain hands. This alteration was done specially for the author by Mr. Sukalle as formerly stated, and not by the factory.

or cause time-saving movements to be more effective, I will be among the first, and the most insistent, to demand it incorporated in my equipment. It will be necessary, of course — always — that it stand up and maintain its claimed-for merit, under actual tests, under the specified conditions where the advantages are supposed to be evident.

On this basis I am still enjoying the personal privileges of successfully using closed trigger guards, and I very cheerfully extend the same privilege regarding cut-away trigger guards to other persons who, for some reason (real or imaginary), may prefer them. The remarks contained in this discussion are not in any way directed at, or intended for, any particular person or persons. They simply consist of a summing up of conclusions and candid opinions, based on experiment, trial, and experience, and passed on for the benefit of others.

SECTION 20

TRAINING LAW ENFORCEMENT OFFICERS. PRACTICAL REVOLVER SHOOTING APPLIED TO POLICE TRAINING.

What can be more important to any community, city, state, or government organization than proper training for law enforcement officers? Who could have more urgent need for actual and practical training in fast, sure hitting, effective revolver shooting than our police and kindred law enforcement officers? Who are more deserving of and should receive more consideration and encouragement along such lines than our police officers? Do they, as a general rule, get it? I'll say not. Are they, as a rule, given any post-graduate training under conditions that are in any way similar to the actual conditions that usually arise, and under which their shooting must be done, when it is done? This is a very important question that is deserving of much consideration. How in the name of common sense can any officer be expected to develop into an alert, quick-draw, rapid fire, sure hit, dead center shot, and bandit exterminator, under all conditions of excitement, surprise, traffic jams, and danger to himself, if he is forced to conduct his training under conditions that never did and never will arise, or are never in evidence, and could not exist at or during any of the actual happenings where his services of such an order may be required, when called on in line of duty to use his gun in protection of life and property?

In a tight spot, under pressure of excitement, heavily weighted with danger, the subconscious mind is the only power that man possesses that can pull him through and help him to fill all the above qualifications; and it is for assisting in the development of subconscious control that the training methods, as are herein contained, have been offered.

While I very earnestly endorse all forms of careful and deliberate regulation target shooting, and firmly believe that all officers should receive such training, I am still more firmly convinced that such training in itself is not sufficient for their practical needs. Under actual conditions of combat which may require the use of guns in thickly settled districts, where the police and other officers are usually required to do such shooting, or die as a result of lack of ability to do it, the necessity for post-graduate training in fast, sure hitting, and positive gun handling performance, to place the officer on an equal footing with the criminal, is readily apparent. There can be no question about such training being absolutely necessary under the conditions that confront our officers.

Such training will pay good dividends on the necessary investment of time and expense required for it, in the way of added efficiency of the of-

Training Law Officers

Shooting While Running

This shooting-while-running training for law officers has been referred to in discouraging terms by many persons who should have known better, and in all probability would have known better if some effort had been made to work out the problems involved, and overcome the difficulties which were so much magnified in their own imagination in connection therewith. Like many of the surprisingly successful results secured by persistent effort on aerial targets and other generally considered unusual revolver shooting combinations, the most important thing needed in connection with the shooting-while-running situation was a liberal application of common sense, persistent effort, study and repeated trial and error experiments, with plenty of determination to make necessary corrections and force "Lady Luck," or success, as the case may be, to at least grin a little on such efforts, even if at first you cannot draw a particularly brilliant full face smile.

Experience in developing and promoting this sort of shooting seems to indicate that a right-handed shooter usually has more uniform success with his shots if delivered while his left foot is down and the right foot is either just leaving or entirely off of the ground. Left-handed shooters would, of course, usually need to reverse this rule. More extensive training seems to show that the shots can be successfully controlled when fired while the feet are in almost any position, as evident in the photos of Mr. Anderson in action. Continued practice seems to develop a body balance that can be maintained while entirely disregarding the probable effect of the foot movement. This condition appears to have been a later and natural development in most of the pupils who continued their practice for any prolonged period of time.

The fact should not be overlooked that in the development of this and similar types of shooting the double-action method of operating the revolvers has been made use of exclusively.

SHOOTING WHILE RUNNING

Officer Ben Anderson shooting while right foot is down. The bull's-eye can be hit quite regularly. Note bullet striking behind the target after having passed through the bull's-eye.

ficers and respect for law and the officers of the law in general, and the known well-trained officers in particular. This has been well-demonstrated within the last three years, during which the super-organized and thoroughly equipped criminal gangs have been either killed off, or so widely scattered as to be practically wiped out. Such results were not and could not have been accomplished by depending solely on the majesty of the law, while continuing the petting and coddling methods for criminals that were in use for several years before the more effective system was adopted and put to work.

This is where the early Western marshals and sheriffs were supreme. They worked among, and became familiar with, the exact conditions that would exist at the time that they would be called upon and it became necessary for them to "strut their stuff." At such times, due to "their familiarity with their subject," they were perfectly "at home," usually very cool, collected, and masters of the situation, through such familiarity and the knowledge gained from such first-hand experience. As the old familiar expression at that time put it, "After the smoke cleared away" there were only two kinds of gun fighters, "The Quick and the Dead." The quick went down in history—the dead went down in "Boot Hill," and history shows that the lawmen held up their end of the argument to an amazing extent as a result of practical experience.

The story today still reads much the same. As Captain Ed. Langrish of the Hartford (Conn.) police force—originator of the Langrish police target—put it, a short time ago, "a police officer these days is about the same as a clay pigeon, liable to be shot to pieces at any minute, and, like the monotonous call at the clay pigeon tournaments, he is usually scored 'Dead.'" One of the reasons is that he is usually working alone, individually, against gangs and gang warfare, for which he is very seldom in any very great way prepared. He very often lacks proper equipment, proper support, liberty of action, or freedom of movement, and is not, as a general rule, trained to act in an executive capacity. Much of this is due to too much meddling, uplifting, reforming, sentimentalism, and **political red tape.**

Most bandits have bullet-proof vests, machine guns, plenty of ammunition, and co-operation. The officer, usually, has no such equipment at hand on the instant. Scarcity of ammunition is usually a condition existing in such situations also. Through too many modern regulations co-operation is not so plentiful, as a rule; also many conflicting regulations for public safety often cause restraint in plenty to delay his action.

It is, and always has been, the writer's candid belief that a properly coached, instructed, and rightly developed crew of **one hundred officers,** trained in fast, sure hitting stunts with revolvers, with **proper equipment** and methods, and who were loyal and dependable to their instructors and

SHOOTING WHILE RUNNING

Officer Ben Anderson running crossways, shooting while right foot is down.

SHOOTING WHILE RUNNING

Officer Ben Anderson running crossways, shooting while left foot is down.

leaders, with plenty of ammunition, and full authority to act and remain active, and would stay on the job until finished, could and would clean out all the bold, bad bandits and bad actors in any of the big cities in a very short time.

This couldn't and **can't** be done by men whose loyalty is divided or who will double-cross each other for gain. But it can be done by selection for absolute loyalty, and the proper systematic training and development of each individual, and thus eventually be incorporated into a superefficient, practically unbeatable, whole.

One of the greatest, if not the greatest, weapon that can be employed against the criminal or ganged-up tough element, would also, through this system, take form and be put into effective use against such element, and that is and ever has been **fear,** the "yellow streak," which all records show, with very few and widely scattered exceptions, has ever and always been much in evidence when the grand and final showdown takes place, contrary to the hero worshiping, romantic chatter of sensational news writers.

Mob psychology—gang psychology, that lives and thrives on a spirit of fear created by co-operation and united effort on the wrong side of the law, would be, could be, and should be created on the right side of the law more effectively and with better results even than among the so-called underworld. This underworld cannot exist, live and operate without support of the so-called and generally considered upper world. That is an often proven fact. Like the weather again, many people talk very much about it, but very little has been done to change or control it.

The feeble efforts generally made against these crime outbreaks in the past were somewhat like a boil on one's neck. A little salve was usually applied and then passive waiting until something "busted," then a great excitement of planning and chatter, and again things settled down. Attention directed towards balancing the budget, cutting salaries, saving cartridges, issuing new rules, and again it happens—**BANG !** then what? The cost of one major crime, in special service (after the crime), special agents, investigators, detectives, under-cover men, etc., with the usual failure of prosecution and conviction, cost the people, through the various departments of the communities, more actual cash, to say nothing about wasted effort, than all the officers in all the big cities, and most of the smaller ones of the entire country, would require for the highest priced instructors and the most intensive training and equipment necessary for developing them, through the shooting classes and other methods of practical instruction, from which they could and would very shortly graduate into experts so proficient that none of the organized gangs could exist in the same section of the country.

These facts have been supported and well-proven in plenty, by the

Training Law Officers

SHOOTING WHILE RUNNING

Officer Ben Anderson shooting first shot with left foot down. Next shot when right foot comes down. 2 shots. Note where they strike back of target. Both well placed hits.

SHOOTING WHILE RUNNING

Left—Officer Ben Anderson running towards target; shot fired while right foot is down. Well placed hit.

Right—Officer Ben Anderson running forward, shooting, while left foot is down. Well placed hit.

history of Montana, and of California, and their vigilantes, and of every frontier or crime-infested district, that were finally aroused to wipe out the criminal element. Crooks of every nature must have support and protection from some source in any community or any country, otherwise they could not exist and operate. If the officers get a little more or even an equal amount of support, financially and otherwise, and the opportunity to develop themselves, the crooks will have to "hit the trail" today just as in every other day, and all through Western history.

Quoting from Emerson Hough, "The Story of the Outlaw": "Each of us knows, or ought to know, that the cities which would select twenty Western peace officers of the old type and set them to work without restrictions as to the size of their imminent graveyards, would free themselves of criminals in three months' time, and would remain free so long as its methods remained in force."

The latest developments in support of the correctness of these statements come from the successful activities of J. Edgar Hoover's organization, generally known as the **G-Men** of The Federal Bureau of Investigation of Washington, D. C., which will be later mentioned with more detail.

Some persons, under the mistaken impression that they are intellectual giants (?), think all of these things can and should be remedied by passing a few more **new** laws. The great American pastime, since prohibition,—the biggest joke ever wished on any nation, was forced on the American people and made it possible to "High Finance" organized crime,—has been to pass laws and also "pass the buck," but the crime situation was still with us, and required something more than either warrants or new statutes and ordinances with which to gag the criminal and obstruct his progress, said criminal having been assisted at times by the very ones who were instrumental in passing, and then hiding behind, such statutes and ordinances (which is also a matter of history), and which, in many cases, have been just a blind, and a new form of "passing the buck." In the meantime our officers were being killed off, two or three every day or so, martyrs to a system of too much politics and "fixers," under the guise of reformers and public service improvement associations.

In some localities if an officer is called in and is forced to kill a criminal, the "book of rules" is called into service and he is very liable to be called on the carpet and severely reprimanded, criticized, penalized, or, as in some recent cases on record, he is prosecuted. Under some sort of sentimental activity, and political propaganda, through and as a result of such conditions, the criminal has had all the best of the deal until after he has been duly tried and convicted beyond appeal to higher and still higher courts. Here is where the criminal lawyer, or more correctly speaking in some cases, the lawyer criminal, usually plays his trumps.

The general public and the public officials must be made to realize

FIVE POSITION TRAINING
Fall to prone position, fire first shot from "on stomach" position (1).

FIVE POSITION TRAINING
Fire second shot from "on right shoulder" position (2).

that what the officers need is proper scientific training in **practical warfare against crime** methods, and the expert handling of such equipment. The most important thing of all that the officers and police departments generally need, and **must have** if they are to be expected to combat crime conditions, is **financial assistance** and backing, to put these training programs over properly, as well as the co-operation and support of the public.

There is no valid excuse for not giving such training to the members of police organizations throughout the country, for the very sufficient reason that there are plenty of men qualified and willing, in exchange for **reasonable compensation,** to devote their time and talents to such training of the officers. There are at present several police departments who are getting fairly well-equipped for such training courses, and the merits of such training are being well-demonstrated by actual and effective results, and a decided scattering in such communities of the bold, bad ganged-up criminals and the crooked law sharks and hangers-on, who help control and protect such things. When the order goes out to shoot to kill, and it is **known** that such officers can and will, if necessity demands, obey the order, it certainly does make a difference, and quickly changes the whole situation.

When a game hunting expedition for various animals, dangerous or otherwise, is being organized, great care is taken to secure the most suitable type of equipment, with an ample supply of the most modern and effective guns and cartridges for the purpose, but when our law officers are sent out, sometimes single-handed, to subdue and bring in either one or perhaps several of the most desperate characters, with established reputations for tough resistance, the fact is quite generally overlooked that the most dangerous animal on earth to hunt is man. When he is pursued and closely crowded and confronted with the realization that danger threatens either his life or his liberty, he can and quite generally does become the most cunning, the most dangerous, and the most resourceful animal that exists in the world, and, as has been so very many times quite convincingly proven when he turns criminal, he is not so easily stopped.

The officer whose duty it may become to engage in this sort of hunt should be well supplied with the very best equipment and weapons available for his purpose, and he should also be trained by the latest practical methods, right up to the last little detail that will develop his skill sufficiently to deal with all situations that may unexpectedly arise in the quickest and most efficient manner, when he is forced to take the trail for such purpose.

Consideration of the various angles that might enter into such situations is what started the writer figuring out these different shooting stunts for law enforcement officers herein outlined and demonstrated. Having made notes and observations from the reports of many gun battles between officers and persons on the opposite side of the law, the evidence seemed

FIVE POSITION TRAINING
Fire third shot from "on back" position (3).

FIVE POSITION TRAINING
Fire fourth shot from "on left shoulder" position (4).

to show that the majority of such affairs occur at distances that are less than thirty-five feet, and very many of them under fifteen feet, consequently the greater part of the training methods for developing speed and proficiency in the many slightly out-of-the-ordinary shooting situations, as outlined, have been worked out at varying distances from fifteen to forty-five feet, which should qualify a man who is reasonably expert at these ranges, to be successful even if he should be forced by necessity to reach out a little farther.

This training is originally started with shooter placed at a distance of fifteen feet from targets. As progress develops they are moved back gradually until working at distances from 35 to 45 feet. The fifteen-yard distance is very satisfactory for general results.

ONE OF THE MORE EXTENDED AND FAVORED SHOOTING PROGRAMS OF THE LEWISTOWN POLICE DEPARTMENT UNDER SUPERVISION OF ED McGIVERN

All members of department to participate in shoot. Follow assignment closely, assist in routine, and pay particular attention to instructor.

DISTANCE

(35)   1st. Shoot double action, slow, 35 feet, five shots.

(35)   2nd. Shoot double action, both hands, alternate, five shots from each gun, total ten shots, 35 feet.

(25)   3rd. Stand with back to target, turn and shoot five shots double action, 25 feet.

(18–35) 4th. Draw and step forward away from target, turn and shoot one shot each time. Keep back turned to target while stepping away from it. Draw for each shot, 18 to 35 feet.

(35)   5th. Room dark, shoot double action, hold flashlight with left hand away from body for safety from opponent's shot, shoot five shots, 35 feet.

(25–35) 6th. Shoot double action, shoot with flashlights directed against eyes of shooter, room dark, distance 25 to 35 feet (facing automobile). Hold flashlight as in No. 5, to locate target.

(25–35) 7th. Shoot double action, room dark, one flash of light for first shot only, other four shots to be fired in total darkness. Use bull's-eye on Langrish target.

(35)   8th. Shoot double action, draw and shoot one shot only each time, firing a total of five shots, distance 35 feet. Draw for each shot. Use head sized target only.

(25–35) 9th. Shoot double action, quick draw and fire five shots each time, distance 25 to 35 feet. Use head sized targets.

(35)   10th. Shoot double action, fall to prone position, shoot five shots, 35 feet. Use head sized targets. Change position of body each shot.

(45)   11th. Shoot double action, run and shoot while running towards target, five shots, starting distance 45 feet, finish at 15 feet from target. Use bull's-eye on chest of upper man size Langrish limbless targets.

Training Law Officers

FIVE POSITION TRAINING

Fire fifth shot from "on stomach" position (5) after changing gun to other hand; training in case of injury.

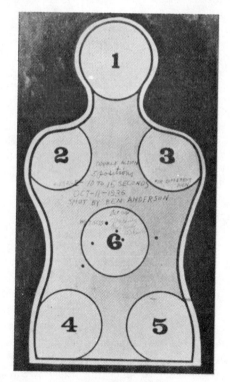

FIVE POSITION TRAINING

Showing the group of shots resulting from the five positions, prone, as shot by Officer Ben Anderson during the demonstration of which the accompanying photographs were made

Fast and Fancy Revolver Shooting

(45) 12th. Shoot double action, running toward man from 45 feet, shoot five shots with left hand while running. (Reverse hands if left handed.)

(20–35) 13th. Shoot double action, run 40 feet crossways, shoot five shots at man target standing in doorway, while running past the opening from right to left, at distance of 20 to 35 feet or more from opening.

(20–35) 14th. Shoot double action, run 40 feet across front of opening of hall or doorway, fire five shots while running from left to right, at distance of 20 to 35 feet or more from opening.

(45) 15th. Run or walk rapidly from 45 feet distance toward Langrish man target, supporting wounded officer with left arm. Shoot five shots double action with free hand.

(45) 16th. Two officers, starting at 45 feet, run or walk rapidly toward Langrish man target, supporting each other with arms locked, each officer shooting five shots double action with gun held in the free hand.

(25–35) 17th. Shooting five shots from each of two guns at same time, double action, both fired simultaneously, total ten shots, distance 25 to 35 feet.

(15–45) 18th. Start at 15 feet, take brother officer's gun (two guns), shoot five shots double action alternately from each gun, while retreating one step backwards between each shot fired, covering wounded officer's retreat.

(15–20–25) 19th. When instructor fires blank cartridge, officer draws gun, fires one shot double action, at head size bull's-eye on chest of Langrish target. Object of this test to develop speed on draw and first shot. Try for—sure hits and split second draws.

(20–25–35) 20th. Draw gun five times, fire one shot double action each time, in response to various surprise or unexpected signals. Use head size bull's-eye on chest of Langrish target at distance of 20 to 35 feet.

With this system of training an officer's quick-draw shooting can be improved and developed so that with a target placed fifteen feet from the shooter a smooth and reasonably sure hit draw can be completed in a period of time bordering closely around 3/5 second to 9/10 second, as shown by the outcome of tests conducted some time ago with the co-operation of several of the officers during one of the police classes. Seldom on this occasion did the completed draw require a full second for the men who had regular training. Only a few instances exceeded a second.

An average shooter, if he has some natural talent along this line, should be able, by persistent practice, to learn to draw a gun from a correctly adjusted holster, constructed to suit him, and score a hit with the first shot in a period of time hovering around the 1/2 second mark. Steady practice combined with close study is undoubtedly the key to success.

Training Law Officers

Officer Ben Anderson demonstrating two-gun training for police.

Training police in aerial target shooting develops speed combined with accuracy. Officer Ben Anderson demonstrating.

Fast and Fancy Revolver Shooting

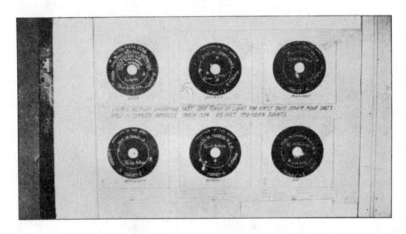

SHOOTING IN THE DARK

SHOOTING IN THE DARK

One flash of light for the first shot only, the next four fired in complete darkness. All shooting double action. (25 feet)

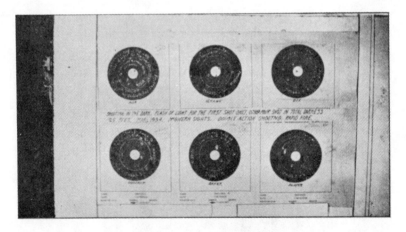

SHOOTING IN THE DARK

One flash of light for the first shot only, the next four fired in complete darkness. All shooting double action. (25 feet) This ability is developed by hip shooting and other forms of practice that make it possible to keep gun pointed by the "feel" of the gun in the hand. March, 1934.

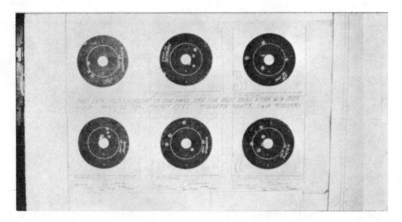

Shooting with aid of flashlight only, no other illumination. (30 feet)

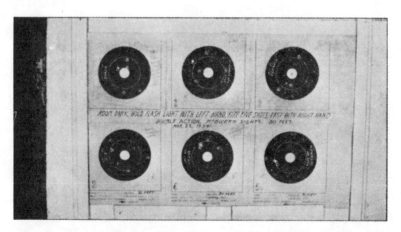

Shooting with aid of flashlight only, no other illumination. (30 feet)

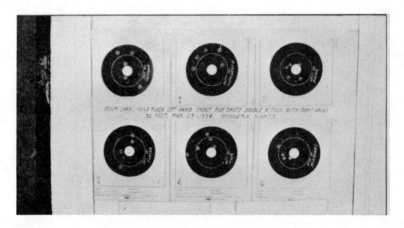

SHOOTING WITH AID OF FLASHLIGHT ONLY

Flashlight held off to one side of the officer, using the gun with the other hand.   (30 feet)

SHOOTING WITH AID OF FLASHLIGHT ONLY

Flashlight held off to the side and away from officer's body for safety measures, while shooting with the gun in the other hand.   (30 feet)

Training Law Officers

TEAR GAS

Mr. Frank J. Fisher representing Federal Laboratories, Inc., Pittsburgh, Pennsylvania, demonstrating to the Lewistown Police Force the effectiveness of his company's tear gas billy, under the supervision of the police instructor who happens in this case to be the author, and who can very highly recommend this equipment. This company manufactures and distributes a full line of gas-handling equipment, Thompson machine guns, bullet-proof vests, steel police shields, armored cars with bullet-proof glass, night flares and about everything that law enforcement officers require for protection and for combating criminal activities.

FIREARMS INSTRUCTION FOR BOY SCOUTS

Ed McGivern instructing Boy Scouts in the use and care of firearms at Annual Scout Camp, June 12, 1935. Not one of these boys has since had a firearms accident.

Fast and Fancy Revolver Shooting

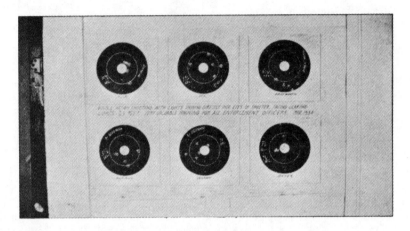

FACING GLARING LIGHTS

Double-action shooting. Officer aided by beam of own flashlight for locating target or driver of car and directing the shots. March, 1934. (25 feet)

Like the shooting-while-running arguments, based mostly on an imaginary basis, the difficulty of successfully teaching officers to face glaring lights and still hit things about where they intend to, and where it should produce the most desirable results, seems to have been based mostly on theory. Determined effort, based on our old friend, the trial and error method, soon produced results in our experiments that were not only flavored with success, but also with many surprises.

The secret of success seems to be more dependent on penetrating the glare in an opposite direction with the rays of a good flashlight. Even the average common variety pocket flash usually gives pretty good results when directed towards the target which is usually supposed to represent the driver of the car whose lights the officers are facing.

For training purposes the large reflector type of flashlights can be used. The glare from two of these, placed in similar position to car lights, are directed into the shooter's eyes. He then directs the light rays of his own pocket flashlight, over and above the headlight glare, and locates the spot or target where he intends placing his shots.

Results here submitted, secured by these methods, have surely provided enough encouragement for further study and experiment along these lines for the benefit of our officers in general.

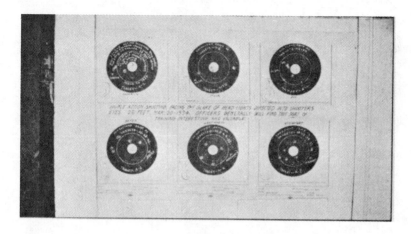

FACING GLARING LIGHTS

Double-action shooting. Officer aided by beam of own flashlight for locating target or driver of car and directing the shots. March, 1934. (25 feet)

FACING GLARING LIGHTS

Double-action shooting. Officer aided by beam of own flashlight for locating target or driver of car and directing the shots. March, 1934. (25 feet)

POLICE TRAINING IN TWO-GUN SHOOTING

Officers Baker, Slater, Dix, Muir, Vehawn, Wentworth. Revolver in each hand shot alternately, one hand, then the other, one shot each time changing quickly, firing rapidly, all shots fired double action. March 20, 1934.

SHOOTING WHILE RUNNING

Officer runs about 35 feet, usually passing 15 feet in front of target, shooting double action. 1934.

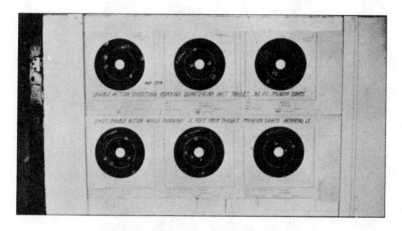

SHOOTING WHILE RUNNING

Officer runs about 35 feet, usually passing 15 feet in front of target, shooting double action. 1934.

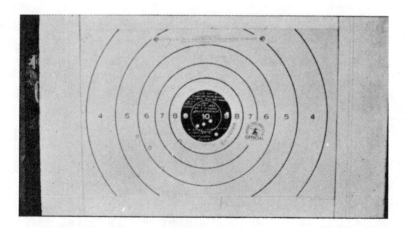

SHOOTING WHILE RUNNING

This target shot by T. Frank Baughmann, special agent of the F. B. I. at Washington, under supervision of the author, Dec. 8, 1936. Running past target. (18 feet)

Courtesy of J. Edgar Hoover, director of Federal Bureau of Investigation, Department of Justice.

Fast and Fancy Revolver Shooting

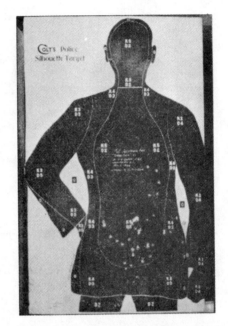

Full automatic fire with Thompson machine gun by W. A. Glavin, special agent, F. B. I. Dec. 3, 1936. Witnessed by the author.

Courtesy of J. Edgar Hoover, director of Federal Bureau of Investigation, Department of Justice. Note five-shot group on chest.

SHOOTING WHILE RUNNING

Target Shot by McGivern While Running from Right to Left

In 1932, '33 and '34, the results secured by police classes very convincingly demonstrated the practical value of training officers to be able to shoot while running, and consistently hit what they were shooting at. The target here submitted was shot by the author in 1934 for a practical demonstration before a group of visiting Montana officers. This target has a five and one-half inch bull's-eye with a one-inch white center, which seems to be of value in this sort of training.

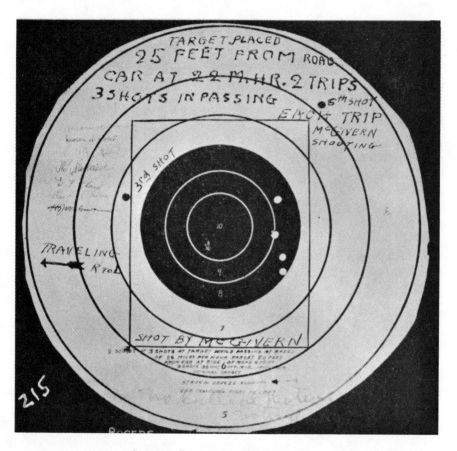

SHOOTING REVOLVERS FROM AUTOMOBILE
Early experiments by McGivern demonstrating shooting from automobile
Courtesy *Outdoor Life*

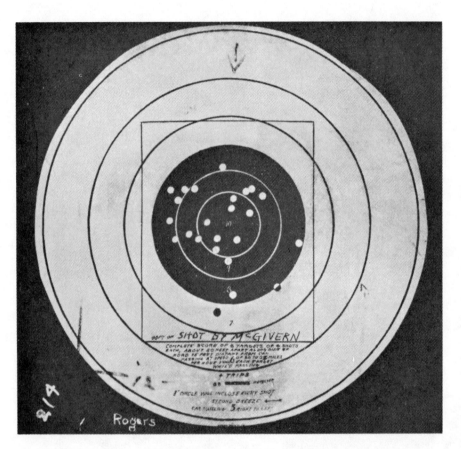

EARLY EXPERIMENTS, SHOOTING FROM AUTOMOBILE
Six targets placed at side of road 15 feet from passing car. One shot at each target, each trip, 4 trips, making 4 shots on each of the 6 targets—24 shots in all.   Courtesy *Outdoor Life*.

Training Law Officers

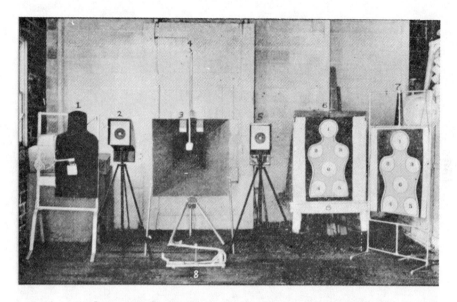

LEWISTOWN POLICE DEPARTMENT'S TRAINING EQUIPMENT

Unit 1—Quick draw target; the iron arm moves the small card in imitation of hand movement of an opponent doing a quick draw when operated by cord and rebound spring.

Units 2 and 5—Koehler Brothers' excellent portable steel target holders and bullet catchers; very practical and convenient equipment.

Unit 3—Three-foot opening X-Ring Products Co. all-steel bullet back stop with centrifugal bullet catching device; a high grade, thoroughly practical piece of shooting equipment, fitted up with various detachable accessories and attachments for police training. Plenty of room for superspeed training and various forms of swinging and otherwise moving targets. Note double swinging rods for crossing target training in place.

Unit 6—Heavy steel back stop for use with heavy caliber revolvers and pistols for quick draw and rapid fire shooting.

Unit 7—Revolving target holder with spring attachment to control time of exposure of target to shooter as may be required and regulated.

Unit 8—Adjustable trap for throwing aerial targets, cans and blocks singly, in pairs or in threes, as desired. Shown in action in Section Five.

THE VAN-AUMATIC TRAPS

Units 9 and 10—Attached to X-Ring steel bullet catching background adjusted and in place for conducting two-man competitive training, as we use this equipment. All shooting on these targets is done double action. As one target is broken another automatically drops into position for the next shot. For developing accuracy and speed combined these traps cannot be excelled for convenience, durability and dependable performance. Deliberate single-action shooting can be done with this equipment also and the distance increased as desired to make regular hitting a little more difficult. These traps and the Duster targets can be secured from Fred Goat Co., 314 Dean St., Brooklyn, N. Y.

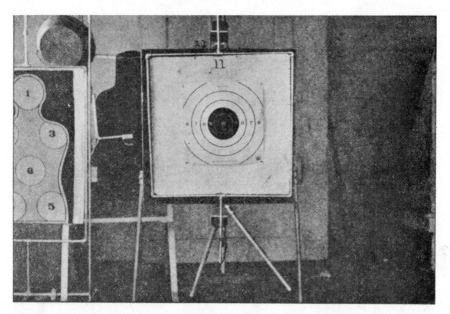

POLICE TRAINING

Unit 11—Front view of revolving target attachment with target facing shooter.   See Unit 12.

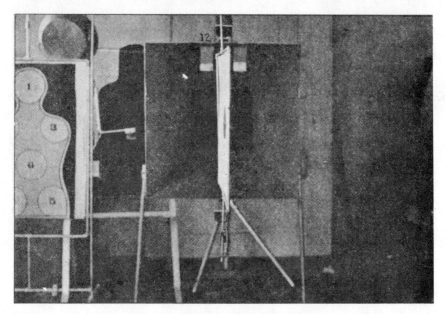

POLICE TRAINING

Unit 12—A practical and convenient attachment for X-Ring steel background arranged to control revolving targets for developing fast action and promoting double-action shooting. This outfit is compact and portable, easily and quickly assembled or removed when desired.

POLICE TRAINING

Duvrock targets held in clips, protected with steel plate. For fast double-action shooting instruction and development. A practical and durable attachment on the X-Ring background. This sort of target set-up creates and holds the interest of the shooters to a surprising degree.

Training Law Officers

POLICE TRAINING BY MODERN METHODS, AUGUST, 1937

Showing Walter Groff shooting from running board of auto which is being driven rapidly past 6 Olympic pattern man targets placed 10 yards from the edge of the road. Five trips, firing 6 shots each trip, gave the following results: 1st trip, 4 hits out of 6 shots. 2nd trip, 5 hits out of 6 shots. 3rd trip, 6 hits out of 6 shots. 4th trip, 5 hits out of 6 shots. 5th trip, 6 hits out of 6 shots. 26 hits out of 30 shots, all fired from .38 S. & W. revolver with 6-inch barrel by the double-action method. This training will develop ability for sure hit performances with a high average of results, with shots well placed. Increased speed and more distance along with other changes which may be considered desirable can be gradually added and no doubt be successfully mastered by more prolonged periods of training.

SHOOTING FROM AUTOMOBILE

In this experiment the Olympic targets are replaced by Langrish targets. Five trips, firing 6 shots each trip, gave good results. 1st trip, 5 hits out of 6 shots. 2nd trip, 6 hits out of 6 shots. 3rd trip, 5 hits out of 6 shots. 4th trip, 5 hits out of 6 shots. 5th trip, 6 hits out of 6 shots. 27 hits out of 30 shots fired, all double-action shooting. August, 1937.

Fast and Fancy Revolver Shooting

SHOOTING FROM AUTOMOBILE

The next experiment shows Walter Groff shooting at targets with 8-inch bull's-eyes placed just above the middle of the Olympic targets. Five trials gave: 1st, 2 hits on the bull out of 6 shots. 2nd, 4 hits on the bull out of 6 shots. 3rd, 3 hits on the bull out of 6 shots. 4th, 2 hits on the bull out of 6 shots. 5th, 3 hits on the bull out of 6 shots. 14 hits on 8-inch bull out of 30 shots. All but two bullets hit the paper squares. All of this shooting is done by the double-action method of operating the revolver.

POLICE TRAINING

Training new class of Montana Highway Patrol in five-position prone shooting, August, 1937, under supervision of the author. Dick Tinker responsible for some of the long range targets in the foreground.

Training Law Officers

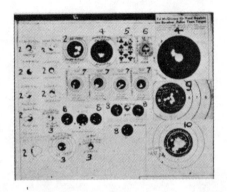

Double-action shooting by pupils. These double-action groups were shot by the following pupils at various distances from 18 to 36 feet: No. 2—Ben Anderson, No. 3—Warren Dix, No. 4—McGivern, No. 5—Vehawn, No. 6—E. Muir, No. 7—Carl Lundberg, No. 8—Joe Young, No. 9—Millington. No. 10—60-shot target, shot by officers Warren Dix, Wentworth, McKnight, Muir, Slater, Goodrich. Fifty shots were fired into the group shown at lower left by Officer Ben Anderson. Target No. 6, top row, was shot by Officer Ernie Muir, who, on another occasion, grouped 50 shots under a quarter at 20 feet. Note excellent groups by Warren Dix on target No. 3, also on target No. 7 by Carl Lundberg, and on center target No. 8 by Highway Patrol Officer Joe Young, and the No. 5 target with five shots on a club spot by Officer Vehawn.

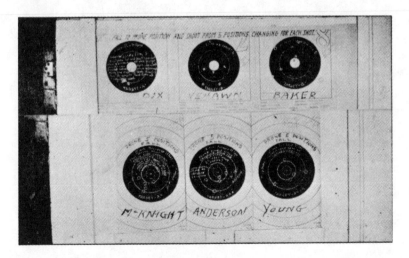

Fall to prone position and shoot one shot from on stomach position, one shot from on right shoulder position, one shot from on left shoulder position, one shot from on back position, one shot from stomach position with gun changed to other hand. Results evident on these targets.

BULLET-PROOF GLASS

The author demonstrates bullet-proof glass. Joe Young of Montana Highway Patrol behind the glass. The glass is held in a solid, well-supported framework, same as a bank fixture, or other office partition would hold it.

Training Law Officers

BULLET-PROOF GLASS

Showing effect of bullet from .45 Colt cartridge fired from a revolver directly at the Pittsburgh Plate Glass Company's bullet-proof glass.   The officer, Joe Young, is perfectly safe behind the bullet-proof glass; the visibility being slightly impaired was the only damage done.

BULLET-PROOF GLASS
"It's your turn now, Joe, to try a shot at that glass."

Training Law Officers

BULLET-PROOF GLASS—JOE TRIES IT

Officer Joe Young shooting the S. & W. .357 Magnum revolver at the bullet-proof glass. The author standing behind Mr. Young instead of behind the glass. Why not? This was demonstrated just outside of the Lewistown Police Headquarters.

BULLET-PROOF GLASS

The Magnum bullet did not go through the glass, but look what a jolt that glass can stand. The author's Magnum and the fired cartridge at botton of glass.

CHIEF OF POLICE A. C. McKNIGHT OF LEWISTOWN, MONTANA

Showing Shoulder Holster Draw with Coat On

Left—The beginning of the hand towards gun movement.

Right—Grasping the gun and releasing it from holster.

Training Law Officers

CHIEF OF POLICE A. C. McKNIGHT OF LEWISTOWN, MONTANA

Showing Shoulder Holster Draw with Coat On

Left—Gun coming out from under coat. Note hammer is protected by the drawing hand to prevent catching on the clothing.

Right—All set for action. Gun can be quickly extended forward on a level with the eye, at the instant that it clears the coat, if so desired.

Any preferred angle and method of pointing the gun may be used in connection with this draw.

Persistent practice develops this draw into a surprisingly fast performance. Very conveniently adapted for use by various law enforcement officers.

The surprise angle possible with this draw is also valuable. It has been successfully completed in four-fifths of a second by trained performers.

SECTION 21

AERIAL TARGET STUNTS AND STATIONARY TARGET PER-
FORMANCES, SELECTED BY THE AUTHOR FROM VARIOUS
EXHIBITION, EXPERIMENTAL AND TRAINING PROGRAMS,
DEVELOPED AT VARIOUS TIMES, OFTEN FOR SPECIAL
OCCASIONS. IN CONNECTION WILL BE FOUND NUMEROUS
SUGGESTIONS SUBMITTED BY THE AUTHOR.

Where conditions are not favorable for aerial target shooting various forms of stationary targets or some sort of swinging or other type of moving targets may be substituted for the aerial targets at the will of the performer. A demonstrator may vary many of the details to suit a special audience, and an instructor may also do likewise for his pupils.

1. Throw target with right hand, draw gun with right hand from cross draw holster on left side and shoot at aerial target.

2. Drop target from shoulder height, draw and shoot at falling target, or shoot a stationary target before object falls to ground.

3. Repeat above with gun upside down when drawn from holster.

4. Draw, toss gun to other hand (either hand), catch and shoot at stationary or aerial target, left-hand border shift or right-hand border shift, as preferred.

5. Throw target with right hand, have assistant toss gun to shooter, catch and shoot at aerial target, or a stationary target, as preferred.

6. Draw gun with left hand, toss gun in air, catch with right hand, and shoot at aerial target, or a stationary target, as preferred.

7. Throw target with right hand, draw gun with right hand from left-hand holster of assistant, and shoot at aerial target.

8. Road agent's spin. Throw any target that may be selected, with gun turned out butt first in motion of surrender to sheriff, spin gun over and shoot target. Target is tossed with gun grip—not with hand. Aerial target forces fast action.

9. Holding revolver upside down, while shooting at aerial target.

10. Gun juggling—throwing targets, etc. Toss gun back and forth to opposite hands—various forms of border shift, after first throwing target in the air. Can be varied as desired.

11. Shooting a stationary and, occasionally, an aerial target by relative position of shadow of gun and target, dependent on conditions—quite often successful when conditions are favorable.

12. Shooter, bending back and over, revolver held sideways, or upside down. Shooter stands with back towards targets, stationary or aerial targets, as preferred.

13. Shooting flying target, bent over table or bench, or other difficult position.

14. Shooting out profiles of Indian heads, cowboys, comic figures, etc., with rifles, revolvers, or pistols, on tin plates. (See photos, Section Thirty.)

15. Lay down gun, on anything conveniently near, throw aerial target with same hand, pick up gun and shoot.

16. Stand on head, supported by assistant, or hang with head down from some suitable support, shoot stationary and flying targets.

17. Shooting rapidly revolving target on string horizontal. Perfect timing necessary.

18. Shooting rapidly revolving target on string vertical. Perfect timing required.

19. Shooting revolving targets on special umbrella type frame work, five targets against time. Double-action trigger manipulation required.

20. Shooting five or six falling targets from specially arranged trap, test against time. This requires double-action operation of revolver.

21. Shooting swinging targets, one stationary and two as they are crossing in front of first target, all broken at same time. Requires perfect timing and trigger control.

22. Shooting aerial targets, two, three, four, five, or six, as at Central Montana Fair, all in the air at approximately the same time, using two throwers. (See photos, Section Five.)

23. Shooting six shots in can while falling, four shots in small cans, etc. (See photos, Section Five.)

24. Shooting four shots through wet clay pigeon without breaking, if possible. (See photos, Section Five.)

25. Shooting through cork in neck of bottle, tossed in air. Knock bottom out without breaking neck of bottle. Short bottles with fairly large neck openings for holding corks should be used. O. K. when conditions are right.

26. Cutting cards edgewise in air, showing similar results and performance of bullet and card as made evident in Peters spark photographs in visible ballistics. (See Section Five.)

27. Cutting or hitting lead discs edgewise in air, pennies, dimes, pills, or what have you. (See Section Five.)

28. Shooting on hands and knees, shooting out behind shooter at stationary or moving targets. O. K. when conditions are favorable.

29. Shooting while lying on back, at flying target, also while lying on stomach, training for fast shooting from awkward positions. Excellent police training when using Langrish stationary police training target.

30. Shooting at five-inch bull's-eyes on 24-inch beaver-board target, five shot while in the air, black, also white bull's-eyes. There is a difference that is very noticeable when this combination is studied, also good police practice when conditions are right. Good groups are possible but require persistent practice.

31. Shooting at 8-inch bull's-eyes at 50 yards, tossed in the air, aerial targets made from the bull's-eyes only of regulation stationary targets mounted on metal or wood discs. O. K. under favorable conditions. Results depend on study and constant practice.

32. Shooting 8-inch bull's-eyes at 25 yards, same conditions.

33. Shooting at two crossing aerial targets coming towards each other while traveling across 15-foot space. Good training to promote quick action. Both targets shot at as quickly as possible after crossing.

34. Shooting two aerial targets going in opposite directions—one gun, two shots. Try getting them as near the central point as possible.

35. Shooting five falling targets from magazine set-up—18 feet high, attempting to hit five in as short time as possible, spaced about 18 inches apart. Time training. **Fast.**

36. Shooting two targets thrown at once, one front, one behind, shooter turning body only, not the feet, for second shot—one gun, single-action, thumb cocking. Good police training. Double-action feature of gun can be used if preferred.

37. Target thrown over left shoulder, turn to right and shoot to rear without moving feet. Another good crook exterminating stunt for police training. (See Section Fifteen.)

38. Target thrown back between legs, straighten up and turn and shoot. (See Section Five.)

39. Throw, draw, and shoot at the target before it passes a line 7 feet from shooter, one gun. Excellent quick draw, combined action training. (Described in Section Seventeen.)

40. Draw and shoot when aerial target appears in air without warning or signal from behind a five-foot high fence or other obstruction. Good police training to develop speed and prompt action. (Described in Section Seventeen.)

41. Throw two targets with right hand, draw with right hand, shoot both with two shots from one gun. Double action of gun required.

42. Shooting from speeding automobile at various sized moving targets and stationary targets also. Good police training to develop speed.

43. Shooting from speeding motorcycle, moving targets, stationary targets, etc. Good police training.

44. Hand grenades, shooting incomers one, two, three, four, five or six in rotation, using two throwers. An excellent speed developing method of training for aerial target development, which ultimately means speed. Double-action method of operating the revolver is favored for this sort of shooting.

45. Rapid fire incomers, Duvrock traps, using one, two or three at a time, also clay pigeons thrown from Remington and Western hand traps, placed at various points and angles. Double-action method of operating revolver is more favorable for this shooting. Targets travel towards the shooter.

46. High flying targets, incomers, and crossing flyers, using two throwers. Developed by gradually increasing the distance from day to day. The key—study and practice—is well exemplified here. Double-action shooting recommended.

47. Can throwing trap, with pole having the feet marked off showing how this stunt was started, and gradually developed to six hits before can could fall to the ground. The marked-off guide is helpful in developing speed. This stunt requires gradual development, prolonged practice and much study. Double-action operation of revolver necessary. (See photos, Section Five.)

48. Jumping handkerchiefs over hurdles with bullets. Plenty of close figuring required—angles and elevations very important. They can be jumped higher than man's head. (See photos.)

49. Clay pigeons from Dupont hand trap throwing towards shooter. Clay pigeons are thrown from 30 yards' distance from shooter, passing over shooter's head.

50. Three aerial targets, two tossed in air, one stationary on ground or other suitable support. Shoot one aerial target, then shoot stationary target, then up and shoot second aerial target. Double-action shooting.

51. Two aerial targets, two short barrel guns, one in each hand same time. "Belly guns." (See Section Six.)

52. Draw and fall and shoot aerial target, also stationary targets placed in various positions.

53. Chicken hunting. Kick target off of toe into the air to about shoulder height, then hit it with the first shot. If missed, shoot again. The idea is not to let the target get away without being hit.

54. Drop coin or handkerchief or can, and shoot as many shots as possible. The time for this stunt is split seconds, timed with special electrical equipment, showing drop meter timing falling objects. For the public's enlightenment.

55. Aerial target tossed, run forward, pick supposed opponent's fallen gun from ground and shoot target. Plenty action—perfect timing required. Excellent training for prompt action in emergency.

56. Rolling can on ground, five shots. Old-timers' recreation, standard old-time stunt, with modern variations.

57. Shooting oranges or can of tomatoes tossed in the air, with new hollow point bullets, Magnum or S. & W. .38/44. Good demonstration of shocking power of new cartridge, which gives surprising results, duplicating stunts formerly done with high power rifles.

58. Shooting guns upside down at targets thrown from behind back to front, over shoulder.

59. Hang target on string, cut string with first shot, hit the falling target with second shot. Prompt action training—requires much practice. Double-action operation of revolver necessary for success.

60. Throwing targets from behind, hitting them out in front, after passing

over shooter's head, singles and doubles, speed development—gun right side up.

61. Lay down gun, throw target, pick up gun from table, chair, box, or floor after throwing, and shoot the target.

SHOOTING STATIONARY TARGETS, AND HUMAN TARGET STUNTS WITH REVOLVERS, USING SINGLE-ACTION METHOD, RAISING HAMMER WITH THUMB AND SQUEEZING TRIGGER FOR FIRING SHOT.

62. Shooting targets out of lady's hands.

63. Shooting targets off of head of assistant, held by belt around head, fastened under chin.

64. Shooting five targets held in hand, fan shape, on small fixture.

65. Shooting cigarette from holder's mouth, or pipe or other holder.

66. Cutting two cards at once, crossed in center and held edgewise to shooter by assistant.

67. Blindfold shot on stationary target, aided by assistant, demonstrating sense of location from former vision and relative position. Study and persistent practice will develop many surprising results in this stunt.

68. Shooter, bending back and over, towards target in rear, revolver held normally in hand but turned down, due to position, either sideways or upside down, as preferred.

69. Three targets at once, split bullet on axe after passing through front target. (See photo, Section 30.)

SUPERSPEED SHOOTING.

70. Ten guns, drop one, pick another, from specially arranged bench, 50 shots fired double action, in 21 seconds on target.

71. One hundred shots, in 47 seconds, using 20 guns, same as above. Requires bench, basket, and special set-up for rapidly changing guns.

72. Shooting the lower small bottle or clay pigeon out from under one placed above it and breaking top one before falling to the ground, less than four inches. One gun, two shots. Quick.

73. Fanning the trigger, five shots at target, double-action gun, special demonstrating gun. Unusual stunt.

74. Shooting five shots from double-action guns by regulation double-action manipulation, in time periods ranging from one second to as low as two-fifths of a second, as shown on verified targets.

(It will be noticed that these groups are controlled within the outline of the hand, and many within the outline of an ordinary playing card.)

QUICK DRAWS FROM VARIOUS TYPE OF HOLSTERS.

75. Drawing from any regulation holsters against pointed, cocked gun, beating the shot from gun so held, due to psychology, sensori-motor impulse, practice, and study. Called "Beating the Drop."

76. Draw and shoot the moving gun hand, on quick-draw set-up of man target. Excellent for police training practice, for hitting opponent's gun hand—right now, and spoil his quick draw. (See photos, Section Twenty.)

77. **Hip Shooting,** after the draw, deliberately placing five shots on five targets placed in a row, without raising gun above belt level, using any position preferred and holding gun in any manner desired. Fast and effective.

78. Quick draws on disappearing targets of various kinds, sizes and shapes. Revolving targets with time limit appearance and disappearance. Excellent police work.

79. Waistband holster draw with gun right side up, either hand, from either side.

80. Waistband holster draw with gun upside down, either hand from either side. Both of these draws are fast, deceiving, and usually effective.

81. The "Behind the Back" draw, holster worn back of hip, butt of revolver turned to any position desired, by adjusting holster on belt. Practice makes this stunt fast and quite deceiving.

82. The cross draw, developed by using breakable targets on man-sized, and shaped, background.

83. The belly draw and twist, relative to opponent. Same training methods.

84. Suspender holster draw and twist, relative to opponent. Same training methods.

85. Shoulder holster draw and twist, relative to opponent's position. Same training methods.

86. Derringer holster draw, from hands-up position, wrist holster. Dangerous to the arresting officer, if not expected. Reversing the situation, this draw can be very effectively used by an officer in a tight spot.

DRAWLESS HOLSTERS.

87. Drawless holster (4-inch gun), tip up, shoot, flip off of belt, shoot again at stationary target, then shoot again at aerial target. Sights can be used when gun comes level with the eye. These holsters can be attached to belts in various ways.

88. Drawless holster. Toss fair sized can or other target out in front, tip up, shoot. Hip shooting on moving target, demonstrating perfect timing, sense of direction and location. Much practice necessary for successful development with this equipment. The results depend on the same principles that are necessarily involved in successful hip shooting.

89. Shooting through pocket of coat, etc., at several targets. Handy police training—favorite gangster trick. Practice develops skill in the same manner as done for hip shooting. Drawing from hip pocket holster, or shooting with hand behind the back.

90. Hideout gun positions and draws, positions as selected and separate from regular habits of carrying guns. Hideout gun positions and draws, from sleeve and from special holster sewed in to replace watch pocket of pants, and various other locations.

In these are included two inside coat pocket draws. Number one has the gun placed in special light leather holster which fits gun snugly and is securely sewed in the desired position on the inside of the coat. The double-action revolver is placed muzzle down and slanting towards the back. Grip is carried high and within easy reach. This is really a "sneak draw." The hand is used to scratch chin or adjust either collar or necktie in a very natural manner, then suddenly dropped to gun butt and the fireworks come into play immediately by using a body twist. This draw is amazingly fast, very deceiving and is quite generally effective as regards hits on targets.

Number two of these draws consists of specially arranged holster or pocket arrangement inside of coat on either side preferred. The double-action revolver is placed with grip down, and the butt to the front with barrel and muzzle slanting back towards arm. The deceptive hand movements are the same as for the Number one draw, only that the gun is drawn and pulled forward by the muzzle with thumb and finger placed on each side of barrel, keeping them and other parts of hand out of the way of the muzzle blast. The shot is fired between finger and thumb by grasping grip (as soon as it comes forward) with the other hand and instantly pressing the trigger and firing the gun by the double-action method, at the same instant that hand comes in contact with gun. This is one of the most deceiving, extremely fast, and deadly-in-results methods of gun producing performances on the list. There are so many ways of moving the hands without arousing suspicion in preparation for reaching the gun that most arresting officers may be caught completely off guard.

Guns carried with holster on inside of leg by web straps fastened around waist and legs, in same manner as suspensories are worn, can be a dangerous combination to face. The inside seam of both pant legs are opened and zipper fasteners inserted and sewed in place, which do not show when closed. Such a gun carrier, with small gun, is hard to locate by regular methods of "frisking" a prisoner and even when handcuffed such prisoner is very dangerous.

The Montana State Highway Patrol favors a method of handcuffing a prisoner's hands around and below his right leg while sitting in seat alongside of driver. The above arrangement of holster and gun would certainly prove very disastrous to the arresting officer if not discovered. In making an arrest even if the prospective prisoner is knocked down and plays "possum" he can very easily reach such a hideout gun or guns, as the case may be, and prove very dangerous. There are many guns that are adaptable to such and similar hideout purposes. There is no attempt being made here to list them all.

91. Hideout gun position and draw from leg of boot. Hideout gun can also be carried on elastic band up sleeve.

92. Hideout gun position and draw from vest pocket. Variety of arrangements possible.

93. Hideout gun position and draw through armhole of vest. Special holsters required.

94. Hideout gun position and draw from hat, etc. Special arrangement necessary.

95. Hideout gun position. Gun carried hidden in bandaged hand and fired, or gun can be drawn and fired with other hand.

96. Modern demonstration of the early day gunman's hand shaking quick draw, which is a "sneak" draw, from coat pocket, or other readily accessible spot, where the disengaged hand may be placed without arousing suspicion, while the hand shaking operations are being carried on.
    This is performed by drawing a short gun with the left hand which is usually placed in or very near the pocket beforehand. The gun is immediately tossed or very rapidly passed to the right hand. These gun handling movements must be positively controlled and correctly timed, so as to occur at just the moment that the hand of the other person is released.

If two men equally expert were to use this trick at the same time sure death for both would be the result. An officer can use it effectively in a case where he is being framed by the glad hand method, and the man in front of the gun will be effectively covered and not able to do any fancy dodging. Even if the covered man's friend butts into the argument from the sidelines with another gun, the man in front of the officer's gun is so completely at the officer's mercy that he can do nothing except what he may be told to do, and command his assistants to lay off. In a tense situation such as this, a shot fired at the officer by some one else would most certainly cause the gun in his hand to be fired instantly, which would be just too bad for the glad hand artist who was leading the officer into the trap.

Several arrangements of Langrish or other targets can be used for training purposes. Practice and study will establish positive control over the hand and gun movements.

97. Aerial target shooting with Derringers, not at all an ordinary accomplishment, but very useful if, and when, needed.

98. Shooting with card over gun at stationary target. Several Langrish targets in several positions. Better system than working without sights. Helpful for developing ability for shooting in the dark.

Fast and Fancy Revolver Shooting

99. Shooting from speeding auto at targets placed at side of road in various positions. Also good police work.

100. Shooting from auto at targets placed on each side of road, right, then left, either alternately or in series, several on one side, then on the other. Excellent police work.

101. Shooting from auto at targets placed alongside of and also hung across road, if conditions allow it, every 25 feet. Police development.

102. Shooting from auto at various targets placed at side of road, on wires or pipes or other supports at intervals, and at different elevations. Police training for quick selection and instant judgment.

103. Same on rig fastened to side of auto-trailer, coming toward shooter, safely placed behind or above elevation of driver and body of car. Fast police training.

104. Same on trailer coming toward and going by shooter, well back from towing car, targets arranged in various positions, imitating driver, passenger. Excellent police training.

Practical Shooting Stunts Adapted to Police Training and Protection of Arresting Officers Entering Stores, Dark Alleys and Other Out-of-the-Way Places, that Are Usually Poorly Lighted, When in Search of Burglars or Other Law Violaters.

As flash-lights are about the only light that an officer could produce to help him under such conditions, he should be trained to shoot well in such situations and be familiar with the problems usually so encountered, and be able to place his shots effectively under such limited lighting conditions. The numerous targets shot by men so trained, that are herein presented, show conclusively that such training is effective, is practical, and is positive in results, and should be considered a necessary part of every law enforcement officer's training.

105. Shooting with the aid of flash-light only in dark, holding light away from body for own protection.

106. Shooting with lights shining in eyes, aided only by flash-light in hand of officer to assist in locating target. Good stationary target groups can be made in this way. (See photos of such reproduced targets.) Many officers have lost their lives under these exact conditions of approach by auto.

107. Locate target by an instant only, flash of light, first shot fired during flash, five shots fired in the dark, after the flash of light, at Langrish target.

108. Shooting in dark with no light. Skill developed by flash of light training, and experience, a necessary and valuable police training angle.

109. Walking forward in supposedly poorly lighted dark alley at command to Halt! Stop! or Hands Up! turn upper part of body only and shoot, instantly. Practice in this stunt will develop surprisingly effective results and is one of the most important things that an officer can become proficient in. When training the performer stands with back to target and shoots at signal. Learning to walk past or away from target so as to be correctly balanced at all times for turning upper part of body only, without shifting the feet in any manner, requires only a moderate amount of practice and reasonable study.

110. The blindfold draw. The performer stands in front of Langrish target, notes location of target, assumes his accustomed position, and is then blindfolded. He draws and shoots one shot each draw, for five trials. It is surprising how rapidly hitting ability can be developed by this method. Very useful training in connection with quick-draw shooting under poor light conditions and for training with flash-lights and other shooting in the dark, and nearly dark, situations. The blindfold draw is also useful in training for shooting when guided by sound only. An electric buzzer may be used to furnish the sound, the performer can be turned around to different positions, relative to the target. He must then locate target by the sound. Any sound that may be preferred by the interested persons can be put into service.

   Shooting, guided by sound only and sense of location, in the dark, can be developed to a surprising degree of hitting ability, by study and persistent practice, with proper and careful coaching.

111. Shooting at target exposed by flash of gun only, in the dark, gun arranged for developing judgment of opponent's position. Police training, study and practice. Artificial gun flash can be substituted for early training.

112. Shooting at head of Langrish target placed behind newspaper, in reading position. Police training.

113. Shooting at head size targets bobbing up from behind protecting cover. Police training.

114. Shooting while running towards Langrish target, five shots on targets. Police work, practical and valuable police training.

115. Shooting while running crossways in front of door opening. Shoot five shots into Langrish target, through opening, travel to right, then to left. Practical police work, and valuable training, not so hard to make effective groups on such targets. Persistent practice is the secret, effective on "holed up" opponent, hiding in entrance or opening of building.

116. Shoot five shots into Langrish target while supporting disabled brother officer with left arm and backing away from target, shooting with right hand. Police training development that is practical, and may prove very valuable experience.

117. Shoot five shots, one each time, at short intervals while running backwards away from Langrish target, but always facing target. Practical police training.

118. Running forward from corner of building or from one side of door opening, which contains Langrish target, turning slightly as target is passed, firing across to side and rear into doorway as body is turned. Continue firing from changing positions. Excellent training in police work, and of practical value.

119. Falling over obstacle, drop with head towards target, shoot once, roll sideways shooting one shot every time body is turned over or position changed. Five positions—on belly, right shoulder, back, left shoulder, then change gun to other hand for last shot. This can be completed in 15 to 20 seconds, for all positions.

   This accomplishment can be very valuable to an officer in some situations. An officer should make a practice of shooting from behind various obstructions such as piled-up merchandise, fixtures, etc., and familiarize himself with all the outlined shooting combinations where flash-lights have been used and demonstrated as effective. It is not so difficult to master as at first considered, before being successfully worked out by practical methods.

   Following are a few novelty stunts worth trying for the experience gained therefrom:

120. Locating target placed behind curtain by shadow, at a signal. Shoot and try to hit target by sense of location from front of curtain. Police training.

121. Shooting bullet-proof glass demonstration, practical police work, for protective methods, etc., officers standing behind glass. (See photos, Section Twenty.)

122. Firing double-action revolver and making hits on target with everything taken out but cylinder and hammer. Crippled gun demonstration in competition with claims made for any other kind of gun's practicability under crippled condition. Hits are possible and can be fairly well-controlled in a pinch.

123. One hand out of commission, unload, reload, shoot five separate targets double action, demonstrations of double-action gun possibilities under wounded person's situation.

124. Shooting guns double action, with only thumb and finger, first, second or third finger. Demonstrating crippled hands, still shooting under urge of self-preservation.

125. Hold gun (revolver) with feet only, any finger to pull trigger. Hits can easily be made on man target.

NOVELTY STUNTS WITH SINGLE-ACTION COLT REVOLVERS.

126. Fanning single-action fast—fastest method known for spraying lead from single-action revolvers. Very effective at short range. Early day stunts. (See photos, Section Eight.)

127. Slip shooting, two hands, single action, accurate and fast, practical and effective. Early day stunts. (See photos, Section Eight.)

128. Single roll, shoot as it comes over. Hits can be made in this manner. (See photos, Section Eight.)

129. Double roll, shoot as they come over. This requires much practice to score hits.

SHOOTING WITH MIRRORS ON REVOLVERS FOR LOCATING AND SIGHTING ON VARIOUS STATIONARY, SWINGING AND AERIAL TARGETS.

Mirrors may be permanently attached to gun or held in the hand, as preferred. Adjustable mirrors, attached to the guns, which can be easily removed when desired, give more satisfactory results.

Single shot pistols are also very well adapted to all sorts of mirror shooting, if preferred to revolvers, by the user. Automatic pistols are not usually successfully used for this purpose.

Specially arranged mirrors can be used for performing almost any shooting stunt that can be done by the regulation method of sighting and firing the shots. If enough study and practice are indulged in very surprising results can be secured.

A few exhibition stunts, worked out at various times, are here listed:

130. Target behind back, mirror and revolver, one mirror, shoot under arm.

131. Target behind back of shooter, two mirrors attached to revolver or pistol. Reflection sighting over head.

132. Revolver held across arm with mirror attached to revolver or held in hand, for shooting stationary targets.

133. Revolver held on top of head with one mirror, shooting stationary targets.

134. Revolver held across arm with mirror for locating and shooting aerial target.

135. Revolver held across arm with mirror for shooting swinging target.

136. Revolver held across arm with mirror, breaking two swinging targets while crossing. Perfect timing and coördination is necessary for success.

137. Revolver held over shoulder with mirror, shooting several targets stationary.

138. Revolver held with mirror attached, looking in front at reflection in another mirror, target placed at left side of shooter. Reflected sighting.

139. Revolver with two mirrors attached, target placed a distance away in line with top of shooter's head while lying on his back. Reflected sighting.

140. Shooting revolver held between legs, pointed back at target, shooter stands with back to target. Sighting is done by looking straight down at mirrors.

TWO-GUN AERIAL TARGET STUNTS AND OTHER COMBINATIONS.

This list of two-gun performances has been developed by combining practical accuracy with fancy stunts that are effective and useful when and if needed.

Fast and Fancy Revolver Shooting

1. Two guns shot almost at same time at two aerial targets while shooter is lying on back. Two guns, one in each hand, targets thrown from a point several feet from head of shooter.

2. Shooting two flying targets tossed at same time, one crossing left to right, the other crossing right to left, both traveling towards center; shoot the first one, then the other, as quickly and as close together as possible.

3. Shooting two flying targets traveling away from center in opposite directions. Spreaders. Quick action is the key to success.

4. Two guns, one in each hand, shooting aerial targets, one in front of shooter, one behind shooter, both targets tossed in the air at same time. The left-hand gun is usually shot at rear target first, then front target with right hand as quickly as possible.

5. Two aerial targets thrown by assistant, draw two guns from Buscadero belt, shoot one target with each gun. This is called "Quick Draw on Doubles."

6. Shooting one stationary target and one flying target at same time, gun in each hand. Stationary target may be held by assistant, who also tosses other target in the air.

7. Two aerial targets tossed at same time, left-hand gun right side up, right-hand gun upside down.

8. Two guns, one in each hand, shooting at two aerial targets while hanging head down from ladder or other convenient equipment, or supported by assistant while standing on head. Same procedure is followed for stationary targets.

9. Shooting two guns at once at one target tossed in the air, tin cans, etc. This is somewhat difficult on account of it being necessary to hold guns close together and parallel instead of triangular as on separated targets, the eye being the point of the triangle in this situation.

10. Shooting two guns at once at two wide angle aerial targets, various distances apart.

11. Cutting two cards edgewise at the same time, one with each gun.

12. Shooting two stationary targets at the same time, placed on opposite sides of shooter, arms extended full length. Shooter stands between, as shown in photo, Section Six.

13. Shooting two stationary targets held one with each hand of assistant. Shooter, with gun in each hand, shoots them simultaneously.

14. Shooting two guns at two targets while being bent backwards over bench or other convenient fixture.

15. Two guns placed on ground several feet in front of shooter. Run, pick up guns, shoot two targets.

Shooting Programs

16. Two guns tossed to shooter by assistant. Catch and shoot two targets.

17. Two guns used at once, shoot at two widely separated targets placed in front of shooter at various distances that may be decided on, and gradually separated until they are finally on opposite sides of shooter.

18. Two guns shot by superspeed double-action method at Langrish targets separated 10, 12, 15 and 18 feet apart. This performance is sometimes added to the two-gun draw demonstration.

19. Thirty-six shots are to be fired by the double-action method at six Langrish targets placed 35 feet from shooter and separated or grouped at various distances from each other.

This modern demonstration is arranged to create a situation somewhat similar to the famous gun battle of the Earps and Clantons in the O. K. Corral, at Tombstone, Arizona, October 26, 1881, which has been written up so much in Western history. As reported, something over thirty shots were fired and about six hits scored.

Two Guns Used for Superspeed Shooting.

20. Hold two guns out in front of shooter about shoulder high, fire right-hand gun, drop, then fire left-hand gun with right hand before dropped gun falls as far as shooter's belt. Practice makes this demonstration unbelievably fast.

21. Shooting two guns at same time, making playing card and hand size groups on various targets under various conditions and while using several types of guns. Superspeed, combined with accuracy, checked with and against mechanical and electrical timing devices. (See photos of properly witnessed and verified targets shot in this manner, giving dates and the serial numbers of the guns used, Section Ten.)

Two-Gun Mirror Shooting.

22. Shooting two opposite targets at same time, using mirrors on each gun, targets stationary, guns held in front of shooter's body, sighted by looking straight down into mirrors.

23. Shooting two targets placed, one in front of shooter, one to rear of shooter, hitting both at same time, using mirrors for sighting the gun that is held over shoulder for hitting the rear target. The other gun is held off hand in front of shooter in regular way. (See photos, Section Six.)

Many of the one-gun mirror shooting performances can be developed into two-gun combinations by study and practice.

Two-Gun Draws and a Few Suggestions.

Any one-hand, one-gun draw can be developed into successful and fast two-gun draws by practice with each hand in turn, then combining them and making slight changes in body positions, which, of course, must be governed by the physical proportions and general build of the individual.

24. Draw two guns from holsters hung at hips on Buscadero belt and shoot five shots from each gun on Langrish target, which is exposed

toward shooter for only three seconds by a quarter turn of the mechanism, which is attached to the X-Ring bullet stopping background, as shown in photo of police equipment.

The Langrish target herein reproduced, which was shot at the Boy Scout's summer camp in June, 1935, and signed by officers and Scouts in charge of the demonstration, was exposed three seconds, but the time required for completing the performance of drawing the two guns and shooting the ten shots was only two seconds, as stated on the target.

25. Drawing two guns from holsters hung low at the hips on two modern crossed belts, somewhat similar to those used in the early days, and firing five shots from each gun at Langrish or similar target placed on a revolving frame, as shown in photo. Target is turned facing towards shooter for three seconds and then turned edgewise. Shooting sixteen such targets in a demonstration for Fox Movietone News, several years ago, resulted in 160 hits out of the 160 shots fired from the two guns.

This type of two-gun draw, with one shot from each gun, placed on a target, can be done in around three-fifths of a second, and some of the witnessed targets herein produced show that the ten shots have been fired in time periods of one and a fifth seconds, and others in one and two-fifths seconds, and the results show good grouping of bullets generally. This would indicate that the time period for the faster two-gun draws and ten shots from double-action revolvers, as indicated by the evidence, would be approximately one and four-fifths seconds on some occasions, and around two seconds on some other occasions. Such performances, completed within periods of time around one and four-fifths seconds and on up to the full three seconds time limit, set by the manipulation of the target, are in reality superspeed demonstrations.

26. Draw two guns, draw with right hand from holster hung on left side front (making a cross draw). Draw gun with left hand from holster hung back of left hip, level with belt, which is sort of a "sneak draw" for the reason that the movement of the right hand takes the attention away from the movements of the left hand. The holster holding the gun for the left hand is not in sight at all from the front. If coat is worn this holster is entirely hidden at all times, giving the impression that officer carries only one gun. Shoot both guns at man target placed on left side of shooter. Shooter stands sideways with left side of body towards target. Langrish target. Deceptive and fairly fast.

27. Two targets placed on opposite sides of shooter, draw two guns from holster at hips. Right gun is shot behind and across the back, at target at left side of shooter. Left-hand gun is shot across stomach, at target placed on right side of shooter, Langrish targets. This is called the back and front cross-fire from Myres Buscadero belt and holster. Pretty fast and usually successful. Requires constant practice.

28. Draw two guns, toss left gun over to right hand, right gun tossed to left hand, passing each other in the air, catching guns in opposite hands and immediately hitting two separate Langrish targets. Complicating and doubling the "Border shift." Spectacular but not fast.

29. Two targets, two guns. Draw guns from holsters on belts of another person, and hit both targets. Dangerous for arresting officer and surprisingly fast.

30. Two guns, McGivern drawless holsters, flip up, shoot two stationary targets from hip, then immediately slip holsters free of belt, shoot two other targets, one with each hand. Guns are not, and cannot be drawn, from holsters in this performance, and the surprise is that the sights can be used when the guns are freed from belt. Accurate shooting can be done with this combination.

31. Two-gun draw, hit two separate targets with guns taken from two specially arranged boot holsters. Deceptive and dangerous to an officer.

32. Two-gun draw. With hide-out guns, from "hands up" position of two Derringer wristband holsters, "or what have you." Myres holsters. Dangerous to arresting officer.

33. Two separate targets placed out in front of shooter, a few feet apart. Draw guns, then with motions of surrendering to officer, with the butts turned front towards officer, spin and fire both guns and hit both targets at practically the same time. This is called "The road agents' spin" doubled to make it more difficult, and adaptable to two opponents. (See photos of how guns are handled.)

34. Two-gun draws and hit two separate targets at the same time from two hip pocket holsters—both guns worn behind shooter.

35. Two-gun draws and hit two separate targets at same time from two inside waistband holsters. Myres holsters.

36. Two-gun draws and hit two separate targets at same time from two cross draw holsters. Myres holsters.

37. Two-gun draws and hit two separate targets at same time from two low hung suspender holsters. Myres holsters.

38. Two-gun draws and hit two separate targets at same time from two Sam Myres shoulder holsters.

39. Two-gun draws and hit two separate targets at same time from two Hardy covered shoulder holsters.

40. Two-gun draws and hit two separate targets at same time from two Berns-Martin push-out holsters.

41. Two-gun draws and hit two separate targets at same time from two E. E. Clark's No. 999 hip holsters.

42. Two-gun draws and hit two separate targets at same time from two button clasp top strap holsters. Myres holsters.

No kind of buttoned down flap holsters are fast unless flap is opened and prepared beforehand. Long buttoned down straps, passing over frame of gun to hold it in holster, when buttoned low on side of holster, is correspondingly slow. This style of strap fasteners are in quite general use. Personally, I do not like them. Our much improved short strap, fastened by clasp button at the top, just over gun grip, which can be instantly flipped open by thumb as hand comes in contact with gun grip, and is then out of the way, has replaced all straps that button low on the side, and is much preferred by us for all such holsters now in use. This arrangement is only a fraction of a second slower than open holsters, yet has all the safety features for keeping gun in holster until intentionally taken out by the wearer.

Two-Gun Shooting While Handcuffed and Leg Ironed. Dangerous Angles for Arresting Officers.

43. Hitting two targets with gun in each hand while handcuffed.

44. Shooting two upper man Langrish targets, placed on opposite sides of shooter, with gun in each hand while hands are handcuffed behind back.

45. Shooting two targets at same time, gun in each hand, handcuffed in front. Right-hand gun is fired across stomach at target on left side of shooter, left gun fired at target straight out in front of shooter. Langrish targets. Also reverse positions.

46. While handcuffed and with ankle irons on, lying on back with gun in each hand, shooting out between upper part of legs at targets held in hands of assistants.

47. Same conditions—handcuffed and ankle irons, head on ground, shooting under stomach back between legs with two guns held out over the heels, hitting two separate targets at same time.

48. Same conditions, lying doubled up on side—two targets, demonstrating angles of danger for officers, handcuffed, leg ironed, knocked down, still can shoot effectively.

49. Lying on back on the ground or floor, while handcuffed and with hands up over head. A person can shoot two revolvers effectively in that position while rolling back and forth only, or by rolling over and over, which makes it possible for him to hit either two or several targets (or persons) placed in various positions and at various angles in relation to his position. Such a person would also be a hard target to hit.

50. A handcuffed person in "hands up" position or with hands down by waist can strike a gun from an officer's hand, and by just following this up with a fall can easily grasp the gun, and by the rolling movements above-described, easily and quickly kill not only one of the officers, but others, dependent entirely on how many shots are in the gun. Such a gun in his hands would also make a vicious club in a man-to-man fight afterwards. The moral for the officer being, either have two guns within easy reach or "don't take chances."

51. An apparently safely handcuffed person taking the gun from officer's holster and pressing the muzzle against the officer's body (as illustrated

Shooting Programs

by Duke Wellington and the author in Section Nine shows a dangerous angle that all officers should guard against. This performance is very fast and, in the case of a real criminal in action, it would mean an immediate farewell for the officer, who would have little, if any, chance to defend himself.

A revolver shooter of any ability is still a very dangerous person even when handcuffed with his hands either behind him or in front, and with leg irons securely adjusted also, if he can by any possibility get hold of guns. This important fact should not be overlooked.

One of the most interesting practical emergency performances that can be studied and mastered by law officers, for use when the situation may present itself, under more or less urgent conditions, and which has been successfully worked out on several occasions which gave somewhat convincing results, consists of shooting revolvers at Langrish limbless man targets, at much longer than usual ranges, and getting very surprising results.

This performance includes shooting at man targets at 100 and 200 yards, and since the advent of the Smith & Wesson .357 Magnum revolver and its amazingly performing cartridge, developed by the Winchester Company, the ranges have been extended to 300, 400, 500 and 600 yards, such experiments being conducted for the purpose of creating interest in the possibilities for the training and development of various law officers along this line of endeavor. When a rifle is not readily available, an officer's reasonably fair ability along this line might possibly change the entire history of an important man hunt.

The results on the witnessed and dated targets, giving gun number and other details, herein reproduced, give a fair idea of the intensely interesting developments possible in this field. Our efforts have only slightly scratched the surface, and deeper research and activity should develop some amazing results in the near future.

This sort of training becomes extremely interesting and quite naturally follows the development of proficiency in the various shooting performances adaptable to the use of law enforcement officers, and outlined in the extensive programs presented.

Attention is called to the fact that there has been no effort made in connection with these shooting programs to introduce disarming methods as usually employed, recommended and taught by various instructors in charge of law enforcement organizations generally. Instead I very earnestly recommend to the reader the most excellent book covering this subject, by the internationally known police instructor, S. J. Jorgensen, Maritime Building, Seattle, Washington.

SECTION 22

J. EDGAR HOOVER, DIRECTOR OF THE FEDERAL BUREAU OF INVESTIGATION, UNITED STATES DEPARTMENT OF JUSTICE.

J. EDGAR HOOVER, Director of the Federal Bureau of Investigation, proved to be the very capable person who was needed to straighten out the recent unparalleled crime situation which, for the past several years, existed in these United States, and which was triumphantly active and defiant until a very short time ago.

The general disregard for law and order and for all of its representatives and enforcement organizations, which resulted in the ruthless murder of law enforcement officers generally, was the very natural outgrowth of the successful and terrifying reign of crime which developed after the World War, and continued practically unchecked up to the time that Mr. J. Edgar Hoover and his supertrained organization, of what is now generally referred to as the **G-Men,** were given proper equipment and full authority to enter the field free of all political red tape, and of the former bugaboos of state boundary lines having any influence or effect towards hampering their movements or interfering with their activities.

Mr. J. Edgar Hoover, and the organization of which he is the director, is without doubt the finest, most thoroughly equipped, and most efficient organization for the successful solution and suppression of crime known to the world at any time in its history. The results secured by this organization since 1934 very conclusively support this statement.

The following letter may help to make clear the foundation on which the marvelous success of the Federal Bureau of Investigation is founded, and also the importance which Mr. Hoover attaches to the need for proper training of officers in the intelligent and effective use of firearms:

FEDERAL BUREAU OF INVESTIGATION
UNITED STATES DEPARTMENT OF JUSTICE
WASHINGTON, D. C.

May 29, 1937.

MR. ED McGIVERN,
Lewistown, Montana.

Dear Mr. McGivern:

As you have requested in your letter of April 23, 1937, I am pleased to make the following statement for inclusion in the new book which you are writing:

There is nothing secret about the manner in which the Federal Bureau of Investigation works. Its formula is a simple one—intensive training, highly efficient and carefully investigated personnel, rigid requirements in education, conduct, intelligence, ability to concentrate, alertness, zeal, and loyalty, plus careful schooling in which we do our utmost to make every man to a degree self-sufficient. He must be a good marksman and have the courage to shoot it out with the most venomous of public enemies. He must know how to take fingerprints and what to do with them afterward. He must learn that no clue, no matter how seemingly unimportant, can be overlooked. He must have constantly before him the fact that science is a bulwark of criminal investigation and neglect no avenue toward this end. And he must realize that no case ever ends for the Federal Bureau of Investigation until it has been solved and closed by the conviction of the guilty or the acquittal of the innocent.

As of possible interest to you, there is also transmitted herewith a publication of this Bureau entitled "The Federal Bureau of Investigation."

With best wishes and kind regards,

Sincerely yours,

ENCLOSURE

J. EDGAR HOOVER.

When in 1934 a Federal law was passed arming the agents of the Federal Bureau of Investigation and giving them full authority to make arrests, the first and greatest step towards the elimination of organized crime took place. The new developments in the activities of the organization seemed to fit well into the general attitude of the members toward the crime situation. Risking their lives against America's most ruthless killers and desperate criminal element did not cause any of the members of the organization to resign. Instead they trained willingly and persistently to become thoroughly proficient in everything that might be required to successfully handle any and all angles of the new problems involved.

One of the first things necessary when Congress gave the F. B. I. weapons and full authority for their use, was to give the men thorough and proper training, and this is exactly what Mr. Hoover made arrangements to do, and he did it in a very thorough manner. This fact I take great pleasure in verifying by witnessed results. I very firmly endorse Mr. Hoover's methods, and I very earnestly recommend that the officials and heads of departments of all law enforcement agencies and organizations follow similar methods of procedure, and make suitable training available to each law enforcement officer in all departments.

All officers, if they carry arms, which I very earnestly believe to be an absolute necessity, should be thoroughly trained in the use of such arms until they are proficient and very positive as to the results which they can secure with them, at various distances and under much varied conditions. Many such possible conditions are outlined herein and may help to make clear the fact that such practical training methods can secure the development of satisfactory results in a reasonably short period of time.

The training given the agents of the F. B. I. under Mr. Hoover's direction include such shooting as herein outlined, while standing, sitting, or running, and various targets are used, such as bull's-eyes and disappearing targets, for the purpose of developing alertness, speed, and accuracy, coupled with quick and positive judgment under emergency conditions. Shooting is also practiced under all sorts of light conditions, both day and night, with various sorts of sight arrangements, and quite often with tracer bullets.

Shooting from rapidly moving cars and developing ability to score hits under such conditions, which is clearly outlined in these pages, is also a necessary item of accomplishment. The ability to quickly take cover and at the same time to get their guns working and effectively score hits on a target—which, during active duty may often be a running man target—is just another of their required accomplishments. Quick draws, sure hits and immediate action, combined with positive judgment and clear thinking under the urge of speed and fast performance throughout, is the goal that such training is designed to reach.

Several interesting examples of the results secured by this method of training in revolver shooting may be found among the illustrations in Sections Ten, Fifteen and Twenty.

The agents are also trained in the use of machine guns, rifles, shotguns and the Colt Monitor automatic rifle, one of the most effective weapons available, all of which constitutes an array of very convincing argument which criminals generally, no matter how desperate, have learned to respect and stay away from.

The Department has proven to be a successful and very much worthwhile institution. Reports show that in the 1937 fiscal year, at a cost of approximately $5,800,000, $41,400,000 was returned to the government in fines, savings and recoveries; 46 convictions were secured under the Lindbergh law, and $6,500 in ransom money was recovered. The agent's most important activity is to get evidence that will stand up in court, the result being that out of the total number of cases that have gone to court, convictions have been secured in ninety-four per cent of them. No other law enforcement or crime investigation organization in history can show such a record. Facts seem to establish the urgent need for such an institution and its record seems to justify the training methods.

SECTION 23

HOLSTERS, BELTS, AND EQUIPMENT.

Many letters coming from men in all walks of life contain inquiries as to which is the **best all-around** holster for a quick draw. One answer will do for these questions—there is no such thing as **one best holster** for everyone. Holsters and belts, like clothes, should be made to fit the individual who plans to wear and use them. They should be constructed, arranged, slanted, and balanced according to his personal peculiarities, his general habits, and, above all, they should be suited to the purpose for which they will be used. When these things are determined and explained clearly to Sam Myres of the S. D. Myres Saddle Company, El Paso, Texas, the proper and best holster for the purpose can be easily secured.

Based on his close contact, association and familiarity with the subject and his practical experience in this field of endeavor, Mr. Sam D. Myres is, in the opinion of the writer, just about the best qualified man in these United States to construct practical pistol and revolver carrying equipment. He has made belts, holsters, and gun harness in endless variety, and is constantly consulted and engaged in the development of new ideas along that line.

Mr. Myres has had many years of actual and practical experience designing and producing fast, serviceable, and, above all, **practical gun harness** for the needs and everyday use of men with whom practical, fast, and sure gun handling was, and is, a matter of necessity, actually being, in their case, a matter of life or death, not a matter of theory or fancy or recreation. Mr. Myres and his son also are practical and very proficient revolver shots and are in constant and almost daily association with some of the finest revolver shots in the country.

Mr. Myres has made special gun harness for many of the most famous rangers, officers and men on the border, where practical fast gun producing methods and quick sure hitting proficiency always was, and still is, an important matter of business and a fairly regular part of the day's work.

Such practically unlimited experience in supplying the needs of this great number and variety of practical gun handling experts should place Mr. Myres in a position to most intelligently advise and direct any person who may be in need of any regular or special belts, holsters or other gun carrying equipment or combination thereof. If Mr. Myres is consulted in this regard, and his advice is followed in connection with a few suggestions and details as furnished by the customer, absolutely satisfactory service will be the result.

We are making this statement from experience. Mr. Myres has made many exceptionally fine two-gun outfits for our use which are adapted specially to the type of gun to be used and the kind of shooting expected to be done with them while in use. The large assortment of very fine holsters, belts, and combinations herein displayed attest our confidence and satisfaction, as practically expressed, by the variety and large assortment of Mr. Myres' product as favored and used in our practical demonstration and experimental work.

We also highly recommend Captain A. H. Hardy's excellent work in the belt, holster and gun harness and equipment department. Captain Hardy, 513 N. Arden Drive, Beverly Hills, California, is one of the foremost all-around fancy exhibition shots who has appeared before the American public. The Captain is also a practical and very proficient competition shot, having several records, high averages, and many winnings to his credit. He is also a very highly qualified shooting instructor. His successful coaching has produced many winners and highly proficient target shots and police revolver team winners and record performers.

Many examples of Captain Hardy's excellent work is in evidence among our assorted equipment. Being a practical performer himself and very expert in the use of pistols and revolvers, he is in a position to apply his knowledge in a practical way to the development and construction of holsters, belts, and various gun carrying equipment required for almost any purpose where such things are needed.

We also use and recommend for certain purposes the Berns-Martin speed holsters and belts which have many desirable features that differ, to a great extent, from most other regulation holsters on the market. These features can be studied from photos on page 386. The photo on page 387 shows the recommended way of taking a gun from a Berns-Martin holster.

In all fairness we must state that study and practice in the use of these Berns-Martin holsters can develop very satisfying speed and in many other ways they also give very satisfactory results, particularly when using the longer barreled heavy caliber revolvers. They also have some outstanding points when using target sighted guns.

Both of these gentlemen, Mr. Berns and Mr. Martin, are expert and practical revolver shots, both having had training and service in the United States Navy. Their practical experience with revolvers and pistols has had much influence in the designing of these holsters. J. E. Berns, 1523 Park Avenue, Bremerton, Washington, will be pleased to furnish any additional information desired.

We also wish to make favorable mention of Mr. E. E. Clark of 1042 West Compton Boulevard, Gardena, California, and his excellent and very practical line of belts, holsters, and equipment for police and law enforcement officers generally. These goods are of excellent quality and workmanship, and have stood every test. They are practical, convenient, fast, durable, and in every way very satisfactory, and, for the special purpose for which they are designed, they are exceptionally well-adapted.

A very fine two-gun outfit on the Buscadero pattern of belt and holsters was made for me by Joseph R. Diekan of 41 Fulton Street, New York. They are shown in the pictures on page 376, accompanied by an excellent suspender holster and several **quick action** flap top holsters. These goods, while in plain finish as shown here, are of the very highest grade material and workmanship. Very excellent and highly satisfactory goods.

The George Lawrence Company, 80 First Street, Portland, Oregon, manufacture a full line of "steer hide" belts and holsters for all models of pistols and revolvers that give very satisfactory service.

The Herman H. Heiser Company of Denver, Colorado, also manufacture a full line of belts, holsters, etc., of excellent quality.

This holster information is here set forth solely for the benefit and guidance of the reader who may be interested in the various types of holsters, such as used herein, being available. The ones listed will take care of every need that confronts the shooter in any line. Any of these men may be depended upon to furnish a holster that is correctly designed for the purpose for which it is intended to be used. These holsters are made from high quality genuine skirting leather. (The only kind, we are informed, and we believe correctly, that is suitable for a first-class holster.) Each individual holster is made to fit the revolver perfectly by being formed over an aluminum model of the arm with which it is to be used.

Three very fine outfits for the two-gun draw are what Sam Myres terms his "Buscadero" belt, and Captain Hardy calls his "Hollywood Special," and a similar one made by J. R. Diekan. These are special belts about three inches wide. They have drop loops on either side for the holsters. This style of outfit enables one to make a fast two-gun draw because the guns drop lower than they do on a straight belt, and thus can be regulated to suit the peculiarities of the wearer. We like these outfits very well indeed, and in our experience with them they have proven most satisfactory. We have had a number of special holsters, for various demonstration stunts, made to order by these veterans of the game, and have found them very satisfactory and well-suited for the particular purposes for which we desired them.

Because of our own experience, we suggest that any reader desiring the best holsters for his personal use apply to any of these men, giving full particulars about himself, his build, and habits, and add a few suggestions about personal peculiarities and preferences. They will do the rest, and you may be assured that you will be fitted with the right holsters for your purpose. This is exactly what we did in our own efforts to obtain proper holsters, and this suggestion is therefore honest in its intention to help the reader solve his similar problems.

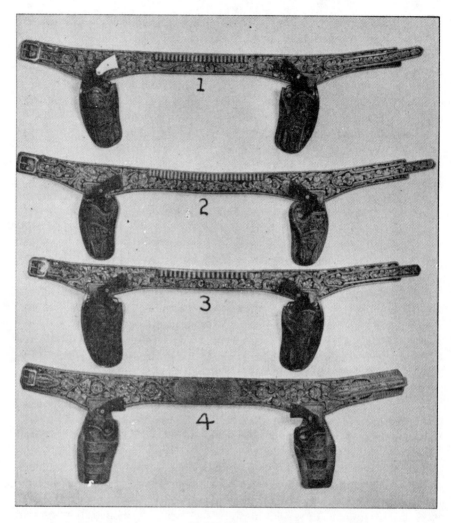

TWO-GUN RIGS

1. Sam Myres Buscadero belt, slanted and hung specially to suit the writer, for .38 Smith & Wesson Military and Police target revolvers, 6-inch barrels.

2. Myres Buscadero belt, two-gun rig, specially constructed for two Smith & Wesson .38-44 McGivern Model target-sighted revolvers, with 5-inch barrels. The hang and slant of these holsters for use with these guns is just right, making a fast and excellent outfit which is much in favor, and used more by the writer than any other combination in our very satisfactory assortment.

3. Myres Buscadero belt built for Smith & Wesson .45 caliber target revolvers, very nicely balanced and arranged for these guns. It will be noted that holsters are spaced so as to hang just slightly more to the rear than the other guns. This is the same outfit that is used with the two left-hand holsters for the back and front cross-fire stunt, as shown in photo on page 269.

(Description continued on next page)

Holsters, Belts, Etc.

4. Captain Hardy's Hollywood Special belt and drop holster. Note these holsters and gun grips are dropped more than any of the other holsters shown. This outfit was built for Colt .38 Officers' Model revolvers, 6-inch barrels. Note these holsters and guns, when in position on shooter, hang almost straight down and just a little farther forward than any of the other holsters.

All of these holsters are interchangeable on the several belts, thus they may be changed around at will. Flat steel springs are built into the shanks of these holsters to the specification of the writer, which stops all buckling or hanging on to the guns during the draw, making it unnecessary to tie them down to the legs as usually done to prevent such occurrences, also making it possible to "set" the grip at any particular angle or degree of hand clearance from the body or belt that may be desired by the person using them.

The author is indebted to Eugene Cunningham of El Paso, Texas, for the explanation of the origin of the name "Buscadero" as given to Mr. Myres' two-gun belts, as illustrated here.

The word "Buscadero" is of Spanish origin. **Buscar** is the verb to search or hunt. The suffix **dero** means "he who is" or "he who does."

Buscudero, then, could be translated as either **the one who hunted** or **the one who was hunted.** In the last mentioned sense it became current from Utah to Cananea in the days of Butch Cassidy and the Wild Bunch (probably was in use long before this, but particularly spread around in Butch's day) as the general name for the outlaws—the men who were hunted.

Showing a very fine and quite ornamental combination of white leather trimmed with black with the author's name carved out on the back center of belt. An excellent piece of work by the artist—Sam D. Myres of El Paso, Texas.

A mate to this excellent two-gun rig was also made for Walter Groff of Philadelphia.

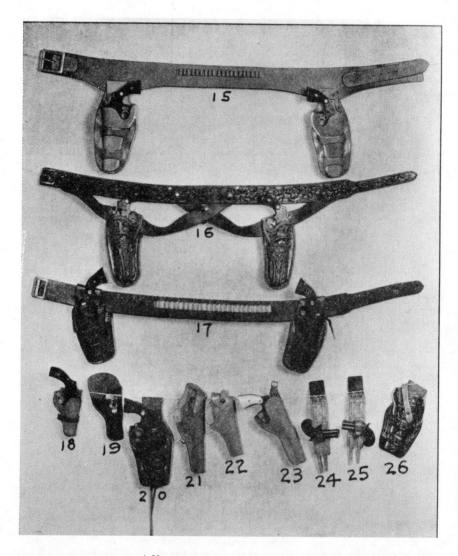

A VARIED ASSORTMENT OF HOLSTERS

15. A fine plain finish two-gun belt by Jas. R. Diekan, 41 Fulton Street, New York. This pair of holsters is set pretty well forward. Interchangeable holsters make it possible to use any kind of revolvers hung at exactly any slant desired by the user. A high quality, very serviceable, durable, dependable, two-gun rig. Holsters do not need to be tied down.

(Description continued on next page)

Holsters, Belts, Etc.

16. Fancy 2½-inch belt by Captain Hardy. Drop straps built and adjusted by Ed Mc-Givern, and two perfectly formed and fitted quick-draw holsters by Sam Myres, specially constructed for two .38 double-action target revolvers. A very satisfactory three-man combination idea that gives excellent results and replaces the old style cumbersome crossed belts; also has many advantages, and is really much more convenient to handle, to adjust and to wear.

17. Hardy's 3-inch plain belt and two of his Texas Ranger style holsters for Colt single-action revolvers, which have been equipped with target sights by the late J. D. O'Meara. This combination makes an excellent outfit.

18. Hardy's compact cross-draw holster used in various quick-draw stunts.

19. Myres' waist band holster, for cross-draw or straight-draw, as preferred. Can be arranged at any location on belt line position around the body that may be preferred. Handy, light, compact, safe. It fastens with a self-adjusting metal clamp that is quite secure, yet easily released when so desired.

20. Shows the detachable Hardy-McGivern (stiff shank) low hung holster for .38-44 Smith & Wesson or .45 Smith & Wesson target-sighted revolvers. This as shown can also be tied down to the leg at bottom if so desired.

21 and 22. Diekan's flap top, snap button, quick-draw holster. The strap and snap button is flipped off with the thumb as hand closes on grip of gun. This holster is within a small fraction of a second of being fully as fast as an open top holster, yet giving gun full protection when closed, and also makes it quite difficult for someone else to lift an officer's gun out in a scrimmage.

23. Diekan's suspender holster. A very handy and satisfactory non-conspicuous holster for use where a gun may be needed quickly, yet can be worn with ordinary street clothes. Handy, effective, yet well and conveniently concealed. Ideal for bank messengers, officials, etc.

24 and 25. Myres' wrist and arm band holsters (right and left) for Remington .41 caliber rim fire Derringer pistols. Good hideout and protection outfit, also for bank messengers, officials, etc., making a very good emergency gun available. Even when held up and with hands in the air these holsters keep these guns within easy reach, if and when the slightest chance is given to draw and shoot. These bands can be worn any place desired on the inside of the forearm (as shown in photo on page 384).

26. Hardy's open-top quick-draw holster, fitted with a detachable (when so desired) strap across top of gun. Excellent attachment when extra security is needed. When strap is snapped around on back of holster, a plain open-top quick-draw holster is the result. A very good all-around combination in a single, high quality holster.

MYRES HOLSTERS

Sam D. Myres and his son, nationally famous leather workers of El Paso, Texas, holster makers supreme, with a few samples of their excellent workmanship. Note the revolver case in center. The writer has one of these which is a work of art.

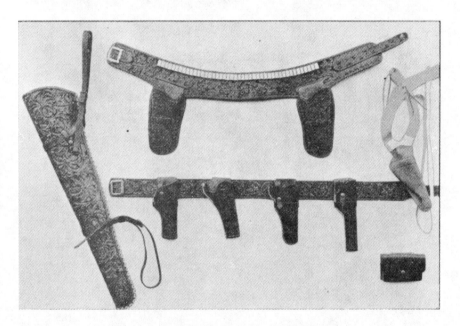

HARDY HOLSTERS—HIGH GRADE WORKMANSHIP

MONTANA HIGHWAY PATROL HOLSTER—FRONT VIEW

The holster adopted by the Montana Highway Patrol worn on the left side—the safest side for an officer's gun if and when he takes his prisoner in the car seat with him. This holster hangs in a safe position, is comfortably worn and is plenty fast. The projecting tip of safety strap is pushed off of the button lock with the thumb as hand comes in contact with gun grip.

MONTANA HIGHWAY PATROL HOLSTER—SIDE VIEW

Showing the hang and position of gun and holster when in place on the left side where it is regularly worn. Note the adjustment of this holster. Keeps gun grip slightly away from the body, always clear and free—ready for a quick grip and fast draw.

The author was pleased to co-operate with the department in arranging the details of slant hang position and general proportions.

Fast and Fancy Revolver Shooting

DUKE WELLINGTON SHOWS ARRANGEMENT OF VARIOUS GUN RIGS

Left—Showing the regulation dropped cross belts, both attached to and supported and held in place by the one belt, which fits snug around the waist. This style of two-gun rig has many admirers and very good fast work can be done when properly adjusted.

Right—Drop-strap two-gun combination, lighter and less cumbersome than the low hung crossed belts, as usually arranged. Adaptable to a variety of adjustments to suit the individual's requirements. (Description No. 16, page 377.)

Left—Diekan's cross-draw holster with snap-off top strap and flap. Safe, convenient, fast, and at the same time gives the gun full protection.

Right—Showing the slanted cross-draw for short barrels, conveniently adjusted to suit the wearer and readily adaptable to fast work.

Holsters, Belts, Etc.

Left—Myres' skeleton shoulder holster.

Right—Myres' covered shoulder holster.

Left—Showing the low hung stiff shank Hardy-McGivern holster which can also be tied down if desired.

Right—Plain leather Buscadero belt and holsters made by Sam Myres for Walter Groff.

The hang and slant of these holsters and the position of the gun grips as shown is ideal for smooth, fast work.

Left—E. E. Clarke shoulder holster, which is also fastened to the belt by a conveniently arranged adjustable strap on back of holster.   A very satisfactory combination.

Right—Showing Myres drop holster for single-action Colt attached to the Buscadero belt. Note slot in upper front of holster to allow the barrel to clear holster just a small fraction of time quicker.

Myres' wrist band holsters for Derringers.   A good hideout combination which can be adjusted and adapted to several positions, locations and purposes.

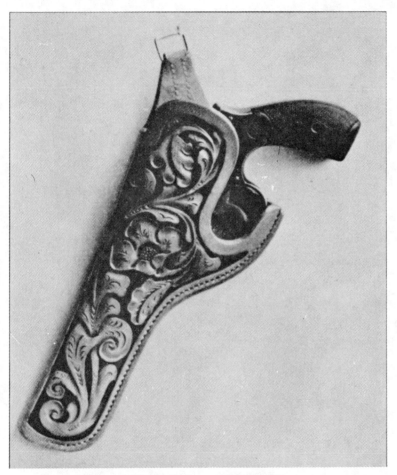

MYRES SUSPENDER HOLSTER
An excellent and convenient holster

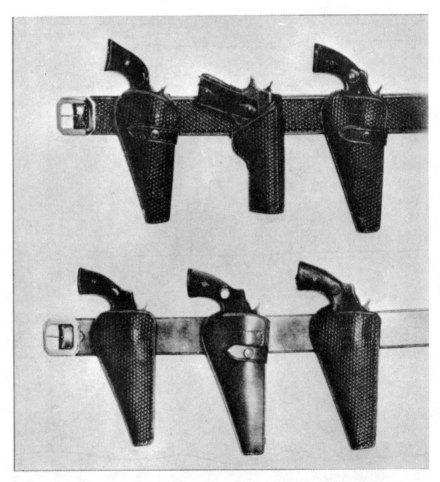

BERNS-MARTIN HOLSTERS

Safety straps are shown on several. The guns come out in front, not out of the top. Cut on next page shows how a gun comes out of these holsters.

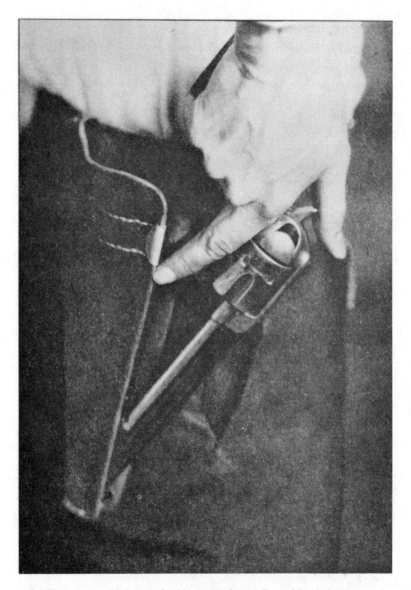

The recommended way of taking a gun from a Berns-Martin holster

SECTION 24

SELECTIONS OF SIGHTS FOR VARIOUS SITUATIONS.

What are the best sights to use on a revolver? I have been called upon to answer this question thousands of times. My answer has usually been: "If there is any such thing as 'the one best set of sights' for every purpose and for everybody's use, I have not been able to make any such very important discovery." The underlying reason for this fact rests on the vital point that there is too much variation in the physical, as well as the mental, make-up and temperament of the individuals who compose the shooting public.

I have, without doubt, put in fully as much study and real effort toward sight building and improvement as any other revolver shooter and instructor in the game, and, thanks to D. W. King, J. W. Weaver, The Lyman Gun Sight Corporation, Col. D. B. Wesson, Vice-President of Smith & Wesson, Inc., and Colt Patent Firearms Company, for their hearty co-operation, I have been fairly successful in securing better results for myself and guaranteeing improved results for my many pupils, through the aid and as a result of the improved sight equipment now available. The main reason for my resolute action along this line was to make it possible for me to pass along these improvements and later methods of development for fast and fancy, yet practical revolver shooting, to police officers and others in various law enforcement capacities, as well as the revolver shooting public generally.

Most of the revolvers used by me in the many tests, experiments and demonstrations in the combined efforts toward **speed** and **accuracy,** have the same sight equipment—the McGivern $\frac{1}{10}''$ gold bead front sight and the standard square notch rear sight one-tenth inch wide. As most of this sort of shooting is usually done at short and medium ranges, the larger sights are recommended for the reason that they can be easily and quickly seen under varied, and sometimes suddenly changing, light conditions. The sights used for other experiments and tests are mentioned in connection with the descriptive matter relative thereto.

Numerous queries have come through the mail, and various arguments have been brought to me for consideration about adjustable sights on revolvers for general use. These call for some consideration at this time. While having my personal preferences regarding sight adjustments and adjustable sights, as generally used on revolvers, I wish to avoid any appearance of attempting to influence others to exactly follow my example. I am giving the account of my experiences and the results of my experiments purely for the purpose of helping others who may be interested in securing similarly successful results, through similar methods of procedure, and who are interested in and seeking such instructive matter as I have tried to have this book contain.

I do not wish to create the impression as many do that my way is the only **correct way**; for me it has been **correct** and very satisfactory. Others may make their own arrangements and choices. Front sights on revolvers are more satisfactory to me always, when fastened securely in some sort of a solidly built and milled-out base on the barrel. These front sights should be interchangeable and easily replaced by means of screws or pins passing through the sides of the base or studs or ribs, also, of course, through the base of the sight, so as to hold it firmly and securely in proper position on the barrel, and not allowing any slack or movement whatever. In other words, when once put in place they must "stay put" until intentionally removed. All adjustments for elevation and windage should be made from, by, and with the rear sight, much the same and in as satisfactory a manner as can be, and very generally is done, on rifles. I perhaps should say quite universally done on rifles.

This arrangement of sights has been nicely handled by D. W. King in his new ventilated rib attachment for revolvers, having micrometer adjustments for rear sight and interchangeable firmly attached front sights, with chromium reflector to illuminate the front bead. The Colt rear sight on the Ace .22 and the Stevens rear sight on the Super Match .38 and the National Match .45 auto pistols handle this situation very nicely, also the King micrometered adjustable rear sight for Colt Woodsman and Hi-Standard .22 auto pistols. The Smith & Wesson rear sight, with the lock screw feature, gives perfect adjustment. This type of sight allows the use of easily interchangeable rear notch slides for all variations in elevation that may be required for any purpose whatever.

When front sights, though interchangeable, are fastened securely in the same position always, it is a very easy and quickly accomplished job to change from one kind of a bead or post or stud, as the case may be, to some other type, when such a change may be desirable. When any sort of long range shooting is indulged in the firmly attached front sight, which is easily interchangeable, is much more satisfactory for the purpose.

For my personal use, and for the work that I am mostly interested in, I do not care very much for any form of round top permanently fixed (integral with the barrel), and as usually termed, military sights, regardless of the arguments so often offered in their favor for quick-draw work, etc. However, it is only fair to call attention to the fact that the military or service sights of today, thanks to the ever-present urge for improvement, have been changed, widened, and built up in various ways until they now come into reasonably close competition with the target sighted guns for certain standard ranges. These permanently fixed non-adjustable sights can be

SUPERACCURATE REVOLVERS AND SIGHT COMBINATIONS

20.   Smith & Wesson .38/44 Outdoorsman, 6½-inch barrel, with small, dull gold bead front sight, D. W. King peep rear sight.   This gun as now adjusted was used on the earlier, up to 300 yards, extended range shooting, with the Peters Hi-Velocity .38 Special cartridges and the Remington Hi-Speed .38/44 S. & W. Special cartridges mentioned.   An absolutely accurate outfit.

22.   Regular .38 Special M. & P. Smith & Wesson 6-inch barrel, equipped with D. W. King special peep rear sight and King-McGivern red bead front sight, interchangeable with fine gold bead, both excellent sighting combinations and used in our first experiments for extended range man target shooting.   Man targets painted white—no bull's-eyes or sighting spots or marks were used as guides.   "Hold center and squeeze 'er off."

23.   Colt Shooting Master .38 Special, fitted with flat topped special U notch rear sight, also made by D. W. King, and a fine gold bead (dull finish) front sight (Colt).   This gun was equipped with special rear sight for the various increased ranges, and used with both Peters high velocity and Remington long range cartridges on our later tests before the .357 Magnum experiments.   Exceptionally accurate gun and satisfactory sight combination. Note the new grip specially designed by Colt for this model.   The tapered barrel adds to the balance and graceful lines also.   All standard factory specifications.

24.   Colt Officers' Model .38 Special, equipped with D. W. King large aperture peep sight and King fine gold bead front sight.   Used by us for several of the shooting experiments. A combination giving excellent results.

Selections of Sights

25. The .38/44 Smith & Wesson Outdoorsman, 6½-inch barrel, with S. & W. adapter, Lyman scope, with special mounts made up and specially fitted and adjusted by Lyman Gun Sight Corp., for our long range experiments with the new high velocity .38 cartridges. This was at that time the supreme combination.

In the face of much opposition we insisted on getting this outfit put together. The results secured justified our faith in the gun, the ammunition and the extra equipment, and started us on our way towards securing many of the results that we were in search of.

26. Smith & Wesson .22/32, equipped with D. W. King white outlined square notch rear sight, and the McGivern gold bead front sight, a fine general purpose combination, quick and easy to handle, and plenty accurate when the shooter does his part properly. "Hold 'em and squeeze 'em" is the secret. This is the model that won the "Any Revolver" Match of the U. S. Revolver Association several times as well as making the record high score.

27. Smith & Wesson K-.22, D. W. King peep rear sight, medium aperture, King-Mc-Givern red bead and interchangeable red post front sight. A surprising combination when using high velocity long rifle cartridges at various distances, occasionally reaching out around 200 yards. The King luminous red post front sight is very satisfactory for the various ranges, and is preferred by many of the shooters who have given these experiments some attention.

28. Standard Smith & Wesson M. & P. .38 Special, equipped with D. W. King square notch rear sight and the McGivern bright gold bead front sight, adjusted for the rapid fire and aerial can shooting and the various combinations and groups of aerial target shooting. A very fast and accurate combination.

29. Smith & Wesson .22 Single Shot Pistol, Patridge sights, for indoor gallery use, McGivern gold bead on back of front sight for outdoor shooting, with interchangeable red and ivory beads to suit occasions. King white outlined square notch rear sight, reversible to black if desired. Accurately superior to the holding ability of the shooter (with perhaps an occasional but very rare exception). This gun and No. 25 will prove equal to any man's holding ability, and "then some." The main grief when using them is the fact that we have no suitable alibis available, if, and when, we are not successful in our efforts to accomplish what we have set out to do. Smith & Wesson rear sights are very conveniently constructed for the various changes herein mentioned; the front sights being stationary are also an aid to easy adjustment when interchanging gold, ivory or red beads or posts, as may be desired. All adjustments, elevation and windage are made by and with the rear sights. Revolver shooting at increased ranges has lost much of the mysterious angles that were once associated with it.

The old system was to sight the revolver at some convenient spot, then watch where the bullets struck. When this bullet catching spot was located, the target was placed in the proper location to catch at least part of the bullets on its surface, and results were noted. Not so today. The revolver is sighted for the exact point it is desired to hit. With the aid of spotting scopes, etc., the results are noted, adjustments are made until the desired results, or a reasonably fair average is secured. Results are then noted and recorded in a much more satisfactory manner than has ever before been possible. New revolvers, new ammunition, new methods, all combined to produce surprising results. "And thus we struggle onward."

built up or cut down to suit the individual so that, with the use of the same brand of standard factory loaded cartridges, or their equivalent, consistent grouping results can be secured at any of the standard ranges for which they have been so fitted.

When it comes to paying the difference between a military sighted revolver and a target sighted revolver of the same model, my personal preference and choice is always in favor of the target sighted gun. For various reasons that have grown out of experience with such guns, I use the target sighted guns for every purpose that revolvers are generally used, and up to the present time I have had no trouble of any kind, and have no complaints whatever to make about the sights giving trouble. The reason for such an attitude is that during the many years some of our preferred guns have been in regular service under much varied conditions, involving the firing of many thousands of shots through them, no trouble has arisen that could be directly charged to the sights. One reason may be on account of the sturdy type of target sights that are favored and used, and which we undoubtedly helped in various ways to develop, and also to make available to the shooting public. Perhaps our very excellent holsters also help to avoid trouble from this source; but there is one thing I am quite satisfied about in my own mind, when any type of sights or any other make of revolver, other than the ones I am using, will help me to secure greater speed or more satisfactory results, I most certainly will be using them. The sight combinations now in use will be found in the particular section devoted to the type of shooting that is under consideration. A fairly complete display of D. W. King's revolver sights will be found illustrated, numbered and identified for the benefit and convenience of our readers. This is a purely complimentary tribute from me, due to the superior quality of King's sights.

As a result of concentrated action and co-operation for better revolver sight activities D. W. King, of the King Sight Company, 171-173 Second Street, San Francisco, Cal., has fitted up and placed on the market various combinations in peep sights that are adaptable to the Smith & Wesson and Colt revolvers and pistols, which are now available for both the long and shorter range shooting. They have proven quite valuable and helpful in certain situations toward getting consistent results. Mr. King has made several types of front sights to be used with these combinations, red beads, which are highly recommended, as well as ivory and gold beads, also hooded front sights of several designs, all of which have proven O.K. in every way in many special experiments.

I have been successful in securing some very satisfactory results by using rear sight slides for Smith & Wesson revolvers, of various heights, for correct elevation at various ranges. Several of these are made with square notches 1/10 inch wide, also similar assortment of slides for the

Selections of Sights

Showing King's ⅛-inch Gold Bead Super-Night Sight and white outlined rear notch mounted on the 3½-inch barrel Magnum revolver. A very fine sight combination for officers on night duty and when shooting where light is none too plentiful.

The Smith & Wesson .22 L.R. Target Pistol, with 10-inch barrel, equipped with the Lyman target spot scope, as used in formerly mentioned experiments up to 200 yards. These two 10-inch barrel target pistols, so equipped, proved to be a surprisingly accurate combination in the hands of several of the shooters who were interested in such experiments. The cartridges used in several of these pistol experiments were Western supermatch and they performed fully up to their name.

rear sights with smaller U notches, for use in the longer range work in connection with the several sizes of front sight beads of various colors. I also have a series of interchangeable rear sights for the various target model Colt revolvers that give the correct elevation for the various ranges when used with the adjustable front sights, made up with an assortment of beads. I have secured very satisfactory results with these several combinations when used on the Colt and Smith & Wesson revolvers.

Step by step this sight question for all purposes, both short range and long range, was studied and worked out by degrees and by repeated trials, and the results were subject to the investigation and opinions of interested and well-informed persons, with nothing of value being intentionally overlooked. We were honestly in search of facts with which to replace theories.

And the facts when assembled seem to rather clearly indicate that, for the fastest or the slowest shooting on stationary targets, moving targets, aerial targets, as well as on all quick draws on targets of various kinds where the revolver is raised high enough for the shooter to look over the gun at all, the sights are necessary for consistent results and should be used.

When shooting under somewhat poor and uncertain light conditions, good sights will usually help to secure much better results than are generally secured when trying to get along without them. The numerous targets reproduced in the police section, were shot with revolvers having gold bead front sights and by the aid of the dim illumination of pocket flash-lights only. Various other targets were shot under purposely arranged poorly lighted conditions, as the descriptions accompanying the targets explain. These were so arranged for practical police training situations similar to those that might be expected to exist where and when our law enforcement officers would be called upon to risk their lives while compelled, in the line of duty, to attempt effective shooting, and will substantially support the statement regarding the use of sights.

The actual results secured in all of the situations listed and described were the result of plenty of study combined with deliberate practice in the use of sights under such conditions. The first sight on all of the guns used for these tests under poor light conditions was the McGivern gold bead front sight, just as issued from the factory. The King spark point gold bead front sights in two styles also give good results under these conditions.

For the law enforcement officer who is on duty mostly at night, I recommend that his gun be equipped with some sort of suitable sights such as has been developed for these and similar conditions. A very excellent combination of sights for an officer who expects to be required to use his revolver mostly at night, consists of the King Super Police Sight, which, in plain English, is a large (steel center) gold bead front sight used

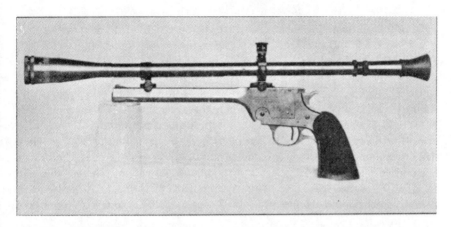

Lyman Target Spot Scope mounted on the Harrington & Richardson 10-inch barrel .22 L.R. target pistol. The two pistols shown here so equipped constitute a superaccurate combination that opens up an interesting field of experiment for the pistol shooters.

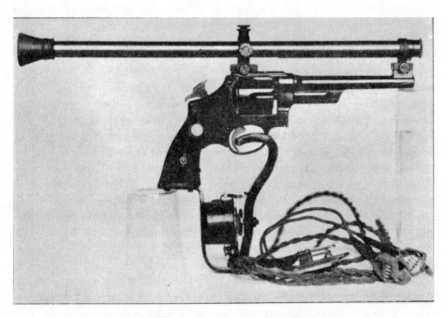

The .38-44 Outdoorsman, with scope attached, was later equipped with an electric trigger releasing device for certain experimental purposes in relation to single-action trigger squeezing. This device will not operate the double-action mechanism even though it appears as if it could do so. It does, however, give a perfect trigger release when the hammer is raised by hand to full cock position. The series of experiments planned by the author in connection with this device at the time it was constructed were never completed on account of illness.

in connection with a white outline set in the frame or around the rear sight notch on target models. They are the best sights for the purpose that I have so far found and can often be seen fairly well under night shooting conditions. Under city lights or even moonlight the large gold bead reflects any light that may come from the rear or above, and the heavy white U outline (semicircular) can be seen under almost any condition where there is any light at all. When the gold shows above the U, you know you are sighted through the notch and can be reasonably sure of a good line shot. Many trials by members of the shooting classes have demonstrated these features conclusively and I believe that there is a reasonable need for these special purpose sights for every officer, when he is on night duty especially. This combination of sights as described can be seen on the photo of the Smith & Wesson .357 Magnum with three and a half inch barrel.

Personally, I make use of and depend on the sights for directing the shots whenver it is at all possible to use them, even when working on the fastest aerial target shooting and other speed performances where it is quite generally believed, by many, that sights are not used. This belief is entirely wrong and should be corrected, which is exactly what I am endeavoring to do. As results show, I have been at least successful enough in this branch of revolver shooting to determine the necessity and value of good sight equipment on revolvers.

I do not attempt to do any of these things without the use and assistance of the various combinations of sights that have been selected for and adapted to the certain performances. Shooting without sights is, with very few exceptions, not productive of overwhelming success with the various combinations of shooting performances herein set forth. Fancy sights are not intended as an expensive decoration for revolvers. They have been developed and improved for the special purpose of better performance and more consistent accuracy. Any man who has developed any consistent shooting ability whatever can do better shooting with sights suitable for his particular kind of work than he can without them.

On the other side of the argument it should be quite evident from the submitted proof that I have devoted considerable time and attention to building up a system for developing sufficient skill to hit various objects while shooting from the hip or below belt level, and other similar forms of quick-draw shooting with one and two guns from various positions; also slip shooting, fanning the hammer with single-action revolvers, and about all of the other gunmen's tricks of shooting without sighting, so widely written up and so generally connected up with the romantic "chatter" of the early West.

While much success with these various stunts has been the result of such study, practice and training along these several lines of gun pointing

Selections of Sights

accuracy, the foundation of it all is, was and always must be, built up from and by much persistent practice with, and the careful use of, suitable sights until the correct "pointing feel" and confidence in sense of direction has been firmly established.   It should at this time be clearly understood that training for "shooting without sighting" should come **after** successful results have been secured by the "correctly sighting" system, and very positively **not before it.**

KING REAR SIGHTS ADAPTED TO PISTOLS AND REVOLVERS

The finest assortment of sights for the revolver shooter ever produced by any manufacturer to date.

1.   King Peep Sight adapted to Colt Woodsman, .38 Super and .45 Auto. and Target Model revolvers.

3, 4.   King Micrometered Windage and Elevation Adjusting Sight adapted to Colt Woodsman pistols with wide rear sight base.

7, 8.   King Rear Sight adapted to Colt Woodsman, adjustable for windage only.

10, 11.   King Windage and Elevation Adjusting Rear Sight for Colt Ace, Super .38 and .45 Autos.

2.   King Rear Notch Slides adapted to S. & W. Target Model revolvers and pistols.

5, 6.   King Interchangeable Peep and Open Discs to fit sights Nos. 3 and 4.

9, 12.   King Rear Sights adapted to Colt Target Model revolvers.

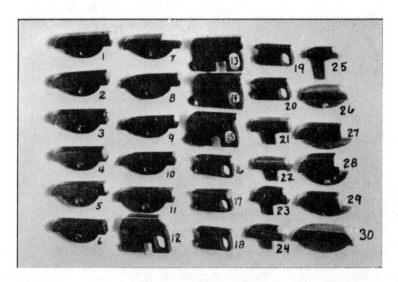

KING FRONT SIGHTS ADAPTED TO PISTOLS AND REVOLVERS

The finest assortment of sights for the revolver shooter ever produced by any manufacturer to date.

1, 11.   King-Call Red, Gold or White Beads.

2, 3.   King-McGivern Red, Gold or White Beads.

4, 5, 6.   King "Patridge" Type Red, Gold or "Kingoid" White "Posts."

7.   King Undercut Black Post Sight.

8, 9, 10.   King 3/32", 5/64" and 1/16" Beads, Red, Gold or White Beads adapted to S. & W. Target Model revolvers and King ramps.

12, 15.   King Red, Gold or White Beads adapted to Colt Officers' Model .22 and Shooting Master.

13, 14.   King Red, Gold or White Post Sights adapted to Colt Officers' Model .38 and Shooting Master.

16, 17.   King Red, Gold or White Post Sights adapted to Colt Woodsman, .22 Officers' Model and Police Positive Target.

18, 19, 20.   King Red, Gold or White Beads for same models as 16 and 17.

21, 22, 23, 24.   King Post and Bead Sights adapted to Colt Ace, .38 Super and .45 Auto.

26, 27, 28, 29.   King Bead and Post Type Sights adapted to S. & W. Target models.

30.   King Super-Police Full Gold Beads with Steel Center adapted to all types pistols and revolvers, Military or Target models.

SECTION 25

SPOTTING SCOPES.

In the writer's opinion, next to the gun the most important and necessary item of any target shooter's equipment is the possession of one or more spotting scopes. This is particularly true of the revolver shooter. This conclusion which caused this statement to be made is well-borne out by the results of our own experience in this field of endeavor as here set forth.

While we confined our revolver shooting to short and medium standard target ranges we were able to get along fairly well in the regular old-fashioned way of shooting a string of shots and then walking up to the target or bringing the target back to us, by mechanical means or otherwise, for inspection. But as the conditions were gradually changed, and the distances, and the accompanying difficulties also increased, the problem of accurately determining the exact location of hits, shot by shot, on the man targets, began to get more unsatisfactory as the changes were more numerous and the targets and distances and conditions were more greatly varied.

Unless we had a full crew at the military range to raise and lower the targets and hold the markers so as to indicate where the bullets were hitting, and also pass information along over the phone, we had to either walk or drive up to the target set-up after each string of shots in order to check up on our progress.

We soon found that at the ranges from two hundred yards on, such procedure soon became rather tiresome, and the greater the distance we were stationed from the target the more monotonous these trips became. For instance, five hundred yards is not only a rather long shooting distance —it is also a rather long and tiresome walk—both ways—to check up results, and it is also a somewhat long ride back and forth in a car, and not so very interesting if repeated many times, which, of course, would be very necessary if close checking of results was desired as a guide towards successful progress.

At about this time we began to see rather clearly that some very important changes in our methods would soon be necessary or the experimental revolver shooting at man targets at the various increased ranges would soon lose its attractiveness, and we, like others, would pass up in disgust what could be a very interesting game if some of the inconveniences could be eliminated.

Much discussion of this angle at this time brought us face to face with the facts that among the most important things necessary for us to secure, would be some sort of dependable spotting scopes, if we were going to

Fast and Fancy Revolver Shooting

SPOTTING THE SHOTS ON LONG RANGE REVOLVER TARGETS
Jim Browne of Big Fork, Montana, shooting the S. & W. .357 Magnum at long range targets. Ed McGivern with Bausch & Lomb prismatic spotting scope calling the shots and checking results.

Spotting the shots from S. & W. .357 Magnum revolver at 600 yards, using the Bausch & Lomb prismatic spotting scope for the purpose. Walter Groff shooting.

Jim Browne of Big Fork, Montana, shooting the S. & W. .357 Magnum at long range targets. Ed McGivern spotting the shots with Bausch & Lomb prismatic spotting scope. Two Bausch & Lomb draw tube spot scopes in foreground.

successfully continue our research experiments for the purpose of ascertaining the reasonable possibilities of revolver shooting at the longer ranges, and the other various intermediate distances as well.

In this situation we were confronted with several problems having various angles that must have careful consideration for our own guidance toward satisfactory progress with such equipment. A thorough investigation of spotting scopes and kindred equipment was now under way, and after looking the entire field over thoroughly and by asking and eventually receiving the advice of various persons of experience with such equipment, the products of the Bausch & Lomb Optical Company seemed to deserve the most favorable consideration, and were quite generally regarded as the most satisfactory instruments for the purpose, when all angles and points of merit were to be considered.

The Bausch & Lomb 20 power draw tube spotting scope which sold for thirty dollars, used in connection with a folding tripod costing ten dollars and fifty cents, was the first one that we put into service, and it proved to be an excellent instrument and gave very satisfactory results at the various ranges. The holes made in the man targets by the bullets from the various .38 caliber cartridges that we were using, were not so difficult to locate.

We next secured the Bausch & Lomb N.R.A. model prismatic spotting scope, with the several extra eye pieces of different power from 12.8X, 19.5X, 26X and up to 36.5X, which gives several optical adjustments suitable for almost any conditions that may be encountered. The substantial wooden tripod, or cradle, as it is called, which runs a little higher in price, allows the observer to be comfortably seated in a chair while spotting the shots (as shown by the photographs taken when scope was in use on the range). This scope can also be seen with the $10.50 folding metal tripod being used for spotting shots while shooting in the prone position. This type of scope sold for $55.00 and the prices for extra eye pieces were very reasonable. The instrument is usually sent out with the 19.5X eye piece for general use, and purchase of the other eye pieces are optional. Any further information desired in relation to these instruments will be cheerfully furnished by the Bausch & Lomb Optical Company, 432 Lomb Park, Rochester, New York.

When the man targets were placed at still longer ranges, and out towards six hundred yards, the Bausch & Lomb 80 mm. team captain's spotting scope was put into service. Four eye pieces are interchangeable in this scope. The several powers represented are 12.7X, 21X, 25.6X, and 32.6X. The sturdy wooden tripod illustrated is adjustable for standing or sitting. This scope, with tripod and packing case complete, costs $275.00 and with extra eye pieces comes around $300.00. This outfit is the most value for the least money that has been produced for the shooting fraternity.

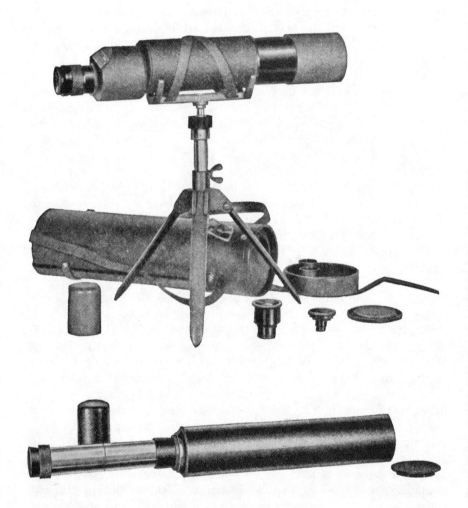

Upper—Bausch & Lomb Optical Company's N.R.A. prismatic spotting scope with four interchangeable eye pieces.

Lower—Bausch & Lomb's 20 power draw tube spotting scope.

These scopes and tripods described with more detail on page 401.

Spotting Scopes

And it is my candid opinion, resulting from the very satisfactory and often quite surprising results secured, that the Bausch & Lomb team captain's spotting scope and accessories comprise the very finest equipment ever designed for that particular purpose.

After the successful conclusion of many experiments the full realization finally dawned on us that what was done last in relation to spotting scopes, etc., should have been done first. The most important and very necessary part of the equipment for the success of the experiments that we were interested in conducting had been neglected and overlooked until almost the danger point of indifference and dissatisfaction had been reached.

Immediately after the spotting scopes were put into service everyone's interest was again aroused and the whole situation seemed changed. We could see clearly where our errors crept in and made headway with some problems that we had not been very hopeful would ever be successfully solved while laboring under the former condition of affairs.

The results secured on the submitted targets support the testimony in favor of the spotting scopes much more convincingly than I can tell it. Personally, I would not attempt to conduct any more such shooting experiments without the aid of first-class spotting scopes. It would be just about as sensible to attempt them without first-class revolvers. In this case we used what we honestly believed to be the very best revolvers obtainable, and we honestly believe that we also possessed and made use of the very best set of spotting scopes that has been made available for the shooters. It is an established fact that the extremely large line of optical goods and instruments of precision produced by the Bausch & Lomb Optical Company has not been excelled by any institution engaged in the manufacture of such products. Their practically unlimited equipment for research, under the supervision of their large force of technically trained experts, and backed by the vast experience resulting from a long period of years spent in highly specialized service, makes this firm the unquestioned leader in the large field covered by their activities in that particular branch of industry.

THE BAUSCH & LOMB TEAM CAPTAIN'S SPOTTING SCOPE

The finest instrument for the purpose ever designed and produced by any optical manufacturer in the history of the shooting game.

SECTION 26

LONG RANGE REVOLVER SHOOTING. TELESCOPES ON
REVOLVERS AND PISTOLS. THE SMITH & WESSON .357
MAGNUM REVOLVER, ITS CARTRIDGES AND ITS ADAPTA-
BILITY FOR THE OUTDOORSMAN. THE TARGET SHOOTER
AND THE LAW ENFORCEMENT OFFICER.

We have often noticed in various **he-man hero** stories wherein were
described hair-raising accounts of situations in which the hero faced death
or capture at the hands of his enemies who had him bottled up behind some
rocks, and he was entirely at their mercy, for the reason that, while they
were out in the open and could watch his every movement and keep close
tabs on his actions, the distance separating them was too great for the
possibility of scoring a hit with a bullet fired from a revolver, yet the man
out in front with a 30–30 carbine could bounce a bullet off one of the rocks
near the hero's head any time said hero made a move.

In the general arrangement of targets for competition, the rifle targets
for two hundred yard use usually have the same sized bull's-eyes as the
revolver targets have for use at fifty yards. On this basis the rifle should be
effective at four times the range of the revolver. In other words, if the
revolver would be capable of registering on a man target at 250 yards the
rifle should have about the same accuracy possibilities at a thousand yards,
and for revolver results at six hundred yards the rifle would necessarily be
put back to 2,400 yards. We will compare these probable results as we
proceed with the account of the revolver shooting tests that we conducted
at the various extended ranges which were suggested to us as a result of
reading the referred-to gunslick hero stories.

As the situation is usually presented, the only weapon available to our
hero was his revolver (make and caliber not always stated), but being a
matter of life or death with any possibility of escape cut off by the man with
the rifle, it was up to our hero to do some accurate long range revolver
shooting in spite of the fact that his author decided the distance was too
far. Yet, as the story goes, the rifle shooter could control his shots perfectly, and could also, at will, lay them on any spot near the hero that
pleased him most.

This was the angle of the game that aroused my interest. Just how far,
is really too far, for a fairly good average revolver shot to smoke out the
man with the rifle. As I became more interested I aroused the interest of
several more persons who were pretty handy with revolvers—not supergun-
slick heroes by any chance, but just fairly proficient performers.

The results of our tests, as demonstrated by a few of the targets herewith produced, would indicate that no man—outlaw, sheriff, hero or otherwise—in possession of anywhere near his right senses, would or could be "damphool" enough to stay out in the open at any distance up to and including six hundred yards, while the experienced modern-day revolver shooter would deliver three shots in his direction with deliberate effort to score a hit.

After studying these various targets carefully it makes quite a difficult problem out of answering the question, **"Just how far is too far?"** for a good revolver shot to smoke out an opponent and make him take to his heels in a hurry, or hunt some good safe protection between him and the revolver shooter with any of the guns and cartridges herein mentioned as having been used in the tests.

These long range activities were conducted in an effort to furnish a fair idea of the probable average number of hits that might reasonably be expected to occur on various types of man targets (not bull's-eyes) at the several distances, during and as a result of carefully conducted trials, **and was very positively NOT done** with any idea of trying to impress on the world in general that we were endowed with any "extra special" ability in this long range revolver shooting field of activity.

I am using, and will continue to use, the word **we** in this case while discussing this class of shooting and experiment, for the reason and as a result of the fact that there were at all times several persons very actively interested and each, in turn, taking an active part in the great amount of shooting necessary to be done in this much varied series of long range experiments while in search of the possibilities that might develop therefrom, which, in turn, might later be used to advantage by, and in the practical training of, officers who are active in the various branches of law enforcement.

In former days it was the usual custom, when long range revolver shooting was indulged in, to select some spot or object as an aiming point which was usually somewhat higher and entirely separate and apart from the target or object to be shot at. Often a few shots would be fired to determine the point of impact of the bullets, then the target or object, if portable, would be moved over and placed where the former bullets had been striking and the shooting would be continued by holding carefully on the aiming point as formerly located.

In some of our earlier attempts we arranged a target holder having a high center pole and on this we arranged a traveling bull's-eye that could be conveniently raised and lowered at will to suit the shooter. This automatically adjusted the aiming point to suit the various experimental loads, standard loads, reloads, and quite oftentimes overloads that were made use of in the attempts to hit the target set-up which was placed below the pole. This adjustable sighting point on an unright pole was quite an improvement over some of the former methods employed by ourselves as well as others, but, at its best, it was only a start in the right direction. The problem has since been solved by improvement in ammunition and sight adjustments.

My friend, Elmer Keith, of North Fork, Idaho, one of the earlier long range revolver shooting enthusiasts, and, in my opinion, about the most successful and proficient large and small game shot with revolvers in this country, developed a system of gold cross-bars spaced at certain intervals across the back of the front sight, that worked out very well for various distances. This sight, I believe, is now available to the public.

Our first fairly successful long range results were secured with Smith & Wesson Military and Police .38 Special, six and a half inch barrel, target revolver. For extra elevation at various ranges we made use of interchangeable rear sight slides of various heights, and a small Sheard gold bead front sight. This combination started us on our way towards getting enough hits on man targets at two hundred yards so that the spectators could at least get some sort of a definite idea about what we were really shooting at.

At this period in our progress D. W. King was called upon to assist and co-operate in solving our revolver sighting problems. He immediately sent along some peep sights with suitable openings for use on revolvers, an assortment of rear sights and a variety of front sights, of all sizes and shapes, colors, and material, and we were then well on our way, as the results secured rather clearly indicated.

Several pistols and revolvers are shown with scopes attached which developed some extremely interesting results, as mentioned in connection with the photos of these guns. An electric pulling device is also shown as part of the experimental equipment used to satisfy our curiosity about certain points of interest to us. The two ten-inch barrel pistols with scopes on were successfully used to break liquor flasks at two hundred yards. Mr. Frank Fish, local gunsmith, was successful in breaking four out of five of these flasks at two hundred yards in the presence of many witnesses.

The Smith & Wesson .357 Magnum revolver, in six inch, six and a half inch and eight and three-quarter inch barrels, holds the lead on all of the extreme ranges on man targets. This .357 Magnum revolver can be had in all of the various sight combinations, and attention is called to the fact that it handles with exceptional accuracy, never equaled by any other one gun, all of the various .38 caliber cartridges, .38 Short Colt's, the .38 Long Colt's, .38 Smith & Wesson Special, the .38 Colt's Special, the .38 Special Superpolice 200-grain bullet, the .38 Special gallery load, the .38 Special Midrange wad cutter or square shoulder 146-grain bullet for target shooting, the .38 Special full charge 158-grain wad cutter or sharp shoulder bullet for target shooting, the .38/44 High Velocity with 158-grain metal point bullet, the .38/44 with full lead bullet, the Western .38 Special cartridge with metal

Fast and Fancy Revolver Shooting

LONG RANGE REVOLVER SHOOTING

This view shows a very good sitting position being practically demonstrated by Jim Browne of Big Fork, Montana, in the long range revolver shooting. This is a position that an officer can use on almost any road or out-of-town location when circumstances may make such shooting necessary, and it will be found productive of very good results. Slight variations may be necessary for various persons. This can be determined by the usual trial and error method until the most satisfactory position has been determined and from there on this form of shooting becomes very interesting and effective.

A somewhat clearer view of the sitting position made use of by Jim Browne and several others during the experiments conducted to determine the probable effective results that could be secured with revolvers at extended ranges on man targets, with a view towards developing a practical training course, along such lines, for the benefit of law enforcement officers.

piercing bullet, and the most powerful and extremely accurate revolver or pistol cartridge ever produced in shooting history, the S. & W. .357 Magnum cartridge brought out by the Winchester Repeating Arms Company, at the request of Smith & Wesson, and now available from all of the other companies.

The machine rest groups shown herewith and made by the Magnum revolver with several of the loads and bullets as carried in the various cartridges mentioned, very positively verify the statements made above relative to accuracy. Many persons have had a mistaken idea and labored under the false impression that the Magnum cartridge, with its rather heavy recoil, had to be used exclusively in the Smith & Wesson .357 Magnum gun, and were not apparently aware that all or any of the other .38 cartridges that are of the .38 Special diameter could be used in the .357 Magnum revolver with much better accuracy, in most cases, than in the general run of standard guns that are built specially for the numerous cartridges mentioned.

These Magnum revolvers, in barrel lengths from three and a half inches up to six and a half inches, have been thoroughly tried out on quick-draw work, aerial target shooting, and on slow deliberate target shooting. They have also given highly satisfactory results at both superspeed double-action shooting and deliberate double action on paper targets at various distances, as plenty of accompanying evidence will clearly show.

Attention is called to the excellent targets shown here shot by Frank W. Millington of Hinsdale, Illinois, with the time periods plainly marked thereon. Attention is particularly directed towards several of the very excellent targets showing quick-draw results, and other exceptionally good targets which were shot by the double-action method by Captain T. Frank Baughmann, of the Federal Bureau of Investigation, while shooting the Magnum revolvers with three and a half and six inch barrels, under my supervision, at the gallery in the Department of Justice building at Washington, D. C.

All of these targets were personally inspected and approved by J. Edgar Hoover, head of the Bureau of Investigation, who, at my request, granted written permission to me for their use in this book for the benefit and guidance of other officers of the law, by witnessing the actual results that can be secured while shooting revolvers **double action.**

The accumulated evidence seems to support my formerly stated belief that the Smith & Wesson .357 Magnum revolver, just as issued from the factory, in the regulation standard factory specifications, with no special order changes of any kind, is the most positive functioning and smoothest operating, as well as the most powerful, accurate and durable double-action revolver ever produced, and comes closer to being the ideal all-around general purpose gun, readily adaptable to all purposes for which

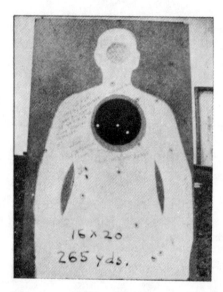

265-YARD TARGET

16 hits out of 20 shots fired from .38-44 S. & W. Outdoorsman with scope sight at 265-yard target; sitting position with back support. Target by Jim Browne. June 3, 1934.

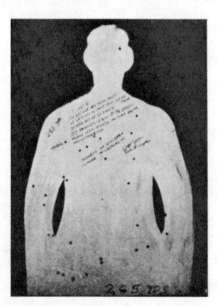

265-YARD TARGET

30 hits out of 50 shots on the first trial of the standard (just as issued) .357 Magnum revolver with plain iron sights. This shooting was done by Jim Browne of Big Forks, Montana, from sitting position with back support.

revolvers and pistols may be used, and handling, as it does, a much more varied assortment of ammunition, suitable for the various purposes, than any revolver or pistol ever made available to the shooting public. All such valuable features being incorporated in one standard model, allows the purchaser to have any length of barrel desired and any standard combination of sights requested.

The Smith & Wesson .357 Magnum revolver is not a remodeled, built over, or converted gun by the addition of an extra cylinder or other special adaptation. It is, instead, the most outstanding achievement of progress and development in the history of pistol and revolver manufacture. The development of the .357 Magnum cartridge and this particular standard model of revolver which so successfully handles it, gave to the pistol and revolver shooters a combination that was at first announcement believed to be both unattainable and impossible.

The successful conclusion of so great an undertaking as to combine such greatly increased velocity with superaccuracy, and such astonishing results in bullet performance as was, and regularly can be, secured on targets as well as in the variously conducted and never equaled, or even closely approached, penetration tests for effective results on game, etc., and have it all incorporated in, and possible to secure with one standard model of revolver or pistol, really compares very favorably, and is in direct line, with the progress now made evident as a result of the research and scientific development of the superaccurate and extremely high velocity rifles, at the present time making their appearance, several of which have already been made available for that group of shooters who desire more dependable bullet performance, combining increased velocity with finer accuracy on targets, fast action and supreme accuracy for more definite and positive results on game, all of which is within reach at the present time.

The .357 Magnum revolver, with its varied assortment of adaptable ammunition, fulfills all of the requirements in the revolver line for the outdoorsman in relation to game shooting, either large or small, results that can be secured being entirely dependent on the skill and ability of the shooter, as has already been quite clearly demonstrated by several noted performers in this field.

The target shooting enthusiast also has his choice of an excellent line-up of cartridges for any sort of target shooting in which he may wish to take an active part, at short and medium, or on out to the extended ranges. The results that can be secured as formerly mentioned in relation to game shooting are dependent entirely on the ability of the shooter himself. It is my candid opinion that there is no man living today whose holding and trigger control can, or for any number of shots ever will, equal the accuracy of the .357 Magnum or of the other high-grade target revolvers available today.

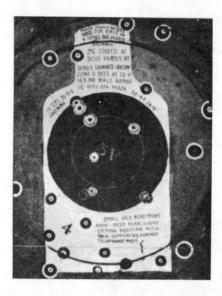

300-YARD REVOLVER EXPERIMENTS
16 hits out of 25 shots on the man target.

Shot by Sergeant Leonard Larson, range officer, June 11, 1933. .38-44 Smith & Wesson Outdoorsman. 6½-inch barrel. Small gold bead front sight. Peep rear sight. Peters High Velocity .38-44 cartridges. Sitting position with back support.

The Smith & Wesson .357 Magnum revolver has brought just as many and as startling changes in the revolver shooting branch of the shooting game as the superaccurate and amazingly high velocity rifles, and their specially adapted cartridges, have brought to the rifle shooting enthusiasts.

For several years the law enforcement officers stationed around and among our border patrol and other law enforcement organizations have been wishing for and requesting someone to bring out a more effective hand gun with which to combat smugglers, gangsters, and the usually desperate outlaw element generally, the main idea being to get a gun that would have more instantaneous and positively definite stopping power than usual when it became a necessity for the officers to use their revolvers on such opponents.

The suggestions for such proposed improvement as usually offered by such officers and others seemed to follow the old and well-worn groove of increasing the diameter and weight of the bullet in order to increase its effectiveness, without giving any thought to the discomfort to the shooter from the resulting heavy recoil that such changes, as suggested in these guns, would

Long Range Shooting

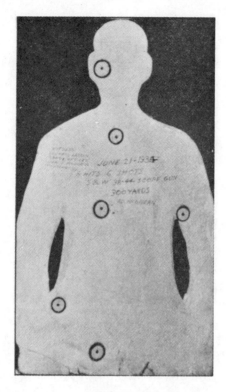

300 YARDS

Shot by McGivern in sitting position with back supported and both hands holding gun and resting on knees. This target was shot with the S. & W. .38-44 scope sighted gun and standard factory loaded .38-44 cartridges having the metal cased point bullets. Range 300 yards. June 21, 1934.

develop. This chatter was continuously going on before the Smith & Wesson .357 Magnum revolver was produced. Now we have in this gun, when necessity demands it, the very qualities which seemed to be so greatly desired by these men, and which they asked for and claimed to be absolutely necessary and positively required for properly stopping and effectively disabling this very element so greatly stressed as so vitally dangerous to the enforcement and maintenance of law and order. And the most agreeable part of it all is that we can have all of these things in one gun without any discomfort to the shooter.

When such emergency demands it the .357 Magnum gun and cartridge will do the work in a very effective manner and is, without doubt, the very

200 YARDS

Target shot by Dick Tinker of Helena, Mont., April 18, 1937. Witnessed by Geo. Lamb, Jas. R. Thomson, Ed Lamb, O. B. Erickson, Sidney R. Roe, Roy D. Jones. 200 yards, S. & W. .357 Magnum revolver. Six shots from sitting position.

best weapon ever put into the hands of the various branches of law enforcement officers. When no such emergency as above-described exists these same officers can use these same guns with any of the standard regulation .38 Special cartridges, from .38/44 down to the lightest target load, and have their choice of a particular cartridge loaded expressly to suit any sort of target practice or other training system that may be desired or otherwise in order.

The Smith & Wesson .357 Magnum revolver does not require that the powerful .357 Magnum cartridge be shot in it always, nor exclusively, as many persons seemed to have believed was the case. It handles all the other .38 Special cartridges equally as well, and, in many cases, better than most of the other .38 caliber revolvers do, and also far more comfortably for the shooter as a general rule.

Personally I find the gun excellently adapted to any shooting problem with which I may be confronted. As an arm with which to train law

Long Range Shooting

300 YARDS	500 YARDS

Left—Target shot by Dick Tinker of Helena, Mont., June 27, 1937. Witnessed by Geo. Lamb, Jas. R. Thomson, Ed Lamb, O. B. Erickson, Sidney R. Roe, Roy D. Jones. 300 yards, S. & W. .357 Magnum revolver. Six shots from sitting position.

Right—Target shot by Dick Tinker of Helena, Mont., May 9, 1937. Witnessed by Geo. Lamb, Jas. R. Thomson, Ed Lamb, O. B. Erickson, Sidney R. Roe, Roy D. Jones. 500 yards, S. & W. .357 Magnum revolver. Six shots (4 hits) from sitting position.

enforcement officers I have found nothing that has given better results. The barrel lengths used for this purpose run from three and a half inches to six and a half inches, and are equipped with various combinations of sights for various experiments.

Some of the short barrel Magnums were fitted with King superpolice night sights for shooting in very poor light. One of the Magnums with the eight and three-quarter inch barrel was fitted up with the King red post front sight and white outlined rear sight, while another was fitted with McGivern sights.

The six and the six and a half inch barrel Magnums were generally fitted with the McGivern gold bead front sight and U bottom rear sight. This is the same combination that was used by Col. D. B. Wesson on his

Fast and Fancy Revolver Shooting

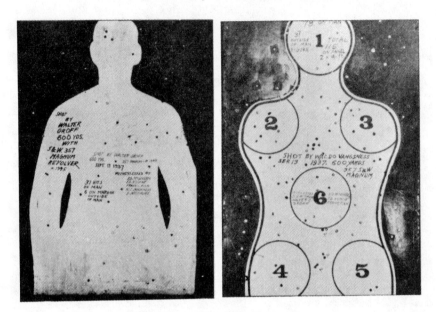

LONG RANGE REVOLVER SHOOTING

Left—Target shot by Walter Groff of Philadelphia with the author's S. &. W .357 Magnum revolver at 600 yards, Sept, 13, 1937. Prone position using plain peep rear and narrow post front sight. 8¾-inch barrel. 37 hits on man. 6 hits on margin of panel. Panel 28 inches wide. 75 shots fired.

Right—Target shot by Waldo Vangsness with author's .357 Magnum revolver at 600 yards, Sept. 13, 1937. Plain peep rear sight. Narrow post front sight. 8¾-inch barrel. 78 hits on man. 37 hits on margin of panel. Panel 2 feet wide. 150 shots fired.

very successful big game hunt in Wyoming in the fall of 1935, ending at the ranch of Ernie Miller near the west entrance of Yellowstone Park where I met him.

On this hunting trip, while using the S. & W. .357 Magnum revolver only, and the Winchester S. & W. .357 cartridge with 1515 f. s. velocity, Colonel Wesson hit an antelope at 125 yards and again at 200 yards, killing it. He was then successful in killing a bull elk at 130 yards with a shot that passed through the animal's lungs. Later, one shot, the first one, shot from the Magnum at a moose at a distance of 100 yards, struck Mr. Moose in the chest and promptly killed the animal. The bullet entered the base of the neck, cut the second rib, passed through the lungs, sheared the eighth rib on the other side, lodged under the skin and was later recovered for inspection.

Long Range Shooting

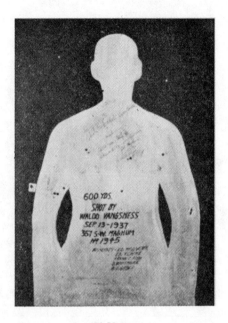

600 Yards

The group of shots on the arm of this target shows the freak occurrence bordering on the improbable, which happens occasionally in spite of the firmly established law of averages, which usually works against the shooter instead of in his favor on most occasions. The shooting was done by Waldo Vangsness and the results constitute the best groups so far secured on the various targets shot from 600 yards with the .357 Magnum revolver, having 8¾-inch barrel and equipped with plain, flat peep rear sight, plain, narrow post front sight, holding gun with two hands and shooting from prone position. The four out of five shots on the chest are one group, and the three out of five shots on the arm, with one just off the arm, and the other one high and to the left of the head, constitute the other group. Such freak grouping as this is not liable to occur often in several thousand shots, if ever again.

The signatures of the witnesses can be clearly seen as written on the target at the time and place when the shooting was done.

These successful big game results amply verify my former statement that this .357 Magnum revolver fulfills all of the requirements for the outdoorsman in relation to game shooting, either large or small, the results being entirely dependent on the skill and ability of the shooter, as stated.

The durability of these guns, as well as the accuracy, seems to be highly satisfactory. I know of one testing gun which still shows no noticeable dropping off in accuracy in the machine rest tests that has fired some twelve thousand rounds of .357 Magnum cartridges, and another that has fired around six thousand Magnum cartridges, and still another with a record of

600 YARDS

The small white spot at the edge of the hill (upper right) is the Langrish Limbless target, as it looks when placed 600 yards from the shooter. Mr. Vangsness is shooting and Mr. Walter Groff is at the right making notes for use when he goes to bat. Frank Fish is spotting the shots with the Bausch & Lomb prismatic spotting scope.   Sept. 13, 1937.

LONG RANGE TARGETS

The targets on the hill were 100 yards behind the targets on the frames; the arrangement of firing points for the targets were at 200, 300, 400, 500, 550, 600 yards at the Company K, 163rd Infantry rifle range, where many of the revolver shooting experiments at various extended ranges were conducted.

Long Range Shooting

What the .357 Magnum revolver bullet did to a prairie dog's head at 75 yards.
Shooting by Russ Whitmore.

Stock attachment made and fitted to the author's .357 Magnum revolver by R. F. Sedgley of Philadelphia.   Note the holes through the rib for attaching mounts for the telescope sight.

THE AUTHOR'S SMITH & WESSON .357 MAGNUM REVOLVER

Equipped with Lyman 438 field scope. This is the revolver which was used for the long range targets mentioned herein, but the scope was not used. Other sights described in connection with targets were used instead.

.357 MAGNUM CARTRIDGES

These are some of the Phil Sharpe type bullets and experimental cartridges used in developing the Smith & Wesson .357 Magnum revolver.

over four thousand rounds to its credit, with approximately eight thousand additional rounds of assorted .38 Special cartridges as well. One of my plentifully used Magnums, in addition to a large quantity of .357 Magnum cartridges, has also fired around twelve hundred of Keith's heavy hand loads on which the cartridge company's test reports show pressures much higher than standard. This gun shows no noticeable ill-effects as yet.

The long range experiments with revolvers, many of the results of which are herewith shown, were conducted over a period of more than six years, starting with the regulation .38 Special revolvers and ammunition,

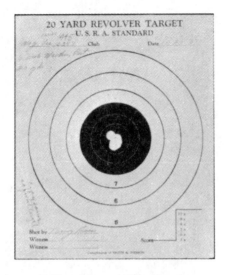

20-Yard Machine Rest Groups

Smith & Wesson .357 Magnum Revolver

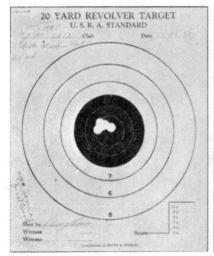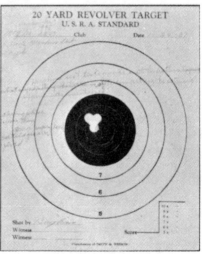

Smith & Wesson .357 Magnum Revolver

Machine rest tests made with the author's Magnum revolver without any adjusting whatever after completing the extensive experiments mentioned, during which more than 8000 assorted superload cartridges were fired.

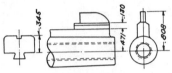

SMITH & WESSON SIGHTS
for 8¾" .357 Magnum at 500 yards

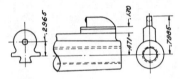

ED. McGIVERN SIGHTS
for 8¾" .357 Magnum at 600 yards

and later stepped along with the new .38/44 cartridges fired from both Smith & Wesson Outdoorsman and Colt Shooting Master revolvers, up to and somewhat beyond 300 yards. Later experiments resulted in the development of the .357 Magnum and the greatly improved cartridges adapted to it.

The experiments were then continued up to and including 600 yards, with the idea of determining about what sort of effective results could be expected by various law enforcement officers and others in relation to the several types of upper man targets in general use for training purposes.

In these experiments to determine probable results and the most favorable type of sights for such purposes, several thousand cartridges were used, the greater part being of the two later types, .38/44 and Magnum, fired by various persons during the many tests made on the numerous occasions.

SECTION 27

SHOULD REVOLVER SHOOTING BE REGARDED AND DEVEL-
OPED AS AN ART OR A SCIENCE, OR A COMBINATION OF
BOTH?   IMPORTANCE AND VALUE OF BODY BALANCE.

Science—Accumulated and systemized knowledge. Skill as the result
of knowledge. Science teaches us to know, and art to do.

Art—Knowledge made efficient as skill; skill, dexterity, or the power
of performing certain actions, acquired by experience, study, or observation;
knack.

Practical revolver shooting, when it enters into fast and fancy shooting
where speed must be combined with accuracy, in all probability should
be considered as an art. A really proficient performer in this field should
rightfully be regarded as an artist, "Quick draw artist," "Two gun artist,"
"Superspeed artist," etc. Regarded as an art, it becomes a sweeping,
flowing thing full of life and action. Regarded strictly as a science, it is
too stiff. It forces the shooter into a feeling of exactitude and he becomes
taut and tense, not only interfering with his free muscular movements
but also, and at the same time, interfering with the fun and the thrill that
arises from the freedom of movement that brings both pleasure and success.
The difference between regarding this branch of revolver shooting as an
art or as a science might be compared with the more or less graceful movements of dancing with a lady partner for pleasure, and the very precise
movements of going through a complicated program of military drill.

Study, practice, and effort towards improvement are quite necessary,
but mechanical exactness is very hard to combine with graceful freedom
of movement, for the reason that freedom of movement cannot be combined
with tenseness and muscular strain.

Tying yourself up in strained and uncomfortable positions in an effort
to be scientifically precise is not productive of fast and accurate revolver
shooting proficiency. It is, of course, very necessary to be correct in fundamentals, but even in these there must be some latitude. No part of the
shooter's body, arms, or legs need be held in any position that does not
allow of considerable variation.

The successive movements required for successful performance of any
one of the fast and fancy shooting stunts can be ever so near correct,
yet utter failure will result if there is not that something combined therewith that makes them one, flowing smoothly and continuously through
from beginning to end. The essence of the idea is to make this sort of shooting an act of enjoyment, one that you can regularly derive thrills from,
rather than a job of hard labor that must be accomplished in pain and
suffering.

Fast and Fancy Revolver Shooting

The shooter who strives for mechancial perfection by trying to build up a series of movements and a shooting position with meticulous attention to detail is sure to fail of accomplishment, and, as a result of such repeated failures, will become one of the many "crabs" who take great pleasure in casting doubt on the accomplishment of others.

Deal with this branch of the game with a sort of liberal conception. Do not try too hard to look like someone else, or to act like somebody else, no matter how outstanding that person may be in this field of endeavor. Learn and observe fundamentals—learn your own peculiarities of physical and mental make-up. Study to develop these into one smooth working whole, and it will be surprising how soon subconscious control can be built up, and amazing progress will reward your efforts.

There is no one else in the world just like you and you can never be just exactly like someone else. You can be just as good, or perhaps you may get to be a still better performer than someone else whom you may now think is almost perfection, but, if you do so, you will have to do it by methods that are adapted particularly to your own physical and mental make-up, and not by trying to follow some sort of a set of blueprints and near scientific rules and regulations.

A plastic surgeon may change the outer appearance of your head and face so as to make you look more like someone whom you may wish to look like, but he cannot change the inside of the upper part of your head, and that is where your development of proficiency must come from, and it must come in a natural way, entirely dependent upon yourself, and on the use you make of your mental equipment, to train, to develop, and to control the physical qualifications with which nature has provided you.

It is quite generally believed and fairly well-supported by results of tests that each shooter is equipped with a sort of mental laboratory of his own, working under natural control, incorporated within himself, which is capable of wonderful action, reaction, and production. Therefore we should make every effort to avoid ruining this individuality with **general formula**—particularly should we endeavor to develop certain exceptional ability that will result in superior individual performance.

Necessity of perfect body balance rather than the rigid sort of fixed positions is extremely important. For extreme rapid fire and rapid aerial target shooting with revolvers, the body must be kept perfectly balanced, very similar to the way that a fast boxer and a good fast tennis player does it, so that instant change of poise and immediate action are always possible without any loss of time.

Standing rigidly and solidly on one's feet is not at all necessary or desirable. Such behavior and the resulting positions are harmful and generally detrimental to successful results. Fast shooting and the necessary action that controls and secures hitting with regularity depend more on properly regulated body balance and correct body movement than on anything else.

Movement of the arms and hands must be combined with body movement toward the definite result made necessary by the situation at hand. Moving the arms and hands independent of the body is not the proper system of directing and correctly controlling the handling of, and the repointing of, the gun or, in other words, correctly maintaining and controlling the pointing of the gun so as to confine all shots to the desired area, during the necessary effort required to overcome the recoil of each shot during a very fast five or six shot string.

When firing a string of shots at a high rate of speed, perfect body balance and correct shifting of the body forward, backward, and sideways, is absolutely necessary to maintain control of the gun pointing, while at the same time controlling the muscular effort required for gun operation and also overcoming the disturbing effect of recoil, and still be successful in having the gun correctly pointed at any certain spot, target, or moving object, when the next shot is fired, constitutes a problem that cannot be handled by the free movement of hands or arms, separate and apart or independent of the movements of the body.

The body movements combined with perfect balance must control and direct the movements of both the arms and hands towards the desired point, while the gun is being lined up, either directly or indirectly aided and governed by the vision, by looking over the sights, or shooting from hip, or arm across the stomach positions, etc., while keeping the eyes focused on the target. The body balance during such movement can be and is maintained in much the same way as balance and correctly directed and properly timed movement is combined and performed on the dance floor.

This body balance combined with arm and hand movement in connection with perfectly coördinated body, leg, and foot movement **is the big trick** of the whole thing. In this sort of shooting the feet and legs play a very much more important part than has ever been generally considered, and as a consequence this important fact has been quite generally overlooked.

The usual and quite generally advanced and recommended rigid target shooting "stance," so very confidently spoken of as "Correct" and "Proper" by persons who have only studied perhaps that one angle of revolver or pistol shooting, will, with many persons, prove detrimental to superspeed when attempting to combine it with accuracy. The result of these fixed, solid, stiff, and permanent, "correct and proper" shooting positions will prove very similar in your speed efforts to the effect of four-wheel brakes on an automobile when they are somewhat out of adjustment.

The fact that during many of my experiments I have been able to accomplish some things that appear to be just slightly, at least, out of the ordinary in the revolver shooting line, is due in almost direct proportion to the departure we have made from fixed rules, fixed "stance," and the cut-and-dried fixed positions recommended by our more or less tradition-ally inclined grandfathers, etc., which we have before, do now, and will hereafter term "The rule of the dead men."

If others have not been successful in mastering the various stunts so greatly different from the usual programs of exhibition and fancy revolver shooting generally, as shown here, the main reason is incorporated in the foregoing explanation. We are confident that it has been very clearly shown that it is the difference in the methods of procedure that secures the results.

Much of our superspeed shooting and most of our surprising success on aerial target shooting is due to, and done by, having the body weight balanced mostly on one foot, while the other foot is used for a sort of brake, or rudder, or stabilizer, with which to control and direct, and also stop movement and body swing, etc., at the desired point. (Note photos of Ted Renfro; note position of feet.) This gentleman, according to official averages, is credited with being about the most proficient all-around trap and other flying target, as well as live bird and game shot with shotguns, in the Trapshooting world, which is the reason why his foot work is pointed out here as a valuable illustration of this point now under discussion. (See Section 5, page 48.)

Soldierly attitudes and fashion plate positions, while very interesting, are not a beneficial or necessary part of this game, and we are making this very plain in this book on revolver shooting, for the express purpose of impressing it on the minds of all who wish to succeed, and perhaps excel in this line of endeavor.

Arguments have been plentiful. How could certain persons perform so differently and so much more consistently than so many others who have attempted these things? The correct answer seems to be in the system used, and in the methods worked out and employed, which were and are, as explained, so entirely different from the ones generally followed by the various persons who have not studied into these particular angles, which we have found, and very firmly believe to be, so very important.

SECTION 28

APPLIED PSYCHOLOGY. THE SHERIFF AND THE KILLER.
THE EXHIBITION SHOOTER.

Here let us analyze some of these tense, fast, positive action situations and explain the psychology angles. Personally, I do not favor technical explanations, for the reason that they generally prove tiresome to the average person, on whose good nature I will impose in this instance.

Let us now, for an example, follow one of several of the famous sheriffs of early West fame as he approaches to confront and arrest a known "bad man and killer," as they were spoken of at that time. According to the traditional "code of the West" which was supposed to have been adopted, recognized, and generally followed, subject to the usual exceptions much as we find in every game, this sheriff must tell his man that he is wanted and is being placed under arrest, and, to make the picture, we will assume he is one of the "wanted men" who is to be taken under the heading of "Dead or alive." Naturally, under these conditions, the situation is **tense.**

Each of these men are (as I will describe them) selected experts at the game of "Fill your hand!" "Go for your iron!" "Slap leather!" "Start yer draw!" "Show your hand!" "Turn your wolf loose!" "Come a-smokin'!" "Cut 'er loose!" "I'm waitin'!" "Get goin'!" "I'm call'n' yeh!" "I'm all set to go!" "Grab your cutter!" etc., which are a few of the many exclamations mentioned as having been used during that period, when inviting a man into a gun fight (which we will refer to later on as the external stimulus), to indicate that the speaker was all ready and willing to start a gun fight, or, as with the wanted man in this case, ready to resist arrest and fight it out, in keeping with the code of the "even break" that most if not all of the noted characters of that time prided themselves on respecting and observing, or at least pretending so to do, which was, by the way, a most important point to be considered, for the very vital reason that after the killing, if there existed reasonable proof that such warning had been given, it was sufficient, in almost all cases, to clear the killer. It often happened that on the basis of the "even break," such warning would cause the "other fellow" to "reach for his gun" or "start his draw" just a very small fraction of a second ahead of the more expert, and later victorious, gun handler, and then such victor could and would very promptly plead "self-defense," on the grounds of—"Boys, you all saw him go for his iron," or "You all saw him grab for his gun," etc., etc. The angles of such a situation furnish a practical explanation of the bearing on, and the great importance of, applied psychology, whether knowingly or unknowingly employed as the controlling element.

Fast and Fancy Revolver Shooting

I will here give an outline of the psychological factors that enter into such situations, and in Section Twelve there can be found a detailed outline and description of how these factors are developed and controlled, what causes them, how they function, and the results.

As mentioned, these two men, sheriff and wanted man, are equally skillful, equally fast and accurate, and, above all, equally determined of purpose. The sheriff has the one advantage (but a very important one) of being on the right side of the law, and not facing the necessity for flight, explanations, or of prosecution—quite a psychological factor. The wanted man had none of these angles in his favor, but he had the backing and the support of friends who were present at the time, who would take care (much as they still do today) of the necessary flight, give protection from capture, and assistance of every nature, if and when needed.

With the sheriff, his position in the community, his standing as a citizen and an officer of the law, and the protection and support of himself as a person and a personality to be reckoned with, in reference to the dignity of the law and of law enforcement, as well as the responsibility placed on him as a result of his oath of office, all combine to produce a psychological situation that has the effect of causing him to be willing to risk his life— which he knows well he is doing—in the discharge of his sworn duty. Here we have the compelling urge.

Now we look at the wanted man. He also realizes his danger, he also realizes his responsibility in exposing his friends and their valuable friendship to danger. He gambles on the long, slim chance that perhaps his well-known reputation as a killer will help him, and, if it doesn't keep the sheriff away from him it will surely have enough of a disturbing effect to make him cautious and thus slow him up a trifle (psychology a-plenty). Mentally and physically he (the wanted man) is well-qualified and knows full well his danger. He is well-prepared, well-equipped, ready and willing, and from successful past **experiences,** much of which is fresh in his **memory,** he has plenty of confidence. He has the mental impulse (still held in reserve) ready to release in response to the proper "external stimulus" that will put his supertrained muscles into instant, positive, and effective action. He is prepared for action under the protective instincts of self-preservation, a "primitive urge" and a "compelling urge" that have affected and influenced man for ages.

The stage is, so to speak, "all set." The sheriff, still outside the building, is mentally reviewing the process and methods of procedure by which he hopes to place Mr. W. M. (wanted man) under arrest or kill him if he must; which eventually will have to be decided on and accomplished before Mr. W. M. can kill him. Here is the only rough place over which nervous energy may have to travel to cause stuttering of the sheriff's sensori-motor impulse to kill, if necessary. The "if" is the stumbling block that may falter the impulse when issued by the sheriff when the signal—movement or word—by Mr. W. M. will cause the external stimulus (eye or ear, sensory) to flash through the sheriff's nervous system and to continue to the conclusion of the situation.

Mr. Wanted Man is within the building under the spell of a watchful, waiting attitude, "all set," with psychological factors all tuned in when Mr. Sheriff steps in through the door. Mr. Wanted Man instantly becomes alert. Each man is surcharged with nervous energy, all prepared for everything or anything that may happen. Who, if either, will walk away—who goes to "Boot Hill"? All psychological factors are at their highest tension. The situation has many serious angles vital to both men. The sheriff speaks his piece, "So and so, you are under arrest." One tense moment. "Yuh can't take me." The release of two external stimuli, one from each to the other—action. The sheriff wins—one .45 bullet ended the battle. The sheriff should win under these conditions due to having his nervous system already working and in order, and having the most of his body in motion, the motor impulses in active operation, nervous energy traveling over almost all of the nervous system. In fact, a sort of physical "warm motor" condition.

Mr. Wanted Man had to go from a sort of standing start. By the rules of the game he couldn't very well kill the sheriff unless compelled to kill him to save his own life, but even then, not until the sheriff had spoken his little piece and declared his intentions. The man in this case, Mr. W. M., who would normally, under such conditions, hesitate just a moment or small fraction of a second, should be the one to lose, where the two men are equally matched. If the sheriff killed him there could be no comeback; if he killed the sheriff there was "hell to pay." Deliberation steps in here—conscious analysis, reflection, choice. All are interrupting factors.

A parallel to this final action, "the shoot-off" without the fancy trimmings, may be taken from the killing of Wm. Bonney, "Billy, The Kid," by Sheriff Pat Garrett in Pete Maxwell's house at Fort Sumner about midnight, July 13, 1881, which happened in an almost darkened room, the only light being a patch of moonlight through a window. The Kid wasn't quite sure of his man, or just who he was. He hesitated, he had his gun out all set to go, he was a wizard at the game, nerve in plenty, perfect control always, positive and accurate in his movements when under pressure of excitement or danger; but uncertainty, hesitation, cost him his life on that occasion. He couldn't see (on account of the dark) or hear (because Garrett never spoke). There was no external stimulus to set Billy, The Kid's motor impulse going, although from reports he must have felt it; his sense of location was also just a little slow. The subconscious warning of danger was held back somewhat by the conscious knowledge of his friend Maxwell's presence (on or near the bed in the room), and he risked his life on the human impulse **not to harm his friend,** something that is overlooked by many persons these days. This kept Billy from shooting until he was sure of whom he would be shooting at. After Garrett's slug hit him, which was a lucky break for Garrett, Billy's motor impulses were interrupted. Garrett performed along the line of applied psychology (rather well applied) on this occasion, to "get" Billy before Billy could get him—a point of importance that rarely leaves the mind of men trained and experienced along such lines, which, as history shows clearly, is a "compelling urge" of great consequence in the consideration of such things.

The psychology of fear in its various forms will also have a great influence in such matters (a factor in both of these cases), even though controlled, as in this case; not fear of facing the issue or even of the outcome, but fear of being just a trifle slow, of being just a little hesitant beyond the margin of safety. Garrett knew that he would have to kill Billy, The Kid, in order to take him, yet he was looking for him. There was no other way out; he made no attempt to sidestep the issue. On one side of the situation we have for consideration Garrett's uncertainty at first, that the man really was Billy, The Kid, but when Billy spoke to Maxwell the voice sounded to Garrett like Billy's voice. Here we have Pat Garrett's external stimulus, sensori-motor impulse, to which he responded, thus fear of the consequences of delayed action urged Garrett's shot to be delivered.

On the other side of this situation we have an entirely different reason for Billy, The Kid's uncertainty of action. We find that it was not fear for himself, which is generally regarded as the most important of all, but instead it was fear for the safety of his friend Maxwell. This fear of making a mistake and injuring one of his loyal friends overrode the personal safety urge and held back Billy, The Kid's shot long enough to give Pat Garrett the deciding advantage, otherwise this scrap of history might have been written differently. Psychology dealt the trumps in that two-handed game of **life and death.**

In contrast to the sheriff's case we will review the situation of the exhibition shooter. We will place him in the same psychological attitude as the sheriff and the killer. He is trained right to the very minute. He stands in front of the crowd (the psychological factor) all set ready to go and conscious only of the concentrated energy ready to be released in the efforts required to break his opponent, in this case being the various combinations of stationary and aerial targets that must be arranged conveniently or thrown in the air when required, for the purpose of enabling him to complete his program, do his duty, and, like the sheriff, fulfill his obligation.

Applied Psychology

Here again our principal actor is all ready, plentifully practiced, mentally alert, physically fit, all nerve connections through frequent use alive and in readiness, with a minimum of resistance in the entire circuit over which the nervous impulses will travel to set up muscular action and complete all movements necessary from the instant of stimulus set up by sense of sight as the targets are tossed and come into his field of vision, with the identical effect of an opponent's drawing movement. Perhaps he sees the tossing movement start, thus gaining a fraction of time, from his memory of former similar experiences, which mentally prompts him that his opponent (the targets) will appear a small fraction of a second later, and, as he is all "wound up," so to speak, his necessary combined movements follow in unbroken series through and over a very familiar sensori-motor path, repeating movements that have been made hundreds of times before. This situation parallels the responsive actions of the gun-fighting sheriff facing the "wanted man."

He is guided instantly for hits by familiar visual images of his gun aligned in proper relation to each target, in turn, as had been done hundreds of times before. The nervous energy simply follows the well-worn grooves of past experiences and his mental and muscular response is perfect.

From the first effort put forth of getting his guns in readiness and announcing to the assisting throwers that he is ready, his conduct on to the finishing moment has been subconsciously controlled action. This holds good through all such shooting whether there be several shots fired at one target or single shots fired at each one of several targets. There is no danger of any physical injury to the shooter—only the fear of missing and being ridiculed for lack of skill. You'll think, not a very serious matter compared with the sheriff's situation, but serious enough in the mind of the exhibition shooter to keep him from missing if it is at all possible for him to avoid so doing. "Psychologically," sure and regular hits are quite as important to the exhibition shot as to the sheriff. Many such men regard criticism and ridicule with as much concern as they would regard the prospect of possible serious injury.

SECTION 29

ANALYZING THE MODERN DEBUNKERS.

I have often read and have also, on many occasions, heard about certain persons who claimed that they knew every gun artist of any importance, and also knew about everything that transpired that was at all worthy of note or of any real consequence in early Western history. I have also read that some such persons make the claim that there never were any real two-gun men, or at least there never was anyone in the Old Days nor is there anyone at the present time who either ever was, or is, capable of shooting two guns at once, and hitting anything with the shots from each gun, while both guns were being fired at the same time, although they do admit that there may have been men who carried two guns at once in holsters and other ways in preparation for emergencies. Such guns were generally carried with either one empty chamber or one empty shell under the hammer for safety, and the other five chambers fully loaded, thus giving them ten shots instead of five ready and at hand when needed, but that such men usually shot only one gun at a time until empty and then switched to the gun that was still loaded, and continued firing with the same hand that fired the other gun, until empty, etc., etc.

These same persons also make many claims that certain famous marshals, like Wild Bill Hickok, Wyatt Earp, Pat Garrett, Bill Tilghman, John Slaughter, Bat Masterson, Billy Breakenridge, Tom Horn, Ed Short, Chris Madson, Heck Thomas and various other famous marshals and deputies, did not deserve very much of the credit that was given them, because they really didn't do anything that anyone else couldn't have done in their places. It all sounds very fine if there really was any truth in it, but when such men, as the only partial list above shows, could live through at least dozens of life and death gun battles with revolvers, usually termed six guns or six shooters, their proficiency and sure hitting ability, under pressure, to say nothing of their courage, could hardly be questioned or in doubt.

We also hear from some of the wise ones that fanning the hammer of the single-action Colt revolvers, in order to release the shots rapidly, and at the same time be able, and reasonably sure of hitting any particular thing, was a myth, and so on down the line until about everything and everybody connected with early Western history has been plucked clean of every item of credit that ever had been connected with them.

In contrast to this general reduction in credit for the more or less meritorious performances, the author would like to know just exactly how such definite and positive first-hand information could have been successfully secured by any one person while covering, as he must, so large an area as was traversed by the early Western routes of travel, and be in personal touch with the many things that transpired, at practically the same time at widely separated points, during the more or less stormy but gradual settlement of that vast area.

When the extreme difficulty of travel, transportation, and communication encountered at that period is taken into consideration, it certainly would be a tremendous undertaking for any one man to accomplish. Still there are reports of some who have taken to themselves full credit for such accomplishment, and who, to show their wisdom as a result of some such imaginary experience, proceed on every available occasion to discredit any and all accomplishments of others of either early or late history.

Let us now give consideration to present-day conditions, wherein it must be admitted that our modern mode of travel and communication is the most efficient that ever existed in human history, yet, just how far does knowledge of present developments travel today, and just how much country will any one man have to cover to find it. Outside of the services of the Associated Press, which were not available in the early days of the West, just how much of the detailed information relative to any particular subject does any one man pick up and completely master for himself. In this particular instance we are interested in and are discussing revolver shooting.

The type of such shooting, as set forth in this book, has for several years been under development and improvement, right out in the open, without any attempt whatever towards secrecy or concealment, and carried on in the vicinity of Lewistown, which is situated right in the exact center of this fairly well-settled state of Montana, on Custer Highway No. 87, which passes right through the center of the city. Yet, with all of our modern methods of transportation and communication, as well as the various mediums of publicity and widespread distribution of the printed word, besides plenty of information that has been released in the form of articles in several of the leading sportsmen's magazines concerning the subject, just what particular person outside of the present writer and his assistants, and the person to whom this book is dedicated, really knew everything right up to the last little detail regarding our activities, our successes or our failures, our personal peculiarities, our methods of procedure, our attempted performances, our accomplishments, our guns, or our special and necessary equipment, or what combinations we had worked out with one gun and with two guns, and how successful we had been with them, before this book was written and made available?

That's the question! Where was there anyone who could positively state that he knew all about it? Just what was or was not done? Just what could or could not be done? Just what was possible and just exactly what was not possible? The last question is still unanswered, and will remain so for some time.

Fast and Fancy Revolver Shooting

If this problem exists today, just how could it have been solved so readily and so positively in the early frontier days. It is quite evident that it could not be. Consequently, I take off my hat to the very proficient gun experts and their, of necessity, very practical and effective shooting ability. These very proficient gun experts of the early West made shooting history that has never had a parallel before or since.

We cannot condemn all of the early day revolver shooters on account of the gross ignorance often displayed by the writers of such reports, and the same rule may very well be applied to the activities of the present day.

SECTION 30

GENERAL SUMMING UP AND REVIEW OF SPECIALTIES, SHOOTING GLASSES, SPECIAL GADGETS, ETC.

This section of the book will be devoted to a general summing up of the contents, along with some mention of the few remaining items of probable interest, which may need a little more definite mention than has so far been given them. Also some mention will be made, along with short descriptions, of various specialties which I believe will be of interest to a great many, if not all, of the readers. I will also take this opportunity, in response to the numerous inquiries that have been received from my many shooter friends concerning the matter, to mention the fact that due to severe and prolonged illness it became necessary for all of my shooting activities to be entirely suspended and my work on this book was interrupted to the extent that its completion, with the assembling of all data, was delayed for a period of around two years.

Among the many things that have been in my favor, and for which I have been quite thankful, and which gives me more or less pleasure to mention at this time, is the fact that I have never found it necessary or desirable to enter the services of any manufacturer of guns or ammunition in order to make a living, or to enable me to follow up and develop and continue to improve, and also continue to enjoy, my shooting hobby.

Shooting has, with me, been much more of a hobby and source of entertainment, along with more or less profitable recreation, than it ever has been of the nature of a regular business or vocation. The necessary research and experiment required for development was a source of revenue in many ways, not the least important of which was the substantial returns, and very effective results secured from and through many cases of firearms identification and kindred activities in relation to court cases in connection with killings and attempted killings, wherein firearms and ammunition of various sorts were involved.

Having been quite well qualified, in other ways, to secure a reasonably satisfactory income entirely separate and apart from any connection with any sort of shooting activities whatever, it never was necessary for me to obligate myself by any contract, understanding or consideration with, or from, any gun or ammunition manufacturer, distributor or agent; consequently I have remained free and unhindered in every way to select and use and recommend for use any product of any maker on its own dependability, durability and merits of performance alone. When finding by actual tests and service that certain products were more satisfactory and desirable for the purpose for which I required them, all of the reports of the results secured with them were presented on this basis. All developments were natural results following the research and various experiments which were conducted with determined effort, definitely directed towards certain desired and sought-for results. Such is the source from which the material for this book was developed.

Why the Numerous Targets, etc., herein Displayed are Dated: The dates appearing on the many photographs and other exhibits which have been presented herewith, in the several sections, rather clearly indicate the periods of time which elapsed between the various series of experiments which were conducted for developing certain performances, along with the necessary skill for the accomplishment of the certain results desired during such certain performances. As quite evident they were not all conducted and developed together and at any one time or during any one limited period, but were developed, one or two at a time, sort of individually and on sometimes widely separated dates, and not intermingling to any extent at any time.

In many cases it was necessary for certain combinations of experiments to be repeated over and over again, until the more important principles could be finally incorporated into a system of routine procedure, with all extra effort eliminated, and the absolutely necessary action reduced to the most consistent minimum possible.

Therefore the showing of such dates in connection with results of these various experiments, as evident on the targets and other exhibits herewith presented, have only one purpose, which is to make evident just about when the particular performance was first made ready for addition to the rapidly growing fast and fancy revolver shooting programs, in keeping with the plans relative to double-action revolvers which are mentioned in the early part of this book.

Exhibition Shooting: A few rules of conduct deserve mention at this point. All deliberate and superaccurate shooting of whatever nature, on any shooting program, should be performed and completed before any superspeed group shooting stunts, or moving and aerial target shooting performances, are attempted.

Preparing for Exhibitions and Demonstrations: At least, a short course of rehearsing, preparation and practice is advisable for even the most expert before attempting to perform and demonstrate any difficult and more or less complicated program in public.

Each of the several items the performer intends to make use of to fill out any selected program that can be concluded within any average showtime period that will be allowed him at, or during, any public entertainment occasion, will of necessity require some special routine arrangement and preparation before attempting their performance before an audience or critical gathering of any kind. "The effect of crowds," the psychology angle, which, as formerly mentioned, can usually be overcome by confidence from being prepared, enters here for consideration.

General Summing Up

Impromptu, or on the spur of the moment, performances are seldom indulged in by experienced performers. Satisfactory success is seldom the result of such conduct. I very seriously advise my pupils against such procedure.

It is well to remember that persons who constitute audiences do not always attend the performances for the purpose of seeing some certain performer be successful in doing his more difficult stunts in high-class form with precision and dexterity. Many of them get a much greater thrill from the possibility that the performer may falter and fail, or in, perhaps, more familiar terms, see him "flop" or "fall down" on his feature performance. Human nature is often like that. There are many people who go to championship prize fights, wrestling matches, and other top-notch athletic and sporting events, for the thrill of the possibility of seeing some "champ" meet his "Waterloo," while there are many others who attend for the pleasure of watching high-class performances, wherein the various participants make good and put on a high-class entertainment for the patrons.

The more unusual, widespread and interesting the reputation may be which some performer is able to build up for himself in any line, the greater the thrill for many people when the great event happens by which he is compelled to step down from his pedestal of success although his position thereon, in all probability, may have been hard earned, and perhaps also richly deserved. This seems to be the order of things in the field of human endeavor wherein we are continuously contending with human rivalry and the reactions of human emotions.

I recall quite clearly one occasion in my own experience, while putting on a revolver shooting exhibition several years ago at the Montana State Trap Shooting tournament where a group of factory representatives were in attendance, and after having been quite favorably treated by "Lady Luck" to the extent that my efforts in a rather varied, and somewhat complicated, program had been quite pleasingly successful, and in response to a request, it was arranged that I would conclude the program with a few attempts to cut some cards edgewise in the air with bullets fired from a revolver, as formerly herein described. When these attempts were made it happened that they were also successful, which caused one of the, no doubt, disappointed critics to step out hurriedly and, with much apparent pleasure and satisfaction, call attention to the fact that they hadn't been "cut through the middle anyhow." The fact that I had been successful in cutting the cards didn't matter—I was still open to criticism for failing to cut them in the exact center. So here we have the source of one of the reasons for my attitude towards over-enthusiastic critics, and against the conducting of "politely obliging" performances.

Trigger Pulls for Exhibition Shooting: Extremely light trigger adjustments, often referred to by Western story writers as "hair trigger actions, etc.," have no place among the equipment of the person performing among groups of persons or around large public gatherings.

Fast and Fancy Revolver Shooting

For all moving and aerial target shooting the revolvers used should have trigger pull adjustments heavy enough to support more than the weight of the fully loaded guns themselves. The importance of this safety measure lies in the fact that when revolvers are moved quickly from side to side, up or down, or swung rapidly from one point to another with an attempt to stop them suddenly, at or in line with some particular point or small object, there is considerable tendency, along with a great liability, if the trigger pull is light, to discharge the gun accidentally and without intent, before the shooter is ready, or prepared for firing the shot.

The slight increase in the weight of the trigger pull is in no way detrimental to the performer if he has any consistent ability, and the safety angle is so very much more improved by this very sensible and, in my opinion, very necessary precaution, that the value of the safety measure so very far overshadows the value of the lighter trigger pulls, that there is really no sensible argument possible in favor of light trigger adjustments.

Full weight standard factory adjusted trigger pulls are recommended by me and also used on all of the revolvers, at all times, for fast work of every sort, and for all moving target or aerial target shooting. No weakened trigger springs or main springs are ever allowed to be put into any such guns. If any weakened springs happen to occur through any reason whatever they are taken out.

Improved and More Suitable Cartridges: The development of the sharp shoulder and wad cutter type of bullet. When the results of some of this sort of aerial target shooting and speedy work with revolvers were first made public in the columns of "Outdoor Life" and other sportsmen's magazines, the noise-makers wailed about the various subloads (reduced loads) and so-called mid-range, short range and gallery loads used in .38 Specials at that time, and quite generally recommended by the manufacturers for mid-range shooting. Along about 1915 the author took these matters up with the several cartridge companies, carrying on much correspondence and later on making many demonstrations with the present form of mid-range blunt-end and square shoulder hollow base bullets for .38 Special cartridges, made from moulds specially designed by and for the present writer, and turned out for him by the Ideal Manufacturing Company, who later, in October, 1925, sold out to the Lyman Gun Sight Corporation.

The story about these bullets and cartridges, which are in high favor today, runs along about as follows: Before 1914 I began experimenting with heavier bullets and better loads of powder for mid-range .38 caliber revolver cartridges, and a little later I became interested in a cartridge put out by the Peters Cartridge Company, who were the first to produce .38 Special cartridges, having the so-called wad cutter bullets. I have shot a great quantity of these Peters cartridges at various times with very satisfactory results. Photos of this cartridge appear herewith along with several similar cartridges, and the 148-grain bullet which was originally developed by and for me through the co-operation of the Ideal Manufacturing Co., and was extensively used by me in my early tests and experiments. The specifications and details and such data as was at hand was later turned over by me to the Winchester Company, and many very satisfactory tests were conducted and surprisingly pleasing results reported, in reference to this cartridge, which was later put on the market by them.

Later, in the latter part of 1919, in company with Mr. P. M. Talcott, the owner of the Ideal Manufacturing Company, I personally assisted, with George Garrison, Mr. Hadley and Mr. Thomas, Remington ballistics engineers, in numerous tests of this bullet, a quantity of which had been cast, sized and lubricated at the Ideal Manufacturing Company's plant in New Haven, and brought to Bridgeport for the purpose. Results then were, and undoubtedly have since been, entirely satisfactory for the reason that the bullet, as now loaded by the Remington Company, is still practically the same in all particulars as the original cast bullets turned out by my original moulds. Photos of several samples and sectional views of such bullets appear herewith.

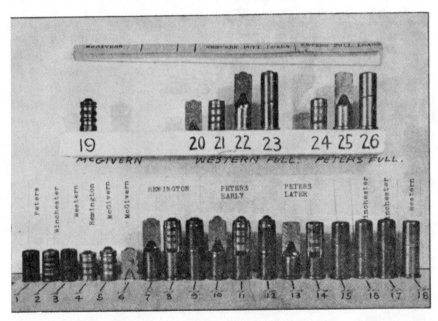

This view, starting with No. 19 on upper left top row, shows the 148-grain bullet No. 358395, designed and developed by the author, as herein fully described, and the various bullets of the same type, which later followed this bullet on the market, as made up and loaded by the various ammunition manufacturing companies to date. They are classified as follows:

Fast and Fancy Revolver Shooting

No. 1. Peters mid range bullet.
No. 2. Winchester mid range bullet.
No. 3. Western mid range bullet.
No. 4. Remington mid range bullet.
No. 5. McGivern 148-grain bullet, full view.
No. 6. Sectional view of McGivern 148-grain bullet.
No. 7. Sectional view of Remington cartridge.
No. 8. Exposed bullet view of Remington cartridge.
No. 9. Full view of Remington complete cartridge.
No. 10. Sectional bullet view of Peters early wad cutter bullet mid range cartridge.
No. 11. Exposed bullet view of Peters early wad cutter bullet mid range cartridge.
No. 12. Full cartridge view of Peters early wad cutter bullet mid range cartridge.
No. 13. Sectional bullet view of Peters latest wad cutter bullet cartridge.
No. 14. Exposed bullet view of Peters latest wad cutter bullet cartridge.
No. 15. Full cartridge view of Peters latest wad cutter bullet cartridge.
No. 16. Full cartridge view of Winchester mid range sharp shoulder bullet cartridge.
No. 17. Full cartridge view of Winchester full load sharp shoulder bullet cartridge.
No. 18. Full cartridge view of Western square shoulder mid range bullet cartridge.
No. 19. McGivern 148-grain bullet showing wide base band and wide grease grooves as originally developed.
No. 20. Sectional bullet view Western 158-grain bullet for full load cartridge.
No. 21. Full bullet view Western 158-grain bullet for full load cartridge.
No. 22. Sectional bullet view of Western full load square shoulder bullet cartridge.
No. 23. Full cartridge view of Western full load square shoulder bullet cartridge.
No. 24. Full bullet view of Peters 158-grain full load wad cutter bullet.
No. 25. Sectional bullet view of Peters 158-grain full load wad cutter bullet cartridge.
No. 26. Full cartridge view of Peters 158-grain full load wad cutter bullet cartridge.

"So All Might See" (1917-18-19)

McGivern's assistant loading cartridges with a machine placed on the running board of the car, so that the "Doubting Thomases" could see what went into the revolver that "scored the hits with such regularity," in the early experiments. Courtesy *Outdoor Life*.

General Summing Up

The Loading Machine which was later turned over to the Ideal Manufacturing Co., loading tool makers in 1919. Courtesy *Outdoor Life.*

This machine was designed and constructed by the author for loading .38 Special cartridges, when using Ideal 148-grain bullet No. 358395, mentioned and fully described herewith as the McGivern bullet, for the purpose of enabling all who might be interested to become familiar with the new type of bullet which was being used in the early successful experiments mentioned in connection with data in this section and elsewhere in these pages.

Many persons, with peculiar ideas relative to revolver ammunition, had their education somewhat improved by a close inspection of this machine and the cartridges which were loaded "right before their eyes" on many occasions.

This machine idea appeared to be of some real value at that time and was turned over to the Ideal Manufacturing Company, makers of loading tools, for further development. But nothing more was done to improve it or to place it on the market so far as the author has been informed.

This excellent bullet is listed by Lyman Gun Sight Corporation as No. 358395, weighs 148 grains, and by slight changes can be arranged to weigh 158 grains, and the moulds can be secured for casting this extremely accurate bullet at the regular price for such equipment. This is practically the same as the factory-loaded bullet now turned out by the Remington Company, and which was used by Mr. F. W. Millington for his excellent 25-yard double-action targets displayed in Section 10, and it is also the bullet in the Remington cartridges used by Mr. Walter Groff, for the greater part of the shooting, shown herein as done by him, much of which appears in Section 10 and also Section 5.

This bullet and some data, relative to the early trials, was turned over by me to the Western Cartridge Company sometime after my return from the East in 1920, and, while various slight changes have been made, the general proportions and design and the very accurate results, also, remain much the same. A considerable quantity of this type of Western cartridge was used in our recent experiments with very satisfactory results.

Later developments by all of the loading companies finally gave us the full 158-grain bullet of this type, with a full load of powder behind it, for 50-yard target shooting and better performance at somewhat increased ranges. In many of the fanning experiments and various other performances, including numerous two-gun tests against time, etc., these full load target cartridges were used, thereby setting aside the aimless "chatter" relative to using "sub" or reduced loads, and similar former criticism.

Now, as regards my opinion of this type of cartridge and bullet, I very much favor both the mid-range and full load in this type of cartridge, for general all-around revolver shooting, and particularly for fast and fancy exhibition shooting, where the spectators have a desire to see the bullet holes on the targets or else watch something "bust" with a decided smack.

Shooting Glasses: Anyone with any sort of serious defect of vision, and also those with only slight defects, which do not appear to be at all of a serious nature, will usually get much better results by using a pair of properly constructed shooting glasses. There are several such products available which are specially designed, corrected and adjusted for that particular purpose.

Such glasses, fitting such specifications, can be secured from The F. W. King Optical Company, Euclid Arcade Building, Cleveland, Ohio; also from W. H. Belz, Optician, 2A, East 44th Street, New York City. Both of these firms make a specialty of shooting glasses, and are fully and properly equipped to grind such glasses to any particular prescription that may be required by the person for whom they are to be made.

Considerable detailed correspondence with Mr. Belz brought the information that, when desired, he can furnish a sort of bifocal combination on a shooting glass that will make it possible for the wearer to use this

General Summing Up

Carl Lundborg, electrical engineer for the A. C. M. Company, Great Falls, Montana, and the author, working on some of the later experimental loads for revolvers. Care and precision are the governing factors. This equipment serves that purpose very nicely, and consists of the Pacific loading tool, Bausch & Lomb low power, wide field, comparison microscope, Ideal powder measure, superaccurate assayor's scales for weighing powder and the Ideal bullet sizer and lubricator. (1935–36)

small reading lens, or short focus portion of the larger glasses to correctly adjust his revolver or rifle sights, also focus a camera, adjust the shutter speeds, and diaphragm openings, etc.,—in fact, do any one of the many things that ordinarily require a change of spectacles or use of an additional magnifying glass, without any such inconvenience being required. Such addition on the lower part of one of the large lenses or on both lenses of the regulation shooting glasses should prove of great value in the way of convenience, time saving and, more important still, more complete and convenient service to the wearer.

I took this matter up with The F. W. King Company but never received the definite answer to this bifocal question. However, correspondence with either of these firms will undoubtedly bring any information desired.

Personally, I have four pairs of shooting glasses with my necessary prescription ground into each of them. The first is clear glass, the next is slight amber tint, the third, similar but fairly strong medium tint, and the fourth, a rather strong combination of amber and greenish tint for overcoming any extremely bright glare from water or snow, or when working on aerial targets against an unusually bright and glaring sky, which situation is encountered only occasionally.

The King Rifleite glass is quite generally highly recommended by many shooters and seems to be a very satisfactory combination for the shooter. If no correction is needed for any sort of defective vision the large lens shooting glasses will prove a very valuable protection for the eyes from flying particles of lead or other metal fragments which occur occasionally and always at unexpected times and places, usually as a result of burst primers or shell rims of rim-fire ammunition, etc. Often particles of powder and the escape of hot powder gas through, or as a result of, some slight defect in gun or cartridge, will cause very annoying temporary, if not permanent, injury to the eyes, which shooting glasses can usually prevent. Aside from this safety angle the tinted glass will prove very helpful and, in most instances, quite beneficial to the average shooter's eyes, while preventing, or at least reducing, the tendency of developing headaches and eyestrain from too much glare from various sources.

The question has often been asked—which should be clearer to a shooter wearing glasses, clear definition of the sights and a slightly fuzzy target, or slightly hazy sights and a clearly defined target? The answer to this seems to be to a great extent dependent on the individual and the special peculiarity of his vision, which an oculist familiar with the case should be able to determine. For my own use and condition, I need clear visibility of the sights and if there must be some slight indistinctness of vision it must be in relation to the target or object being used or regarded as the target.

I shot clay pigeons at the traps with the shotgun quite successfully for years before I ever saw the exact outline of such target distinctly while it was in the air. One day when I went to the traps with a properly fitted and corrected pair of shooting glasses I wondered and asked questions, and was very greatly surprised to learn that most of the shooters had had that clear vision in their favor before I even knew that such a thing was possible, yet I had been scoring a fairly high average. Since securing properly corrected shooting glasses the average and all relative conditions have gradually improved, and I have not since experienced any very noticeable difficulty, when using revolvers, in securing clearer visibility of both sights and targets, much better in fact than had ever been possible before securing such glasses.

My candid opinion must therefore be expressed as firmly believing that the average person will do better shooting, generally, through the use of correctly fitted and properly corrected shooting glasses. All such adjustments, fitting and corrections should be made in accordance with the individual's special requirements. All other questions, which are more or less of a technical nature relating to such matters, should be referred to the judgment of a fully qualified oculist.

My personal requirements along this line have been very well taken care of by Dr. Edouard Sutter, Optician and Optometrist, of Lewistown, Montana, and the results secured through his services and co-operation have been exceptionally pleasing and very satisfactory in every way. I can very sincerely recommend Mr. Sutter's services to any person who may be in need of assistance with any problem involving correctly constructed and accurately adjusted glasses for any special purpose.

Bullet Art: Shooting out the profiles of persons and animals, along with numerous other designs, has always been considered The Masterpiece of the exhibition shooters' program, and, like many other shooting performances, attempts have been made to add a great deal of mystery to such performances, and any instruction or information relative to this branch of shooting game has been very carefully withheld and the great secret of success carefully guarded. There was often more or less "chatter" of the nature that it was necessary to be the seventh son of a seventh son and have great and mysterious artistic talent handed down, for several generations, to the lucky person who was selected by destiny to do such shooting. All of which would be quite interesting, if true.

This form of shooting has always been considered exclusively a rifle shooter's game, but, like aerial target shooting and various other similar stunts, it seems quite possible that by persistent and systematic effort much headway could be made by revolver and pistol shooters along this line of endeavor by adapting sights, positions, and holding methods to this special purpose of accomplishment, and, when such adjustments have been made, successful results should follow persistent effort, and bullet art become a not too difficult thing for a number of pistol shooters to master.

It is here made quite plain, by a system of procedure that has been quite simplified, that almost anyone who can hit any sort of very small object at short range, with a .22 rifle, pistol or revolver, and who has any sort of memory for repeating past performances, following familiar routine and making similar motions repeatedly, should eventually master this seemingly great mystery.

As here made evident by the accompanying reproductions of photos made especially for use with the descriptive matter of this particular subject, any suitable design can be sketched out on a sheet of paper or on a cardboard, and when proportioned to suit the interested person the outline should then be clearly marked, as shown in the original line drawings reproduced herewith. The next step is to perforate the card or paper with either a small punch or some sort of coarse needle, taking care to follow the outline correctly and to have the perforations or holes spaced from about three-quarters of an inch to around one inch apart, on the paper or card that is to be used as a pattern. Care must be taken to have a hole come directly on each and every one of the main points of the design, particularly on all corners or sharp points and intersections of lines. If a line runs into a circle or other important point of a design, the spacing must be arranged so that a hole will be placed exactly at the ending point of the line. The shorter curves are usually made more easy to visualize and follow by making the holes just a little closer together than on ordinary straightaway lines.

When the drawing has been completed as wanted, and the perforated pattern has been made from it by the method above-described, the operator is ready to etch out his design with punch marks on a tin plate or cardboard, which will now constitute the target, as it will hereafter be referred to, meaning the material on which the design will be shot.

When all of the design has been etched on the surface of the target, remove the pattern and place the target in whatever receptacle or other equipment you may have selected or arranged for holding it, and start shooting. The pattern of the design may be etched lightly so that it is not easily seen by anyone but the shooter, or etched more deeply during the early trials for clearer visibility by the shooter, and then later on can be etched more lightly again as more skill is developed.

At first, progress is made and familiarity with the design is developed by shooting off the little spots or etching marks, one at a time, from the visible guide left by the pattern, and later on when the design has been shot several times memory will begin to step in and make the shooter aware of the fact that there are a certain number of bullets distributed in a certain direction at some certain angle and in some certain shape or formation, which forms the key, or starting section, of that particular design, and each section of the design which follows thereafter consists merely of a continuation of the same system of distribution and relative arrangement, the result of which is dependent on the extent to which such familiarity with the design has been developed.

It now becomes quite important that a sincere attempt should be made to memorize the particular direction in which the lines run, and the number of bullets required to be used for each particular line or section of the design, and when it becomes possible to clearly recall such details regarding these groups of bullet holes and the relative forms, angles, and directions in which they were arranged when formerly shooting out the design, it should soon become possible for any portion of the hat, head, face, chin, nose, or other part of the profile to be reproduced at will, then, by combining these various groups of bullets in their correct relative arrangement, the result should be the completed profile.

When this period of progress has been reached it is simply a question of application and study, combined with persistent practice, whereby the performer can develop sufficient skill to complete the designs with all of the shots properly located, directed, and guided by memory only, without any sort of visible guide.

Any new design can at first be made by following a pattern, then learned from and by repetition. Several designs can be learned in this

way and the program varied to suit occasions. The process of development is the same for all.

Rifle shooters usually sit down or kneel on one knee, and lean the left
elbow on the other knee, which enables them to have positive control
over the gun, and the correct spacing of the bullets (note photo of Captain
Hardy), and the usual range used by the better performers is from nine to
twelve feet. Pistol and revolver shooters should secure somewhat similar
results by assuming a sitting position with the back supported against
something fairly solid, any sort of firm support will answer the purpose,
and then secure absolute steadiness and positive control over the gun by
making use of both hands to hold the gun, while supporting both the hands
and gun by use of the knees, in various ways.

The accompanying photos (pages 457 and 458) show several views of a
very good two-handed position adaptable to this and similar kinds of
shooting. Variations can, of course, be made to suit the individual's
preference. The distance for pistols and revolvers, if and when attempting this kind of work, should not be more than around seven to ten feet.
This sort of shooting is like several other types described in detail in these
pages. It is strictly a short range game. Adding difficulties does not
improve results. Any one who, at short range, can place his bullets
reasonably close to a small spot, should, by application and study, be successful in learning this game of Bullet Art, and like often occurs with other
shooting stunts, it is sometimes surprising what progress can be made by
some persons with a reasonable amount of study and persistent effort.
Simpler designs, with few lines, are good to practice on at first and gradually
branch out as ability for spacing and outline develops. Many opportunities will present good subjects. Persons with a little drawing ability can
usually be found who can make simple designs that will be suitable for re-
producing, or they may be secured from books containing some of the early
instructions in drawing and designing easily available around bookstores
and news stands, or distributors of school supplies.

Several Indian heads and other figures herewith reproduced show the
bullet art work of Mr. Adolph Topperwein and Captain A. H. Hardy, two
of the foremost performers in this field. Accompanying these will be
found various designs submitted by the author, the outline of the boy's
head having been shot out by him in 1913, or twenty-five years ago
(1938).

Mr. Topperwein and Captain Hardy, as a result of much experience,
and more or less continuous practice, do this sort of shooting with rifles
without requiring any outlines or marks to guide them, and it is only a
reasonable belief that many pistol and revolver shooters should, and
eventually may, be able to do the same thing if the suggestions herein
presented are followed. Many more difficult things than this form of

Fast and Fancy Revolver Shooting

shooting have been successfully accomplished and completely mastered by and with the use of revolvers, and as a result of confidence and determination.

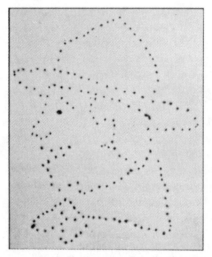

This profile, intended to somewhat resemble young Emmett McGivern, the boy in the photos displayed in Section 5, was shot out on a tin plate by the author in 1913.

Mr. Adolph Topperwein and the author at Great Falls, Montana, with everything ready and in order for Mr. Topperwein's exhibition. Note assortment of objects at left of foreground to be used as aerial targets and the tin plate on improvised background at the right on which Mr. Topperwein shoots out the profile of the Indian head, as reproduced herewith.

General Summing Up

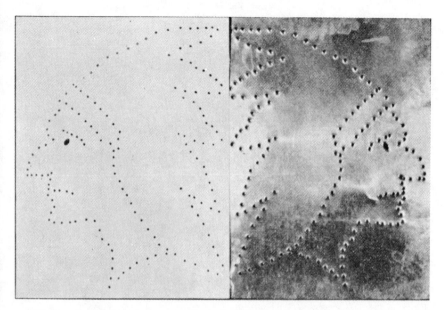

The front view and the back view of the Indian head shot out on a tin plate with bullets fired from .22 rifles by Adolph Topperwein during his shooting exhibition mentioned herewith.

Captain A. H. Hardy shooting out Indian head and other profiles with bullets from a .22 rifle. Note the excellent position adopted by the Captain for this sort of shooting.

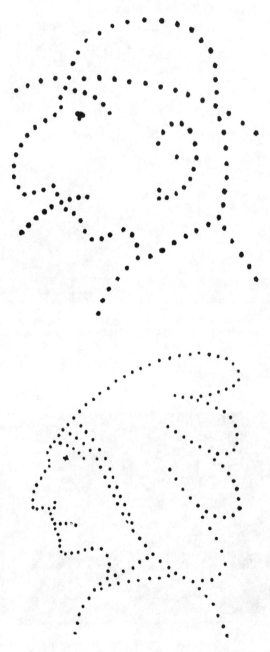

Two excellent profiles shot with .22 rifle by Captain A. H. Hardy of Beverly Hills, California.

General Summing Up

This design, composed of the author's name and figures 1937 in connection with the words "bullet art," was arranged for the express purpose of illustrating the proper handling of spacing in relation to short and long curves, square corners, straight lines, and various combinations of curves, square corners and straight lines, all used together as in the figures 1937.

Almost every sort of line, loop and curve that may be required for any sort of profile design, is combined in this design and the arrangement of the spacing necessary in this combination should be a satisfactory guide for any design that may be encountered in this field of endeavor.

It is for this special reason that this particular design has been selected and carefully worked out, and is herewith presented.

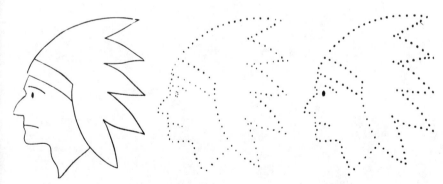

View One—Shows Indian head drawn in with plain outline, which is then perforated with small punch or pinholes properly arranged and spaced, thus forming a pattern for placing bullet holes to form a profile design.

View Two—Shows punch marks on plate as made by end of punch passing through holes in pattern, called etching the design, in preparation for shooting it out with bullet holes.

View Three—Shows the completed bullet art design of Indian head.

The same routine as described on the preceding page is used for this cowboy design and for all of the other designs until such time as the operator is able to make them from memory and without visible outlines and guides.

The racing stable attendant and the "winnah" of the "darby."

General Summing Up

Bullet Art Patterns, outlined and punched, or perforated patterns for the Bullet Art designs here presented, can be secured through the author, on special order, for $3.50 each. Other designs can be adapted to this type of shooting at a price of $5.00 to $8.00 each. Patterns for names can be worked out for around $5.00 to $10.00 and up for each design, depending on the nature of the design desired.

Suitable Material for Bullet Art: Plain tin plates, which come in sizes of 20″ x 28″ and 20″ x 30″, are generally preferred by most shooters who indulge in this sort of performance. Good results can be secured by using fairly heavy cardboard, sizes 22″ x 28″ and about six or eight ply, which is heavy enough to support itself without buckling or breaking apart where the bullet holes form the design, even when the bullets are placed fairly close together.

"Two-gun Ike" chases the tenderfoot up the road and—

(See next page)

Fast and Fancy Revolver Shooting

When shooting out the designs on either of these materials, the plate or card, as the case may be, should be supported on the back by some material similar to the wooden boxes in which window glass is usually shipped, one of which is shown holding one of the tin plates in preparation for Mr. Topperwein's bullet art performance, clearly visible in the photo showing him and the author with all arrangements complete for his shooting exhibition (page 448).

Guns Adaptable to Bullet Art: It is not the author's intention to suggest any particular gun to anyone for this particular purpose. Any .22 caliber repeating rifle, with sights properly adjusted, will answer the purpose.

Any .22 revolver or automatic pistol, with sights adjusted properly, will also answer the purpose. Among these may be mentioned the Smith

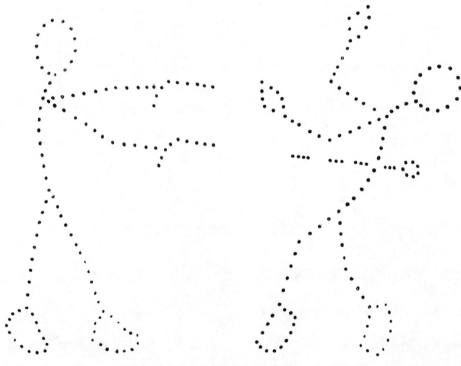

The tenderfoot is finally perforated by a slug from one of "Two-gun Ike's" t-rusty guns.

& Wesson K-.22 revolver, the Colt Officers' Model .22 revolver, the Harrington & Richardson Sportsman .22 revolver, the Colt Woodsman .22 Automatic pistol, and the High Standard .22 Automatic pistol. All of these guns are bored and chambered for the .22 long rifle cartridge. All are accurate and dependable. The inexpensive .22 short cartridges can be successfully used in the several revolvers mentioned.

A later model of the High Standard Automatic pistol is specially bored and adjusted for .22 short cartridges only, and is surprisingly accurate and dependable in operation, functioning perfectly and capable of surprising performance with these inexpensive cartridges. On account of this economy feature and the very satisfactory results of thorough trials, this gun is highly deserving of very favorable mention where and when automatic pistols are under consideration. This pistol can be secured from the High Standard Mfg. Company, 151 Foote Street, New Haven, Conn.

Special Grips for Special Reasons: For those who may be interested in securing specially constructed revolver grips with which to carry on shooting experiments of a special nature for their own satisfaction and interest, a reproduction of a composite photograph is herewith presented, showing four views of excellent revolver grips made for the author, to certain desired specifications, by the Kearsarge Woodcrafts Company of

SPECIAL GRIPS FOR SPECIAL REASONS

Warner, New Hampshire, under the supervision of Charles B. Wendell, Jr., director.

Note the three styles of thumb rest developed for special purposes and for conducting certain experiments in search of definitely desired results.

The two lower grips are very well proportioned and readily adapted to the two-handed hold (page 457), which has been extensively used for various short and long range accuracy tests and experimental performances where slightly more positive control over the gun than is usually secured may be desired. When using these grips for this style of two-handed holding, the thumb of the right hand can be placed in the thumb rest groove, and the thumb of the left hand very conveniently overlaps the right thumb, and both can, and usually do, assume a comfortable position, which also places the left thumb in a very convenient location for rapidly cocking the hammer. This two-hand hold and relative position of all parts mentioned is quite clearly made evident in the photograph (page 458) showing the left side view of the hands in position on the gun.

The upper grip design is one of the later developments in grip construction, resulting from various experiments conducted in an effort to produce something that would reduce the disturbing effect and shock of recoil on the upper part of the hand of such persons as may be over-sensitive to the jarring effect of recoil at that point, and the dimensions have been so well controlled that this grip is suitably proportioned for small and medium-sized hands, something which has not been available heretofore in any grip of somewhat similar construction, but which the author believes has been very much needed.

The view at upper left (page 455) shows this grip with both sides rounded and nicely proportioned so as to be slightly wider than usual at the upper part where most of the shock of recoil is felt by many persons when shooting the more powerful cartridges now available, which give somewhat increased and more disturbing recoil.

This grip, which was designed by the author, and which, in all probability, will hereafter be referred to as the McGivern grip, has a small built-in filler block back of the trigger guard and also an extension below the bottom of the grip straps, as shown in the view at right. It also has a built-in portion for increasing the width and filling the curved hollow in upper part of frame and back strap, of both Colt and Smith & Wesson revolvers, making the back of the completed grip a gradual and uniformly continued curve entirely free of any narrow places, raised portions or irregularities, leaving a smooth, evenly rounded surface in contact with the hand of the shooter.

Many shooters enjoy playing around and experimenting with various combinations of so-called superloads, and this type of grip should be quite an improvement, and much more comfortable to use under such conditions than the usual regulation grips heretofore available.

General Summing Up

Showing a very good sitting position using two hands for holding and operating the revolver, which is suitable for various positive control performances. This position is not offered with the usual titles of "correct" and "proper" and no claim is made that it should be adopted by every one, but merely offered as one of the sitting positions which have proven satisfactory and effective for the author and many others when certainty of results was very urgently desired.

The right forearm is resting on the leg just back of the knee, the forward part of the right foot is resting on the back part of the left foot, and the right heel is resting firmly on the floor. There is no discomfort felt while in this position. The right leg can be moved up or down or sideways, much or little, as may be desired, carrying the arm and gun with it to any point of line-up found necessary. The elevation of gun can also be changed by the movement of the right arm to just exactly the degree required. With practice this position can become the much talked of "Dead center hold."

The internationally known shooting authority, E. C. Crossman, has written some excellent and convincing articles on the holding of revolvers with two hands for extremely accurate results at various ranges. We therefore have a very proficient and quite well recognized authority endorsing the most important principles involved in this sort of shooting.

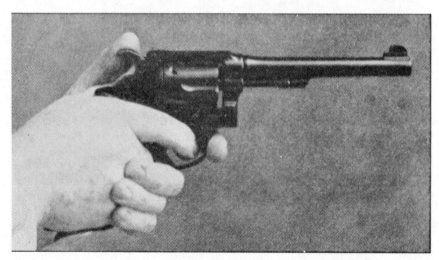

Showing view of right side of two-handed position used for deliberate holding while in sitting position for all shooting where extreme care of placing shots is desired.

Note the hammer is cocked for each shot with the thumb of the left hand. Note position of thumb ready for cocking movement. This system of raising the hammer does not in any way disturb the hold or make it necessary to move any other part of either hand except the trigger finger.

The K-.22 revolver being used here is equipped with the Smith & Wesson "hump-backed" hammer, which is an outstanding improvement of real value.

Showing left side of a very good two-handed position for both short range and long range revolver shooting. This is the hold used in connection with the sitting position shown herewith (page 457).

Showing a very effective two-handed hold for revolvers without resting hands on any support. A steadying combination useful in many situations.

The Smith & Wesson Hump Back Hammer is a very valuable new and outstanding development in the way of a fast, sure and comfortable cocking spur on revolver hammers, where and when a considerable amount of hammer raising for rapid single-action revolver shooting is necessary to be performed within limited time periods.

There is no cramping of fingers necessary, no undue strain required, and the liability of thumb slipping from hammer spur and causing accidental discharge and the usual annoying circumstances resulting therefrom has been very greatly lessened and in all probability entirely eliminated.

This hammer has been proclaimed by many of the foremost revolver shooters of this country as one of the most outstanding and valuable improvements in revolver construction which has been developed in many

General Summing Up

years. This type of hammer has been very thoroughly tested and favorably recommended by the author. This style hammer can be secured on all Smith & Wesson revolvers when so specified.

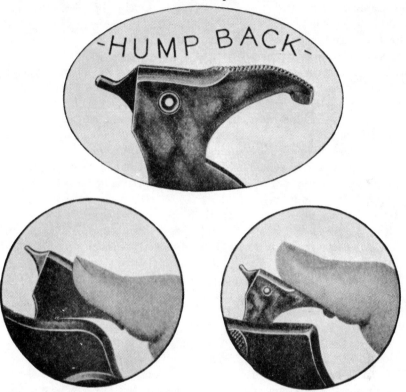

COCKING THE CONVENTIONAL HAMMER   COCKING THE HUMP BACK HAMMER

The McGivern Front Sight, consisting of a large gold bead, the circular outline of which is arranged to be even with the sides and top of a one-tenth inch wide post front sight, was developed for use on revolvers for the special purpose of fast, accurate shooting under all sorts of light conditions on both stationary and various forms of moving targets. This sight is so constructed, due to its square top, that it establishes absolutely positive elevation in connection with the easy and quick visibility of the rounded surface of the brilliant gold bead.

Most of the various bead sights heretofore available were sadly lacking in this very important point of establishing the positive and correct elevation level, when looking over them, which is an absolute necessity with any front sight for revolvers, if consistent results are to be secured with any degree of regularity. Any front sight for revolvers which does not give correct and easily determined elevation without delay, due to required deliberation, can never be successfully productive of satisfactory results in the branch of revolver shooting which is under discussion in these pages. The McGivern sight can be secured on Smith & Wesson revolvers as standard factory equipment, and can be secured for Colt and other revolvers, etc., from the D. W. King Sight Co., 171 Second Street, San Francisco, California.

Correct Sighting: Holding under or holding center? There has been much discussion as to which system of holding and sighting is the more positive and certain of results for general exhibition shooting purposes.

In the early section on Aerial Target Shooting (Section 5) the slightly lower holding system was quite thoroughly explained and the reasons given why it was useful and somewhat desirable in the certain situations therein described.

For the sort of objects generally used as targets for fast and fancy revolver shooting the system of holding center seems to be the more effective and convenient, particularly when reasonable speed and fairly consistent accuracy are to be combined.

When shooting at the various sized objects, such as are used for general exhibition purposes, and which, as a rule, are held and supported in various unusual ways, it is generally a very difficult matter to use any other method than the "center hold."

In support of this opinion the author takes the liberty of mentioning the fact that Charles Askins, Jr., who is one of the foremost revolver shots in America, expressed himself in recent writings, in favor of, and as also making a practice of, "holding center," which, in plain terms, means lining up the sights at the exact spot where you wish the bullet to strike.

From this it would appear to be a fairly well-supported decision, when the author advises the "center hold" as more generally effective and adaptable for the shooting activities in which we are here more particularly interested, and which on occasion may also involve the human target holding feature, as herein described.

Holding Targets in the Hands: When targets are held in the hands while being shot at, they should be held in the end of clipper clothespins for safety, but if they are to be held in the fingers they should be held with the extreme tips of the index finger and thumb only, just pinching the extreme edge very lightly and never by holding the finger over or around the top of target with the thumb extending under or around the lower edge of the target, so that the bullet must be so placed as to strike between the thumb and finger. This system of holding makes a danger zone all around the outer edge of target, while by holding only one small part of the edge at the point where tips of thumb and finger pinch it, leaves the entire target exposed and clear for the shooter. (See page 461.) This is the system used for holding targets in the hands during all such exhibition shooting programs in which the author took an active part.

General Summing Up

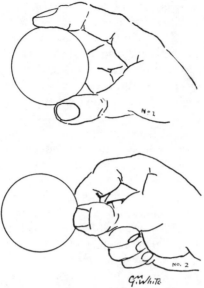

G. White

No. 1. The wrong way to hold targets if and when they are to be shot at while being held with the fingers.

No. 2. The right way to hold targets when they are to be shot at while being held in the hands.

Holding Targets on the Head: If it is considered necessary and desirable by all parties concerned in such a situation, and the revenue is sufficient for the apparent risk involved by adding the element of danger to a fancy shooting exhibition, which is always considered present by the spectators when targets are placed on the head of an assistant for the purpose of shooting them off, the method usually used by the author, on numerous occasions, when such events were featured, is here described and recommended, and consists of the following procedure: A soft leather strap, about three-quarters of an inch wide, is arranged to fit comfortably over the head and fasten under and slightly to one side of the chin with a buckle or with one or several snap buttons which are arranged so as to be adjustable for a snug fit.

The top part of this strap covering the head is reinforced with firm leather to the thickness of around five-eighths of an inch and tapered off at each end. In this reinforcement five holes are punched, one in the center and two on each side of center, spaced about one and a half inches apart. These holes should be of a size to fit small sticks similar to the skewers used for pinning roasts together in meat markets, or some of the simpler shaped sticks used for holding ice cream novelties and lollipops, etc. On these sticks the targets can be fastened by various means, or, if composition balls are used, they are simply placed over the sticks and

— 461 —

held in place by the ever-present open hole in the side of such targets. If Duvrocks or other disc-form targets are used they can be attached to the sticks with plaster of Paris or melted resin, or the same compound from which the composition balls are made. Bending the strap around the head causes these targets to assume a sort of fan-shaped formation. The sticks can be any length desired by the persons most seriously concerned in the performance. Arranging them so they will project about one and a half inches or so below the bottom of the target, makes a fairly good margin of clearance, but, of course, such details must depend on the spectacular effect desired, and the confidence and dependable skill of the performers.

There is no noticeable jar, if and when these small sticks are struck with the bullets while passing through the targets when held in this manner. While I do not advise attempts at this sort of shooting without unusual care and safety precautions, with plenty of careful preparation in advance of the actual event, the fact remains that this stunt has been successfully performed a great number of times on my programs without even a close approach towards an accident. Yet it must be kept in mind at all times that the unexpected may happen any moment, and the information is here handed out without any recommendation, suggestion or encouragement that this stunt be adopted without due consideration and knowledge relative to the risk involved.

For listing this information I may be severely criticised by some, whereas if I leave this information out of the book I would be just as severely criticised by others for so doing, the result being that it is here presented with the urgent warning to be quite sure of the correctness of everything before attempting the stunt, and, above all, be careful.

McGivern Drawless Holsters can be secured, complete with belt, two holsters and fittings, from Sam D. Myres of El Paso, Texas, the cost ranging from $30.00 to around $75.00, depending on the style and finish desired. Hardware only, such as swivels and clasps complete for attaching to the shanks of holsters and for attaching swivels to belt blocks, can be supplied by Frank Fish of Lewistown, Montana, for $4.00 for single holsters and $7.50 a pair for double holsters.

Weaver Machine Rests and **Telescope Sights,** used and recommended by the author and favorably mentioned elsewhere herein, can be secured from W. R. Weaver, El Paso, Texas.

Smoothed-up Revolver Actions: Shortened hammer falls, special wide hammer spurs for more comfortable, fast, single-action shooting under regulation rapid-fire target shooting conditions, along with special improvement on hammer action and trigger pull arrangement, etc., on the .45 Colt Auto pistol, can be secured from J. D. Buchanan, 1280 Sunset Boulevard, Los Angeles, California.

Benjamin Air Pistol, recommended by the author as very satisfactory

General Summing Up

and practical for training purposes to develop careful holding and control of the trigger finger, has adjustable sights and a correctly adjusted and excellent trigger pull, is dependable and durable, and not expensive to operate. Barrel is correctly rifled and shoots very accurate lead bullets. Can be secured from Benjamin Air Rifle Company, 807 Marion Street, St. Louis, Mo.

Stop Watches, accurate and dependable, adjusted and arranged for special as well as regulation timing operations, can be secured from the Pastor Stop Watch Company, 43 East Main Street, Waterbury, Conn., whose products are extensively used and highly recommended by the author.

Gun Slick, an excellent product, recommended and used when working in, and smoothing up, the mechanism of double-action revolvers, as described herein, can be secured from Outers Laboratories, Onalaska, Wis.

Pacific Loading Tool, powder scales and accessories, as used in our various experiments, and highly recommended as a result, can be secured from The Pacific Gun Sight Company, 355 Hays Street, San Francisco, Cal.

Bullet-Proof Glass, as demonstrated herein, can be secured from the Pittsburgh Plate Glass Company, Pittsburgh, Pa. Any information desired relative to this product and its many uses, along with plans and specifications for installation in various fixtures and arrangements, will be promptly forwarded by the company in response to inquiry.

Van-Aumatic Traps and the excellent 1⅝-inch flat Duster Targets, fully described in Section 20 relating to training of officers, can be secured from the Fred Goat Company, 314 Dean Street, Brooklyn, N. Y.

Badger Spotting Scope Tripod, and jointed tube extension, a handy light-weight, convenient accessory, can be secured from Badger Shooters Supply Company, Owens, Wis.

One of the author's .36 caliber cap and ball Colts without the top strap. This was considered one of the most dependable guns of this type in its day. This gun can be fanned and works O.K. for slip shooting also.

Fast and Fancy Revolver Shooting

One of the author's formerly owned cap and ball Remington revolvers, considered an excellent gun in its day. Can be operated much the same as the single-action Colt cartridge guns of today. This gun is now the property of Wm. H. Fisher of Baltimore, Maryland.

Muzzle Loading Cap and Ball Revolvers, as shown herewith, can be fanned and used for slip shooting in a very similar manner to the way it is done with single-action Colt cartridge guns.

Supplies for Cap and Ball Revolvers: Can be secured from E. M. Farris, Portsmouth, Ohio, secretary National Muzzle Loading Rifle Association.

Gas Equipment and Machine Guns: Bullet-proof vests, armored cars, etc., for law enforcement officers, can be secured from Federal Laboratories, Pittsburgh, Pa.

The Scott Automatic Nite Site: This is an electrical device in the form of a small, but powerful, searchlight which operates from a battery. It is compact and practical and very effective for the purpose for which it was developed, that of enabling law enforcement officers to quickly locate a target in the dark, and just as accurately place the bullets fired from their revolvers as if operating in daylight. Some claims are made that the Nite Site is more accurate in the hands of many persons than the average shooting done by them under similar circumstances would be in daylight.

The Scott Automatic Nite Site is undoubtedly the greatest contribution to protective equipment ever offered to law enforcement officers. This device is really a scientifically correct precision instrument built with skill and exacting accuracy, is durable, practical and extremely dependable and effective. Regulation revolvers, submachine guns and sawed-off shotguns can be equipped with this device, affording an impregnable defensive weapon for use by officers at night.

Every experienced law enforcement officer realizes the danger that must be faced and the perils encountered in trying to apprehend or capture dangerous criminals operating under cover of darkness. With the Scott

General Summing Up

Nite Site the officer has a device that searches out the suspect in his hiding place, penetrating the gloom of darkness and turning the officer's gun into an instrument of deadly accuracy.

This device with battery costs somewhere around $75.00 when fitted to a revolver, and the special holster for carrying the gun equipped with the device sells for $5.00 extra. This is a very practical piece of equipment, and not a plaything in any sense of the word. Excellent shooting can be done with it at night and it is claimed the arrangement is such that the officer is not exposed by the back reflection of the light when in use.

The writer has not had the opportunity to test this combination out thoroughly as yet, under the various conditions which would be probable and liable to exist when such device would be required and pressed into service by the law enforcement officers. However, general reports received from other sources seem to support the belief that this equipment is all that is claimed for it.

Any additional information can be secured from The Scott Nite Site Company, Inc., 519 Equitable Building, 6253 Hollywood Boulevard, Hollywood, Calif.

Showing engraving on Smith & Wesson .357 Magnum revolver which can be secured on order through the factory.

Engraving on Smith & Wesson .357 Magnum revolver which can be secured on order through the factory.

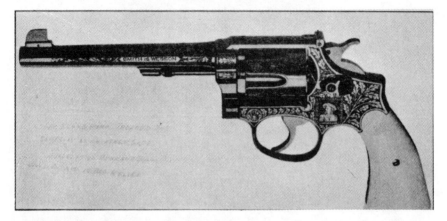

Showing engraving on Smith & Wesson revolver by R. J. Kornbrath, 284 Asylum Street, Hartford Conn.

Engraving by R. J. Kornbrath, 284 Asylum Street, Hartford, Conn., Mr. Kornbrath is equipped to do any sort of engraving, gold inlays and ornamentation of every nature, on any type or make of pistols, revolvers, rifles, etc. Individual and exclusive designs of any nature can be furnished on special order.

Fast and Fancy Revolver Shooting

HOLDING TARGETS ON HEAD

The author shooting target from head of assistant with .38 caliber target revolver. Curley Dunlop's Dude Ranch at Half Moon Pass, Montana.

MIRROR SHOOTING

Walter Groff performing with revolvers used in connection with mirrors.

Left—Shooting with aid of mirror at target placed to the side of shooter.

Right—Shooting with the aid of mirror at target placed to the front of shooter.

JUMPING HANDKERCHIEFS
The author jumping handkerchiefs over hurdles with bullets fired from revolvers.
Courtesy *Outdoor Life*

Fast and Fancy Revolver Shooting

Emmett McGivern demonstrating some interesting pistol shooting combinations. Back to target. Using mirror to sight pistol.

DOUBLE MIRROR SHOOTING

Back to target, using two mirrors to sight pistol. The reflection in the upper mirror controls the success of this stunt.

General Summing Up

HITTING THREE TARGETS WITH ONE BULLET

Bullet passes through the center target, then is split by the axe blade, and divides to break the two targets on each side of the axe.

When making preparations for this performance the gun is sighted so that the bullet will strike above line of sight. The edge of the axe projects slightly below the center target. The sights are aligned on the edge of the axe below the target, and when the shot is fired the bullet strikes above the point of aim and, hitting the center target, passes through to come in contact with the edge of the axe blade and is thus split. The divided parts being separated by the axe blade then strike the two targets placed at each side of the axe.

Care in placing the axe exactly upright and arranging the targets in proper relative position to the axe blade, is the key to success with this performance. The shooter does not align his sights on any part of the center target but just under it on the exposed edge of the axe blade.

THE AUTHOR ARRANGING SWINGING TARGETS FOR EMMETT McGIVERN

The position of the hands show the method of releasing two swinging targets to be hit with one bullet while passing each other at the central point of travel. The assistant steps away before the shot is fired, of course.

This is a very practical method of training for developing positive control over the exact instant at which any certain shot can be released.

Perfect timing by the shooter is quite necessary for success with this and similar performances.

General Summing Up

CONCLUSION

In bringing this book to a close it is the author's most sincere hope that the revolver shooting data, suggestions and methods of instruction may result in saving the lives of many of our law enforcement officers, to whose lot it may fall, in the line of duty, to be compelled to use their revolvers while attempting to capture or subdue some of the desperate criminals who make such procedure necessary.

While my shooting activities of the future, for a time at least, will undoubtedly, of necessity, be somewhat limited, my enthusiasm and interest in the coaching and instructing of law enforcement officers will be just as sincere and active as ever.

Much of my time and efforts of the future will be directed towards developing and promoting practical and effective training methods for law enforcement officers in general.

It was with the desire that in the final summing up, law and order would continue to be supreme, that the practical shooting development programs were undertaken and worked out as herein presented.

SECTION 31

THE GUN FIGHTER!

Franklin Reynolds, writer of Western fact yarns, who knows his subject thoroughly, gives us here just a little food for thought relative to the outstanding frontier character—"The Gun Fighter!"

"Gun fighters! Relentlessly and without explanation fate drove persons of peculiar characteristics into the Western frontier. There the environment developed them and made them what they were. But just what it is that is incorporated in the make-up of any particular individual that renders him **the gun fighter,** fits him so completely into **such environment** and puts him in that class, is still an unanswered question.

The accomplishment of gun-fighting is not peculiar to the men in any walk of life, of any age, of any degree of education or wealth, of any station in society, of any race, creed, or color. It just crops out, here and there unannounced, unquestioned, and seldom, if ever, understood. Cultivated by some, but in the hands of others, it appears a gift from the gods.

Gun-fighting! The art of **slapping leather** and **burning powder**—the **talent** of **dropping** the other fellow with a minimum loss of time, to the accompaniment of the fewest possible, **if any,** bullet holes in the anatomy of the **fastest man!**

The Gun Fighters were, and are, a class apart. Not always heroic and fearless, as some suppose, not always worthy of esteem, not always the flashing and dashing **caballero** of skillful ride and gallant manner, they were, all of them, possessed of certain characteristics. **But, common to them all, was that characteristic rampant fever of gun-play!**

Gun Fighters were not just some picturesque quintessence of fiction —they were **REAL!** There was a good and valid, a comprehensible reason for **Gun Fighters**—for **the** dry gulching **gun man,** none!

The Gun Fighter did many things worth while in Western history. He trapped and brought to Judge Colt's justice the **malo hombre** who ambushed and murdered the Ranger in the Big Bend. He encased in sudden and terrible death the rustlers who killed the stock association detectives! He brought to a gory end those who killed boys, robbed trains, stole from the Indians, the miners, the banks, the express company, the stockmen! He did not stay his hand to wipe out those who burned and pillaged, and did worse! **Such was the Gun Fighter!**

The Gun Fighter and **not the army**, restlessly wandering and drifting, impatiently moving across the face of a continent with blazing guns, conquered that continent, tamed a savage land, and yet more vicious men, red and white. **The Gun Fighter lived,** thumbed the hammer and

The Gun Fighter

fingered the trigger, and died—but not in vain! He made the West for the cattleman, the sheepman, the merchant, and the hoeman! **The Gun Fighter** was, and is, one of the many sorts of freaks of human nature!

His environment was not one of austere conventionality such as breeds sophisticated courtesy. Rather, it should be described as "raw whiskey and sweat-stained rags for his bloody wounds, raw whiskey also to wash the lead from the bullet holes in his body." These are not dainty expressions, but **The Gun Fighter** was not a dainty man nor the frontier an elegant place to live! He was often a noble man, even perchance viewed at his worst. Not the princely nobility bowing and smirking over the lily-like hand of a lady of the court, but his was the nobility of manhood! He could, and did, face the inevitableness of a cruel and bitter nature with the same smile he wore when he greeted a friend. With death he walked, hand in hand—with death he rode, stirrup to stirrup!

His was the quality of courage that took long chances—asked no quarter and gave none—with the frontier. The absolute necessity for every man to become "his own law" as well as his own doctor and the preserver of his own existence helped materially to make conditions what they were, with a high premium on the accomplishment of gun fighting. Witness a list of notable pistoleers and gun fighters picked at random:

BILL LONGLEY, a bashful farm lad, was first among the **Gun Fighters** to appear across the bullet-scarred horizon because he had been abused by the Texas (Negro) State Police in the period of Reconstruction.

JOHN WESLEY HARDIN, son of a Methodist preacher, who shoved forty men, or more, through the portals of eternity, became the saltiest in the corral when he learned, at the ripe old age of sixteen years, that the only difference between a big man and a little man was the equalizing medium of a six-shooter.

BEN THOMPSON, small and swarthy, started life a fish peddler in Austin, became a knight of the green cloth, and died with his boots on because the "knack" of swiftly unharnessing a gun and shooting straight settled itself on his shoulders.

JOHN H. "DOC" HOLLIDAY, coughing and sallow, a dentist from Georgia, went West for his health. He found it more lucrative to pull aces from the bottom of a deck than aching molars from a jawbone. This would have been suicide had it not been for his reputed ability as a gunman.

JOHN RINGO, sad, mysterious and dangerous. Top-hand of Tombstone's pistoleers and a university graduate who read the classics, and could quote page after page of Shakespeare.

CLAY ALLISON, "the curly wolf of the Washita," black haired, black eyed, black bearded, and of black moods. The cripple who used a Winchester for a crutch and "treed" town after town without meeting a marshal ready and willing to match his draw—Clay Allison from Tennessee.

Fast and Fancy Revolver Shooting

MELVIN KING was a soldier in the frontier cavalry, a recruit from the effeminate East, and the army's contribution to the gallery of those who consistently embedded bullets in saloon fixtures and then died with gun smoking.

BILLY, THE KID, deadliest killer of them all, followed his star from New York's slums to the Lincoln County war, armed with six shooters, the ability to use them and **always** the willingness to "let the hammer drop."

HENDRY BROWN, alternately outlaw and marshal, made Caldwell, Kansas, good because he was **so bad** morally and **so good** at burning powder —until he was hung for bank robbery and murder.

From Missouri came TOM HORN to develop an ability with six guns that made him one of the most famous of Indian scouts, deputy sheriffs, stock association detectives, Pinkerton operatives, soldiers and killers.

JOHN SLAUGHTER, sheriff of Cochise County, was one of Arizona's wealthiest ranchers. He did not hesitate to use his .45's to rid the Territory of an undesirable citizen or a score of them, when occasion demanded.

LONG-HAIRED JIM COURTRIGHT, eagle-eyed, sharp-featured marshal of old Fort Worth in "them good old days," fugitive from elsewhere, had pre-eminent standing among the slingers of the sixes until a gambler **softened** him and "dusted him off" with a .45.

JAMES BUTLER "WILD BILL" HICKOK, Beau Brummel of Abilene, was a professional law enforcement officer and bad man exterminator, the outstanding hero of early Western fiction, and one of the most famous **Gun Fighters** and the complete master of his lethal cap-and-ball Colt.

LITTLE BASS OUTLAW was disposed to be so wholly disagreeable that the other rangers could not tolerate him. For "the good of the service" he was asked to resign when the Rangers **needed good** men, and yet, there was not a man on the Ranger rolls who was his peer with belt guns.

HARVEY LOGAN, credited with being one of the fastest, was made into an outlaw and driven to the rim-rocks because he happened to love the daughter of a man who disliked Logan, and who was, at the same time, powerful and influential in the Little Rockies.

DALLAS STOUDENMIRE, tall and stalwart, two-gun marshal of wild old El Paso, killed more than his share of bad men. He was a professional peace officer when he arrived from New Mexico to strut for his brief hour or two and die with a belly loaded with whiskey and lead.

BUTCH CASSIDY's accredited dexterity and accuracy with a cylinder gun saved him the necessity of many killings.

JOHN R. HUGHES of Illinois, Texas Ranger Captain, was "Boss of the Rio" because the outlaws soon learned that their draw against his was a bad deal—for them.

TEMPLE HUSTON, eccentric son of the beloved General Sam of Lone Star fame, eloquent orator and able lawyer, was one of the gun-fighting clan.

The Gun Fighter

CAPTAIN BILL McDONALD, who established for the Rangers the reputation of "one riot, one ranger," was a native of Mississippi. This bodyguard of Presidents Theodore Roosevelt and Wilson shot his way to eternal fame and glory. He was one of the outstanding Ranger captains of all time.

JOHN SELMAN, Confederate Veteran, Scout in the Lincoln County war, exterminator of more than twenty bad men, and the El Paso officer who played **the game** with John Wesley Hardin and won, while they watched each other in a backbar mirror.

GEORGE SCARBOROUGH, ex-ranger and deputy United States marshal, who downed Selman in El Paso and was downed near San Simon, Arizona, by Harvey Logan.

BILL TILGHMAN, "valiant old soul behind the star," who spent most of his more than threescore years and ten in the harness, only to die in a boom oil town because of his carelessness in handling a bad man of the jazz generation (the worst of the breed).

FRANK HAMER, another Ranger Captain, the man who fingered the trigger of a Browning automatic rifle and hastened Clyde Barrow and Bonnie Parker through the gates of the great beyond, is one of the few men using a revolver as well with one hand as with the other.

TOM HICKMAN, whose demonstrations with his six shooters have entertained the crowned heads of Europe, another Ranger captain and fast draw artist.

To such men revolvers are the everyday tools of their trade and their life insurance also. Proficiency in their use is a necessity—not a novelty.

And so—the roll may be called—on and on without end. The **Gun Fighters** of yesterday and today pass in solemn, silent review, in flesh and blood, in memory and tradition—sharp-eyed, romantic, daring, charming men who laughed at death, hung their lives on their front sights, and challenged the world!

All were the **individuals** comprising **the class.** It was not always a matter of courage—it could not have always been a matter of necessity, for some were not called upon to kill. It was not inclination, for many disliked taking life. It could not have been fear, for not always did they make an effort to evade **the meeting.** It was not reckless bravado, because unless they were cautious souls they did not last long.

But, whatever it was, it made **The Gun Fighter! The Gun Fighter** made the West!

Wherever he was found he was a striking individual. One of the breed that was, in many instances, loved, respected, and trusted. In others, hated, hunted, and dared, by some emulated, by others dodged, and the object of, and subject to, every human passion that may be harbored in a human breast.

Fast and Fancy Revolver Shooting

The Gun Fighters! From everywhere they came to play their parts on the old Western scene, to bedazzle and inspire in their own inimitable and swaggering way, "cat-walking and cat-eyed," and—to make frontier history famous, and, in some cases, notorious! Also making "six shooter" and "six gun" history and romance so outstanding that no amount of argument or criticism has been able to lessen its interest compelling appeal.

The Gun Fighter, aside from all their other accomplishments, developed a literature. To the people of no other section of American life has a literature been devoted. **The Western Story** is because of **The Gun Fighter** and the traditions he established.

INDEX

A

Index

Index

Index

Index

Index